Medical Communication
Defining the Discipline
Second Edition

Theodore A. Avtgis, Ph.D.

Professor and Director, School of Communication Studies
The University of Akron
Adjunct Associate Professor, Department of Surgery
West Virginia University School of Medicine

E. Phillips Polack, MD, MA, FACS

Clinical Professor, Department of Surgery
West Virginia University School of Medicine
Wheeling Hospital
Wheeling, WV

Kendall Hunt
publishing company

Book Team
Chairman and Chief Executive Officer *Mark C. Falb*
President and Chief Operating Officer *Chad M. Chandlee*
Vice President, Higher Education *David L. Tart*
Director of Publishing Partnerships *Paul B. Carty*
Senior Developmental Coordinator *Angela Willenbring*
Vice President, Operations *Timothy J. Beitzel*
Senior Permissions Coordinator *Caroline Kieler*
Cover Designer *Faith Walker*

Cover image © Shutterstock.Com

www.kendallhunt.com
Send all inquiries to:
4050 Westmark Drive
Dubuque, IA 52004-1840

Copyright © 2011, 2017 by Kendall Hunt Publishing Company

ISBN 978-1-5249-3352-4
Text ISBN 978-1-5249-2247-4

Published in the United States of America

Dedication

This book is dedicated to students of any background or discipline who are interested in the integral partnership that is healthcare, and for our children, Aiden Avtgis and Julie Polack.

T.A.A.
E.P.P.

Brief Contents

Contents

Background and Philosophy

The title of this book, *Medical Communication: Defining the Discipline,* refers to some unique and groundbreaking perspectives on communication in the practice of everyday healthcare. This project is the result of a multidisciplinary effort to address the requisites that are currently underserved by scholars in both communication and healthcare. By breaking out of our silos, we were able to forge a new direction in medical communication by combining both theory and research from many disciplines and present it in a way that will be meaningful for anyone, regardless of discipline, to become more literate regarding healthcare choices and obtain essential skills to effectively be a patient as well as treat a patient. In fact, we made it a point to overcome the existing "turf" wars that currently exist in fields such as health communication and health psychology.

This perspective is informed not only by existing research, but by the fact that we are drawn from the disciplines of communication and surgery studies respectively. We have gone to great lengths to include scientific evidence to bring forth concepts and communication practices that have been found to be effective and in the best interest of all parties in the medical encounter. Perhaps the most important result of this effort is the fact that communication-related issues lead to thousands of deaths annually and, in our estimation, should be considered unnecessary and preventable. In the end, the goal of this text is to increase patient safety and increase the health literacy of the reader in an attempt to make a better and more health-conscious society.

This text is written in a way as to provide the information needed to increase communication accuracy in a variety of contexts that will result in:

- A greater understanding of the cultural mosaic that is medicine
- Increased 'mindfulness' as to the value of professionalism
- Increased understanding of the values that are essential to the ethical practice of medicine
- Greater understanding of the importance of technology in the delivery of 21st Century healthcare
- Increased patient and practitioner satisfaction
- Reduced costs and liability
- Increased happiness for both patient and practitioner
- Reduced patient and practitioner stress
- Increased patient compliance
- Increased medical literacy for all who navigate the healthcare system

Features of this Text

Medical Communication: Defining the Discipline presents material in a flexible format that provides scientifically sound and accurate coverage for those who want to become better healthcare providers and for those who want to become more informed patients.

Chapter Objectives focus on the overall concepts, theories, and skills

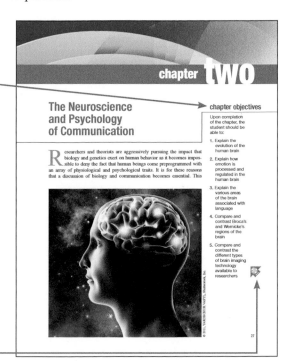

Web Icons send you to additional online material, such as interactive activities, flash cards, and links

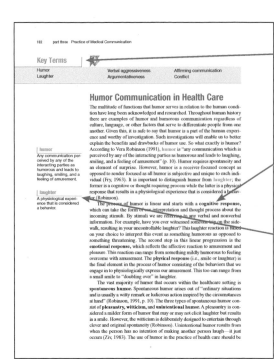

Key Terms List directs you to the important specific terms

Highlighted Concepts indicate important information explained in the text and defined in the Glossary

Running Glossary provides easily accessible definitions to all key terms

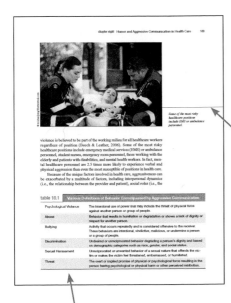

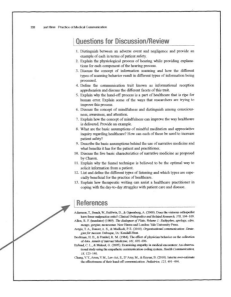

Full Color Photos further illustrate chapter content

References comprehensively list all sources and research utilized in each chapter

Tables visually depict important and sometimes complex concepts

Conclusion succinctly summarizes and reinforces chapter content

Figures visually depict important and sometimes complex information

Questions for Discussion/Review provide an opportunity to further consider chapter concepts

Organization of the Text

Part One: Foundations of Medical Communication

Part I introduces the reader to the concept of medical communication and an overview as to why communication is of paramount importance in healthcare. These data are compelling and provide the necessary rationale that frame the rest of the text.

Chapter One, *The Imperative of Medical Communication?* introduces the reader to the basic reason why the study of communication in everyday practice is critical to reduce error and increase patient safety. Models and myths of communication are presented to dispel folklore from science and provide a foundation for understanding the communication process.

Chapter Two, *The Neuroscience and Psychology of Communication* explores the evolution and composition of the human brain with an emphasis on how language and communication is processed and produced. The specific portions of the brain related to communication are identified and discussed. New brain 21st Century imaging technology is introduced and discussed in terms of its potential impact for investigating the communication process.

Chapter Three, *The Physiology of Temperaments, Communication Traits, and Predispositions* exposes the reader to human temperament and personality traits and how such predispositions to behave influence our ability to communicate. Disorders associated with the brain and personality are identified; as well as a discussion on the perception process.

Part Two: Context and Types of Medical Communication

This section of the book introduces a variety of healthcare environments within which communication is a critical component for both the practitioner and the patient. These environments are constrained by culture, gender, and literacy. The studies that are cited are squarely rooted in social science as opposed to being a product of radical philosophy or other agenda-laden approaches. The unique contexts (environments) in which healthcare is practiced require special understanding of the different types of communication that can occur, and that should occur, to maximize patient safety and assist the patient and/or the practitioner in utilizing communication in a 'mindful' and purposeful way.

Chapter Four, *Gender in Communication: The Influence on Competent Communication within Health Care* introduces the concepts of sex versus gender and dispels some of the myths that currently exist by focusing on the science of the social behaviors and predispositions leading to illness and disease as influenced by biologic sex. Communicative differences in disease and illness presentation are also presented in order to make the healthcare practitioner more mindful of the meaningful physiological and psychological differences that are attributed to both sex and gender.

Chapter Five, *Body Language: The Science of Nonverbal Communication*, explores how various aspects of nonverbal communication can affect the relationships as well as how such nonverbal attributes can assist in better navigating those relationships within the culture of healthcare. Cultural aspects of nonverbal communication such as use of time, grooming, and so on are discussed and suggestions provided.

Chapter Six, *Intercultural Sensitivity and Behaviors* provides a background for understanding how culture can adversely affect your health and the practice of healthcare. The cultural influences on the perceptions of people are discussed along with suggestions for how a provider can effectively navigate potential cultural barriers. Specific perceptual biases, based on culture, are presented as well as ways of demonstrating and becoming mindful of cultural empathy.

Chapter Seven, *Health Literacy: The Not So Silent Epidemic*, explores the concept of literacy and health literacy and how low levels of literacy serves as a major contributor to an environment in which threats to patient safety and ineffective communication are commonplace. Populations particularly susceptible to low levels of literacy are identified and ways of diagnosing low literate patients are presented. Once identified, several tests are offered and discussed as ways to not only assess literacy but as opportunities for the healthcare practitioner to adapt their communication in a way that serves both the needs of the patient and the effectiveness of their treatment.

Part Three: Practice of Medical Communication

Chapter Eight, *Humor and Aggressive Communication in Health Care* explores the physiology and psychology of humor and humor use. Research shows how humor can be used effectively by healthcare practitioners in order to better facilitate the healing process. This chapter also presents the growing epidemic of both physician and communication based aggression. The constructive and destructive sides of aggressive communication are presented.

Chapter Nine, *Medical and Relational Information Processing* provides a comprehensive understanding of the nature of information processing. The physiology and psychology associated with both hearing and listening are presented. Psychological barriers to listening are identified and ways of maximizing effective message transmission and reception are provided. The concept of 'mindfulness' and listening to the narrative of the patient are discussed in terms of their implication for the healthcare provider. Techniques for questioning a patient in order to maximize patient information giving are provided. Therapeutic narrative expression for the provider is also addressed with some specific approaches for engaging in such expression.

Chapter Ten, *Theories of Health Communication* are outlined so as to give students an overview of the published data and theory building that has greatly expanded in recent years on the topic of health communication.

Chapter Eleven, *Assessment and Training within Healthcare: Training the Trainers,* provides the fundamental tools that are needed in order to develop, present, and assess an effective training session. The focus on skills provides the reader the tools necessary to set both instructional and behavioral objectives for training on any healthcare topic. Vehicles for delivery and effective behaviors are presented as a way to assist in successful training outcomes.

Part Four: Medical Communication in Tributary Situations

Chapter Twelve, *Informed Consent and Apology* exposes the reader to the language of medical error and the various implications and responsibilities associated with such error. The informed consent process is discussed in detail with a focus on methods through which healthcare providers can more effectively relay important information to the patient. The philosophy of apology and techniques for effective apology are offered as well as a legal perspective indicating specific state laws and the impact and implications such laws have on the apology process.

Chapter Thirteen, *Professionalism, Ethics, Social Media, and other Medical Communication Technologies* explores the many different types of professions that are present within the healthcare field. The responsibilities and training background of professions in both the medical and allied health fields are discussed. Patient needs are presented as well as a detailed accounting of the various choices and legal issues associated with end-of-life care, such as the do not resuscitate order and cultural assumptions about organ donation.

Chapter Fourteen, *Medical Communication Technology: Currents and Futures,* exposes the reader to the future of medicine and healthcare in general. The impact of using electronic health records and other technology on the practice of medicine is discussed with a specific focus on patient confidentiality and possible threats to secured patient information. Other technological advances regarding medical techniques, methods of education, robotics, and SMART technology are discussed with implications for the future.

Student-Oriented Pedagogy

Because of the evidenced-based culture that pervades healthcare, we recognize the importance of providing objective and unambiguous ways of assessing student learning. Therefore, we have integrated within each chapter several features that serve to move the student toward a successful experience and the instructors with quality measures of learning outcomes. Some of these include:

- **Learning Objectives** help students focus on the overall concepts, theories, and skills discussed throughout each chapter
- **Key Terms** direct the students to the specific terms that are important in each chapter
- **Running Glossary** provides an easily accessible definition to all key terms within the text

- **Highlighted Concepts,** bolded throughout the text, are thoroughly explained within the chapter and also appear in the Glossary for further study
- **Figures and Tables** visually depict important and sometimes complex concepts within each chapter
- **Chapter Summaries** provide a synopsis of themes and concepts presented and discussed throughout each chapter
- **Questions for Discussion/Review** provide the student an opportunity to further consider the concepts introduced throughout each chapter
- **References** provide the reader a comprehensive list of all sources and research utilized in the writing of each chapter
- **Glossary** provides a comprehensive list of definitions for all key terms and highlighted concepts introduced in the text

Instructional Online Enhancements

Both students and instructors will have access to online content that is integrated chapter by chapter with the text to maximize the principles and enrich student learning. The Web access code is included on the inside front cover of the textbook and provides the purchaser of the book the ability to reference all of the online material.

Student Web Content

- Video and audio interviews and commentary that provide further information and insight into the concepts discussed in the book
- Vignettes based on real situations with full analysis and debriefing to illustrate the principles under investigation
- Flash cards offer an interactive version of the key terms and their definitions
- A running glossary to serve as an easily accessible reference when reading the text
- Web icons indicate additional online exercises and information for each chapter

Instructor Web Content

- Detailed chapter outlines highlight the central ideas for each chapter and also serve as instructor lecture notes
- Comprehensive test bank offers over 1,200 questions in a variety of formats to best assess student learning and knowledge
- Supplemental teaching materials (sentinel articles, film supplements, and suggested readings for students)

Complete PowerPoint slides present major concepts in the chapter and can be made available to students or used exclusively for instructor lectures

Acknowledgments

We would like to acknowledge the following individuals for working with us to ensure that this book was all that it could be and more. First and foremost, thanks to our families who served as a constant support and source of encouragement throughout the writing of the book. Secondly, thanks to our colleagues from both Medicine and Communication Studies who provided the data from which this text was created.

From Kendall Hunt, we want to thank Paul Carty (Director of Publishing Partnerships) for taking a chance on this groundbreaking book and for "seeing what we wanted him to see," Angela Willenbring (Senior Developmental Editor) for keeping things clean, neat, and on track (as always), as well as a host of others who have worked diligently to deliver a book concept that we believe will have significant impact on the communication process during the everyday practice of medicine.

The following individuals have assisted us greatly in the generation and refinement of our drafts for the second edition. We greatly appreciate their expertise and time as their efforts ensured that the process stayed on course: Lori White (RHIA), Rural Emergency Trauma Institute and Janice Vanchure (RHIT), Physicians Transcription and Support Services. We would also like to thank the following professional colleagues for assisting at key times throughout this project: Andy Rancer, Ph.D., Susan Wieczorek, Ph.D., University of Pittsburgh Johnstown; Valerie Satkoske, Ph.D.; Deb Lassard, BSN MA JD; Patricia Liebman; Cindy Marsh, MBA BSN; Angelo Georges, MD; Kenneth Nanners, MD; Dennis Neiss, MD, MMM, CPE; Thomas Gadacz, MD; David Kappel, MD; Kimberly Auten, BSN; Cassandra Prezzia; Ellen Freeman, and F. Dean Griffen.

Finally, to the students who have attended the Medical Communication classes that were offered at West Virginia University, you were some of the most patient and tolerant "experimental subjects" vs. "test subjects." You allowed us to test the concepts and approach of this book, and you provided the feedback for refinement. Thanks to all!

Theodore A. Avtgis, (Ph.D., 1999, Kent State University) is Professor of Communication Studies and Director of the School of Communication at the University of Akron. He is also an Adjunct Associate Professor in the Department of Surgery at West Virginia University. Dr. Avtgis has authored over 60 peer-reviewed articles and book chapters on organizational communication, communication personality, and their impact on the practice of healthcare. His work has appeared in journals such as the *Journal of Trauma, Journal of Surgical Education, Communication Education, Management Communication Quarterly,* among others. He is co-author of ten books and has served as Editor-in-Chief of *Communication Research Reports* as well as co-founder of *Medical Communication Specialists.* Among several awards, he was recognized as one of the Top Twelve Most Productive Scholars in the field of Communication Studies (between 1996–2001), recognized as a member of the World Council on Hellenes Abroad, USA Region of American Academics, and in 2009 named as a *Centennial Scholar of Communication* by the Eastern Communication Association and the 2011 recipient of the ECA Past Presidents' Award.

E. Phillips Polack, (MD, 1971, West Virginia University, MA, 2006, West Virginia University) is Clinical Professor of Surgery at West Virginia University. Dr. Polack's initial book, *Applied Communication for Health Professionals*, was published in 2008. He has lectured widely in the topic of provider-patient communication, mindfulness and teamwork, at all levels of the health care hierarchy. He is past Governor of the West Virginia Chapter of the American College of Surgeons, and has been an instructor in communication at the *Clinical Congress* of the American College of Surgeons. He has served as Visiting Professor in both residency programs and major academic institutions including the *Canadian Surgical Forum* in 2007. He currently practices plastic surgery at Wheeling Hospital, Wheeling, West Virginia, where he serves as Chairman of the Committee on Ethics and on the Clinical Palliative Care Service.

part One

Foundations of Medical Communication

chapter one

The Imperative of Medical Communication

Upon completion of the chapter, the student should be able to:

1. Explain the evolution of contemporary healthcare

2. Explain the need for effective communication within healthcare in general and within the medical team in particular

3. Explain the five axioms of applied healthcare communication

4. Compare and contrast the various models of communication

5. Explain the 10 misconceptions of communication

B ack in 2011, we defined medical communication as the pragmatic approach to the everyday navigation through, and the interpersonal encounters between, all healthcare providers and their patients. The definition was intended to describe an applicable discipline for those who physically or psychologically interface with the human condition. Over the past 40 years, communication within health care has been studied extensively. A central component of this concerns both the provider's ability to gain patient compliance and the patient's ability to accurately relay their narrative of illness to the provider. Simply put, our ability to effectively and appropriately communicate directly impacts our ability to provide quality care and to fully engage in our own recovery respectively.

Patients frequently have both social and medical needs that can be immense given the complexity or seriousness of the illness. According to the September 17, 2014 "Dying in America" report by the Institutes of Medicine (IOM), approximately 40% of all medical spending is secondary to unrealized

© Monkey Business Images/Shutterstock.com

3

key terms

communication	effectiveness	source message channel
communication competency	hand-off communication	receiver [SMCR]
continuous quality	SBAR	uncertainty management theory
improvement (CQI)	sentinel event	[UMT]
crew resource management		
(CRM)		

communication

The process of a source stimulating meaning in the mind of a receiver by means of verbal and nonverbal messages.

or unmet social support on the part of the healthcare provider. Contributing factors to this lack of social support can be attributed to factors such as low levels of literacy, language and cultural barriers, inadequate nutrition, unsafe housing, family violence, mental illness, and most significantly, worn out and exhausted family healthcare providers. We use the term provider in reference to every individual family member or healthcare professional who provides care for a patient concerning her/his health throughout the duration of life; from birth to death.

In 2007, the Agency for Health Care Quality Research reported that in the United States, more people die as a result of miscommunication in the healthcare setting (approximately 42,000) than die in automobile accidents (approximately 41,115), and almost as many die from breast cancer annually (approximately 45,000) (Polack & Avtgis, 2011). Therefore, the focus on **communication** and communication competency or the understanding of communication works has a central role in the multi-disciplinary practice of safer patient care. Kizer, in 2002, noted that upward of 80% of the care of a patient is provided by nonphysicians which further emphasizes the central importance of communication competency for all of those providing patient care. In a study looking at hospital care within the United States, Leonard, Graham, and Bonacum (2004) revealed stunning findings indicating that communication-related problems are the proximate cause of 70% of sentinel events or an event causing risk/serious injury or death to the patient. Of this 70%, 75% of those patients die.

In the practice of modern medicine, healthcare providers owe a great debt of gratitude to Ernest Armory Codman (1869–1940) who is considered the founding father of the patient safety movement. Codman opened a 12 bed proprietary (i.e., for profit) hospital which he referred to as the "End Result Hospital" in Boston where he advocated the following revolutionary concepts:

1. *The patient should know how much things cost.*
2. *The patient should know what sort of results their doctor achieves for patients predicated on evidence-based data (i.e., research that is data driven via the scientific method) and that such care follow the ancient obligations of Hippocrates which include beneficence (i.e., doing good) and non-maleficence (i.e., doing no harm)* (Hippocrates [400 B.C.] Epidemics Part XI).

Tables 1.1 and 1.2 display the Hippocratic Oath: Modern Version and the Hippocrates' Epidemics Part XI 400 B.C. respectively.

table 1.1	The Hippocratic Oath: Modern Version

I swear to fulfill, to the best of my ability and judgment, this covenant:

I will respect the hard-won scientific gains of those physicians in whose steps I walk, and gladly share such knowledge as is mine with those who are to follow.

I will apply, for the benefit of the sick, all measures [that] are required, avoiding those twin traps of overtreatment and therapeutic nihilism.

I will remember that there is art to medicine as well as science, and that warmth, sympathy, and understanding may outweigh the surgeon's knife or the chemist's drug.

I will not be ashamed to say "I know not," nor will I fail to call in my colleagues when the skills of another are needed for a patient's recovery.

I will respect the privacy of my patients, for their problems are not disclosed to me that the world may know. Most especially must I tread with care in matters of life and death. If it is given to me to save a life, all thanks. But it may also be within my power to take a life; this awesome responsibility must be faced with great humbleness and awareness of my own frailty. Above all, I must not play God.

I will remember that I do not treat a fever chart, a cancerous growth, but a sick human being, whose illness may affect the person's family and economic stability. My responsibility includes these related problems, if I am to care adequately for the sick.

I will prevent disease wherever I can, for prevention is preferable to cure.

I will remember that I remain a member of society, with special obligations to all my fellow human beings, those sound of mind and body as well as the infirmed.

If I do not violate this oath, may I enjoy life and art, respected while I live and remembered with with affection thereafter. May I always act so as to preserve the finest traditions of my calling and may I long experience the joy of healing those who seek my help (Lasagna, 1964).

table 1.2	The Epidemics (Part XI)

*As to diseases, make a habit of two things—**to help**, or at least **do no harm**. The art has three factors, the disease, the patient, and the physician. The physician is the servant of the art. The patient must cooperate with the physician in combating the disease (Hippocrates, 400 B.C.).*

In 1917, Codman became the first chairman of The American College of Surgeons Committee of Standardization which ultimately led to the 1952 formation of the Joint Commission on Accreditation of Hospitals later named the Joint Commission on Accreditation of Health Care Organizations (JCAHO) which is the nation's primary organization for patient safety and hospital oversight. The JCAHO advocates **Continuous Quality Improvement (CQI)** by utilizing a peer review method (i.e., programs that are reviewed by outside experts and programs of equal status) (Levinson & Dunn, 1989). The CQI process is effective in fostering discussion of medical error and fallibility, including sentinel events, and allows for self-critique and introspection. There is one immutable truth concerning patient safety and in that there will be error. The most important facet to this is how the

continuous quality improvement (CQI)

A process based on evidenced based standards that are derived by the scientific method and result in improvement of patient care.

sentinel event

An event causing or risking serious injury or death to the patient.

error is addressed. Sentinel events are called "sentinel" for a reason; they signal the need for immediate investigation and response (Joint Commission, 2014). To quote the 18th-century English poet Alexander Pope, "To err is human, to forgive is divine" (Pope, 1711).

How Safe Is Health Care?

Even though Ernest Codman, back in 1914, strongly encouraged transparency in health care, little was written on or discussed regarding the topic. It was not until 77 years later that Leape, Brennan, and Laird (1991) published an article on hospital-based error. Evaluating the hospitals stays of approximately 30,000 patients within the state of New York, 4% or approximately 1200 patients were in some way injured and the approximately 66% of these injuries were preventable. The major communication-related error was providing double doses of medication or poor "hand-off" communication. While it is difficult to fully digest the impact of communication errors within health care, these findings shed interesting light into an otherwise controllable risk. The Leape et al. finding does not include those patients who never access the hospital system; such is the case of patients in nursing homes, outpatient clinics, community health centers, etc. However, the findings were so dramatic from a patient safety perspective, that the IOM, assessing hospital safety, issued their now famous *To Err is Human* report (Kohn, Corrigan, & Donaldson, 1999). This report reflects data analyzed from 1984 and shows error that accounts for between 44,000 and 98,000 deaths per year. The outrage by the American public resulted in the 2001 document by the IOM, which established goals and objectives to establish multidisciplinary team practice for safer patient care (Shine, 2002). A protocol was established designed to reduce error by half by the year 2005. In 2010, the Office of Inspector General for Health Care and Human Services noted that hospital error contributed to the deaths of 100,000 patients on Medicare alone in a single year.

In a 2013 article published in the *Journal of Patient Safety*, it was shown that between the years of 2008 and 2011, 210,000–440,000 patients who go to the hospital for care suffer from some type of preventable harm that directly contributes to their death (James, 2013). In fact, James argued that the number of serious but not fatal incidences that attributed to preventable harm is 10–20-fold higher than that. These statistics make hospital harm, the third leading cause of death in America behind only heart disease and cancer that are first and second respectively. These data suggest that the American healthcare system has become complacent. Recall the initiative of the IOM's recommendations that were to reduce error by 50% when they were estimating around 100,000 incidences. The 2013 report suggests that we are dealing with numbers of error that quadruple this. It would seem that such data serve as a clarion call for standardized education in medical communication. While there are some general principles guiding competent communication, a large part of communication is contextual and there are certain elements of communication that are unique to the healthcare setting.

The Healthcare Team

Health care begins at the moment when an individual accesses either on a routine or emergency basis any member who is considered a healthcare provider be it a hospital, office, or clinic setting; hospital, nursing home, or at home, etc. One of the most valid concepts of safe patient care can be found in the notion of the healthcare team. Hackman and Johnson (2004) distinguish between a **group** and a **team** in that a group consists of several individuals who come into contact with each other but maintain their distinct and individual interests and concerns. A team, on the other hand, is a group of individuals who come together to create a joint product and that joint product, in terms of patient care, is to help the patient by doing no harm and being able to establish a collaborative partnership with the patient in a spirit of mutuality. Sharpe and Faden (1998), citing the ground breaking book by Paul Starr (1982) titled *The Social Transformation of American Medicine,* discuss the cultural shift in the relationship between healthcare providers and their patients. More specifically, they discuss the profound shift in healthcare culture from what was once a **paternalistic model** where the provider had all of the power and acted upon the patient. The patient was seen as a passive participant in their own treatment. However, as society evolves, we presently find ourselves in a **mutuality model** in which both patient and provider act in unison with one another to create the best possible solution based on not only the disease but also other influences such as social and economic factors. This shift in care is attributed to the result of the Vietnam War in the 1960s and the Civil Rights Movement in the early 1970s when common citizens began to question power structures around them. One of the largest power structures that were being questioned was health care.

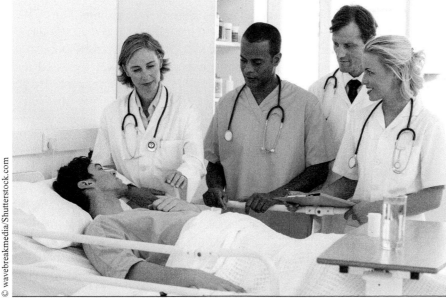

Healthcare teams focus on patient safety.

© wavebreakmedia/Shutterstock.com

crew resource management (CRM)

A management system based on the concept of error that results from a breakdown in interpersonal communication, leadership, and decision-making.

As the team concept began to flourish in health care, other industries were also creating related types of partnerships. One such industry was that of aviation. The concept of **Crew Resource Management (CRM)**, emerged as valuable concept for team function. CRM can be traced to the early work of psychologist John C. Flanagan (Flanagan, 1954). Flanagan developed the Ethical Incident Technique to evaluate behaviors that were believed to determine success or failure of aircraft pilots. Using post-Korean War data, Flanagan focused on specific behaviors that distinguished good pilots from bad pilots. Carrying this initial work forward, Helmreich (1997) determined that the majority of pilot error was a direct result of poor communication, poor team work, and ineffective collective decision-making. Such failures become readily apparent when voice data recorded was retrieved from the Potomac River when Air Florida Flight 90 crashed into the 14th street bridge in the Washington D.C. area on January 13, 1982. The Boeing 737 was taking off in a snow storm. Neither pilot had much experience flying in such weather. The pilot was described as a quite person who was previously suspended for not following standard checklist protocols. The co-pilot had told the pilot four times that to spite what the instrument panel was indicating, it did not reflect the reality of the situation in which they would not clear the bridge upon take off. The end result was that 78 people died in the crash.

In a similar effort, Merritt and Helmreich (1996) studied 13,000 pilots from 16 different countries from around the world. They researched the impact that culture has on compliance in team decision-making. The findings indicated that culture exerts great influence on compliance behavior. More specifically, pilots of Asian extraction were very concerned about respect and the concept of "face" (i.e., respect for another person's self-concept) and reported that speaking up to a superior was not the correct thing to do. In western cultures, 98% of pilots from the United States and Europe reported that voicing concern in the face of error was the correct thing to do. In light of this revelation, Crew Resource Management principles were seen as transferrable to other high stress industries regardless of culture. Thus CRM was readily accepted as an effective tool. This led Leonard et al. (2004) to develop the mnemonic checklist known as **SBAR** which stands for <u>s</u>ituation, <u>b</u>ackground, <u>a</u>ssessment, and <u>r</u>ecommendation. SBAR was designed and mandated to be used in the delivery room at the Kaiser Permanente Health System. However, this checklist has been applied to other types of practice throughout the healthcare systems. An example of this can be seen in the pre-hospital setting. Consider a paramedic has evaluated and stabilized a patient at the scene of an accident and is ready to transport the victim to the hospital. He transmits a radio message based on SBAR: *Situation*—Paramedic Dan Jones with an 18-year-old female involved in a car versus truck head-on collision. *Background*—There is significant front-end compression, and the air bags were deployed. The patient was a restrained driver. *Assessment*—The patient is semi-comatose and has a large chest contusion, multiple glass lacerations to the forehead and scalp. *Recommendations*—Two large bore IVs have been started. The patient is on a backboard with CID and neck lock. We will transmit the cardiac rhythm strip, and we are on our way to your facility.

SBAR

A pneumonic device developed to increase the efficiency of information exchange, thus reducing the chance of human error. SBAR stands for **S**ituation, **B**ackground, **A**ssessment, and **R**ecommendations.

While simple mnemonic device may simply be inadequate for every situation and may require much more information, what we are confident about is the fact that devices such as the SBAR assist in the standardization of information and allows, in high stress situations, a person who is practiced in the use of the mnemonic, a degree of psychological comfort in times of chaos and uncertainty.

Changing the Culture of Health Care

Culture can be defined as those traditions, customs, norms, beliefs, values, and thought patterns that are passed down from generation to generation (Avtgis, Rancer, & Liberman, 2012). James Reason (1990), considered the father of error analysis, stated that changing behaviors for an entire culture is like swatting a single mosquito to eliminate an entire mosquito infestation. In fact, the only solution to truly eliminate a mosquito infestation is to drain the swamp that provides the habitat for survival. True to this thought, Reason argued that although we cannot change the human condition, we can change the condition in which humans work. Regarding healthcare culture specifically, any change in communication will need to take place within individuals at all levels of the hierarchy. According to Polack, Richmond and McCroskey, (2008), two major factors in bringing about cultural change are **education** and **training**. Education is the process of imparting knowledge whereas training refers to the acquisition of demonstrable skills so as to perform a specific task in a specific way. Both education and training are operationalized through language. Language comprises both syntax and semantic symbols and thought-bound cultural assumptions. Thus, language is the vehicle through which culture is passed from one person to another (Matsumoto, 1990). In an effort to summarize a series of studies targeted at cultural change regarding the importance of communication training within health care, Polack, Avtgis, Rossi, and Shaffer (2010) developed five axioms regarding assumptions about medical communication.

1. *Leadership* is a communication skill, and not a medical skill. Leadership is multidisciplinary and includes communication studies and other social scientific disciplines including psychology, management, and sociology. As such, it becomes clear that leadership theory and behavior are best acquired via the social sciences as it is the application to the practice of health care that provides the basis for effective human performance.

2. *Perception* and *interpretation* are individual events and thus will always be subjective in nature rendering them imperfect. As we indicated earlier in this chapter, communication competence consists of both effectiveness and appropriateness in the pursuit of understanding how communication works (Infante, Rancer, & Avtgis, 2010). However, of the two elements of communication competence, it is the appropriate dimension that varies much more greatly based on the context in which the communication occurs. For example, time is one such contextual factor. The SBAR acronym probably would not have been accepted as

effectiveness

A dimension of communication competence that reflects the ability to achieve one's goals.

an effective communication tool 30 or 40 years ago due to the nature of medicine being paternalistic. In other words, the team concept did not exist and input from people of lower status than that of the physician was not valued. A paramedic would not think to make suggestions to a physician regarding suggested treatment strategies.

3. *Team is a relationally based concept, and not a medical concept.* To be a member of team assumes that there is an increased level of interdependence and trust among team members. A properly functioning team requires members to have an understanding of the idiosyncratic interpersonal behaviors and team rules and norms that allow all team members to be successful. According to Larson and LaFasto (1989), effective team members demonstrate eight strategies consisting of clear and inspiring team goals, maintain a result-oriented team structure; assemble competent team members who strive for unified commitment, develop a collaborative climate that rewards interdependent performance, follows standards of excellence, provides extrinsic reward and punishment for team performance, and applies the principles of leadership.

4. *The concept of a perfect world is unrealistic and as such, should not be the focus of any communication skills training.* When dealing with human conditions and human relationships, one cannot easily navigate the idiosyncratic nature, dynamics, and complexities of human behavior. The concepts of jealousy, biases, and stigmas are fraught throughout most interactions and they are only compounded by the fact that health care is a complex intermeshing of many different people predicated on power and hierarchy. However, through the communication education process, we hope that people exposed to communication training and evidenced-based research will come to understand the differences between people who are effective and successful communicators and people who are ineffective and unsuccessful communicators.

communication competency
The ability to relay information in an effective and socially appropriate way or understand how communication works.

5. *Change cannot occur locally if it is not nurtured globally.* Communication competency training efforts can only be truly successful if the organization embraces such efforts at all levels of the organization. This takes a cultural change to reflect that communication best practices should be an ongoing goal that has bottom-line results. In other words, patient safety, economic efficiency, and employee morale all are improved through communication education and training. However, it should be noted that substantially changing an organization's culture is a difficult process that takes time and resources to accomplish.

In contemporary medicine and health care, there is a cultural assumption that the practice of medicine is a "pure science" and the social scientific side of such practice is frequently discredited or overlooked in the contemporary evidenced-based culture that we currently find ourselves (Sackett, 1997). Even in light of this, the Accreditation Council for Graduate Medical Education (ACGME) mandated that effective July 1, 2011, all postgraduate residency educators must instruct their trainees in compassionate care and interpersonal communication as a core competency. Despite this call, communication skills training within postgraduate residency programs remains an exception and not the norm. One only needs to consider the patient safety data and percentage of burnout of health workers to see that communication is key to increasing patient safety and reducing costly employee turnover.

Rapid Advancement

Throughout history, including the time of Hippocrates (400 B.C.), communication or language has been the primary vehicle through which the healthcare provider establishes trust with the patient. This relationship development is critical for effective care. Recall that the Hippocratic Oath specifically refers to medicine as a science and an art and that concepts such as empathy, understanding, and warmth are equal if not more important than any surgery or medication (Lasagna, 1964). Advances made in medicine since 400 B.C. were relatively slow until the mid-19th century. However several of those advances were truly revolutionary. For example, in 1846, William Morton gave the first public demonstration of ether anesthesia in the 'ether dome' at Massachusetts General Hospital in Boston. Famous surgeon John Collins Warren was scheduled to remove a tumor from the jaw of his patient. Morton, who was a trained dentist, set up the ether dome so that the patient could breathe ether such that within three minutes the patient fell into a "state of insensibility." Warren wrote that the patient did not experience any pain at the time although he was aware that the operation was proceeding. In 1858, Edward K. Squibb began to manufacture medical products that were cleaner, safer, and more standardized than most medications at that time. These included ether, chloroform, and cocaine.

Regardless of the magnitude of medical advancement, patient trust has always been an important issue. Peabody (1927) noted that the secret to patient care is simply caring for the patient. The first 50 years of the 20th century, primarily as a result of World War I, saw incredible advancements in medical treatments and procedures. In 1928, the accidental discovery of penicillin provided the world with its first antibiotic. Sir Alexander Fleming published his findings on how mold that had grown on a culture plate prevented the growth of the staphylococcus bacteria. He published his findings in 1929 in the *Journal of Experimental Pathology*. Up until that time, staphylococcus bacteria was responsible for much of the morbidity and mortality at that time and now could be contained. While all of these and many other advancements pushed forward the science of medicine, scholars warned that we cannot forget the three key factors concerning the art of medicine put forth by Hippocrates. First, the patients' narrative which reflects what the patients know and understand about their ailment. Second, clear and effective/competent communication between the provider and the patient. Third, there needs to be a nurturing of trust that reflects knowing the beliefs, attitudes, cultural background, and socio-emotional health of the patient. Although, being mindful of such patient information allows us to collaborate with the patient in a mutual collaboration regarding the most effective and appropriate treatment.

Such collaborative processes between patient and provider are not only just best practices, but they also have bottom-line economic outcomes as relationship building also increases a patient's compliance with provider recommendations. According to DiMatteo (2004), noncompliance or lack of patient adherence to a recommended treatment regimen costs the U.S. healthcare system billions of dollars each year. Sullivan, Kreling, and Hazlett (1990) argued that hospitalization due to patients not properly taking their medication, costs the United States approximately $13.35 billion annually. Noncompliance has become such a significant issue that Kane, Huo, Aikens, and Hanauer (2003), isolating noncompliance as a single risk factor for poor outcomes, argued that lack of compliance results in approximately 125,000 deaths annually just within the U.S. healthcare system.

As much as 40% of all patients engage in noncompliance depending on how complex or difficult the provider's recommendations are perceived to be (Haynes, McDonald & Garg, 2002). In fact, depending on the degree to which the recommendations involve significant life style changes such as changes in diet, increased exercise, smoking and drinking cessation, or modification of other habits, noncompliance can be as high as 70% (Brownell & Cohen, 1995). When patients are asked to take multiple pills, noncompliance can be as high as 80% (Graveley & Oseasohn, 1991).

Another significant factor that influences compliance is health literacy. According to the U.S. Department of Health and Human Services (2000), health literacy is defined as "the degree to which individuals have the capacity to obtain, process, and understand basic health information and services needed to make appropriate health decisions." Compliance with health recommendations can be extremely difficult when an individual cannot read or does not understand even the simplest of written instructions. Williams, Parker, and Baker (1995) assessed 2500 patients for accuracy of compliance with medical recommendations. The results indicated that 42% misunderstood directions for properly taking medication on an empty stomach and 25% could not recall their next appointment date and time. Almost 60% were unable to understand a typical informed consent document. The quality of the relationship between the patient and the provider also can work for more effective compliance. O'Malley, Forrest, and Mandelblatt (2002) found that when patients believe that their provider communicates well and encourages the patient's active participation, the patient is more motivated to adhere to the instructions.

The concept of culture has also been implicated as a factor in determining the level of patient compliance (Copper, Gallo, & Gonzales, 1999). However, more recent research indicates that the quality of relationship that is forged between the patient and provider is far more influential in determining the level of compliance than any cultural factors including ethnicity, age, and gender (Jahng, Martin, & Golin, 2005).

One cannot underestimate the role that mental health has on any given patient behavior. Compliance is no different. In a meta-analysis (i.e., a study that looks at many other related studies and treats each of the previous studies as one piece of data), DiMatteo, Lepper, and Croghan (2000) found that patient noncompliance is 27% higher if the patient is depressed and 30% higher if the patient has end stage renal disease (Martin, Williams, Haskard, & DiMatteo, 2005). However, there are individual factors that influence a given patient. For example, the patient may not understand they are depressed and this unawareness may manifest itself in physical ailments in a way to keep the patient from confronting the stigma of mental illness. Such an unawareness or fear of stigmatization may result in the patient's resistance or increased anxiety related to disclosing their psychological symptoms to the provider (Docherty, 1997). In terms of the provider, some barriers to compliance include the provider's lack of knowledge about depression, poor training in psychiatry, and reluctance, due to time limitations, to engage in discussions about the emotional states of the patient (Carney, Dietrich, & Eliassen, 1999).

The Basics of Communication

The student of health care, regardless of the specific profession one is entering, must remember that medical communication is very contextual. While contextual, there is a basic science to communication that transcends any given context. More specifically, the science of communication studies involves a combination of rhetoric or the ability to strategically use language to appeal to emotions, goodwill, and/or logic and social psychology which is the systematic study of social behavior. This study of social behavior is primarily conducted through the scientific method in order to understand personality, attitudes, motivations, and behaviors. Through the combination of rhetoric and social psychology, verbal and nonverbal behaviors can be systematically investigated and theories can be derived. Polack et al. (2008) defined communication as the "process of a source creating meaning in the mind of the receiver through verbal and nonverbal messages" (p. 17). While there are literally dozens of ways to define communication, there are basic elements common to most.

Process reflects something that is ongoing with no actual beginning or ending. For example, a nurse engages in an aggressive exchange with a difficult patient. In an effort to end the episode, the nurse walks out of the examining room. At what point did the aggressive exchange begin? When the patient first spoke? When they entered each other's field of vision? This question is impossible to answer, based on the assumption that communication is a process. **Meaning** reflects the idiosyncratic way in which people make sense of stimuli. For example, you may use the word "nice" when referring to a colleague's performance during a particular procedure. However, you may also use the word "nice" when that same colleague knocks over a piece of monitoring equipment. In these examples, most people would interpret the first response as communicating approval and communicating sarcasm in the second response. The **verbal** aspects of communication include **syntax** which is the digital language or the actual words that are used, and **semantics** which is the analog language or the meanings of the words that are used. Finally **nonverbal** aspects of communication reflect all of the other aspects of communication that do not involve words. These aspects can include voice inflection, tone, speech rate, body movement, eye behavior, touch, among others.

Models of Communication

There literally are dozens of models of communication that have been developed over the past 60-plus years. We will focus on two of the most influential models for mapping out the communication process. The first model was developed in 1960 by David Berlo. Known as the Source Message Channel Receiver (SMCR) model of communication, it includes elements of the **source** or the person who encodes or creates the message, the **message** or the information being sent, the **receiver** or the person(s) who receives the message in order to give the message meaning or decode the message. Figure 1.1 illustrates Berlo's SMCR model.

The second most significant model of the communication process is the **McCroskey Model of Communication** (1968). This model incorporates all of the aspects of the SMCR model and highlights the concepts of **noise** and **feedback**. Noise is an element of communication that is omnipresent throughout all elements of communication and can be present before and/or after any given communication act (Infante et al., 2010). Noise can be considered anything that can distort or encumber the communication process. Types of noise can include intrapersonal noise or the psychological states of the communicators, interpersonal noise or relational climate between the communicators, and physical noise or the physical environment in which the communication takes place. Feedback reflects any information via verbal or nonverbal communication that is sent in reaction to a message. Such feedback results in feedback-induced adaptation. According to Infante et al. "feedback-induced adaptation means that a source can adapt to a receiver's feedback by altering his or her subsequent messages and responses" (p. 66). Figure 1.2 illustrates the McCroskey Model of Communication.

source message channel receiver [SMCR]

Communication model proposed by David Berlo that highlights the concepts of source, message, channel, and receiver.

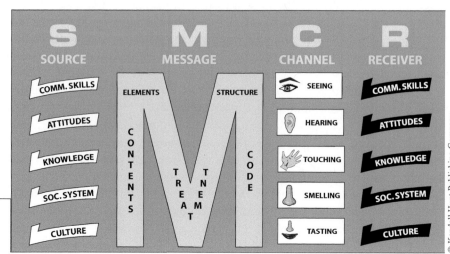

© Kendall Hunt Publishing Company

figure 1.1

Berlo SMCR Model

A model of the ingredients in communication

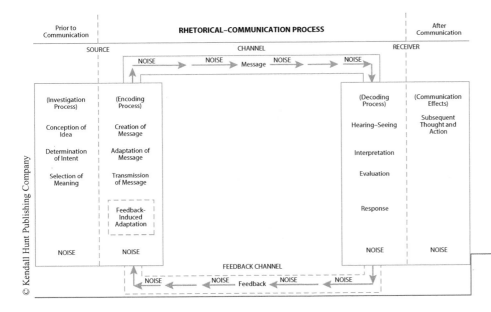

figure 1.2

The McCroskey Model of Communication

As illustrated in this section, the communication process is fluid, dynamic, and complex. We will now discuss the concepts of how interpersonal goals and motivations that people have when communicating can have a profound impact on not only communication processes in general, but also how they affect healthcare communication specifically.

Communication Goals

When we communicate with other people, we generally engage in such a behavior in order to achieve some desired outcomes. Generally speaking, there are four goals that are pursued through communication. The first goal is to **build relationships**. We communicate to create and establish many different connections that can include personal and professional connectedness and networks. From an evolutionary perspective, communicating to build relationships also includes survival needs in that by being connected to others, we increase our probability of survival as there is strength in numbers and that strength is realized via relationships with others.

The second goal of communication is to **influence others**. We communicate with other people in order to get them to think, feel, and/or behave in certain ways. Communication is the primary vehicle in the practice of influence. Whether we want to form thoughts, feelings and behaviors; reinforce thoughts, feelings, and behaviors; or change thoughts, feelings, and behaviors we need to implement effective communication strategies.

The third goal of communication is to **understand**. This reflects the use of communication to understand the world around us. For example, on September 11, 2001, many people engaged in communication with complete strangers or co-workers whom they never had a previous conversation simply in order to understand what was occurring regarding the 9/11 terrorist attacks. Such communication can serve to clarify, probe, or engage in debate to name but a few.

The fourth goal of communication is to **reduce uncertainty**. Communication allows us to reduce feelings of vulnerability or reduce the unknown. For example, a patient who is experiencing a significant amount of uncertainty regarding a particular condition may ask questions such as "What if this happens?" "What if that happens?" "What do I do now?" "Will insurance cover this?" "Who will be performing the procedure?" These are but a few of the communication strategies designed to reduce uncertainty. People engage in a great of uncertainty reduction behavior particularly at the beginning of relationships (Berger & Calabrese, 1975). There are several levels of uncertainty reduction that move from the most general and rather insignificant to the most specific and most significant. The first layer of uncertainty reduction is known as **cultural uncertainty reduction** and includes communication designed to reveal basic assumptions about others based on easily recognizable yet sometimes insignificant characteristics. Some of these characteristics include a person's race, gender, accent, and so on. The next level of uncertainty reduction is known as the **social level of uncertainty reduction** and reflects revealing things that are less easily recognizable such as age and general world view but still, similar to the cultural level, tends to be more superficial in nature. **Psychological uncertainty reduction** reflects an understanding of another person's attitudes, beliefs, and values. The **intimate level of uncertainty** is the highest level of uncertainty reflecting the least uncertainty due to the fact that it requires all of the previous three levels of knowledge plus the ability to tailor messages in ways that fully account for the other person's potential reaction.

While it has long been assumed that all people seek to reduce uncertainty, sometimes uncertainty simply cannot be reduced or people do not want it reduced. In 2001, Dale Brashers developed Uncertainty management theory (UMT). Brashers (2001a) believed that uncertainty was a multifaceted concept that can fulfill important functions if we do not treat it as something that is universally bad or something that needs to be reduced or eliminated. For example, if someone is faced with terminal illness, he or she would probably benefit (psychologically, physically, or both) from the concept of hope and miracle. Both of which require a degree of uncertainty.

Consistent with this example, UMT is based on a person's ability to "manage," not "reduce," uncertainty. Some people can be comfortable with high levels of uncertainty (e.g., "I trust my physician, so that is all I need to know."); other people are only comfortable when uncertainty is at a minimum (e.g., "I was up all night printing out all of the available information about my condition."). A person's tolerance for uncertainty is based on three factors: (a) the meaning a person attaches to the uncertainty, (b) the role that the person's behavior plays in response to uncertainty, and (c) the communicative and psychological strategies used to manage uncertainty (Afifi & Matsunaga, 2008; Infante et al., 2010).

In a study of how illness affects uncertainty, Brashers (2001b) investigated how patients who were HIV positive experience and manage the

uncertainty management theory [UMT]

A theory that explains how people react to health-related uncertainty.

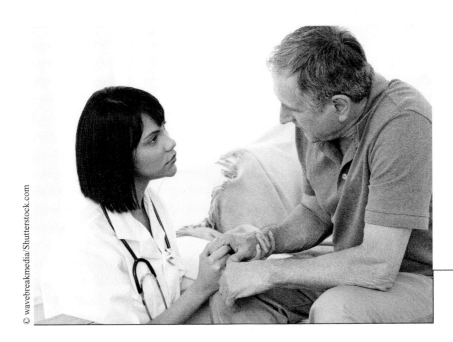

Expressing concern and caring makes others feel appreciated.

uncertainty. The findings indicate that some patients may actively seek out healthcare professionals who encourage uncertainty in an effort to provide a sense of hope or a chance of some other beneficial outcome. By doing this, it provides the patient with a sense of control, optimism, and hope (Seligman, 1990). Hope is very important in health care. Frank and Frank (1991) argued that a patient's belief in hope reduces stress, anxiety, and increases survivability. Investigating support among patients with small cell carcinoma of the lungs, Temel, Greer, and Mukikansky (2010) found that patients who link standard treatment with supportive or palliative care survive longer. These data illustrate the power of quality relationships and supportive communication in patient healing. Figure 1.3 illustrates this process of uncertainty management.

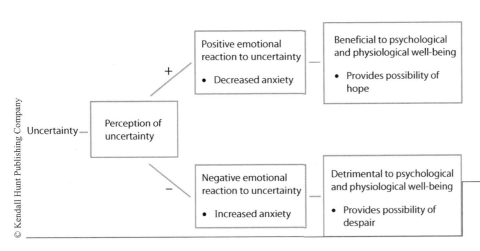

figure 1.3

Model of the Uncertainty Management Process

Misconceptions of Communication

As with other types of knowledge, knowing what effective communication is and how to put it into practice within health care are but pieces of the larger puzzle. What needs to be addressed are the misconceptions that people have about communication. It is well documented in the organizational training literature that to be effective in achieving improved communication, one must first dispel any false information the participants have prior to the new knowledge being introduced (Avtgis et al., 2012). Polack et al. (2008) outlined the 10 most common misconceptions of communication.

Misconception #1: **Words have meaning.** This misconception leads to a great deal of misunderstanding among people. Meanings exist in people, not in words (Polack & Avtgis, 2011). When we refer to the concept of meaning within people, we are referring to both the sender(s) and/or the receiver(s). Most words that are contained in the dictionary have multiple meanings. It is only in the context of the delivery (i.e., environment), the linguistic channels used (e.g., tone of voice, speech rate, and so on), nonverbal behaviors (e.g., facial expressions and body posture), and syntax (i.e., the order of the words) of the sentence that determines the meaning in the mind of the receiver. The meaning of a particular word to a sender may or may not be the same for the receiver.

Misconception #2: **Communication is a verbal process.** In fact, communication is a dynamic process that involves both verbal and nonverbal behaviors. How you send a message can create as much meaning and sometimes even greater meaning than the actual message itself. Most of the effect or emotion that we attach to messages comes from the ability to express oneself nonverbally. In a very real way, the nonverbal behavior we use is the determining factor in the successful relaying of verbal messages.

Misconception #3: **Telling is communicating.** The concept of telling someone something is reflective of only considering the needs of the source without regard to the receiver. In the interpersonal communication models presented earlier, the sender encodes a message and then sends it to the receiver, but this is only the beginning of the communication process. People develop this misconception because of their failure to acknowledge the active role played by the receiver. In fact, people who believe this misconception have no understanding that the receiver actually attaches meaning to the source's message. This process of attaching meaning to the source's message is primarily based on the receiver's background and experience. An example of this misconception can be seen in the amount of recall and understanding of information a patient has after a meeting with a physician. Silverman, Kurtz, and Draper (2005) reported that patients recall only 50% to 60% of the information given to them by physicians. Dunn et al. (1993), focusing specifically on patients with cancer, reported that during the initial medical interview patients only remembered 45% of the "key points" of the process. The key points are the most important information as determined by medical oncologists (i.e., cancer specialist). As one can imagine, the diminished recall of the patient in general, and the patient with cancer in particular, can be attributed to the uncertainty and anxiety associated with such a situation.

Misconception #4: **Communication will solve all of our problems.** Communication can be the cause of conflict and can exacerbate an already existing conflict. In a **conflicted dyad** (i.e., two people who are in a conflict with one another), communication can actually serve to escalate the conflict into a verbally aggressive exchange (e.g., use of verbal attacks such as attacking another person's competence or character).

Communication is the essential component to effective problem-solving, yet this same communication can create new problems. For example, consider a nurse–practitioner who has suggested to a patient that he or she needs to lose weight. The nurse practitioner's motivation for such a suggestion can be entirely altruistic and professional in terms of acting as a responsible health counselor who is offering sage advice to the patient. However, depending on the mindset of the patient, this suggestion can be interpreted as valuable input or an attack on the patient. In the end, communication can be used to create, escalate, or solve problems.

Misconception #5: **Communication is a good thing.** Communication is a tool, and similar to all tools, it can be used for good or bad and can serve to fix or break things. Communication should be considered **amoral** or something that is without moral characteristic. For example, consider the fact that Adolph Hitler, Abraham Lincoln, Martin Luther King Jr., Joseph Stalin, and Mother Theresa all used communication in various ways. It was not in the communication itself that was valued as good or bad but

© wavebreakmedia/Shutterstock.com

People who believe telling is communicating are forgetting about the role of the receiver.

in the implementation and outcomes of such communication. In terms of an example in health care, a hemostat is a good tool for clamping bleeders (i.e., bleeding blood vessels), but if you use it improperly or throw it in anger, it becomes a weapon.

Misconception #6: **The more you communicate, the better.** As is with many things in life, it is not the amount of something but the quality of something that matters most. For example, if a healthcare provider tells a patient that they need to increase their intake of quality protein, they are advocating that the patient behave in a certain way and to a certain degree. They are not saying that the patient should only eat protein or consume it at massive levels; only an increase in intake. Too much protein intake would also be detrimental to the patient and have the opposite effects. Communication can be thought of in the same way. A competent communicator knows that balance of when to and when to not communicate. This balance is based on the particular people and the particular relationship between the two.

Misconception #7: **Communication can break down.** When there is difficulty in communicating with another person, it is common for people to say that the communication "broke down" or that there was a "communication breakdown." Given that communication is an ever-present process with no real beginning or ending, there is at no time an opportunity for it to stop, much less break. It is important not to confuse the concept of incompetent or ineffective communication with "communication breakdown." For example, during **hand-off communication** an abundance of information is exchanged between the person relinquishing their duties and the person who is taking over those duties. Hand-off communication is the information exchanged between the outgoing party and the incoming party regarding health and general information pertaining to patients and patient care. When a nurse is ending a shift, there is a particular protocol or "hand-off" procedure that must be followed to reduce the possibility of error with regard to a lack of or inadequate instruction from one party to the next. Such issues can include patient status, medication allergies, patient complaints, family issues, and so on.

hand-off communication

Information exchanged between the outgoing party and the incoming party regarding health and general information pertaining to patients and patient care.

Misconception #8: **Communication is a natural ability.** Communication is a learned process. Training and education are crucial in the development of competent communication. Some examples of the importance of learning and communication competency can be seen in children who, in the early months of life, are able to utter a full spectrum of phonemes (sounds) but are unable to put these phonemes into a coherent language until approximately two years of age. It is because of this developmental process that scholars advocate that children learn foreign languages between the ages of two and six years. Similar to your chosen healthcare vocation, none of us were "born" into that specific skill set. The development of skills was a direct result of educational and training efforts. Therefore, we should approach the development of communication competency as we would any other skill that is critical to our success as a healthcare professional.

Misconception #9: **Interpersonal communication is intimate communication.**
Interpersonal communication can include anything from acquaintances interacting to the closest of friends interacting. Most of us have plenty of practice
in general interpersonal communication and little experience with intimate
communication. **Intimate communication** can be defined as communication
that involves disclosure of significant magnitude from one or both interaction partners. This is in contrast to **interpersonal communication,** which is
any communication that occurs between two parties. It is important for the
healthcare practitioner to understand the reasons that you ask a patient certain
things and avoid asking other things. Although routine questions may make
perfect sense to you in the context of the clinical setting, these routine questions may or may not make sense to the patient. Therefore, it is important
that when asking questions of the patient, even if there is a remote possibility
that the question could be perceived as intrusive or "none of your business,"
you should provide a rationale for the question so as to avoid any confusion
in distinguishing appropriate from intimate questions. For example, a young
woman with a sore throat may be surprised when you evaluate all of the
lymph node—bearing areas for swollen glands. The patient may not understand why it is necessary for you to palpate the groin area where there is a
chain of lymph nodes. By explaining the reason for your need to inspect the
groin region, you are providing the patient a degree of control and avoiding
any misinterpretation of your actions and intent.

Misconception #10: **Competent communication is effective communication.** Larson, Backlund, Redmond, and Barbour (1978) defined communication competence as an ability to demonstrate knowledge of appropriate
communication in any given situation. To be truly competent, one must be
able to move beyond simply being effective. In fact, many scholars argue that

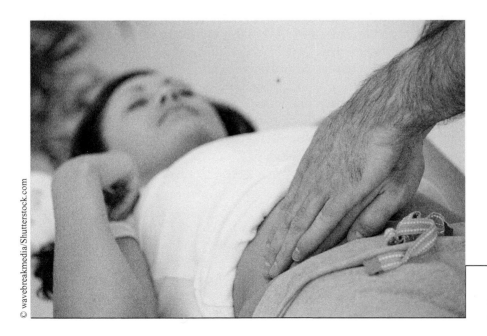

© wavebreakmedia/Shutterstock.com

*Why should you always
explain your actions and
intent during an exam?*

communication competence contains both appropriateness and effectiveness dimensions (Infante et al., 2010; Spitzberg & Cupach, 1984). As discussed earlier in this chapter, both effectiveness and appropriateness are critical to efficient information exchange. For example, when considering the team-oriented nature of medical care, one is in a constant relationship with other members of the team. With that said, there are relationships among healthcare team members that need to be maintained and respected. Thus, by including appropriateness in the communication competence equation, we can not only achieve our goals, but we also can do so in a way that does not damage the relationship with a person with whom we will need to rely on for the foreseeable future. The bottom-line effects of utilizing competent communication include the following: Increased patient and general workplace safety, reduced medical error, reduced costs, increased job satisfaction of personnel, reduced liability, and increased patient perception of caring—**Perceived Empathy.**

Conclusion

The goal of this chapter was to present a brief history of communication in health care and introduce some basic concepts and assumptions about the study of competent communication and health outcomes. Medical error and its connection to ineffective communication are major concerns that have been shown to cost billions of dollars annually. Several approaches to error reduction were presented and discussed. One example of this was crew resource management.

Five axioms of communication in health care that serve as the foundation for our approach to healthcare communication were outlined. The process of communication and the key components of that process were identified and defined. The concept of uncertainty and how people react to uncertainty, especially when it comes to their health, was shown to be a complex process. The uncertainty management theory informed us that uncertainty is not always bad and, in fact, can serve to provide people with hope. Also presented were the 10 common misconceptions about communication. By presenting these misconceptions, we can address any faulty thinking about the communication process. These basic concepts and ideas serve as the foundation from which to present and discuss more advanced ideas of medical communication.

Questions for Discussion/Review

1. What role do you think the concept of communication plays in the ancient physician obligations of beneficence and nonmalfeasance? How do you think these two obligations should be communicated to the patient?
2. Discuss the concept of error in health care. How does error in health care differ from error in the aviation industry?
3. Discuss the basic assumptions of crew resource management. How has this management theory been used within healthcare organizations?
4. Define the components of SBAR and provide a health-related example of how SBAR can be used to effectively relay information.
5. Discuss the four categories of uncertainty reduction.
6. List the five axioms presented in this chapter and provide an example for each axiom.
7. List and define the basic concepts of the SMCR model of communication.
8. Distinguish between feedback and feedback-induced adaptation. How can the knowledge of each of these communication concepts be beneficial to a healthcare practitioner when communicating with a patient?
9. Present the basic assumptions of the uncertainty management theory and how treating uncertainty as a multifaceted concept can serve both patients and practitioners well.
10. Identify 3 of the 10 misconceptions of communication and give an example in your own life of how such a misconception resulted in negative outcomes.

References

Agency for Health Care Quality Research. (2007). *How many patients die from medical mistakes in U.S. hospitals?* Retrieved from http://patientpatientsafety.com/questionp=310,

Afifi, W. A., & Matsunaga, M. (2008). Uncertainty management theories: Three approaches to a multifarious process: In L. A. Baxter & D. O. Braithwaite (Eds.), *Engaging theories in interpersonal communication: Multiple perspectives* (pp. 117–132). Thousand Oaks, CA: Sage.

Avtgis, T. A., Rancer, A. S., & Liberman, C. (2012). *Organizational communication strategies for success* (2nd ed.). Dubuque, IA: Kendall Hunt.

Berger, C. R., & Calabrese, R. J. (1975). Some explorations in initial interaction and beyond: Toward a developmental theory of interpersonal communication. *Human Communication Research 1,* 99–112.

Berlo, D. K. (1960). *The process of communication.* New York: Halt, Rinehart & Winston.

Bio. (2014). *Alexander Fleming biography: Biologist, scientist (1881–1955).* Retrieved from http://www.biography.com/people/alexander-fleming-9296894.

Brashers, D. E. (2001a). Communication and uncertainty management. *Journal of Communication, 51,* 477–497.

Brashers, D. E. (2001b). HIV and uncertainty: Managing treatment decision making. *Focus: A guid to AIDS Research, 16,* 5–6.

Brownell, K. D., & Cohen, L. R. (1995). Adherence to dietary regimens I: An overview of research. *Behavioral Medicine, 20,* 149–154.

Carney, P. A., Dietrich, A. J., & Eliassen, M. S. (1999). Recognizing and managing depression in primary care: A standardized patient study. *Journal of Family Practice, 48,* 965–972.

Copper, P. L., Gallo, J. J., & Gonzales, J. J. (1999). Race, gender, and partnership in the patient-physician relationship. *Journal of American Medical Association, 282,* 583–589.

DiMatteo, M. R. (2004). Social support and patient adherence to medical treatment: A meta-nalysis. *Health Psychology, 23,* 207–218.

DiMatteo, M. R., Lepper, H. S., & Croghan, T. W. (2000). Depression is a risk factor for noncompliance with medical treatment: A meta-analysis of the effects of anxiety and depression on patient adherence. *Archives of Internal Medicine, 160,* 2101–2107.

Docherty, J. P. (1997). Barriers to the diagnosis of depression and primary care. *Journal of Clinical Psychiatry, 1,* 5–10.

Dunn, S. M., Butow, P. N., Tattersall, M. H., Jones, Q. J., Sheldon, J. S., & Taylor, J. J. (1993). General information tapes inhibit recall of the cancer consultation. *Journal of Clinical Oncology, 11,* 2279–2285.

Edelstein, L. (1943). *The Hippocratic oath: Text, translation, interpretation.* Baltimore, MD: Johns Hopkins University Press.

Flanagan, J. C. (1954). The critical incident technique. *Psychological Bulletin, 51,* 327–359.

Fleming, A. (1929). On the antibacterial action of cultures of a penicillium, with special reference to their use in the isolation of B. influenza. *British Journal of Experimental Pathology, 10,* 226–236.

Frank, J. D., & Frank, J. B. (1991). *Persuasion and healing: A comparative study of psycho-therapy.* Baltimore, MD: The Johns Hopkins University Press.

Graveley, E. A., & Oseasohn, C. S. (1991). Multiple drug regimens: Medication compliance among veterans 65 years and older. *Research in Nursing Health, 14,* 51–58.

Hackman, M. Z., & Johnson, C. E. (2004), *Leadership: A communication perspective* (4th ed.). Long Grove, IL: Waveland.

Haynes, R. B., McDonald, H., & Garg, A. X. (2002). Interventions for helping patients to follow prescriptions for medications. *Cochran Database System Review, 4.*

Helmreich, R. L. (1997). Managing human error in aviation, *Scientific American, 276,* 62–67.

Infante, D. A., Rancer, A. S., & Avtgis, T. A. (2010). *Contemporary communication research,* Dubuque, Iowa: Kendall Hunt.

Institutes of Medicine (2014). *Dying in America: Improving quality and honoring individual preferences near the end of life.* Retrieved from http://www.iom.edu/Reports/2014/Dying-In-America-Improving-Quality-and-Honoring-Individual-Preferences-Near-the-End-of-Life.aspx.

Jahng, K. H., Martin, L. R., & Golin, C. E. (2005). Preferences for medical collaboration: Patient-physician congruence and patient outcomes. *Patient Education and Counseling, 57,* 308–314.

James, J. T. (2013). A new evidence-based estimate of patient harms associated with hospital care. *Journal of Patient Safety, 9,* 122–128.

Joint Commission. Definition of sentinel event. Retrieved on August 27, 2014 from, http://www.jointcommission.org/topics/hai_sentinel_event.aspx

Kane, S., Huo, D., Aiken, J., & Hanauer, S. (2003). Medication nonadherence and the outcomes of patients with quiescent ulcerative colitis. *American Journal of Medicine, 114*(1), 39–43.

Kizer, K. (2002). Patient centered care: Essential but probably not sufficient. *Quality and Safety in Health Care, 11,* 117–118.

Kohn, L. T., Corrigan, J. M., & Donaldson, M. S. (1999). *To err is human: Building a safer health system. Committee on Quality of Health Care in America.* Washington, D.C.: National Academy Press.

Larson, C. E., Backlund, P. M., Redmond, M. K., & Barbour, A. (November, 1978). *Assessing communication competence.* Paper presented at the Annual Meeting of the Speech Communication Association, Falls Church, VA.

Larson, C. E., & LaFasto, F. M. (1989). *Teamwork: What must go right/what can go wrong.* Thousand Oaks, CA: Sage.

Lasagna, L. (1964). The Hippocratic Oath (Modern Version). Retrieved on 08/27/14 from http://www.pbs.org/wgbh/nova/body/hippocratic-oath-today.html

Leape, L. L., Brennan, T. A., & Laird, N. M. (1991). Incidence of adverse events and negligence in hospitalized patients: Results of the Harvard Medical Practice study. *New England Journal of Medicine, 324,* 370–376

Leonard, M., Graham, S., & Bonacum, D. (2004). The human factor: The critical importance of effective team work in communication providing safe care, *Quality and Safety in Health Care, 13,* 185–190.

Levinson, W., & Dunn, P. M. (1989). Coping with variability. *Journal of the American Medical Association, 261,* 2252.

Martin, L. R., Williams, S. L., Haskard, K. B., & DiMatteo, M. R. (2005). The challenge of patient adherence. *Therapeutics and Clinical Risk Management, 1,* 189–199.

Matsumoto, D. (1990). Cultural similarities and differences in display rules. *Maturation and Emotion, 14,* 195–214.

McCroskey, J. C. (1968). *An introduction to rhetorical communication.* Englewood Cliffs, NJ: Prentice-Hall.

Merritt, A. C., & Helmreich, R. L. (1996). Human factors on the flight deck: the influence of national culture. *Journal of Cross-Cultural Psychology, 27,* 5–24.

O'Malley, A. S., Forrest, C. D., & Mandelblatt, J. (2002). Adherence of low income women to cancer screening recommendations. *Journal of General Internal Medicine, 17,* 144–154.

Peabody, F. W. (1927). The care of the patient. *Journal of the American Medical Association, 88,* 877–888.

Polack, E. P., & Avgtis, T. A. (2011). *Medical communication: Defining the discipline* (1st ed.). Dubuque, IA: Kendall Hunt.

Polack, E. P., Avtgis, T. A., Rossi, D. C., & Shaffer, L. (2010). A team approach in communication instruction, a qualitative description. *Journal of Surgical Education, 67,* 125–128.

Polack, E. P., Richmond, V. P., & McCroskey, J. C. (2008). *Applied communication for health professionals.* Dubuque, IA: Kendall Hunt.

Pope, A. (1711). *To err is human, to forgive is devine: An essay on criticism. Retrieved from http://www.quotationspage.com/quotes/Alexander_Pope/*

Reason, J. (1990). *Human Error,* New York: Cambridge University Press.

Sackett, B. L. (1997), Evidenced-based medicine, *Senior Perinatal, 21,* 3–5.

Seligman, M. E. P. (1990). *Learned optimism: How to change your mind and your life.* New York: Pocket Books.

Sharpe, V. A., & Faden, A. I. (1998), *Medical harm,* Cambridge, England: Cambridge University Press.

Shine, K. I. (2002). Health care quality and how to achieve it. *Academic Medicine, 77,* 91–99.

Silverman, J., Kurtz, S., & Draper, J. (2005). *Skills for communicating with patients* (2nd ed.). Oxford, U.K.: Radcliffe Publishing.

Spitzberg, B. H., & Cupach, W. R. (1984). *Interpersonal communication competence.* Beverly Hills, CA: Sage Publications.

Starr, P. (1982), *The social transformation of American medicine.* New York: Basic Books.

Sullivan, S., Kreling, D. H., & Hazlett, K. (1990). Noncompliance with medication regiments and subsequent hospitalizations: A literature analysis and cost of hospitalization estimate. *Journal Res Pharmico Economics, 2,* 19–33.

Temel, J. S., Greer, J. A., & Mukikansky, A. (2010). Early palliative care for patients with metastatic non-small cell lung cancer, *New England Journal of Medicine, 363,* 733–742.

U.S. Department of Health and Human Services. (2000). *Healthy People 2010.* Washington, DC: U.S. Government Printing Office. Originally developed for Ratzan SC, Parker RM. (2000). Introduction. In *National Library of Medicine Current Bibliographies in Medicine: Health Literacy.* Selden CR, Zorn M, Ratzan SC, Parker RM, Editors. NLM Pub. No. CBM 2000-1. Bethesda, MD: National Institutes of Health, U.S. Department of Health and Human Services.

Williams, M. V., Parker, R. M., & Barker, D. W. (1995). Inadequate functional health literacy among patients at two public hospitals. *Journal of the American Medical Association, 274,* 1677–1682.

chapter two

The Neuroscience and Psychology of Communication

chapter objectives

Upon completion of the chapter, the student should be able to:

1. Explain the evolution of the human brain

2. Explain how emotion is processed and regulated in the human brain

3. Explain the various areas of the brain associated with language

4. Compare and contrast Broca's and Wernicke's regions of the brain

5. Compare and contrast the different types of brain imaging technology available to researchers

R esearchers and theorists are aggressively pursuing the impact that biology and genetics exert on human behavior as it becomes impossible to deny the fact that human beings come preprogrammed with an array of physiological and psychological traits. It is for these reasons that a discussion of biology and communication becomes essential. This

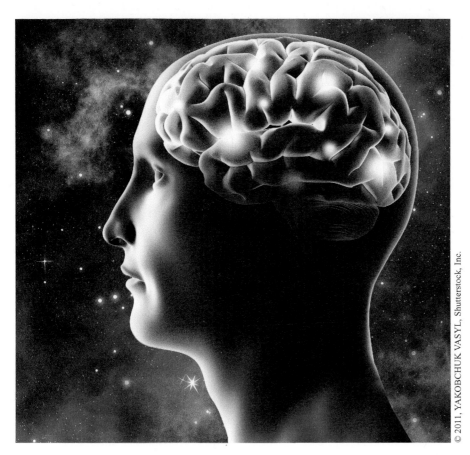

© 2011, YAKOBCHUK VASYL, Shutterstock, Inc.

chapter is dedicated to the presentation of the basic anatomy of the brain, the neurological processes specifically associated with communication, and the specific research tools and methods available to researchers interested in seeking biological explanations for communication behavior.

The Human Brain

The human brain is the most sophisticated communication system in the world and contains approximately 100 billion **neurons** (nerve cells). Each of these nerve cells, on average, connects to 1,000 other neurons. This results in approximately 100 trillion **synaptic connections** (Gazzaniga, Ivry, & Mangun, 2008). To illustrate such complexity, consider your brain activity while reading the introductory paragraph. The paragraph consisted of a cluster of black impressions that make sense to you because your brain interprets these as letters or symbols; this involves orthographic memory. You then attribute meaning to each of these symbols (i.e., **semantics**). If you choose to read the introductory paragraph aloud, you then incorporate memory centers of how the words are supposed to sound (i.e., phonological memory).

The human brain is a complex web of neurons that send pulses of electricity through hundreds of miles of wires composed of tiny brain cells. The reading example just illustrated occurs in less time than it takes you to blink your eye. In fact, much of the neurological processes occurring in your brain happen involuntarily or without much thought or conscious attention. Throughout this chapter we will refer to nerve cells or neurons. These neurons look much like a "fried egg" with the white of the egg being the **cytoplasm** and the yellow center being the **nucleus.** Understanding the basic structure of the neuron is important because the nucleus contains **deoxyribonucleic acid (DNA),** which hold bytes of biologic instruction. These instructions contain information such as how tall a person will be and other physical, psychological-based, communication-based, and temperament-based traits. Figure 2.1 illustrates the anatomy of a neuron.

The brain is so dynamic that whenever a person learns something new, the wiring in the brain changes (Kandel, Schwartz, & Jessell, 2000). These changes occur in the structure of the neuron even when the simplest of information is acquired. Thus, the brain is functionally organized and reorganized on a continual basis. When we refer to learning, we are not distinguishing between simple (e.g., how to properly lock a garage door) and complex (e.g., how to determine the best way to invent money). Instead, **learning** is the acquisition of information that was not previously known. This concept of the brain being malleable is known as brain plasticity, and the creation of newly generated neurological connections is known as **neurogenesis.**

orthographic memory

Memory centers associated with the retention of letters and symbols.

phonological memory

Memory centers associated with the recall of language sounds and style.

brain plasticity

The capacity for change or malleability of the brain.

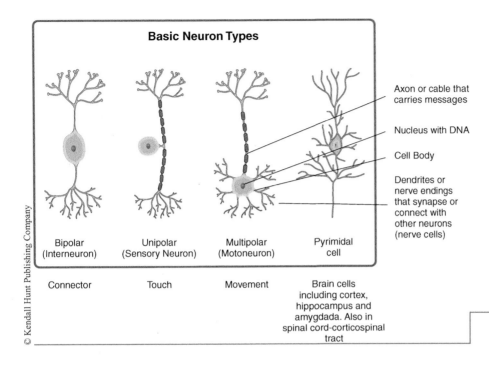

Basic Neuron Types

Bipolar
(Interneuron)

Unipolar
(Sensory Neuron)

Multipolar
(Motoneuron)

Pyrimidal
cell

Axon or cable that
carries messages

Nucleus with DNA

Cell Body

Dendrites or
nerve endings
that synapse or
connect with
other neurons
(nerve cells)

Connector

Touch

Movement

Brain cells
including cortex,
hippocampus and
amygdada. Also in
spinal cord-corticospinal
tract

© Kendall Hunt Publishing Company

figure 2.1

The Anatomy of a Neuron

The Evolution and Anatomy of the Brain

All of the information that we have concerning human brain function is an accumulation of research conducted by biologists who study the tissues of the brain, experimental psychologists who study human behavior, cognitive neuroscientists who study how the tissues relate to behavior, and evolutionary biologists who study how the human brain has developed over millions of years. Evolutionary biologists believe that the human brain has developed in three distinct phases or components. The first phase or component is known as the **lizard brain,** which is considered to be the most primitive portion of the brain, known as the **brain stem.** The brain stem serves as the regulator for normal bodily functions such as breathing, heart rate, and sleeping patterns. The second phase or component is considered the **mammalian or midbrain,** which sits atop the brain stem and is responsible for behaviors that are more representative of animal behavior than that of exclusive human behavior. The four main functions of the midbrain include the following: (a) fighting behavior, (b) feeding behavior, (c) fleeing behavior, and (d) reproductive behavior. The third phase or component is considered the human brain or **cerebral cortex.** Cortex is Latin for "bark." The cortex comprises the surface of the brain and shares electrical communication with both the mid-brain (i.e., mammalian brain) and the brain stem (i.e., lizard brain). The cerebral cortex (i.e., human brain) looks slightly like a "walnut shell," yet each region is highly specialized with sections dedicated to speech, vision, movement, and memory. These three components allow us to breathe, see, laugh, and move, among countless other functions.

lizard brain (brain stem)

The most primitive portion of the brain; also known as the brain stem. Responsible for breathing, heart rate, and sleeping patterns.

mammalian brain (midbrain)

A part of the brain that sits atop the brain stem and is responsible for behaviors that are more representative of animal behavior than that of exclusive human behavior. Also known as the midbrain. Responsible for fighting behavior, fleeing behavior, feeding behavior, and reproductive behavior.

cerebral cortex

The surface of the brain that shares electrical communication with both the midbrain and the brain stem. Responsible for speech, vision, movement, and memory.

The Human Brain

As just discussed, the cerebral cortex is what distinguishes humans from other species. The cerebral cortex is the key to executive (i.e., higher-level) brain functions such as thought, movement, perception, and behavior (Fig. 2.2). The cortical (bark) brain surface is about 233 to 265 square inches in size. For perspective, this would be about the size of one or two pages of newspaper. To fit into the skull, it is compacted into folds (also known as **gyri**) and grooves (also known as **sulci**). The **frontal lobe** handles motor skills (including speech behavior) and cognitive functions of higher thinking and reasoning, which include movement, perception, and behavior. The **parietal lobe** receives and processes all touch and pain sensations from the body. The **temporal lobe** processes auditory information from the ears. Within the temporal lobe, the **auditory cortex** is responsible for interpreting auditory information from the ears and transmitting that information to the parietal lobe. The auditory cortex is also involved in long-term memory (see spoken word in Fig. 2.7). The **occipital lobe** processes visual information from the eyes and immediately transfers this to the parietal lobe for comprehension (Wernicke's area) and the frontal lobe for speech production (Broca's area). Within the occipital lobe, the **angular gyrus** stores memory for words (see written language in Fig. 2.8.).

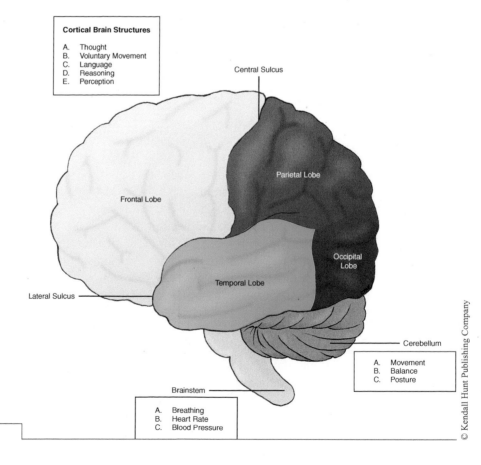

Cortical Brain Structures

A. Thought
B. Voluntary Movement
C. Language
D. Reasoning
E. Perception

Central Sulcus

Parietal Lobe

Frontal Lobe

Occipital Lobe

Temporal Lobe

Lateral Sulcus

Cerebellum

A. Movement
B. Balance
C. Posture

Brainstem

A. Breathing
B. Heart Rate
C. Blood Pressure

figure 2.2

Brain Structures

After reading the previous section on the human brain, a person may be thinking: "How did we come to know so much about the regions of the brain and their functions?" Korbinian Brodmann (1868–1918) used the staining techniques developed by Franz Nissl to identify specific areas of brain function. This technique involves the staining of the neuron's cell body when activated. Brodmann was able to map the cerebral cortex into 50 distinct areas. This system is widely used today to teach the anatomy of the brain. The specific regions of the cerebral cortex, using **Brodmann's classification system,** are identified with a "BA" followed by the particular region of the brain. For example, Broca's area is identified as BA 44-45 and Wernicke's area is BA 22. Figure 2.3 shows Brodmann's classification system.

The Limbic System. The **cingulate cortex (gyrus)** or limbic lobe of the brain is between the **cingulate sulcus** and the **corpus callosum** (Fig. 2.4).

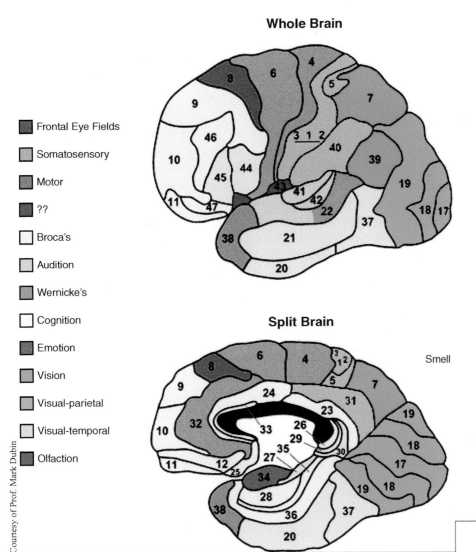

Whole Brain

Frontal Eye Fields
Somatosensory
Motor
??
Broca's
Audition
Wernicke's
Cognition
Emotion
Vision
Visual-parietal
Visual-temporal
Olfaction

Split Brain

Smell

Courtesy of Prof. Mark Dubin

figure 2.3

Brodmann's Classification System

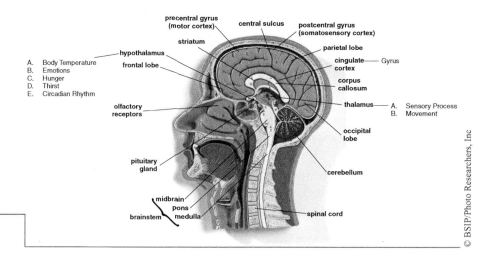

A. Body Temperature
B. Emotions
C. Hunger
D. Thirst
E. Circadian Rhythm

A. Sensory Process
B. Movement

© BSIP/Photo Researchers, Inc

figure 2.4

The Cingulate Cortex (Gyrus)

The limbic system is made up of the primitive brain, which controls behaviors essential for survival such as finding food and self-preservation, and the modern brain, which controls higher level functions such as motivation and emotional behavior (Fig. 2.5).

The phrase "limbic system" was coined by Maclean (1949), who borrowed the term from Paul Broca, who in 1878 used the term "le grand lobe limbique" to describe the ring of the forebrain structures surrounding the midbrain. The first research indicating that the limbic system was involved in human communication was conducted by Smith (1941). Smith noted that stimulation of the **anterior cingulate cortex** elicited vocal activity in monkeys. This vocal activity research was furthered by Myers (1975) and colleagues who argued that the **prefrontal cortex** and, to a lesser degree, the **anterior temporal cortex** control the expression of emotion during social interaction. These higher level cortices (i.e., the prefrontal cortex and anterior temporal cortex) assist in our ability to remain rational as opposed to being entirely emotionally driven in our behavior.

In the human brain, the largest web of connections is between the prefrontal area and the traditional limbic (emotional) brain (see Fig. 2.5). This may be why human beings experience a greater variety of emotions and feelings than any other mammal. Some of these emotions and feelings include wrath, fright, passion, love, hate, joy, and sadness. When one accounts for mixed emotions such as jealousy (a mixture of anger and insecurity), possible emotional experiences number in the hundreds. Although evolution has afforded birds the ability to display some signs of affection, reptiles, amphibians, and most other species are void of such capacity for emotional experience. As mentioned earlier, the limbic system controls behaviors that are necessary for survival, allowing humans and all other animals to distinguish between things that are agreeable (not dangerous) from things that are disagreeable (dangerous). The limbic system also allows for the tendency of females (of many species) to nurse and protect their babies, induces playful moods (**ludic**) to regulate behavior, and is responsible for some functions of memory.

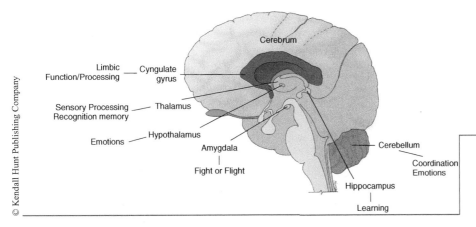

figure 2.5

The Limbic System (Amygdala, Hypo-thalamus, Thalamus, Cingulate Gyrus, Hippocampus)

It is important to keep in mind that the brain and its respective regions are interdependent and in constant communication with one another. Therefore, the limbic and mammalian brain communicates via neural cells to the prefrontal cortex and the anterior temporal cortex. This allows humans to produce symbolic language and engage in skillful intellectual tasks such as reading, writing, and performing mathematical calculations. Maclean (1973) argued that the cerebral cortex is the generator of great ideas or the mother of invention and the father of abstract thought.

Emotion and the Human Brain. The experience of emotion is not a function of any one specific area of the brain such as the limbic system (Feinstein et al., 2009). Instead, the experience of emotion is better conceptualized as a circuit that involves five different brain structures linked together through nerve bundles (see Fig. 2.5). The first area is known as the **hypothalamus.** The hypothalamus is generally associated with thermal regulation (i.e., maintaining our core body temperature), sexuality, combativeness, hunger, and thirst. However, this brain region also plays a role in emotion in that pleasure and rage are associated with the lateral regions, whereas the medial region is associated with aversion or avoidance behavior, displeasure, and a tendency for uncontrollable and loud laughing. Although associated with the experience of emotion, the hypothalamus is more responsible for emotional expression (i.e., emotional behaviors such as crying, laughing, or rage) as opposed to the actual creation of that emotional state (i.e., how the brain processes the emotional experience). The second area of the brain involved with emotion is the **anterior thalamic nucleus.** This area is associated with emotional reactivity. **Emotional reactivity** refers to how people cope with pleasant and unpleasant events. The **cingulate gyrus** is the third area involved in emotion. Although generally associated with coordinating smell and sights with pleasant memories of previous emotional experience, the cingulate gyrus is also involved in the emotional reaction to pain and the regulation of aggressive behavior. Early animal experiments revealed that animals subjected to the destruction of the cingulate gyrus became totally tame in nature, thus reinforcing the link between this region and emotional expression. The **hippocampus** is the fourth area of the limbic system and is associated with recent memory but is more so linked to long-term memory (i.e., storing previous experience and knowledge) as opposed to short-term memory. The final area associated with emotion is the **amygdala,** which is considered the center for friendship, love, affection, fear, rage, and aggression. However, the primary function of the amygdala is to identify possible danger in an effort to self-preserve. The amygdala is most commonly associated with the "fight or flight" response (Fig. 2.6).

In a study exemplifying the importance of the limbic system and its connection to emotion, Feinstein et al. (2009) reported a case study based on a patient named "Roger." This research team studied Roger for 14 years. Roger, born in 1952, contracted herpes simplex (viral) encephalitis (inflammation of the brain) at the age of 28. As a result of this infection, his limbic system was totally destroyed. The only observable disability associated with his destroyed limbic system was his inability to remember anything that happened since he contracted his infection. The conclusions of this study indicated that humans can indeed live without a limbic brain. Further, it was noted that with damaged emotional circuitry, the default emotion is one of feeling better as opposed to feeling worse. Emotions therefore serve to get in the way of feeling good (Feinstein et al., 2009). Simply put, our brain chemistry is calibrated toward pleasant feeling and can be confounded by emotional processes. When these emotional processes are not present, there is a general state of pleasantness.

Jorge Moll and Ricardo de Oliveria-Souza (2008) reported interesting findings concerning the human cerebral cortex (higher brain) and emotionality. The authors argued that the subdivision of the frontal cortex is referred to as the **ventral medial prefrontal cortex (VMPFC)**. The VMPFC is located above the eye sockets and affects moral judgment in everyday situations. By everyday situations we are referring to the many interactions and situations we experience on a daily basis. More specifically, this portion of the brain controls prosocial sentiments such as guilt, compassion, and empathy (Moll et al., 2007). The findings suggest that compassion and empathy are VMPFC

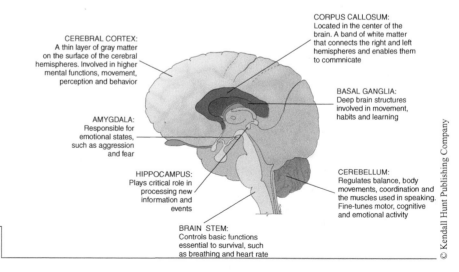

figure 2.6

Brain Structure of the Limbic System

CEREBRAL CORTEX:
A thin layer of gray matter on the surface of the cerebral hemispheres. Involved in higher mental functions, movement, perception and behavior

CORPUS CALLOSUM:
Located in the center of the brain. A band of white matter that connects the right and left hemispheres and enables them to commnicate

BASAL GANGLIA:
Deep brain structures involved in movement, habits and learning

AMYGDALA:
Responsible for emotional states, such as aggression and fear

CEREBELLUM:
Regulates balance, body movements, coordination and the muscles used in speaking. Fine-tunes motor, cognitive and emotional activity

HIPPOCAMPUS:
Plays critical role in processing new information and events

BRAIN STEM:
Controls basic functions essential to survival, such as breathing and heart rate

© Kendall Hunt Publishing Company

controlled and are triggered by states of sadness and affiliation that originate in the limbic (i.e., emotional) brain. These findings were a result of an experiment comparing neurologically "normal" people with those with VMPFC damage in a task of making moral judgments in different situations. Overall, the findings indicate that people with VMPFC damage were more likely to use a utilitarian ethical perspective (i.e., had the willingness to sacrifice the welfare of the individual for the welfare of the group). An example of the moral dilemma used in this study was the following: Given a choice of pushing a single individual into the tracks of a runaway train (thus killing the person) to save the lives of five workers down the track line, what would you choose? (Moll et al., 2007).

Thus far, this chapter has been dedicated to the introduction of basic brain-related concepts, the current state of cognitive neuroscience, and an example of what researchers are investigating with regard to brain function and behavior. In summary, cognitive neuroscience is the study of the mind as it is manifested in the human brain, whereas neuroscience is the study of the nervous system including structure, function, evolution, development, genetics, biochemistry, physiology, pharmacology, informatics, computational neuroscience, and pathology (Koenigs et al., 2007). Perhaps Kandel and colleagues (2000) provide the most concise description of this endeavor. "The task of neural science is to explain behavior in terms of the activities of the brain. How does the brain marshal its millions of individual nerve cells to produce behavior, and how are these cells influenced by the environment. . . ? The last frontier of the biological sciences—their ultimate challenge—is to understand the biological basis of consciousness and the mental processes by which we perceive, act, learn, and remember" (p. 6).

Language and the Human Brain.   Humans have experienced problems associated with language for as long as they have had the capacity to use language. Problems associated with language production and use are so prevalent that entire disciplines such as linguistics and speech pathology are dedicated to understanding and remediating them. The understanding of how language production and comprehension are organized in the brain was largely shaped by a number of studies conducted in the mid-19th century.

In 1861 a French physician, Paul Broca, published a groundbreaking case study of a patient name "Tan." The subject was named Tan because the only word he could speak was "Tan" (Broca, 1861). Tan was capable of understanding and comprehending questions asked of him. However, when Tan attempted to answer those questions, he was able to use gestures and other nonverbal communication behaviors competently but could not speak more than the single word "Tan." For example, if asked "How are you?" Tan may intend to respond "Just fine, how are you?" but his spoken words would be articulated as "Tan tan, tan tan tan?" Upon Tan's death, Broca performed a postmortem examination (autopsy) of Tan's brain and revealed a large lesion (tumor) in the left inferior frontal cortex. The results from this autopsy led Broca to conclude that Tan's speech problems were a result of this lesion. As such, this section of the left inferior frontal cortex is known as **Broca's area**. This syndrome

cognitive neuroscience
A scientific discipline concerned with the mind as it is manifested in the human brain.

neuroscience
A scientific discipline concerned with the nervous system including structure, function, evolution, development, genetics, biochemistry, physiology, pharmacology, informatics, computational neuroscience, and pathology.

(i.e., being able to comprehend language yet unable to produce the desired speech) is known as **Broca's aphasia.** In the 150 years since Broca's report, many studies of brain injury from etiologies such as vascular accident (stroke) or neoplasm (brain tumors) or infection (abscess formation) have supported the original claims made by Broca (Price, 2000).

Following Broca's findings, Carl Wernicke (1874) described the symptoms of several patients who showed the opposite symptoms to those of Tan—these subjects had problems with language comprehension but not with speech production. The patients could produce language as well as any other person, but the utterances were meaningless. Further, these subjects could not comprehend the meanings of words or sentences that were spoken to them. All subjects passed hearing tests, so the lack of comprehension could not be attributed to deafness. Upon autopsy of these subjects, Wernicke found a lesion in the left posterior superior temporal region. This region is known as **Wernicke's area**. This syndrome of having the ability to produce language yet an inability to comprehend language is known as **Wernicke's aphasia.**

Recent developments in brain imaging techniques such as positron emission tomography (PET) and magnetic resonance imaging (or MRI, which will be discussed later in this chapter) have confirmed the findings of both Broca and Wernicke (Price, 2000). This entire body of work concerning the neural organization of language in human beings has led to understanding of the axiomatic principles regarding the way verbal communication is organized within the brain. First, for most people who are right-hand dominant, language is always located in the left hemisphere. However, for people who are left-hand dominant, language can be located in either the right or left hemisphere or in a mixture of both hemispheres (Knecht, Drager, Deppe, Bobe, Lohmann, & Floel 2000). Second, the brain centers that control language production are separate from the brain centers that control language comprehension. It is no coincidence that the **left inferior frontal cortex** is close to, and receives many projections to and from, areas involved in motor (movement) planning and production. In the case of language, motor planning and production take the form of speaking, which involves the converting of mental ideas into motor actions that produce acoustic signals. Similarly, the **left posterior superior temporal cortex** is close to, and receives many projections from, the areas involved in the processing of auditory (hearing) signals. Words must be heard before they can be understood. Therefore, both Broca's area and Wernicke's area are connected by dense fiber tract called the **arcuate fasciculus** (Figs. 2.7 and 2.8), thus allowing for the efficient interaction between these two regions.

Speech and the Human Brain.   As indicated in earlier chapters, communication is defined as the process of a source creating meaning in the mind of a receiver through verbal and nonverbal messages (Polack et al., 2008). This process involves encoding or the production of language. **Encoding** is the process of taking an already conceived idea and getting it ready for transmission (Infante, Rancer, & Avtgis, 2010). When we organize and convey a message, we do so primarily through the **primary auditory cortex**. Speech sounds such as syllables and phonemes are neural commands within Wernicke's area of speech comprehension that are sent through the arcuate fasciculus to Broca's area of speech production, stimulating the motor strip that controls the organs of speech. Such speech organs include the mouth, lips, tongue, palate, and vocal cords. These speech organs produce an acoustic signal (see Fig. 2.7). This process just described is the biological explanation for the encoding process. Once the message is encoded, it is sent to the listener for decoding. **Decoding** is the process of taking the stimuli that has been received and giving those stimuli meaning through individual interpretation and perception (Infante, et al., 2010). The message travels via a **channel,** which is the means by which a message is conveyed from the source to the receiver and concerns our five senses (i.e., hearing, seeing, smelling, tasting, and touching). According to Richmond and Gorham (1998), a message is approximately 30% visual, 25% auditory, 30% auditory and visual, and 15% kinesthetic (touch).

Hearing and the Human Brain   The way in which people interpret the written word is considerably different from the way in which the spoken word is interpreted. Biologically, the written word initially stimulates our **visual cortex**, which is located in the occipital lobe. Although the stimuli are received by the visual cortex, they are not interpreted or translated. Instead, the stimuli are transferred to the angular gyrus where memory for visual words is located. This electrical circuitry is then advanced to Wernicke's area through the arcuate fasciculus. If we were reading the written word aloud, then the circuitry would advance through Broca's area on the left inferior frontal cortex and finally to the motor cortex (see Fig. 2.8).

Repetition of Heard Speech

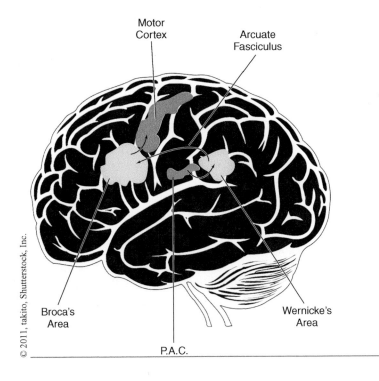

Motor Cortex

Arcuate Fasciculus

Broca's Area

Wernicke's Area

P.A.C.

© 2011, takito, Shutterstock, Inc.

figure 2.7

Brain Areas Involved in the Production of Speech

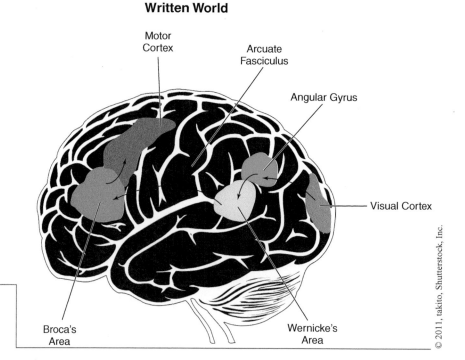

Written World

Motor
Cortex

Arcuate
Fasciculus

Angular Gyrus

Visual Cortex

Broca's
Area

Wernicke's
Area

© 2011, takito, Shutterstock, Inc.

figure 2.8

Brain Areas Involved in the Comprehension of the Written Word

Thus far, this chapter has presented the anatomy of the brain and the brain structures associated with speech, comprehension, and language. The technology available to researchers interested in brain function and its association to psychological and communication behavior has provided incredible insights into explaining why people behave as they do and understanding as to how the brain and its function can aid in the development of effective interventions for circumventing antisocial behavior. The next section will review the technologies available to researchers interested in studying the human brain.

Brain-Imaging Technologies

Although it is informative and valuable to discuss our understanding of how the brain operates and its relationship to the human experience, such a conversation without a basic understanding of how the results were obtained would be a disservice to the reader. As such, this section is dedicated to the presentation of the available technologies commonly used in studies of the human brain. As mentioned earlier in this chapter, before such technologies, the one way to study the brain was by autopsy. Of course, a postmortem inspection of a human brain does not allow for the study of "process" or "dynamism"—only the biology of the organ. The following technologies have allowed researchers to study the living brain without significant risk to the subject. These technologies consist of the *electroencephalograph (EEG), computerized axial tomography (CAT), magnetic resonance imaging, functional magnetic resonance imaging (fMRI), magnetoencephalography (MEG), single photon emission computerized tomography (SPECT), and position emission tomography.*

EEG

The **electroencephalograph (EEG)** is an electrical recording from the scalp and is used to understand brain function. The brain has densely compacted cortical tissues consisting of white and gray matter. These cortical tissues give off small electrical impulses measured in millivolts. These signals can be picked up by electroencephalography using a number of electrodes attached to the scalp. Depending on the study and desired degree of precision, anywhere from 32 to 256 electrodes can be used. The advantage of using EEG technology over other types of technology is the rapid response from the brain. For example, the sampling rate is approximately every 4 milliseconds, whereas functional magnetic resonance imaging, to be discussed later in this chapter, uses slower mechanisms for measurement. EEG affords the researcher almost instantaneous brain reaction to any given stimuli. For example, if we were to show you a picture of a person who you greatly disliked, using EEG technology we could record your instantaneous physiological reaction to that person's image. This would occur so fast that you would not even be aware of it. Therefore, the speed at which activation is detected is a strength of EEG. However, this technique is limited to studying the surface regions of the brain and is less effective when studying structures deep inside the brain (e.g., amygdala) as a tool for measurement of dynamic brain function.

CAT

Computerized axial tomography (CAT) is a technique that has, for the most part, been replaced by the MRI in the dynamic study of brain function. In the CAT scanner, the patient is put in a tube that moves around the person and takes many thin sliced x-rays. These two-dimensional images can then be reformatted by a computer to make three-dimensional static images. The CAT scan was developed in the 1970s and does expose the person to a certain degree of radiation. However, given that CAT scan relies on ionized radiation (x-rays) as opposed to extremely powerful magnetism as used in MRI, the CAT scan is effective for people with conditions that would put them at risk for exposure to high levels of magnetism (e.g., tattoo ink containing lead, metal plates, metal shavings, and other metallic materials that can be contained within the human body), but unlike functional MRI, it is a static not dynamic evaluation of the brain.

MRI and fMRI

Earlier in this chapter we discussed the concept of neurons (nerve cells) that contain a nucleus. Each cell is composed of atoms with negatively charged electrons orbiting around the nucleus of the atom. Unlike the CAT technique, **magnetic resonance imaging (MRI)** and **functional magnetic resonance imaging (fMRI)** evaluate brain function without radiation exposure. Figure 2.9 describes the process utilized in MRI and fMRI.

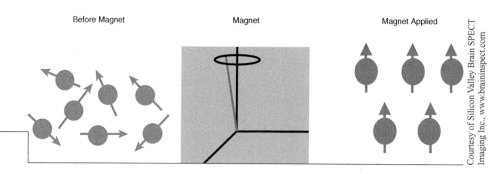

figure 2.9

Effect of Magnetism on the Atom

Generally, the atoms that orbit around a nucleus have no fixed orientation, but when exposed to powerful magnetism (as in the MRI machine) they take on an orderly structure. The magnets found in these machines range from 0.5 to 3.0 Tesla units. To put the power of these magnets in perspective, one Tesla unit equals 10,000 gauss. The Earth's magnetic field varies between 0.3 and 0.7 gauss units. Therefore, the magnetic force used in MRI can range from 5,000 to 30,000 times the force of gravity. This is a powerful magnet. By applying this external magnetic field to a specific part of the body, the atoms in that part of the body align in a fixed direction, as opposed to when there is no such external magnetism and the atoms are then aligned in many different directions (see Fig. 2.9). When the magnet is applied, all of the atoms can align to the right, left, up, or down. The direction is not important, but the fact that they are all aligned in the same direction is. This alignment of atoms allows for an image of the soft tissues of the brain (or any other part of the body that is of interest to the physician or researcher) to be recreated. The main difference between MRI and fMRI is that MRI imaging is more concerned with the physical anatomy (static image), whereas fMRI is concerned with brain activation and blood flow.

In fMRI there is an assumption of relationship between brain activity and blood flow. This relationship was originally described by Charles Roy and Charles Sherrington (1890), and the concept evolved into the technique known as **blood oxygen level-dependent contrast (BOLD)**. BOLD assumes that the signals detected by the MRI scanner change according to the oxyhemoglobin concentration of the blood. Simply put, those areas of the brain that are getting more oxygen are considered functioning and thus, the term functional MRI is used. For example, if you ask someone to wiggle their thumb, the brain region responsible for such a movement would appear on the scan in a different color (usually red) as representing activity or function. Such technology allows researchers to identify the complex activation of various brain systems associated with any given task or behavior. In summary, the chaotic activity of the atoms are oriented in a fixed way that allows an image or shadow to be created that indicates whether the anatomy of the brain is either normal or abnormal. When you add the BOLD concept, you can not only determine anatomical structure, but also what structures are or are not functioning.

MEG

Magnetoencephalography (MEG) is a "newer" technology that has some significant advantages over MRI in that it is much faster in process and can obtain accurate information down to milliseconds in evaluating nerve cellular activity. This device is similar to MRI in that it uses magnetic detection coils with the assistance of an extremely sensitive instrument called the **superconducting quantum interference device (SQUID).** The MEG provides researchers with brain imaging/measurement capability that is reflective of both EEG and MRI.

MEG technology has several disadvantages, two of which consist of the multimillion dollar cost for such as device and the size/weight of the machine, which can be in excess of 8 tons. However, beyond the cost and size issues, MEG has the capacity to unlock information that is frequently missing from data gathered by other imaging techniques, which is a direct analysis of the nervous system at the cellular level.

SPECT

Another common and less expensive method for gaining functional information about the brain is through the **single photon emission computerized tomography (SPECT)** scan. SPECT uses a radioisotope (usually technetium to reveal a color signal of blood flow; Fig. 2.10). SPECT imaging is particularly effective in researching/assessing dementia, cognitive decline, psychiatric disorders, mood disorders, anxiety, autism, or attention deficit disorders.

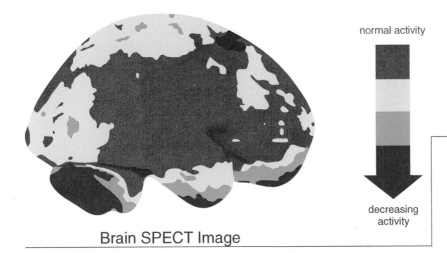

normal activity

decreasing activity

Brain SPECT Image

figure 2.10

Single Photon Emission Computerized Tomography Image of the Human Brain

Note: From http://www. braininspect.com.

PET

Position emission tomography (PET) requires that a radioactive glucose (sugar) tracer be placed in a patient or subject. Similar to other scanning techniques (e.g., MRI), the PET has a tube that scans the brain based on an

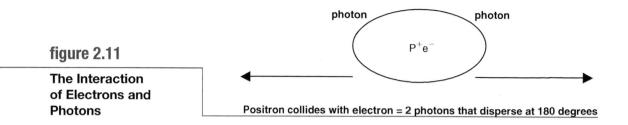

figure 2.11

**The Interaction
of Electrons and
Photons**

assumption similar to that of BOLD. That is, the more radioactive glucose a cell consumes (in this case, brain cells), the more active the cellular activity is determined to be. However, the less radioactive glucose consumed, the less the cellular activity is determined to be. PET technology dates back to the 1950s, when it was determined that particular classes of **radioisotopes** made possible the ability to obtain medical images. These isotopes are **positron emitting.** For example, if a positron collides with an electron, they are completely destroyed at 180 degrees to create two photons, which are then picked up by the PET scanner. Figure 2.11 illustrates this process. When a sugar molecule is tagged with the positron-emitting isotope, it is unlike the functional MRI or SPECT, which records blood flow. Instead, the PET scan shows whether there is or is not function (as opposed to the degree of function) in an area and is valuable in cognitive neuroscience when investigating brain activity.

Conclusion

This chapter introduced you to the human brain and the relationship between brain function and human behavior. The evolution of the brain resulted in the development of higher-level functions that are exclusive to human beings, none of which are more important than the ability to communicate. The intricate brain processes that are in constant interaction with one another were presented and discussed. For example, the interaction between Broca's area and Wernicke's area is necessary for production and comprehension of speech.

Emotion and how it is manifest in the brain was presented and shown to be a product of several neurological structures that account for the production and experience of emotion. In fact, emotion is complex, yet it seems to be an experience that when suppressed, as when the limbic system is completely destroyed, results in an overall "positive state of mind" in the person. Therefore, emotions can serve to confound the human experience. We concluded this chapter with a brief description of the technologies available for researchers interested in researching the physiology of human communication. These technologies vary in their specific imaging technology. For example, EEG relies on detection of electrical impulses, whereas MRI relies on high levels of magnetism. Researchers will continue to explore ways to unlock the intricacies of the human brain and its effect on human communication.

Questions for Discussion/Review

1. Why would it be important for someone interested in healthcare communication to have an understanding of the human brain and its various processes?
2. Describe the evolution of the human brain, and discuss the functions associated with each phase of development.
3. Discuss the Brodmann classification system in the production and experience of emotion.
4. Describe the role of the limbic system in the production and experience of emotion.
5. Discuss what is meant when we say that the limbic system can have confounding effects on the otherwise "positive" state of the human mind. Provide an example for your answer.
6. Describe the role of the amygdala in the experience of emotion.
7. Distinguish between cognitive neuroscience and neuroscience.
8. Describe Broca's area of the brain, how it was named, and the symptoms and neurological explanation for Broca's aphasia.
9. Describe Wernicke's area, how it was named, and the symptoms and neurological explanation for Wernicke's aphasia.
10. Discuss the six neuroimaging techniques discussed in the chapter and what makes them different from one another.

References

Broca, P. (1861). Remarques sur le siege de al faculte du language articule: Suivies d'une observation d'aphemie. *Bulletin de la Scoiete Anatomique de Paris,* 330–357.

Feinstein, J., Rudrauf, D., Khalsa, S., Cassell, M., Bruss, J., & Grabowski, T. (2009). Bilateral limbic system destruction in man. *Journal of Clinical and Experimental Neuro Psychology, 17,* 1–19.

Gazzaniga, M., Ivry, R. B., & Mangun, G. R. (2008). *Cognitive neuroscience: The biology of the mind* (3rd ed.). New York: W. W. Norton and Company.

Infante, D. A., Rancer, A. S., & Avtgis, T. A. (2010). *Contemporary communication theory.* Dubuque, IA: Kendall-Hunt.

Kandel, E. R., Schwartz, J. H., & Jessell, T. M. (2000). *Principles of neural science* (4th ed.). New York: McGraw Hill.

Knecht, S., Drager, B., Deppe, M., Bobe, L., Lohmann, H., & Floel, A. (2000). Handedness and hemispheric language dominance in healthy humans. *Brain, 123,* 2512–2518.

Koenigs, M., Young, L., Adolphs, R., Tranel. D., Cushman, F., & Hauser, M. (2007). Damage to the prefrontal cortex increases utilitarian moral judgments. *Nature, 446,* 908–911.

Maclean, P. D. (1949). Psychosomatic disease and the "visceral brain": Recent developments baring on the Papez theory of emotion. *Psychosomatic Medicine, 11,* 338–353.

Maclean, P. D. (1973). *A triune concept of the brain and behavior.* Toronto, Canada: University of Toronto Press.

Moll, J., & de Oliveira-Souza, R. (February/March, 2008). When mortality is hard to like: How do we juggle evidence and emotions to make a moral decision. *Scientific American,* 30–35.

Moll, J., de Oliveira-Souza, R., Garrido, G. J., Bramati, I. E., Capparelli-Daquer, E. M., & Paiva, M. L. (2007). The self as moral agent: Linking the neural basis of social agency and moral sensitivity. *Social Neuroscience, 2,* 336–352.

Myers, R. E. (1975). Neurology of social behavior and the affect in primates: A study of prefrontal and anterior temporal cortex. In K. J. Zulch, O. Creutzfield, & G. C. Galbraith (Eds.), *Cerebral localization* (pp. 161–170). New York: Springer-Verlag.

Polack, E. P., Richmond, V. P., & McCroskey, M. C. (2008). *Applied communication for health-care professionals.* Dubuque, IA: Kendall-Hunt.

Price, C. J. (2000). The anatomy of language: Contributions from functional neuroimaging. *Journal of Anatomy, 197,* 335–359.

Richmond, V. P., & Gorham, J. (1998). *Communication, learning and affect in instruction.* Acton, MA: Tapastry.

Roy, C. S., & Sherrington, C. S. (1890). On the regulation of the blood-supply of the brain. *Journal of Physiology, 11,* 85–118.

Smith, W. K. (1941). Vocalization and other responses elicited by excitation of the region cingulares in the monkey. *American Journal of Physiology, 133,* 451–452.

Wernicke, C. (1874). *Der aphasiche symptomenkomplex.* Breslau, Poland: Cohen and Weigert.

chapter three

The Physiology of Temperaments, Communication Traits, and Predispositions

I n Chapter 2 we introduced the basic components of the brain and the role of the brain in the production and comprehension of communication. Chapter 3 will extend this conversation to present a discussion on the role of temperament and the development of psychological and communication traits and how these traits are displayed in our behavior and influenced by brain function. By understanding these predispositions toward behavior and their biological bases, we can better understand how and why people behave the way they do and how such behavior is difficult, but not impossible, to change.

chapter objectives

Upon completion of the chapter, the student should be able to:

1. Explain the three biological processes involved in the production and projection of symbolic language

2. Compare and contrast the PEN model of temperament with the OCEAN model of temperament

3. Compare and contrast the different types of communication apprehension

4. Explain the different inherited brain disorders that adversely affect communication

5. Compare and contrast the various types of intelligences

© 2011, Andresr, Shutterstock, Inc.

Key terms

autism spectrum
communication apprehension (CA)
G-factor/general intelligence
OCEAN model of personality
PEN model of temperament

schema
serial position effect
sociocommunicative
    orientation [SCO]
sociocommunicative style [SCS]

talkaholism
temperament
trait
willingness to communicate
    (WTC)

Human Biology and Communication

Human beings are the only species on earth capable of producing and using words. When people communicate they engage three processes necessary for the production and projection of symbolic language. **Respiration** is the first process and involves the **air producing mechanism.** Air passes across the vocal cords, which engage the **voicing mechanism.** The voicing mechanism is a process where the vocal cords tighten to produce vibration. This vibration passes into the nasopharynx and palatal area (Fig. 3.1). The positioning and function of the throat, palate, tongue, lips, and teeth result in **articulation.** "Proper articulation" results in the proper position of each element in this process. Therefore, our native language, or the language we are immersed in and first learn to use, and the dialect with which we learn our native language all determine proper position. For example, people born and raised in New Orleans will have a different English dialect than people born and raised in Boston. Articulation is a result of higher-order brain function and is known as **phonology** (see Fig. 3.1).

For human beings to relate to one another, they must exchange verbal and nonverbal symbols (Polack, Richmond, & McCroskey, 2008). As of 2007

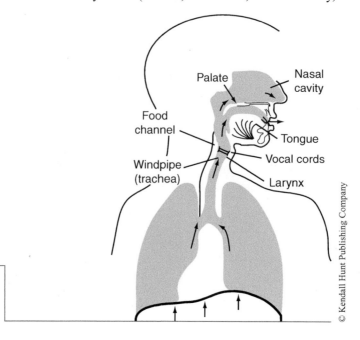

figure 3.1

Physiological Elements Involved in Symbolic Language

© Kendall Hunt Publishing Company

there were approximately 5,000 oral languages being practiced by human beings (Klopf & McCroskey, 2007). Not one of the 5,000 languages is spoken or understood by a majority of humans. However, Mandarin Chinese is spoken by more people than any other language. **Language** is constructed of words (symbols), syntax (word sequence), and grammar (rules for use). Although all languages contain these three elements, fewer than 100 of the 5,000 spoken languages have a written form. It is widely believed that written language is a form that evolved from a human desire to record historic events. Generally speaking, writing is considered more accurate than oral expression for recording history because when information passes through multiple people, it can be either intentionally or unintentionally distorted (McCroskey, 1998).

Traits and Temperaments

When people speak of personality traits, they are referring to any one of thousands of individual characteristics that comprise a person's unique behavioral and thought patterns. Temperaments, however, reflect more global aspects of a person's behavior and, as such, there are fewer temperaments than there are traits. Traits can be defined as a pattern of thought and behavior (Polack et al., 2008), "any distinguishable, relatively enduring way in which one individual differs from others" (Guilford, 1959, p. 6), or "a construction or abstraction to account for enduring behavioral consistencies and differences" (Mischel, 1968, pp. 4–5). However defined, the common thread among these and most every other definition of a trait is the concept of consistency. Traits or predispositions can come in many forms. For example, consider the way that children learn language. Although any one language is learned, the ability for people to recognize **phonemes** (i.e., any sounds that are distinct to a language) of any language is apparent at birth. In fact, the brain's language

| traits

Enduring characteristics that uniquely distinguish one person from another person.

photos.com

Written history is considered to be more accurate than oral expression.

center (located in the left hemisphere) shows development even before birth (Pinker, 2002). When every person has the capacity to acquire language, this type of trait is known as a **generalized human trait** or a trait that any person in any place can possess. **Individual human traits** come from genetic influences. That is, not everyone on the planet has the capacity for the trait—only people who possess your family's specific genetic or inherited attributes. For example, in 2007 there was a television commercial for the cholesterol-lowering drug Vytorin that indicated that cholesterol levels are not simply a function of a person's diet, but also a function of the genetic pool of inherited genes that predisposes you to having certain levels of cholesterol. You may know someone who has greatly modified their diet and regularly engaged in physical activity in an effort to lower cholesterol levels only to find that these efforts did little to assist in lowering their cholesterol levels. In this case, a drug is needed to mediate the genetic tendency for having high cholesterol levels because other changes in the environment (e.g., healthy diet and exercise) were no match for the genetic predisposition for high cholesterol.

temperament

A person's default or overall reaction to stimuli in their environment.

Temperament can be considered super-traits or clusters of related personality traits. A temperament is a person's default or overall reaction to stimuli in their environment. Much of the work on temperament can be attributed to Hans Eysenck (1947). Eysenck (1990) forwarded his "big three" model of personality, which serves as the gold standard for understanding temperaments (Eysenck & Eysenck, 1976). The big three personality factors comprise the PEN model of temperament (Eysenck & Eysenck, 1985), which consists of psychoticism, extraversion, and neuroticism. **Psychoticism** or sociability reflects the degree to which people range on a continuum from being socially likable (low in psychoticism) to socially irritating and aggressive (high in psychoticism). **Extraversion** reflects the degree to which people range on a

PEN model of temperament

Known as the big three model of personality consisting of psychoticism, extraversion, and neuroticism.

What kind of temperament would you expect these women to possess? (Collection)/Thinkstock

Creatus © Getty

continuum from being outgoing (high in extraversion) to being socially avoidant (low in extraversion). **Neuroticism** reflects the degree to which people range on a continuum from being emotionally unstable (high in neuroticism) to being emotionally stable (low in neuroticism). It is believed that all psychological and communication traits are a function of the big three factors.

Eysenck's work was expanded by Costa and McCrea (1985), who developed the "big five" model of personality. The big five is also known as the OCEAN model of personality, reflecting the Eysenck dimensions of neuroticism and extraversion but dividing psychoticism into the three dimensions of conscientiousness, agreeableness, and openness to experience. **Openness to experience** is the degree to which people seek out varied experiences, are imaginative, and are creative. People who are low in openness to experience are more concrete and practical with more narrow interests (such as being regimented in their life). **Conscientiousness** is the degree to which people are dependable, organized, reliable, and responsible. People who are low in conscientiousness are undependable, disorganized, impulsive, and irresponsible. **Agreeableness** is the degree to which people are compassionate, pleasant, good-natured, warm, and sympathetic. People who are low in agreeableness are unfriendly, aggressive, argumentative, and cold. There has been an abundance of evidence supporting both the big three and big five conceptualizations of personality. Both the PEN and OCEAN approaches serve as good theoretical and practical models for understanding and studying human temperament. In fact, psychobiologists have linked the various dimensions of temperament to combinations of various brain systems within the limbic system.

> **OCEAN model of personality**
> The big five model of personality contains dimensions of conscientiousness, agreeableness, open to experience, extraversion, and neuroticism.

Opposite ends of conscientiousness—where does your personality fall on the scale?

Opposite ends of conscientious-ness—where does your personality fall on the scale?

Biologically Determined Traits

communication apprehension (CA)
A communication trait that refers to the degree of fear or anxiety associated with either real or anticipated communication with others.

Communication Apprehension.   The trait of communication apprehension (CA) was developed by James McCroskey (1970) and is defined as the degree of fear or anxiety associated with either real or anticipated communication with others. Recent research indicates that as much as 70% of communication apprehension is genetic or inherited. Further, CA affects approximately 20% of the general population. Imagine the effect of trying to provide care for a patient or communicate with a collegue who is high in communication apprehension. The study of communication apprehension is important because it can adversely affect the quality of life for the person who suffers from it. In fact, research shows that an average American's most common phobia is giving a public speech. To put this in perspective, the fear of death is third on the list (Richmond & McCroskey, 1992).

The amount or degree of communication apprehension experienced by people ranges from feeling apprehension with every communication exchange (trait CA) to feeling apprehension in certain circumstances or situations (state CA; e.g., experiencing anxiety when you ask a question of a particular physician). In addition to trait CA, there are four other dimensions of communication apprehension. **CA-group** is fear or anxiety associated with communication in group settings, **CA-meeting** is fear or anxiety associated with communication in formal meeting settings, **CA-interpersonal** is fear or anxiety associated with communication in dyadic situations, and **CA-public** is the fear or anxiety associated with giving a public speech. When we say that communication apprehension has a genetic basis, what we are saying is that it is extremely difficult, if not impossible, to alter the trait. However, the estimated 30% of CA that is not explained by genetics could possibly be altered by skills training and remediation efforts. This is similar to the cholesterol example mentioned earlier in this chapter in that one can eat healthy foods and exercise only to experience little decrease in cholesterol levels; similarly, a person can take a speech writing or public speaking course and only experience a slight decrease in communication apprehension levels. Figure 3.2 shows the CA continuum.

In the general population, 5% of people are high in communication apprehension, 15% have low communication apprehension, and the remaining

figure 3.2

**Continuum
of Communication
Apprehension**

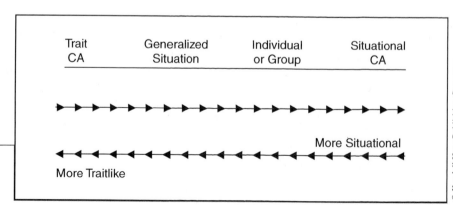

people experience "normal" levels of communication apprehension. It should be noted that just because a person falls within the normal range (i.e., within 1 standard deviation above and below the mean) it does not necessarily mean that they are free from experiencing apprehension when communicating. **Situational CA** is defined as anxiety experienced when communicating in a specific situation or with a specific person or persons.

One of the most effective ways to assess a person's level of communication apprehension is through the **Personal Report of Communication Apprehension (PRCA)**. The PRCA is a 24-item measure developed to assess a person's overall communication apprehension, communication within groups, communication within meetings, communication at the interpersonal level, and communication in public settings. Table 3.1 displays the PRCA-24 and scoring instructions for each dimension of communication apprehension.

The total score can range from 24 to 120. The higher the score, the more the person experiences communication apprehension. To compute the total

table 3.1	The Personal Report of Communication Apprehension

Directions: This instrument is composed of 24 statements concerning feelings about communication with other people. Please indicate the degree to which each statement applies to you by marking whether you (1) *strongly agree*, (2) *agree*, (3) *are undecided*, (4) *disagree*, or (5) *strongly disagree*.

1. _____ I dislike participating in group discussions.
2. _____ Generally, I am comfortable when participating in group discussions.(R)
3. _____ I am tense and nervous while participating in group discussions.
4. _____ I like to get involved in group discussions.(R)
5. _____ Engaging in a group discussion with new people makes me tense and nervous.
6. _____ I am calm and relaxed while participating in group discussions.(R)
7. _____ Generally, I am nervous when I have to participate in meetings.
8. _____ Usually I am calm and relaxed while participating in meetings.(R)
9. _____ I am very calm and relaxed when I am called upon to express an opinion at a meeting. (R)
10. _____ I am afraid to express myself at meetings.
11. _____ Communicating at meetings usually makes me uncomfortable.
12. _____ I am very relaxed when answering questions at a meeting.(R)
13. _____ While participating in a conversation with a new acquaintance, I feel very nervous.
14. _____ I have no fear of speaking up in conversation.(R)
15. _____ Ordinarily I am very tense and nervous in conversations.
16. _____ While conversing with a new acquaintance, I feel very relaxed.(R)
17. _____ Ordinarily, I am very calm and relaxed in conversations.(R)
18. _____ I'm afraid to speak up in conversations.
19. _____ I have no fear of giving a speech.(R)
20. _____ Certain parts of my body feel very tense and rigid while I am giving a speech.
21. _____ I feel relaxed while giving a speech.(R)
22. _____ My thoughts become confused and jumbled when I am giving a speech.
23. _____ I face the prospect of giving a speech with confidence.(R)
24. _____ While giving a speech, I get so nervous I forget facts I really know.

Note: From McCroskey, J. C. (1982). An introduction to rhetorical communication (4th ed.). Englewood Cliffs, NJ: Prentice-Hall.

The PRCA measures a person's communication apprehension.

scores for the PRCA and the total score for each context of communication, follow the following steps:

1. Reverse code the items that are marked with (R). These are items 2, 4, 6, 8, 9, 12, 14, 16, 17, 19, 21, 23). For the following items, if you answer with a **5** replace it with a **1**; if you answer with a **4** replace it with a **2**; if you answer with a **2** replace it with a **4**; if you answer with a **1** replace it with a **5**.
2. Once the items are reverse scored, total the scores by summing the following items:
   a. Total CA level: Sum all of the items.
   b. CA-Group Discussion Level: Sum 1, 2, 3, 4, 5, 6.
   c. CA-Meeting Level: Sum 7, 8, 9, 10, 11, 12.
   d. CA-Interpersonal Level: Sum 13, 14, 15, 16, 17, 18.
   e. CA-Public Speaking Level: Sum 19, 20, 21, 22, 23, 24.

To give you an idea as to how your scores compare to national norms, see Table 3.2.

table 3.2	National Norms for Communication Apprehension (CA) Scores	
Scale	**Mean**	**Standard Deviation**
General Trait CA	65.60	15.30
Group CA	15.40	4.80
Meeting CA	16.40	4.80
Interpersonal CA	14.50	4.20
Public Speaking CA	19.30	5.10

Note: From McCroskey, J. C., & Richmond, V. P. (1996). Fundamentals of human communication: An interpersonal perspective. Prospect Heights, IL: Waveland Press.

Treatment for Communication Apprehension.   According to Richmond and McCroskey (2005), communication apprehension can be treated by two methods: **systematic desensitization** and **cognitive restructuring.** Systematic desensitization is a treatment for communication apprehension that utilizes relaxation techniques to build a greater threshold for the experience of apprehension associated with the specific communication event resulting in anxiety reduction. Cognitive restructuring reflects the reinterpretation of thoughts and cognitions associated with communication situations. Through restructuring the apprehensive or threatening thoughts into nonapprehensive and nonthreatening thoughts, the overall anxiety associated with the communication event will decrease. Although both of these treatments have been met with some success, this success only results in the reduction of communication apprehension by 7% to 10%. Simply put, the amount of benefit achieved by such treatments is small when compared to the amount of time required for these treatment methods.

Given the limited benefit associated with both treatment methods, pharmaceutical interventions have been much more successful. More specifically, the use of antidepressant/antianxiety disorder drugs such as Paxil has been very effective in the reduction and, in some cases, the elimination of communication apprehension. It should be pointed out that communication apprehension is not the same as a depressive disorder. Although the two may be related, they are distinctly different from one another because communication apprehension is narrowly defined as a unique communication trait and depressive disorder is defined as a more global perception of self (Richmond & McCroskey, 2005).

Shyness.   **Shyness** is the predisposition to be timid and reserved when engaged in social interaction. According to Philip Zimbardo (1977), shyness can be considered a discomfort that is associated with many different social situations. A person who is shy experiences discomfort communicating in interpersonal settings, small group settings, and the like. However, it is important to distinguish between shyness and communication apprehension; shyness reflects a tendency to be reserved in any and all contexts, whereas communication apprehension is a fear associated with either real or anticipated communication with another person or person(s). In the general population, 80% of people consider themselves to be shy or were shy at times during their lives (Berger, Baldwin, McCroskey, & Richmond, 1983; Zimbardo, 1977). The implications of shyness for both the patient and healthcare professional are great. The effects of shyness can result in incomplete information gathering, information giving, or information verification on behalf of both the patient and provider. Therefore, the ability to identify people with shyness and provide messages that are nonthreatening and preferably mediated (e.g., email) will reduce the effects of shyness on effective information exchange.

Willingness to Communicate.   **Willingness to communicate (WTC)** is defined as a person's willingness to initiate communication with others (McCroskey & Richmond, 1987). This trait is also believed to be partly genetic

willingness to communicate (WTC)
A person's willingness to initiate communication with others.

Digital Vision

Most people will say they are shy or were shy at some point in their life.

in nature (50% to 60%). People who are high in WTC enjoy approaching or seeking out people for conversation. People who are low in WTC will tend to avoid initiating communication with other people. WTC is easy to detect because all one needs to do to get an indication of a person's WTC is to witness their waiting room behavior. When waiting for the scheduled appointment are they "immersed" in a book? Are they staring at their cell phone? Or are they looking right at you waiting for you to make eye contact so that they can communicate with you? As has been stated several times throughout this book, becoming mindful of others' behaviors and using that information to develop the most strategic communication choices are our central goals.

As we did with shyness, it is important to distinguish between people who do not want to initiate communication (WTC) with people who fear communicating (CA). People who are low in WTC develop clever ways to avoid initiating communication. For example, Chesebro and McCroskey (2002) identified six specific behaviors that individuals with low WTC engage in: (1) they avoid "talk sessions" or communication intensive situations; (2) they will avoid both official (e.g., work groups) and unofficial (e.g., employees who "hang out") small groups; (3) they will sit in "out of the way" locations in large meetings (e.g., in the back of the room or along the walls), avoid any seating position that would constitute the focal point of communication (e.g., sitting in the front row); (4) they will try to occupy the most inconspicuous seat in small-group settings; (5) they tend to choose occupations that are lower in "talk" demands such as engineering, computer science, and other research-intensive positions that have less of a face-to-face communicative demand; and (6) they tend to take the submissive role in dyadic communication in that they will use **powerless language** strategies. Powerless language is language that communicates to the other person insecurity, low power, low status, and low expertise. Some examples of powerless language use include **tag questions** or questions that are attached at the end of a statement such as "you know?" or "right?" and **verbal qualifiers,** which is language that is used at the beginning of a message that detracts from the credibility of the sender such as, "I may be wrong but. . . ." or "You probably already covered this earlier but . . ."

The Willingness to Communicate Scale is found in Table 3.3. Take a moment and complete the scale and find out where you fall on your willingness to communicate:

The total score can range from 0 to 100. The higher the score, the more willing the person is to communicate with others. To compute the total score for the WTC scale and the total score for each context of communication, follow these steps:

To calculate the score for:

a. WTC-Group Discussion Level: Sum 8, 15, 19; divide this total by 3. Scores above 89 = high WTC-Group; scores below 57 = low WTC-Group.
b. WTC-Meeting Level: Sum 6, 11, 17; divide this total by 3. Scores above 80 = high WTC-Meeting; scores below 39 = low WTC-Meeting.

table 3.3	Willingness to Communicate Measure

Directions: Following are 20 situations in which a person might or might not choose to communicate. Assuming that you have free choice to either engage or not engage in communication, determine the percentage of times you would choose to initiate communication in each type of situation. Indicate in the space at the left what percent of the time you would choose to communicate. Choose any numbers between 0 and 100.

_____ 1. Talk with a service station attendant.
_____ 2. Talk with a physician.
_____ 3. Present a talk to a group of strangers.
_____ 4. Talk with an acquaintance while standing in line.
_____ 5. Talk with a salesperson in a store.
_____ 6. Talk in a large meeting of friends.
_____ 7. Talk with a police officer.
_____ 8. Talk in a small group of strangers.
_____ 9. Talk with a friend while standing in line.
_____ 10. Talk with a server in a restaurant.
_____ 11. Talk in a large meeting of acquaintances.
_____ 12. Talk with a stranger while standing in line.
_____ 13. Talk with a secretary.
_____ 14. Present a talk to a group of friends.
_____ 15. Talk in a small group of acquaintances.
_____ 16. Talk with a garbage collector.
_____ 17. Talk in a large meeting of strangers.
_____ 18. Talk with a spouse (or girlfriend/boyfriend).
_____ 19. Talk in a small group of friends.
_____ 20. Present a talk to a group of acquaintances.

Note: From McCroskey, J. C., & Richmond, V. P. (1996). Fundamentals of human communication: An interpersonal perspective. Prospect Heights, IL: Waveland Press.

c. WTC-Interpersonal Level: Sum 4, 9, 12; divide this total by 3. Scores above 94 = high WTC-Interpersonal; scores below 64 = low WTC-Interpersonal.

d. WTC-Public Speaking Level: Sum 3, 14, 20; divide this total by 3. Scores above 78 = high WTC-Public Speaking; scores below 33 = low WTC-Public Speaking.

e. WTC-Stanger Level: Sum 3, 8, 12, 17; divide this total by 4. Scores above 63 = high WTC-Stranger; scores below 18 = low WTC-Stranger.

f. WTC-Acquaintance Level: Sum 4, 11, 15, 20; divide this total by 4. Scores above 92 = high WTC-Acquaintance; scores below 57 = low WTC-Acquaintance.

g. WTC-Friends Level: Sum 6, 9, 14, 19; divide this total by 4. Score above 99 = high WTC-Friends; scores below 71 = low WTC-Friends.

h. To compute the total scores for WTC, add the total scores calculated for WTC-Stranger, WTC-Friends, and WTC-Acquaintance; divide this total by 3. Scores above 82 = high WTC; scores below 52 = low WTC.

Implications for the Quiet Person (high CA, shyness, and low WTC).   Western society puts such a heavy influence on communication competency that people who possess traits that adversely affect competent communication are at a great disadvantage on both personal and professional levels. For example, data indicate that people who are quiet or possess high levels of CA, shyness, or low WTC are perceived to be less credible, less competent, less likely to be a leader, less intelligent, and more anxious. These types of expectations are developed as early as kindergarten. Students who are quiet tend to be seen by others in the following seven ways: (1) they are less intelligent; (2) they are perceived as having learned less than they actually do; (3) they are expected to obtain lower grades and overall grade point average; (4) they are expected by the teacher to perform at low levels; (5) they are more nonverbal in efforts

How do others typically perceive quiet students?

Photodisc by Nick White

to avoid communication (e.g., looking down at the floor to avoid interaction); (6) they prefer large lecture classes as opposed to small classes because there is less probability of being called on during class; and (7) if in a dormitory, they tend to select rooms that are at the end of halls where there is considerably less traffic (McCroskey & Richmond, 1996). In social settings, quiet people are perceived as less friendly, tend to be in monogamous relationships (because starting and developing new relationships can be very uncomfortable for quiet people), and tend to get married immediately after school (high school or college) (McCroskey & Richmond, 1996).

In terms of professional outcomes associated with quiet people, they tend to do poorly in interview settings; are terminated more often; and, when terminated, are less likely to litigate because of the "communication load" associated with protracted legal action (Richmond & McCroskey, 2005). Therefore, when faced with communicating with a quiet colleague or patient, you can make the person more comfortable by using encouragement, focusing on their positive skill sets, not forcing them into communication-intense situations, and avoiding putting them in leadership positions where communication would be a necessary skill.

Talkaholism. **Talkaholism** is a predisposition to engage in compulsive communication behavior (McCroskey, 1993). This trait is also genetically based and reflects people who are intensely driven to communicate. High talkaholism affects 5% of the population. Talkaholics are people who are less concerned with the content of the message than they are with the fact that they keep talking. In fact, these types of people have experienced relational or professional difficulty because of their compulsive talking. Perhaps you know of someone who is always speaking, but what they are saying is rarely of interest or relevant. Further, this same person may be one that other people

talkaholism

A predisposition to engage in compulsive communication behavior.

Mediaimages/Photodisc

Do you know someone who is a talkaholic?

tend to avoid because they do not have time to spend communicating with the talkaholic. It should be noted that the ability to engage in "chitchat" is extremely beneficial in our society and a necessary skill for many professions (e.g., pharmaceutical sales). However, talkaholism is a compulsion and, similar to other compulsions, the person cannot help themselves. It is at this level that the compulsive communicator regularly irritates the targets of such communication episodes. This trait is measured through the Talkaholism Scale and is presented in Table 3.4. Complete this measure to calculate your score on the trait of talkaholism.

To calculate the score for talkaholism:

1. Sum scores for items 2, 3, 5, 7, 8, 10, 11, 14.
2. Sum scores for items 13 and 16.
3. Complete the following formula:

Talkaholic Score = 12 + total from step 1 – total from step 2.

The range of possible scores should be between 10 and 50. Although most people score below 30, those who score between 30 and 39 are borderline talkaholics, meaning that they are able to control their talking most of the time, but there are instances where they find it difficult to be quiet, even though it would be in their best interest to do so. People who score 40 and higher have a true compulsion to talk and as such are considered high in talkaholism.

table 3.4	Talkaholism Measure

Directions: The following questionnaire includes 16 statements about talking behavior. Please indicate the degree to which you believe each of these characteristics applies to you by marking, on the line before each item, whether you (5) *strongly agree* with the statement; (4) *agree* with the statement; (3) *are undecided* with the statement; (2) *disagree* with the statement; or (1) *strongly disagree* with the statement. There are no right or wrong answers. Record your first impression because it is usually the correct one.

_____ 1. Often I keep quiet when I know I should talk.
_____ 2. I talk more than I should sometimes.
_____ 3. Often, I talk when I know I should keep quiet.
_____ 4. Sometimes I keep quiet when I know it would be to my advantage to talk.
_____ 5. I am a "talkaholic."
_____ 6. Sometimes I feel compelled to keep quiet.
_____ 7. In general, I talk more than I should.
_____ 8. I am a compulsive talker.
_____ 9. I am not a talker; rarely do I talk in communication situations.
_____ 10. Quite a few people have said I talk too much.
_____ 11. I just can't stop talking too much.
_____ 12. In general, I talk less than I should.
_____ 13. I am not a "talkaholic."
_____ 14. Sometimes I talk when I know it would be in my advantage to keep quiet.
_____ 15. I talk less than I should sometimes.
_____ 16. I am not a compulsive talker.

Note: From McCroskey, J. C., & Richmond, V. P. (1996). Fundamentals of human communication: An interpersonal perspective. Prospect Heights, IL: Waveland Press.

Sociocommunicative Orientation (SCO) and Sociocommunicative Style (SCS).
In 1983 Robert Norton developed the idea of **communicator style**, which is
a trait defined as the way people use verbal and paraverbal behavior to signal
how literal meaning should be taken, interpreted, filtered, or understood
(Infante, Rancer, & Avtgis, 2010). More recently, this stylistic distinction
was furthered with the development of the sociocommunicative style (SCS)
and the sociocommunicative orientation (SCO). Sociocommunicative
style refers to how others see your communicative behavior, whereas
sociocommunicative orientation refers to a person's self-perception of
their communicative behavior. Both the SCS and SCO are considered
communication traits because our self-perceptions are enduring and so
are the perceptions that others have of us. Therefore, these perceptions are
relatively stable.

Both SCS and SCO consist of two independent dimensions of **assertiveness** and **responsiveness** (Richmond & Martin, 1998). Assertiveness reflects
the degree to which people are able to stand up for their position or rights,
whereas responsiveness reflects the degree to which people show compassion,
empathy, and other orientation for another person. According to McCroskey,
Richmond, and Stewart (1986), assertiveness and responsiveness are two of
the three critical components of interpersonal communication competency; the
third is **versatility,** or the degree to which people can adapt their assertiveness and responsiveness to specific people and specific situations. The assertive
person tends to issue requests (whereas the aggressive person tends to issue
demands without concern for the receiver). The responsive person is a person
who is immediate (appears psychologically close) to others. It should be noted
that just because a person is highly responsive, they are not necessarily submissive. The responsive person does not necessarily yield their rights to the
other person. The truly competent person is able to not only determine which

**sociocommunicative
style (SCS)**
How other people view
your communicative
behavior.

**sociocommunicative
orientation (SCO)**
A person's self-
perception of his or
her communicative
behavior.

iStockphoto

*Is this behavior assertive
or aggressive?*

situations call for assertiveness, responsiveness, or both, but also possesses the ability to engage the appropriate communication strategies.

Androgyny. The trait of **androgyny** reflects a person's tendency to appropriately use both masculine and feminine communication styles (Bem, 1974; Wheeless & Dierks-Stewart, 1981). Masculine communication behaviors tend to be more assertive, whereas feminine styles tend to be more responsive. Androgyny, then, is a combination of the Greek words andros, or man, and gyne, or woman. The most competent communicators are able to shift in their male and female communication styles with ease and effectiveness as the situations dictates. The practice of androgynous communication style is based on the traditional Western concept of masculine and feminine behavior. Given the fact that healthcare is inclusive of all people, the most accessible and effective communication style would be that which is adaptable, flexible, and capable of being understood by the most people.

Psychological Traits and Communication Behavior

As eluded to earlier in this chapter, a person's personality can be defined as the total psychological makeup of an individual comprising experiences, motivations, attitudes, beliefs, values, and behaviors. The sum of these characteristics make each person unique (Hollander, 1976). Although there have been more than 100 separate personality traits identified by social science researchers, a handful of these have provided an abundance of evidence for explaining and predicting a person's behavior. The following represent some of the most important psychological traits in explaining communication behavior:

- **Adventurousness.** This is defined as the degree to which a person likes to experience new and novel situations. A person who is high in adventurousness is always willing to try novel situations, tends to be more talkative, and is task driven. The person who is low in adventurousness is cautious, is less talkative, and generally fosters feelings of inferiority.
- **Authoritarianism.** This is a predisposition "to rely on structure and rules for determining what is right and wrong" (Avtgis, Rancer, & Madlock, 2010, p. 133). A person who is high in authoritarianism seeks to dominate over other people when interacting; rarely seeks out information from others in lower status; and values hierarchical structure, rules, and systematic procedures (Adorno, Frenkel-Brunswik, Levinson & Sanford, 1950). The low authoritarian is more trusting of others, has less regard for hierarchical structure, and does not strive to dominate others when interacting.
- **Dogmatism.** This trait similar to authoritarianism is defined as being rigid in belief systems as to what is right and wrong. Unlike authoritarians, dogmatics are unwilling to consider the viewpoints of others (Rokeach, 1960). A person who is high in dogmatism tends to be closed-minded and rigid with a high respect for authority. Their interaction style is one of certainty with little regard for dissenting opinions or viewpoints. The low

dogmatic tends to be more flexible in opinions and viewpoints and tends to have less respect for authority.

- **Emotional Maturity/Emotional Intelligence.** Emotional maturity/ emotional intelligence reflects the degree to which people are able to understand, recognize, regulate, and productively utilize their emotions. In fact, according to Goleman (1997), there are five dimensions to emotional intelligence consisting of *knowing one's emotions* (self-awareness), *managing emotions* (appropriate emotional management), *self-motivation* (being able to use emotions productively to achieve a desired goal), *recognizing emotions in others* (empathy), and *handling relationships* (skills in handling the emotions other people are experiencing). Those who display a high degree of emotional maturity/intelligence are stable, calm, and well balanced. They are flexible in their communication and adapt well to different situations. However, people who are low in emotional maturity/intelligence tend to be in conflict with others and regularly engage in hostile communication behavior.

- **Locus of Control.** Locus of control reflects the degree to which people interpret events in their life as resulting from their own ability and purposeful effort (i.e., **internal locus of control**) or from chance, luck, or fate (i.e., **external locus of control**) (Rotter, 1966). Research indicates that people with an internal locus of control experience lower levels of communication apprehension (McCroskey, Daly, & Sorensen, 1976), are less aggressive when communicating with other people (Avtgis & Rancer, 1997), are more satisfied with their work (Spector, 1988), and are less persuadable than people with an external locus of control (Lefcourt, 1981).

- **Machiavellianism.** Machiavellianism reflects the degree to which people will say and do whatever needs to be said and done to achieve a desired goal or outcome. People who are high in Machiavellianism are concerned with making good impressions on others because it is easier to get someone to do something when they have a favorable opinion of you (Becker & O'Hair, 2007). Some common vocations for Machiavellians include sales, clergy, and even healthcare because getting a patient to comply with a regimen may take some persuasive skills and strategic communication. Therefore, being high in Machiavellianism is not good or bad in and of itself. Instead, the high Machiavellian should be judged on how they use their skill and outcomes associated with such behavior. For example, a good doctor is a person who can relate to a multitude of patients with different backgrounds, interests, life spaces, and dreams. The successful physician will be able to tap into these areas in an effort to get the patient to comply with, or take charge of, his or her treatment.

The personality traits reviewed here offer valuable insights into individual differences in communication behavior. Researchers are beginning to explore actual brain differences associated with people who possess these traits in varying levels. The ability to determine the types of traits another person possesses, whether it be a colleague or a patient, is invaluable for both professional success and patient safety.

How does a doctor work with different patients and successfully persuade them to comply with their treatment?

Photodisc

Disorders of the Inherited Brain Adversely Affecting Communication

Unlike other communication texts, the fact that this book is targeted at healthcare professionals requires us to take a unique perspective and approach to the discussion of communication and the brain. People working within healthcare regularly come in contact with patients and families who suffer from brain disorders that adversely affect efficient and competent communication, among a myriad of other issues. Therefore, this section is dedicated to presenting several disorders of the brain and their manifestation on communication behavior.

Attention Deficit Hyperactivity Disorder. **Attention deficit hyperactivity disorder (ADHD or AD/HD)** is a disorder of focus and behavior associated with a decrease in frontal lobe activity (Zemetkin, Nordalh, & Gross, 1990). This decreased frontal lobe activation becomes especially prominent when patients with ADHD are asked to concentrate on a task. People without ADHD have the opposite activation patterns. That is, there is increased frontal lobe activity, especially when the subjects are asked to concentrate. By demonstrating the functional differences in the brains of subjects with and without ADHD, researchers are able to establish real differences in brain activity. Communication patterns of the patient/family member with ADHD may be that of incoherent conversation, rapid topic switching, and poor listening skills.

Autism Spectrum. **Autism** is a neurological developmental disorder affecting social and communication behavior. One in 175 American children are affected by autism whereby there is accelerated brain growth. The brain growth in a child with autism is similar to that of normal children from birth until 2 years of age. It is between 3 and 6 years of age when the brain of the child with autism grows abnormally, resulting in brain mass that is 10% larger than there nonautistic counterparts (Kantrowidz & Scelfo, 2006). Autism is a spectrum disorder, meaning that it ranges in scope from disorders such as Asperger's syndrome, which is the highest functioning of the spectrum, to RETT's syndrome, which is the most severely disabling form (Goldberg, 2008). Because the brain is responsible for so many aspects of both verbal and nonverbal communication, problems in communication behavior become apparent when the areas responsible for producing and interpreting communication signals are damaged or abnormal. Two disorders that result in marked problems in communication behavior are autism and Asperger's syndrome.

Autism is a disorder with three core features (*DSM-IV*; American Psychiatric Association, 1994; a diagnostic handbook for mental health professionals). The first feature is *impairment with social interaction* and includes a lack of eye contact and a difficulty developing peer relationships. The second feature, *impairment of communication,* includes a delay in spoken language and the inability to adequately initiate or sustain a conversation with other people. The third feature is *repetitive or stereotyped patterns of behavior, interests, and activities.* People diagnosed with autism display diverse levels of intelligence and language abilities. Given that the degree of severity of all three features can vary greatly between any two people with autism, the different combinations of symptoms that exist comprise what is known as the **autism spectrum.**

| **autism spectrum**
The degree of severity in the symptoms of autism characterized by different combinations of developmental factors.

Children with autism exhibit atypical developmental patterns in that their communication and social skills begin to lag behind children of the same age. Some children with autism can actually experience a deterioration of the language and social skills that were previously developed. A small percentage of children with autism remain mute throughout their entire life, others may speak only single words or continuously repeat certain phrases, and some may have the requisite skills to communicate effectively (e.g., large vocabulary, grammar skills) but are unable to follow social rules for sustained conversation (e.g., turn taking, other-orientation, topic appropriateness). Nonverbally, the behavior of the child with autism is difficult to interpret because facial expressions and movements may not match the verbal messages that they are sending (e.g., difficulty in making and maintaining eye contact and smiles and frowns that are incongruent with their verbal messages). This incongruity can result in high levels of ambiguity and uncertainty for the receiver of such messages.

People within the autism spectrum who experience these social and communication problems, but to a lesser degree than the autistic child, are diagnosed with **Asperger's syndrome (AS).** People with this condition are sometimes referred to as having high-functioning autism because they often show a normal or superior intelligence.

The ability for scientists and health professionals to identify abnormal brain structures associated with autism is difficult. Some studies report post-mortem (autopsy) findings of the autistic brain. Taken as a whole, the autistic brain appears to be larger and heavier than the normal brain (Herbert, 2005). It is believed that the *cerebellum, amygdala, frontal lobes, basal ganglia, hippocampus,* and *brain stem* are all affected by this disorder (Baron-Cohen, 2004). Figure 3.3 highlights these brain systems.

A variety of abnormalities within the neurons (brain cells) occurs within these structures. These abnormalities range from how densely packed the neurons are to an overall reduction in neuron size. Neuroimaging studies indicate that individuals with autism have high brain activation in certain areas and low activation in others. Thus, pinpointing what role each brain region may play in the disorder is difficult to determine. Researchers are currently comparing images of normal and autistic brains to determine the

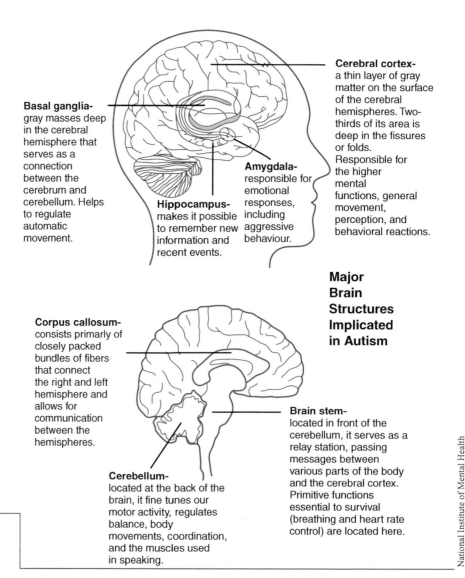

Cerebral cortex- a thin layer of gray matter on the surface of the cerebral hemispheres. Two-thirds of its area is deep in the fissures or folds. Responsible for the higher mental functions, general movement, perception, and behavioral reactions.

Basal ganglia- gray masses deep in the cerebral hemisphere that serves as a connection between the cerebrum and cerebellum. Helps to regulate automatic movement.

Hippocampus- makes it possible to remember new information and recent events.

Amygdala- responsible for emotional responses, including aggressive behaviour.

Major Brain Structures Implicated in Autism

Corpus callosum- consists primarily of closely packed bundles of fibers that connect the right and left hemisphere and allows for communication between the hemispheres.

Cerebellum- located at the back of the brain, it fine tunes our motor activity, regulates balance, body movements, coordination, and the muscles used in speaking.

Brain stem- located in front of the cerebellum, it serves as a relay station, passing messages between various parts of the body and the cerebral cortex. Primitive functions essential to survival (breathing and heart rate control) are located here.

National Institute of Mental Health

figure 3.3

Main Brain Structures Involved in Autism

exact difference in functioning in hopes of developing specific theories of brain system function in autistic spectrum disorder. Some promising therapies are being tested to reduce the effects of autism. For example, Dawson et al. (2010) tested the effects of the **Early Start Denver Model (ESDM),** which is a comprehensive developmental behavioral intervention on children with autism spectrum disorder. This behavioral therapy focuses on improving social interaction and communication (e.g., increasing eye contact and rewarding appropriate communication behavior). The results of this 2-year training indicate significant improvement in intelligence quotient (IQ) score and adaptive behaviors. Improvement in autism reflects moving from a diagnosis of autism to a pervasive developmental disorder, a less severe form within the autism spectrum.

The Human Brain, Intelligence, and Communication

When it comes to the human brain and our individuality, we can be certain in saying that every human brain is uniquely wired (Kandel, Schwartz, & Jessell, 2000). This assertion is based on three general assumptions that we hold to be true:

1. *Different regions of the brain develop at different rates in different people.*
2. *No two people's brains have the same information stored in the same way in the same place.*
3. *Every person is intelligent. Certain intelligences may not show up on a standard IQ test, but there are many different ways of being intelligent.*

Perhaps one of the most robust discussions in psychological circles revolves around the concept of **intelligence** (Moffitt et al., 1993). What does it mean to be intelligent? A task force of the American Psychological Association sought to determine the answer to this question and defined intelligence as "the ability to understand complex ideas, to adapt effectively to the environment, to learn from experience, to engage in various forms of reasoning, and to overcome obstacles by taking thought" (Neisser et al., 1996, p. 77).

In early studies of intelligence, it was assumed that there was one universal definition for intelligence (Spearman, 1927). This definition, referred to as the G factor or general intelligence, was measured by standardized tests such as the **Stanford-Binet IQ assessment,** which yields a single measure of intelligence. The originator of the intelligence construct was Alfred Binet, also known as the father of all modern intelligence tests. Binet believed that intelligence can be assessed in three distinct ways. First, the **medical method of intelligence** assesses anatomical, physiological, and pathological signs of inferior intelligence. Second, the **pedagogical method of intelligence** assesses intelligence through educational or acquired knowledge. This type of assessment is based on the degree of accumulated knowledge that a person possesses. Third, the **psychological method of**

G-factor/ general intelligence

A conceptualization of intelligence that assumes intelligence is unidimensional and universal across people.

intelligence assesses intelligence based on direct observation and assessing behavior considered intelligent in nature.

Louis Thurstone (1938) identified seven distinct kinds of mental abilities that can be considered a level of intelligence: *verbal comprehension, numerical ability, spatial relations, perceptual speed, word fluency, memory,* and *reasoning*. These multiple dimensions of intelligence were assessed through the **Primary Mental Abilities Test** (Thurstone & Thurstone, 1941). In one of the most widely accepted multidimensional concepts of intelligence, Howard Gardner (1983) developed the **eight-factor model of intelligence** consisting of the following:

1. **Linguistic intelligence:** The ability to use language both as an aid to thinking and when communicating with others.
2. **Logical-mathematical intelligence:** The ability to think logically and to solve mathematical problems.
3. **Spatial intelligence:** The ability to use images that represent special relations between and among objects.
4. **Bodily-kinesthetic intelligence:** The ability to learn and execute physical movements.
5. **Musical intelligence:** The ability to discern among pitch, rhythm, and other aspects of music.
6. **Interpersonal intelligence:** The ability to communicate and engage in effective social relationships with others.
7. **Intrapersonal intelligence:** The ability to understand one's self including emotions and cognitions.
8. **Naturalistic intelligence:** The ability to identify patterns in nature and to determine how individual objects fit into the larger whole or pattern.

Gardner's multifactor conceptualization, although intuitively pleasing, did not necessarily lend itself to effective assessment (Aiken, 1997). Because of this inability to measure these dimensions, a more condensed approach to intelligence was created. Sternberg (1985) developed his **triarchic theory of intelligence.** This theory contends that intelligence is composed of three factors: **componential intelligence,** the mental abilities more closely related to traditional concepts of intelligence such as a score on an IQ test; **experimental intelligence,** the ability for creative thinking and problem solving; and **contextual intelligence,** the ability to be practical or display "street smarts." The triarchic approach to intelligence is valuable to education at all levels including traditional classroom learning, patient education, and patient literacy because it provides an opportunity to create curricula that can effectively tap into all different types of intelligence and improved learning in addition to patient safety.

As illustrated in this section, intelligence has been oversimplified and misinterpreted by many theorists and researchers. It is only until recently that the concept of multiple intelligences has been readily accepted and allows for the finding of unique attributes (intelligences) of each individual. Each person has particular strengths, as determined by their neurologic attributes. Given this, communication skills can vary greatly; when a person communicates about an area or subject in which he or she lacks a particular intelligence, he or she may be incorrectly categorized as being unintelligent and communicatively incompetent when, in fact, that particular subject or area of discussion may not be within their realm of cognitive strength and this leads the receiver to an incorrect conclusion about the sender's attributes.

Attention Span and Communication.   The concept of attention and a person's ability to truly attend to a message is an important topic when discussing communication because it serves as a regulator to effectively sending and receiving messages. There is one major truth about attention and adult learners: Adults have short attention spans (Chesebro & McCroskey, 2002). In fact, 10 minutes is believed to be the maximum time that people are able to focus with any intensity on a message (Hoveland, Janis, & Kelley, 1953). With this in mind, any message should contain the most important material within the first minute, with the remainder of time spent on less important aspects of the message or those aspects that do not take too much cognitive effort. The reason for ordering information in this way is that the brain processes messages for detail and such processing takes a lot of cognitive effort. Thus, providing the core concepts early in the message results in improved understanding because there is more "energy" available for processing.

Throughout this book there have been many references to the fact that messages contain both a verbal and nonverbal component. Therefore, when we suggest that the brain is involved in processing messages for details, we are also referring to the processing of nonverbal messages and cues. Who decides which parts of messages are important and which are not? The receiver is the one who chooses to attend to certain things in a message and avoid others. For example, the interpreting of facial emotions that are tied to messages

How long is your attention span?

is available to be processed should the receiver choose to interpret them. These primary emotional expressions are sadness, anger, fright, surprise, and happiness (Ekman & Friesen, 1975). It is believed that because these emotional expressions are universal in nature, meaning that all humans engage in such expressions regardless of cultural background, these emotionally charged stimuli tend to be more memorable to the human brain. Therefore, they garner greater attention from the brain than other sorts of emotional expression. We would be remiss if we did not implicate the amygdala in the processing of emotion and the fact that it is charged with the neurotransmitter dopamine. Therefore, if the brain detects any emotionally charged event, the amygdala releases dopamine into the system. This charge of neurotransmitter (dopamine) is perhaps the main reason why emotionally charged messages and experiences tend to be more easily recalled.

When it comes to the human brain and attention, perhaps one of the biggest myths emphasized by the modern business world is that of the ability to multitask. It is common knowledge in neuroscience that the brain focuses on concepts in a sequential order. Simply put, it puts its energy into one task at a time (Kandel et al., 2000). There is an old saying when referring to a person with limited coordination that states, "He can't walk and chew gum at the same time." In fact, he can because both of these functions are processed by separate neurological networks located in separate areas of the brain. Attention is considered a **cortical resource** that is deployed when we take in information from the environment. A cortical resource is any attribute of the brain that assists in information processing. Further, we only take in one concept at a time, making it biologically impossible to take in more than one concept at a time and efficiently process it. The implications of such sequential processing on communication are multifold. First, relay important information early and with appropriate nonverbal expression. If the information is of critical importance, then relay that both verbally and nonverbally; if the information is not critical in nature, then use the appropriate nonverbal behavior to indicate such noncritical information. No matter how interesting the incoming communication is, the human brain is only capable of so much in terms of effective processing. To illustrate this point, reflect back on the first day of a job; there was so much information regarding procedures, protocols, and processes that after approximately 10 minutes of being bombarded with this information, you very may well have "tuned out" much of the information. Even information that was critical to you performing your job duties effectively may have become victim to information overload.

Information Selectivity and Hurdles in Communication.   James McCroskey and Virginia Richmond (1996) identified five major hurdles for selecting and processing information in the environment: *selective exposure, selective attention, selective perception, selective retention*, and *selective recall*. **Selective exposure** reflects a person's conscious or unconscious decision to place himself or herself in a position to receive messages from a source. The decision to be exposed to stimuli is based on four factors. First, **proximity** reflects the easier the access a person has to a stimulus, the more likely it is to be noticed. For example, it is much easier to reference a medical website such as www.webmd.com than it is to look up information in a medical textbook. Second, utility refers to the more useful a stimuli is to a person, the more likely it is to be noticed. A healthcare professional who, through her preliminary investigation, determines that a particular treatment will be useful is more likely to seek out the relevant information pertaining to that treatment. Third, **involvement** reflects the more involved a person is with a topic, the stimuli related to that topic will most likely be attended to. If a surgeon has scheduled a patient for a surgical procedure, you must know the anatomy and technical aspects of performing the procedure prior to proceeding. Fourth is **reinforcement**, suggesting that the more desired outcomes are experienced with certain stimuli, the greater the probability that the stimuli will be attended to in the future. If a medical treatment you have observed results in positive outcomes, you will probably seek out information relevant to this treatment in the future.

     Selective attention reflects the second hurdle in information processing and communication consisting of which stimuli actually get our attention. Although we cannot always control the types of messages that we are exposed to, we have a greater degree of control over what messages will receive our attention. Thus, all attention is selective as opposed to objective in nature. The average adult's short-term memory is approximately 14 to 20 seconds in length. The human brain works faster than people are able to talk. When a subject or topic interests us, we will pay attention to some parts of the information while ignoring other parts. This selective attention to information is influenced by five factors: *attention span, novelty, concreteness, size,* and *duration.* **Attention span,** as mentioned earlier in this chapter, is short in adults and even shorter for children. It can be defined as the amount of time and intensity a person can exert on incoming stimuli. Human beings can never pay "full attention" to a message. This is why the need for redundant messaging is important for long-term recall. When we refer to **redundancy** we mean that a message is sent (a) *in the same way with the same channel* (e.g., orally repeating the same message), (b) *in the same way via another channel* (e.g., orally delivering the message and also having the message in writing), (c) *in different ways using the same channel* (e.g., orally delivering the message then altering the message and orally delivering the altered message), and (d) *in different ways via another channel* (e.g., orally delivering the message and having an altered form of the message in writing). For example, consider how redundancy would be used in delivering the following message to a patient: "You have the 'flu'." This message may be altered with words like "influenza," "bug," or "viral infection."

     Novelty reflects the concept that things that are unusual or out of the ordinary will tend to get our attention. Novelty, in the sense we are using it here, is context specific. For example, what is termed *novel* for a psychiatric ward is far different from what is *novel* for a neonatal intensive care unit. **Concreteness** is the concept that people pay attention to communication that affects them or that they can relate to. It is common in healthcare education that a person within the specific specialty teaches those aspiring to

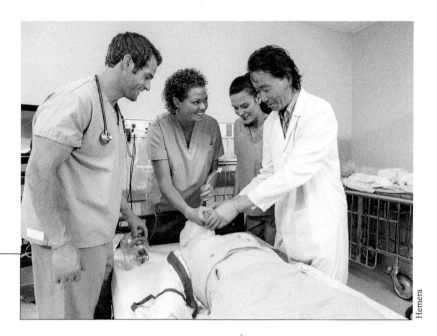

People pay closer attention to communication that affects them or relates to them.

be in that specialty. For example, nursing students who want to specialize in pediatrics will probably relate better to an instructor who can connect with the struggles of being a nursing student in pediatrics than they could an oncology (cancer) nurse practitioner who treats only adult patients. **Size** assumes that things that are out of normal proportion (e.g., being too large or too small) will tend to draw our attention. When things are in their expected proportion we tend to skim over them. For example, a person with normal skin tone probably will not draw our attention, but a person with a big, swollen extremity (arm and/or hand) would tend to draw our attention because it is out of the ordinary. **Duration** reflects the extremely short or extremely long communication encounters that tend to decay people's attention. What consists of something being "too short" or "too long" depends on the specific culture and context within which the communication takes place. For example, the definition of what constitutes communication that is too short and too long during a surgical procedure is different than when making small talk between work shifts.

The third hurdle in information processing and communication involves **selective perception,** or the process of attributing meaning to some messages while ignoring others. Messages do not carry meaning but provide us the stimulus from which to attribute meaning to them. Different people will attribute different meanings to the same message. For example, read aloud the following sentences with emphasis on the bolded word:

> **Please** hand me that retractor.
> Please **hand** me that retractor.
> Please hand **me** that retractor.
> Please hand me **that** retractor.
> Please hand me that **retractor.**

As is evidenced in this message exercise, the emphasis on one word can drastically change the meaning we attribute to it. Several core factors contribute to selective perception: *ambiguous messages, lack of redundancy, lack of schema, biases,* and *lack of prior experience.* **Ambiguous messages** are imprecise and ripe for misunderstanding. Ambiguity is commonly associated with the use of abstract rather than concrete language use. Therefore, the more concrete a message is (e.g., "I need 2 ccs" versus "a little more"), the less likely it is to have significant ambiguity. However, even the most concrete messages can result in ambiguity because interpretation is based on the receiver's attributes, not the attributes of the sender. **Lack of redundancy** reflects that when messages are bound or constricted without any redundancy (e.g., lack of nonverbal communication, verbal message or medium of another sort such as a patient's chart), there is a greater probability of problematic interpretation. **Lack of schema** reflects the lack of organizing ability. According to Avtgis, et al. (2010), perceptual schema is "how we are 'wired' to organize information. We develop set patterns in terms of how we organize stimuli" (p. 11). We generally organize stimuli based on four categories: *physical attributes* (e.g., "This patient is obese"), *role attributes* (e.g., "She is a nurse in the radiology department"), *interaction attributes* (e.g., "That surgeon is very verbally aggressive"), and *psychological attributes* (e.g., "The wife of this patient is insecure and suspicious of any doctor"). **Biases** are cognitive controls that people place on incoming stimuli that influence the interpretation of the stimuli into a desired path. From a behavioral standpoint, this can be illustrated in a nurse who has a dislike for people who smoke. Therefore, when she encounters a patient who reports smoking behavior, she may be less friendly and attentive to the needs of the patient, even if she does not intend to do. From a cognitive standpoint, people have neurobiological biases for processing information. For example, in the individual who is right-brained dominant, art/music stimuli will be more efficiently absorbed and retained. This is also considered the nonverbal side of the brain. For the individual who is left-brained dominant, there will be a preference for mathematics, language, and science. The left side of the brain is considered the verbal side of the brain. **Lack of prior experience** reflects that when people do not have previous similar experience with which to compare present stimuli, they are less likely to be preprogrammed to tune in to certain types of messages over others. For example, a physician assistant with 20 years of experience in medical practice will have a different perspective on handling a difficult patient than would a physician assistant (PA) who was just credentialed and starting a new job. The experienced PA will have years of knowledge and experience from which to compare the present situation, whereas the newly credentialed PA will only have limited, if any, experience addressing patients who are being difficult.

Selective retention is the fourth hurdle to information processing and communication reflecting the ability, or inability, to store information in long-term memory. Committing something to long-term memory is a conscious process that can be either enhanced or inhibited by five main factors. **Highlighting of information** is the first factor in that information that is highlighted tends to be more memorable than that which is not. Verbal and nonverbal highlighting of information provides the listener with cues not only as to which information is more important than others, but also which information is more worthy of being committed to long-term memory. For example, when giving a patient instructions, those instructions may contain both information that is important (e.g., frequency of medication dose) and information that is not as important (e.g., getting rest and relaxation). To be a competent communicator one needs to develop the ability to highlight information that is important because that increases the chances that the information will be stored in long-term memory. Redundancy refers to the concept that the more someone uses or accesses something, the more likely they are able to remember it. That is why people will often study or practice something in multiple ways to commit it to memory. Informing a patient of a treatment regimen and then having the patient repeat that regimen back to you in their own words is a device that is commonly used to create redundancy (teach back) for the patient to make the information more easily retainable and understandable. Schema is the fourth factor involved in selective retention and reflects the need for an idea or experience to have an assigned place to be stored in the brain. That is, the brain has abilities to accommodate an incredible amount of experience and knowledge given it is able to make the appropriate neurological connections. Therefore, if the brain is unable to provide the appropriate schema for which to store an idea or experience, it will not be retained. **Adaptation** refers to whether or not the information or stimuli is useful or adaptable to the receivers needs. Simply put, if the information is relevant to the receiver of the information, there is a greater probability that it will be retained in long-term memory. However, if the receiver perceives that the information is irrelevant or not useful, there is very little chance that this information will be retained. Human beings are self-centered by nature

schema

Factor of selective retention reflecting the need for an idea or experience to have an assigned place to be stored in the brain.

Why is redundancy important when giving patients instructions?

Ken Brofsky/Valueline Collection

in that information from the environment is deemed valuable only if it concerns them directly. People are concerned with that which immediately can affect them, not hypothetical situations that affect "people in general." The final aspect as to whether information will be retained concerns whether the important information is the first or the last thing presented. Hoveland, Janis, and Kelley (1953) investigated whether topics covered at the beginning of a message (i.e., **primacy principle**) or at the end of a message (i.e., **recency principle**) were more memorable and persuasive. The findings of this effort indicated that information presented near the beginning or at the end of the message is more likely to be retained than information presented in the middle of the message. This multiple effectiveness (i.e., information that is being presented near the beginning and at the end of the message being retained in equal amounts) is known as the serial position effect (Ley, 1988).

The fifth and final major hurdle in information processing and communication is **selective recall.** Selective recall refers to the storage of information (McCroskey, 1993). Unlike selective retention, which reflects the ability to store information, selective recall reflects the ability to access or make available the specific memory from storage. Most effective recall requires triggering events known as **context** (environment) that allows you to enact the stored information from memory. This concept is particularly relevant in healthcare where healthcare professionals are required to remember thousands of facts throughout a professional career. Given the sheer amount of information needed to be retained by healthcare professionals, cognitive triggers are greatly needed to facilitate recall. Such memory access triggers can come in the form of a familiar situation, patient faces or symptoms, a book, television show, pneumonic devices, and so on.

serial position effect
In persuasive communication the concept that messages, according to when they are presented, can be more effective in terms of being memorable and persuasive (i.e., information presented near the beginning and at the end of the message).

Conclusion

This chapter presented information on how personality exerts influence on our behavior and ability to communicate. Traits and temperaments were discussed in terms of the various differences in brain activity that are associated with these different traits and temperaments and how these processes affect our communication. We highlighted the importance of several communication traits to indicate how both patients and healthcare professionals are predisposed to communication that can serve as an incredible advantage or an incredible impediment to successful interaction. We presented literature on the importance of general personality traits and how things such as how we see outcomes in life, our willingness to follow structural hierarchy, and our tendency to say and do whatever is necessary to achieve desired goals influence personal and professional outcomes as well as those of the receiver.

A detailed discussion of autism spectrum disorder was provided because of its prevalence in society, its influence on healthcare, and its effect on the brain and brain development. The neuroscience behind several promising research efforts on the disorder were presented because autism spectrum disorder primarily concerns communication and social interaction. This discussion on the brain was then expanded to include the concepts of intelligence, multiple intelligences, and the complex aspects of attending to stimuli. This discussion concluded with a presentation of the many hurdles that can adversely affect attention and how the brain's ability to process information can be slowed considerably.

Questions for Discussion/Review

1. Describe the three processes necessary for the production and projection of symbolic language.
2. Distinguish between trait and temperament and explain the relationship between the two.
3. Distinguish between generalized human traits and individual human traits. Provide an example for each.
4. Explain the PEN model of temperament. Define the three dimensions explained in the model.
5. Explain the OCEAN model of personality, and define the five main dimensions.
6. Define two types of communication traits and how they affect communication behavior. Provide an example for each.
7. Describe the two methods of treating communication apprehension.
8. Define three types of personality traits and how each trait affects communication behavior. Provide an example for each.
9. Explain the developmental differences in the brain of children with autism when compared to the nonautistic brain.
10. What are some of the distinguishing features of children suffering from Asperger's syndrome and other types of autism spectrum disorder?
11. Discuss how the study of intelligence would be of value for studying communication in healthcare.
12. Explain Gardner's eight factors of intelligence and how they compare to the triarchic theory of intelligence.
13. Discuss how attention is a factor for healthcare professionals and what types of things a person can do to improve their attention.
14. Describe the five major hurdles for selecting and processing information in the environment. Provide an example for each.
15. Explain how the lack of redundancy and ambiguous messages can inhibit information processing and communication.

References

Adorno, T., Frenkel-Brunswik, E., Levinson, D., & Sanford, R. (1950). *The authoritarian personality.* New York: Harper & Row.

Aiken, L. R. (1997). *Psychological testing and assessment* (9th ed.). Boston, MA: Allyn & Bacon.

Avtgis, T. A., & Rancer, A. S. (1997). Argumentativeness and verbal aggressiveness as a function of locus of control. *Communication Research Reports, 14,* 441–450.

Avtgis, T. A., Rancer, A. S., & Madlock, P. E. (2010). *Organizational communication: Strategies for success.* Dubuque, IA: Kendall-Hunt.

Baron-Cohen, S. (2004). The cognitive neuroscience of autism. *Journal of Neurology, Neurosurgery, and Psychiatry, 75,* 945–948.

Becker, J. H., & O'Hair, D. H. (2007). Machiavellians' motives in organizational citizenship behavior. *Journal of Applied Communication Research, 35,* 246–267.

Bem, S. L. (1974). The measurement of psychological androgyny. *Journal of Consulting and Clinical Psychology, 42,* 155–162.

Berger, B. A., Baldwin, H. J., McCroskey, J. C., & Richmond, V. P. (1983). Communication apprehension in pharmacy students: A national study. *American Journal of Pharmaceutical Education, 47,* 95–102.

Chesebro, J. L., & McCroskey, J. C. (2002). *Communication for teachers.* Boston, MA: Allyn & Bacon.

Costa, P. T., & McCrae, R. R. (1985). *The NEO personality inventory manual.* Odessa, FL: Psychological Assessment Resources.

Dawson, G., Rogers, S., Munson, J., Smith, M., Winter, J., & Greenson, J. (2010). Randomized, controlled trial of an intervention for toddlers with autism: The early start Denver model. *Pediatrics, 125,* 17–23.

Ekman, P., & Friesen, W. (1975). *Unmasking the face: A guide to recognizing emotions and facial expressions.* Englewood Cliffs, NJ: Prentice Hall.

Eysenck, H. J. (1990). Genetic and environmental contributions to individual's differences: The three major dimensions of personality. *Journal of Personality, 58,* 245–261.

Eysenck, H. J. (1947). *Dimensions of personality.* London: Routledge and Kegan Paul.

Eysenck, H. J., & Eysenck, S. (1976). *Psychoticism as a dimension of personality.* Hodder & Stoughton, London.

Eysenck, H. J., & Eysenck, M. W. (1985). *Personality and individual differences: A natural science approach.* New York: Plenum Books.

Gardner, H. (1983). *Frames of mind: The theory of multiple intelligence.* New York: Basic Books.

Goldberg, J. (July/August, 2008). Re-thinking Jeffrey Goldberg. *The Atlantic Monthly.* Retrieved December 26, 2010, from http://www.theatlantic.com/magazine/archive/2008/07/re-thinking-jeffrey-goldberg/6869/.

Goleman, D. (1997). *Emotional intelligence.* New York: Bantam.

Guilford, J. P. (1959). *Personality.* New York: McGraw-Hill.

Herbert, M. R. (2005). Large brains in autism: The challenge of pervasive abnormality. *Neuroscientist, 11,* 417–440.

Hollander, E. P. (1976). *Principles and methods of social psychology* (3rd ed.). New York: Oxford University Press.

Hoveland, C. I., Janis, I. L., & Kelley, H. H. (1953). *Communication and persuasion.* New Haven, CT: Yale University.

Infante, D. A., Rancer, A. S., & Avtgis, T. A. (2010). *Contemporary communication theory.* Dubuque, IA: Kendall-Hunt.

Kandal, E. R., Shwartz, J. H., & Jessell, T. M. (2000). *Principles of neural science* (4th ed.). New York: McGraw Hill.

Kantrowicz, B., & Scelfo, J. (November 27, 2006). What happens when they grow up? *Newsweek, 46–53.*

Klopf, D. W., & McCroskey, J. C. (2007). *Intercultural communication encounters.* Boston, MA: Allyn & Bacon.

Lefcourt, H. M. (1981). *Research with the locus of control construct: Vol. 1. Assessment methods,* New York: Academic Press.

Ley, P. (1988). *Communication with patients: Improving satisfaction and compliance.* London: Chapman and Hall.

McCroskey, J. C. (1970). Measures of communication-bound anxiety. *Speech Monographs, 37,* 269–277.

McCroskey, J. C. (1982). *An introduction to rhetorical communication* (4th ed.). Englewood Cliffs, NJ: Prentice-Hall.

McCroskey, J. C. (1993). Identifying compulsive communicators: The talkaholic scale. *Communication Research Reports, 10,* 107–114.

McCroskey, J. C. (1998). Serial communication process. In J. C. McCroskey, J. A. Daly, M. M. Martin, & M. J. Beatty (Eds.). *Communication and personality: Trait perspectives.* Cresskill, HJ: Hampton Press.

McCroskey, J. C., Daly, J. A., & Sorensen, G. (1976). Personality correlates of communication apprehension. A research note. *Human Communication Research, 2,* 376–380.

McCroskey, J. C., & Richmond, V. P. (1987). Willingness to communicate. In J. C. McCroskey & J. A. Daly (Eds.), *Personality and interpersonal communication* (pp. 129–156). Beverly Hills, CA: Sage.

McCroskey, J. C., & Richmond, V. P. (1996). *Fundamentals of human communication: An interpersonal perspective.* Prospect Heights, IL: Waveland Press, Inc.

McCroskey, J. C., Richmond, V. P., & Stewart, R. A. (1986). *One on one: The foundations of interpersonal communication.* Englewood Cliffs, NJ: Prentice-Hall.

Mischel, W. (1968). *Personality and assessment.* New York: Wiley.

Moffitt, T. E., Caspi, A., Harkness, A. R., & Silva, P. A. (1993). The natural history of change in intellectual performance: Who changes? How much? Is it meaningful? *Journal of Child Psychology and Psychiatry, 24,* 455–506.

Neisser, V., Boodoo, J., Bouchard, T. J., Jr., Boykin, A. W., Brody, N., & Ceci, S. J. (1996). Intelligence: Knowns and unknowns. *American Psychologists, 51,* 77–101.

Norton, R. (1983). *Communicator style: Theory, application, and measures.* Beverly Hills, CA: Sage.

Pinker, S. (2002). *The blank slate.* New York: Viking Press.

Polack, E. P., Richmond, V. P., & McCroskey, J. C. (2008). *Applied communication for health professionals.* Dubuque, IA: Kendall Hunt.

Richmond, V. P., & Martin, M. M. (1998). Sociocommunicative style and sociocommunicative orientation. In J. C. McCroskey, J. A. Daly, M. M. Martin, & M. J. Beatty (Eds.). *Communication and personality: Trait perspectives* (pp. 133–148). Cresskill, NJ: Hampton Press.

Richmond, V. P., & McCroskey, J. C. (2005). *Organizational communication for survival: Making work, work* (3rd ed.). Boston, MA: Allyn & Bacon.

Richmond, V. P., & McCroskey, J. C. (1992). *Communication apprehension, avoidance and effectiveness* (3rd ed.). Scottsdale, AZ: Gorsuch Scarisbrick.

Rokeach, M. (1960). *The open and closed mind.* New York: Basic Books.

Rotter, J. B. (1966). Generalized expectancies for internal versus external control of reinforcement. *Psychological Monographs, 80,* (Whole no. 609).

Spearman, C. (1927). *The abilities of man.* New York: MacMillan.

Spector, P. E. (1988). The development of the work locus of control scale. *Journal of Occupational Psychology, 61,* 335–340.

Sternberg, R. J. (1985). *Beyond IQ: A triarchic theory of human intelligence.* New York: Cambridge University Press.

Thurstone, L. L. (1938). *Primary mental abilities.* Chicago, IL: University of Chicago Press.

Thurstone, L. L., & Thurstone, T. G. (1941). Factorial studies of intelligence. Chicago, IL: University of Chicago.

Wheeless, V. E., & Dierks-Stewart, K. (1981). The psychometric properties of the Bem sex-role inventory: Questions concerning reliability and validity. *Communication Quarterly, 29,* 173–186.

Zemetkin, A. J., Nordalh, T. E., & Gross, M. (1990). Cerebral glucose metabolism in adults with hyperactivity of childhood onset. *New England Journal of Medicine, 323,* 1361–1366.

Zimbardo, P. J. (1977). *Shyness: What it is, what to do about it.* Reading, MA: Addison-Wesley.

part two

Contexts and Types of Medical Communication

Gender in Communication: The Influence on Competent Communication within Health Care

chapter objectives

Upon completion of the chapter, the student should be able to:

1. Compare and contrast the various psychological differences between men and women

2. Compare and contrast the differences in physiology according to gender

3. Explain some of the major differences between male and female healthcare providers

4. Compare and contrast the manifestation of various diseases as they relate to the patient's biological sex

5. Explain the differing relational outcomes for both the patient and the healthcare professional based on the biological sex of the patient and the healthcare professional

The studies of medicine and health care are studies of science. However, because this science is a product of, and practiced on, human beings, particular human factors must be considered when advancing medical treatment and technology. Perhaps one of the most culturally significant factors is that of gender. Our society is replete with popular psychology books indicating vast differences in the thoughts, feelings, and behaviors that exist between men and women. However these popular books portray gender differences, there is credible and evidenced-based research

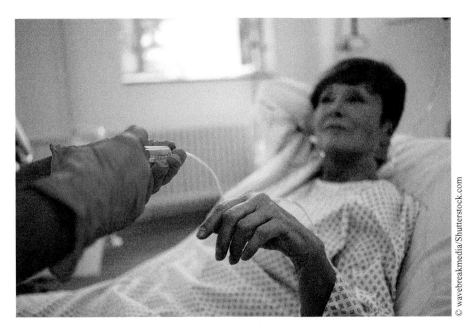

© wavebreakmedia/Shutterstock.com

that indicates important differences in the way men and women approach health care and the reactions that the different sexes exhibit in relation/response to treatment.

This chapter will introduce the concepts of gender and sex and illustrate meaningful differences between men and women regarding disease susceptibility and the unique needs and tendencies that go along with treating patients based on whether they are male or female. Issues related to the sex and gender of the healthcare professional will also be introduced, and suggestions about how to practice health care in a mindful way that includes accounting for gender and sex of both the provider and the patient will be offered.

Definitional Issues

In most conversations, the terms *gender* and *sex* are used interchangeably. However, when studying the differences between men and women regarding the use of communication, gender and sex are very different from each other and as such reveal different ways to categorize people and their communication behavior. **Sex** is defined as the classification of living things as man or woman according to their reproductive organs and functions assigned by

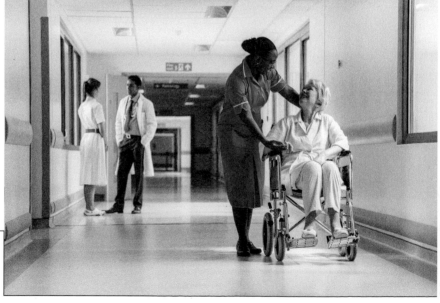

Healthcare providers need to be mindful of unique needs when practicing medicine.

© Spotmatik Ltd/Shutterstock.com

chromosomal complement (Weizmann & Pardue, 2001). **Gender,** however, is a person's self-representation as a man or woman or how that person is responded to by social conventions based on the individual's gender representation. Gender, similar to sex, is rooted in biology but is shaped by environment and experience (Weizmann & Pardue). According to Polack, Richmond, and McCroskey (2008), communication is mostly a product of gender, not sex, with 98% of what and how we communicate being attributed to gender and only 2% to biologic sex.

Physiological Differences

The sex differences, as opposed to gender differences observed in the communication between men and women, may very well be a function of physiological processes and psychology. According to John Medina (2008), there are definitive *genetic* and *neuroanatomical* differences between men and women that account for behavior.

Some differences exist between males and females including physical size. The average man is 10% taller, is 20% heavier, and has 35% more upper-body strength than the average female (World Health Organization, 2010). However, these physical differences are minimized when one considers strength in proportion to body mass (Fausto-Sterling, 1992). Although U.S. women have a longer life expectancy than U.S. men (79.8 years versus 74.4 years), little credible data exists to indicate significant "physical" differences between the sexes, and worldwide, women live longer than men (Barford, Dorling, Davey, Smith, & Shaw, 2006). However, social science research has

© Ruslan Guzov/Shutterstock.com

Why do you think women have a longer life expectancy than men?

emphasized differences in the degree of risky behaviors that people engage in. Most notably, men tend to engage in risky behaviors such as smoking, heavy drinking, and poor diet, which may account for much of the differences in mortality data between the biologic sexes (McCartney, Mahmood, Leyland, Batty & Hunt, 2011). Another major factor is the male reluctance to routinely consult a primary care physician when in states of wellness. This lack of proactive treatment results in late diagnosis and loss of opportunity for effective treatment translating to reduced survival in men (Wang, Freemantle, Nazareth, & Hunt, 2014).

Although there are a few studies indicating biological differences between men and women, most research indicates culture as being the main reason for any meaningful differences. To exemplify the power of culture as a "behavior-shaping" influence, a recent study revealed that highly anxious female math teachers "transfer" their math anxiety onto their elementary students. More specifically, there was an intra-gender transfer of math anxiety from female teachers to female students. This phenomenon was not evident in their male counterparts (Bielock, Gunderson, Ramirez, & Levine, 2010). The "gender-culture" transfer was a result of the teacher's own anxiety and the teacher's expectations of how competent or incompetent females are in mathematics. This type of result can create a condition known as **learned helplessness** (Peterson, Maier, & Seligman, 1993). Learned helplessness is an acquired disorder in which a person experiences disconnection between their own effort and the relationship of that effort to successfully achieving goals. For example, a young girl who is told that she suffers from math anxiety may use a "biologic" excuse to explain away her poor math performance. In attributing failure in mathematical ability to something beyond her control, she does not engage in the required study behavior necessary to achieve success in mathematics, thus reinforcing the "biologic" explanation for the lack of mathematical ability. This finding is systematic of the nationwide reduction of women enrolling in the hard science, technology, engineering, and mathematics (STEM) disciplines at the university level. This is also true about the ability to give public presentations. Many people report high levels of communication apprehension being due to some sort of "communication" gene. Little evidenced-based data links genetics to the ability to effectively communicate. On the other hand, there are myriad studies indicating that preparation and practice are linked to competent communication skills.

Within medicine, this hard science bias can be seen in the fact that 47% of medical school graduates in 2012 were women (AAMC, 2012). The gender gap in medicine is larger than in any other profession. Women physicians make 63 cents for every dollar male physicians earn. It should be noted that this discrepancy may not necessarily be a result of gender differences or discrimination but more so because of the specialty choice. Women may be picking lower-paying specialties or organizational arrangements (e.g., health maintenance organization positions) that end up affording the female physician less salary in exchange for more control of their personal time. This includes the choice of lower-paying specialties (e.g., family medicine

| **learned helplessness**

An acquired disorder where a person experiences a disconnect between their own effort and the connection of that effort to successfully achieving goals.

[women in 2011, 54.3%] versus colorectal [women in 2011, 39%] or plastic surgery [women in 2011, 28.9%]). Males tend to dominate the higher-paying specialties (e.g., orthopedic surgery [women in 2011, 13.6%]); currently the residency programs are predominately filled by males.

Taken as a whole, genetic differences between males and females are apparent, but as of today, these differences do not necessarily translate into actual behavioral differences between men and women regarding their communication behaviors. This is not to suggest that such genetic differences do not exist, but it is something that needs to be investigated further.

Sex and Personality Differences

As presented in Chapter 3, the concept of personality and behavioral tendencies has revealed some interesting differences between males and females. Among the big five personality traits of *openness, conscientiousness, extroversion, agreeableness,* and *neuroticism* (OCEAN), women score higher than men in agreeableness (representing increased levels of compassion and cooperation) and neuroticism (representing increased levels of anxiety, anger, and depression) (Harasty, Double, Halliday, Kril, & McRitchie, 1997). According to Sandra Bem (1974), there are two major categories of gender for which people can be classified: **masculine** or **feminine.** It is important to remember that gender reflects a psychological orientation as opposed to the biological distinction associated with sex. The masculine classification represents tendencies that are traditionally associated with men such as competitiveness, aggressiveness, assertiveness, and being task focused. The feminine classification represents tendencies that are traditionally associated with women such as cooperativeness, nurturing, responsiveness, and being relationally focused.

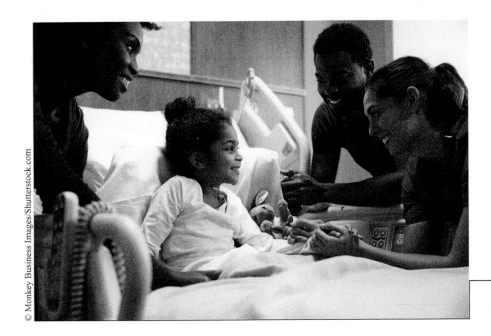

© Monkey Business Images/Shutterstock.com

What characteristics does an amiable person display?

Generally speaking, gender orientation is best conceptualized as two continua consisting of an **assertiveness continuum** (masculine) and a **responsiveness continuum** (feminine) (Figure. 4.1).

Considering these dimensions, where a person falls on the assertiveness and responsiveness continua determines their social style (Merrill & Reid, 1981). That is, particular combinations of varying levels of assertiveness and responsiveness comprise the four social styles of gender. The word *styles* refer to how other people perceive a person's behavior. The **amiable style** represents a person who is low in assertiveness and high in responsiveness. People with this style are generally focused on relationships, enjoy interacting with others, and value the relationship over task completion (Richmond & Martin, 1998). Figure 4.2 shows the amiable style. (The "II" symbol reflects where a person would register on the continua.)

The **analytic style** represents people who are low in assertiveness and low in responsiveness. A person with an analytic style may come across as cold, aloof, and interested in logic and facts over that of relationships (Richmond & Martin, 1998). According to Merrill and Reid (1981), these types of people tend to rely on objective evidence and are slow and methodical in decision-making. However, when decisions are rendered, the analytic will tend to stand by them if questioned by others. Figure 4.3 shows the analytic style.

[--]
Nonassertive   Assertive

figure 4.1

The Assertiveness–Responsiveness Continua

[--]
Nonresponsive   Responsive

[II --]
Nonassertive   Assertive

figure 4.2

The Amiable Social Style

[-- II]
Nonresponsive   Responsive

[II --]
Nonassertive   Assertive

figure 4.3

The Analytic Social Style

[II --]
Nonresponsive   Responsive

The **driver style** represents a person who is high in assertiveness and low in responsiveness. A person who is a driver generally has clear objectives and will engage in behaviors to achieve their desired goals (Richmond & Martin, 1998). According to Merrill and Reid (1981), the driver tends to be impatient, action oriented, independent thinking, and power driven. Figure 4.4 shows the driver type.

The final social style is that of the **expressive style,** which reflects a person who is high in assertiveness and high in responsiveness. The expressive type tends to value interpersonal relationships but is equally task-focused (Merrill & Reid, 1981). In fact, these people are action oriented but utilize intuition in their decision-making while also being creative and adaptable (Richmond & Martin, 1998). Figure 4.5 shows the expressive type.

Taken as a whole, these four social style distinctions provide meaningful ways of categorizing people based on combinations of traditional male and traditional female behavior. There has been much debate as to which type is the optimal social style to use or possess. The result of such debate indicates that the optimal combination of assertiveness and responsiveness is contingent on the specific situation (Merrill & Reid, 1981). However, the key to effective, competent, and mindful communication is to be versatile in the social style you utilize. For example, think of the social style of a highly regarded surgeon, nurse, or physical therapist. What type of style do these people tend to engender? Would the practitioner's patients be better off if the healthcare practitioner was able to engender multiple styles? The answer is yes.

© Uber Images/Shutterstock.com

What social style does a highly regarded practitioner engender?

Gender and the Patient–Provider Dyad

As healthcare professionals, there is often an assumption that when we speak of the patient–provider relationship, we are speaking about these social roles as if they were void of gender influence. These social roles dictate that both patient and provider take on distinct and prescribed patterns of behavior and that these behaviors are influenced by gender. However, certain aspects of this relationship transcend gender. That is, the healthcare provider usually operates from a **disease framework** **[algorhythmic and reductive],** which primarily focuses on the patient's history, physical examination, and laboratory factors that contribute to a medical diagnosis in an effort to develop adequate treatment. The patient, however, usually operates from an **illness framework** **[psychosocial narrative],** primarily focusing on the affective state of the patient including their fears, anxieties, expectations, feelings, and perceptions about illness (Stewart, Brown, Weston, McWhinney, McWilliam, & Freeman, 2003). How these fears and anxieties are experienced are unique to each patient or based on the specific contextual factors at the time the illness occurred. For example, an undergraduate student might go to the infirmary with a common cold (i.e., upper respiratory infection). The healthcare practitioner, who is operating from a disease framework, might wish to withhold antibiotics, whereas the student may want the "quick fix" believing that antibiotics can bring about a cure in time for final exams. This need to be better for final exams constitutes the contextual factors surrounding the illness. In this case, the illness is secondary to the impact that the illness has on the student's upcoming social schedule (i.e., final exams). The healthcare practitioner is concerned with explaining the drawbacks of treating a virus with unnecessary antibiotic therapy that is reserved for bacterial infections, not a common cold that is caused by a virus (not a bacterium).

disease framework

A primary focus on the patient's history, physical examination, and laboratory factors that contribute to a medical diagnosis in an effort to develop adequate treatment.

illness framework

A primary focus on the affective state of the patient's fears, anxieties, expectations, feelings, and perceptions about illness in an effort to develop adequate treatment.

[-- II]
Nonassertive   Assertive

figure 4.4

The Driver Social Style

[II --]
Nonresponsive   Responsive

[-- II]
Nonassertive   Assertive

figure 4.5

The Expressive Social Style

[-- II]
Nonresponsive   Responsive

Male and Female Healthcare Providers

The differences in communication between men and women that have been chronicled thus far are much further reaching than simple generalized interaction patterns that become apparent in everyday conversations. For example, men are generally better at systematizing (i.e., the desire to analyze and explore systems and rules), whereas women are better at empathizing and social support (Baron-Cohen, 2003). Such differences have also been observed in the practice of medicine and health care. Empathy, and the ability to effectively express it, is of great importance to an effective healthcare provider. A study by Bylund and Makoul (2002) revealed that female physicians tend to communicate with greater levels of empathy when communicating with their patients than male physicians. Further, other studies reveal important verbal and nonverbal behavioral differences between men and women, which include patient reports of having more interpersonal-like interactions with female physicians and finding them to be good listeners (Hall, Irish, Roter, Ehrlich, & Miller, 1994). The behavior of the physician was also found to be affected by the gender of the patient. More specifically, the female physician–female patient dyad tends to be the most interactive and prosocial in nature with marked changes in the female physician's behavior when the patient is male. For example, the interaction between the female physician and the male patient has more interpersonal conflict and results in more negative feelings for both participants by the end of the medical interview (Hall et al.).

In direct contrast to the findings just presented, Roter, Hall, and Aoki (2002) conducted a meta-analysis of gender studies. A **meta-analysis** is a type of study that investigates the results of previous studies on a certain

Photographee.eu/Shutterstock.com

The female physician-female patient dyad tends to be the most interactive and prosocial.

topic to determine a common statistic or tendency across studies. Roter et al. sought to investigate previous studies on gender and medical care to determine how significant, if at all, gender really is in medical care. The results revealed that there were no real differences between male and female physicians in terms of the amount of information given or the manner in which the information was relayed. Taken as a whole, all of the research on gender in medicine and health care needs to be interpreted carefully because the vast majority of physicians participating in these types of studies were primary care physicians with little or no data coming from medical specialties or subspecialties (e.g., surgery).

The Engendered Patient

There has been a long-standing critique of medicine indicating that the developments and research within the medical field have almost exclusively focused on the male and his ailments as opposed to considering both males and females in the development of treatments. This disparity is primarily due to the patriarchal nature that traditional medicine has historically displayed. In fact, it was not until the establishment of the National Institutes of Health's (NIH) Office of Research on Women's Health (ORWH) that there was a realization in the scientific community that women's health, which was thought only to relate to biologic sex differences, needs to be expanded far beyond the traditional concept of reproductive health to consider the health status of women in general and across their lifespan (Pinn, 1999). Women and men are very different biological entities whose health, experience of disease, medication, and treatment are equally different and as such require approaches that are tailored to each other.

The inadequate treatment of women in pain has been attributed to the subjective nature of how men versus women describe pain and pain symptoms. Given that medicine and medical advances have been predicated on the male experience, the results that women's experience of pain is taken less seriously and women receive less treatment is not surprising (Berg, Ketley, & Merkatz, 1999). Such differences are believed to also be true for reactions to medications, tendencies toward particular disease states, and a host of other medically related influences and outcomes.

Focusing on time spent with the patient, findings from the U.S. Department of Health and Human Resources Literature Review of Effective Sex and Gender Based Systems/Models of Care (2007) suggest that cardiologists tended to assess patients of the opposite gender with greater specificity. Female cardiologists pay more attention to female patients 48% of the time, and the male cardiologist pays more attention to male patients 59% of the time. Compare these statistics to male cardiologists spending more time with female patients 74% of the time and female cardiologists spending more time with male patients 70% of the time. Clearly there is a systematic distribution of time based on both the patient's sex and the physician's sex.

Even in light of these statistics, most cardiologists are uneducated as to the gender disparities in communication in terms of how males and females

© Monkey Business Images/Shutterstock.com

Chronic diseases can be treated differently based on the sex of the patient.

describe symptoms. For example, male patients present themselves as being interested in the cause of the chest pain resulting in their descriptions of pain and symptoms in concrete terms (e.g., "I have pain in my chest going into my left arm that radiates up into the left side of my neck"). Female patients, however, tend to present in a more stoic way, describing their pain and symptoms in diffuse and abstract ways such as "I feel funny" or "I feel weird." Generally speaking, the language that males use seems to match the expectation of the physician. This matching of language and physician expectation serves to solidify arguments for medicine being paternal in nature. Males tend to list their symptoms in chronological order, whereas females are less specific. Because of this less specific language in the presentation of symptoms, diagnosis is sometimes missed. Women commonly use words such as *terrifying, tiring,* or *intolerable* to describe their symptoms. Given this, physicians determine that these descriptors are exaggerations, often resulting in the women's descriptors not being taken as an accurate reflection of the situation or condition. There are both knowledge and communication gaps between men and women regarding cardiac medicine. Some argue that the ability of healthcare professionals, regardless of the type of medicine being practiced, to accurately diagnose many conditions in the opposite sex patient is compromised by large gaps in knowledge of both communication tendencies and biomedical information. These gaps are exacerbated by long-standing cultural foci on the male norm in the communication of health and disease (Brittle & Bird, 2007).

Building toward Tomorrow

All of the literature reviewed, thus far, indicates that there continues to be disparities in medical care between men and women in that intervention and treatment tend to be developed in a "one size fits all" fashion. However, there are specific needs of patients that move well beyond the biological. In a 2003 article entitled "Culture in Medicine's Culture of No Culture," Janelle Taylor argues that for young physicians to demonstrate competence, they must show a mastery of medical knowledge. The competency in the human or psychosocial aspects of medicine is not of interest to young physicians. More specifically, the patient's story, the emotional experience, and the specific life events from which the patient experiences illness are not considered. These relational data from a patient's life are regarded as extraneous to the "real" problem. The gap in the education process regarding the psychosocial aspects of medicine can be clearly seen in comparisons between nurses and physicians. Relationships, comfort giving, and empathetic communication are mainstays of the nursing curriculum. However, when it comes to physician education, such issues are only beginning to be addressed. This is evidenced in the Accreditation Council for Graduate Medical Education's six core competencies; one of which is communication.

Throughout this text we refer to the *healthcare context.* This term is meant to be reflective of many areas of medical care including outpatient clinics, nursing homes, and psychiatric hospitals. However, the most complex of all these healthcare contexts is the hospital setting. The hospital setting is where the most resources are spent and the most advances in care and the risks that come along with that care are present. Although the term *hospital setting* refers to a specific context, the amount of variation from one hospital setting to the next can be profound. For example, the relationships between physicians and nurses in one institution may be characterized as distant and cold, whereas another institution may characterize this relationship as being family like.

Communication Competency and Its Outcomes

Research indicates that there is a strong relationship between hospital employee satisfaction and patient satisfaction (Kaldenberg & Regrut, 1999). Findings such as this have prompted efforts on behalf of hospital human resource departments to invest greater resources into the hiring of "patient-oriented" personnel and to establish comprehensive training programs. Such efforts are believed to result in hospital patient-oriented personnel who have an ability to communicate effectively and achieve common goals. In a study investigating such hospital personnel in Boston, New York, and Dallas, Gittell, Fairfield, Bierbaum, Head, Jackson, and Kelly (2000), focusing on 338 specific healthcare providers and 878 hip and knee arthroplasty (joint replacement) patients, found the following:

- Greater levels of relational competence
- A 53% reduction in the length of the average hospital stay
- A 22% increase in patient perception of quality medical care
- A 7% increase in patient reports of being pain free in postoperative assessment
- A 5% increase in patient postoperative mobility

As these data indicate, all members of the hospital are involved in caring for patients. This involves the use of both feminine and masculine communication styles. These bottom-line results are in accordance with compliance efforts such as the 2008 mandates requiring hospitals to survey patients to assess the quality of medical care. In fact, hospitals risk losing a large portion of their funding from Medicare and Medicaid should there be substandard performance. This survey is available to the general public at www.hospitalcompare.hhs.gov. This new approach in assessing hospital effectiveness is considered a valuable tool in the new consumer-driven health system (Donaghue, 2007), and reinforced by the Affordable Health-care Act of 2010.

As for the patient, there appears to be differences in what male and female patients want from healthcare providers. Although both males and females highly value the amount of time that is spent with the care provider, women value the care provider's ability to answer questions clearly, the provider's preparedness concerning the patient's specific situation, and quality participation from everyone in the healthcare encounter (including the receptionist, nurses, and so on). This last fact is of particular importance because in today's highly technological healthcare environment, 80% of patient care is interdisciplinary in nature and provided by nonphysicians (Kizer, 2002). It appears that women tend to have a better understanding of the interdisciplinary nature of the healthcare process than do men. For men, one of the most valued aspects of health care is the degree to which the care provider takes a personal interest in them and their medical condition. Further, men also value the emotional content of the interpersonal communication encounter with their provider. It is these factors that are the greatest predictor of male patient satisfaction with the quality of their health care.

Conclusion

Throughout this chapter, we introduced the concepts of gender and sex and how these factors influence the practice of health care and the perceptions and expectations of both the patient and provider. Gender and gender differences with regard to the practice of medicine will continue to be a significant issue for all aspects of health care. As presented in this chapter, men and women react differently to treatments, medications, and a host of other health-related factors including disease susceptibility. Healthcare professionals need to understand the communication and relational expectations that are typical of women and men. By understanding such differences, the practitioner can mindfully craft messages and treatments that result in optimal care for the patient.

The studies reviewed in this chapter reveal that there are real and significant differences between the sexes and their health. Although there is much anecdotal (i.e., nonscientific) evidence indicating unimportant differences, good sound science indicates that not only is it prudent for the practitioner to consider the patient's gender when developing treatment, but it also is considered smart medicine because gender and sex are but additional factors that make a patient, their experience, their illness, and their story unique from other patients.

Questions for Discussion/Review

1. Distinguish between sex and gender. Why are both important factors for healthcare professionals?
2. Identify and discuss some physiological differences between men and women regarding health and health care.
3. Discuss some of the neuroanatomical differences between men and women.
4. Discuss the relationship between personality and a person's gender.
5. Define each of the four types of social styles and give examples of the types of communication associated with each.
6. Compare and contrast the disease framework from the illness framework.
7. What are some possible outcomes/implications associated with the healthcare provider and patient being of different genders? Being the same gender?

References

Aamc. (2012). Women in academic medicine satistics and medical school statistics. Retrieved on November 2, 2014, from www.aamc.org/download/305282/data/2012.

Barford, A., Dorling, D., Davey Smith, G., & Shaw, M. (2006). Life expectancy: Women now on top everywhere, in *BMJ, 332,* 808.

Baron-Cohen, S. (2003, April 17). They just can't help it. *The Guardian.*

Bem, S. L. (1974). The measurement of psychological androgyny. *Journal of Consulting and Clinical Psychology, 42, 155–162.*

Berg, M. J., Ketley, J. N., & Merkatz, R. (1999). *An agenda for research on women's health for the 21st century Vol. 2.* Bethesda, MD: National Institutes of Health. Publication 99–4386.

Bielock, S., Gunderson, E. A., Ramirez, G., & Levine, S. C. (2010). Female teachers' math anxiety affects girls' math achievement. *PNAS, 107,* 1860–1863.

Brittle, C., & Bird, C. E. (2007). *Literature review on effective sex-and-gender-based systems/ models of care-office of women's health, U. S. Department of Health and Human Services.* Retrieved from http://www.womenshealth.gov/owh/pub/genderbased.cfm.

Bylund, C. L., & Makoul, G. (2002). Empathic communication and gender in the physician patient encounter. *Patient Education and Counseling, 48,* 207–216.

Donaghue, E. (2007, July 25). Communication now part of the cure: Movement has begun to help doctors listen and patients understand. *USA Today,* 7D.

Fausto-Sterling, A. (1992). *A myths of gender: Biological theories about men and women.* New York: Basic Books.

Gittell, J. H., Fairfield, K. M., Bierbaum, B., Head, W., Jackson, R., & Kelly, J. (2000). Impact of relational coordination on quality of care, postoperative pain and functioning, and length of stay: A nine hospital study of surgical patients. *Medical Care, 38,* 807–819.

Hall, J. A., Irish, J. T., Roter, D. L., Ehrlich, C. M., & Miller, L. H. (1994). Gender in medical encounters: An analysis of physician and patient communication in a primary care setting. *Health Psychology, 13,* 384–392.

Harasty, J., Double, K. L., Halliday, G. M., Kril, J. J., & McRitchie, D. A. (1997). Language-associated cortical regions are proportionately larger in the female brain. *Archives of Neurology, 54,* 171–176.

Henrich, J. B. (2004). Women's health education and initiatives: Why have they stalled? *Academic Medicine, 79,* 283–288.

Kaldenberg, D. O., & Regrut, B. A. (1999). Do satisfied patients depend on satisfied employees? Or, do satisfied employees depend on satisfied patients. *QRC Advisory, 15,* 7–12.

Kizer, K. W. (2002). Patient centered care: Essential but probably not sufficient. *Quality and Safety in Healthcare, 11,* 117–118.

McCartney, G., Mahmood, L., Leyland, A.H., Batty, G.D., & Hunt, K. (2011) Contribution of smoking-related and alcohol-related deaths to the gender gap in mortality: evidence from 30 European countries. Tob Contr 20: 166–168. doi:10.1136/tc.2010.037929. PubMed: 21228431.

Medina, J. (2008). *Brain rules.* Seattle, WA: Pear Press.

Merrill, D. W., & Reid, R. H. (1981). *Personal styles & effective performance.* Radnor, PA: Chilton.

Peterson, C., Maier, S. F., & Seligman, M. E. (1993). *Learned helplessness: A theory for the age of personal control.* New York: Oxford.

Pinn, V. W. (1999). Women's health research: Progress and future directions. *Academic Medicine, 74,* 1104–1105.

Polack, E. P., Richmond, V. P., & McCroskey, J. C. (2008). *Applied communication for health professionals.* Dubuque, IA: Kendall Hunt.

Richmond, V. P., & Martin, M. M. (1998). Sociocommunicative style and sociocommunicative orientation. In J. C. McCroskey, J. A. Daly, M. M. Martin, & M. J. Beatty (Eds.), *Communication and personality: Trait perspective* (pp. 133–148). Cresskill, NJ: Hampton Press.

Roter, D. L., Hall, J. A., & Aoki, Y. (2002). Physician gender effects in medical communication: A meta-analytic review. *Journal of the American Medical Association, 288*, 756–764.

Stewart, W. F., Ricci, J. A., Che, E., Morganstein, D., & Lipton, R. (2003). Loss productive time and cost due to common pain: Conditions in the U.S. work force. *Journal of the American Medical Association, 290*, 2443–2454.

Taylor, J. S. (2003). Confronting "culture" in medicine's "culture of no culture." *Academic Medicine, 78,* 550–559.

United States Department of Health and Human Services. (2007). *Literature review of effective sex and gender based systems: Models of care.* Retrieved from http://www.4women.gov/owh/multidisciplinary/reports/GenderBasedMedicine/ Question6.cfm.

Wang, Y., Freemantle, N., Nazareth, I., Hunt, K. (2014, July). Gender differences in survival and the use of primary care prior to diagnoses of three cancers: An analysis of routinely collected UK general practice data, *TLOS1, Vol. 9* (7), Retrieved from http://www.plosone.org/article/fetchObject.action?uri=info%3Adoi%2F10.1371%2Fjournal.pone.0101562&representation=PDF.

Weizmann, T. M., & Pardue, M. L. (2001). *EDS. Exploring the biologic contributions to human health: Does sex matter?* Washington, D.C.: National Academy Press.

World Health Organization. (2010). *What do we mean by sex and gender?* Retrieved from http://www.WHO.INT/gender/whatisgender/en/index.html.

chapter five

Body Language: The Science of Nonverbal Communication

chapter objectives

Upon completion of the chapter, the student should be able to:

1. Compare and contrast the functions of nonverbal communication

2. Compare and contrast the components of nonverbal communication

3. Explain the seven universal facial expressions of emotion

4. Compare and contrast the different ways that people can conceptualize time

5. Explain the role of patient stigma in healthcare

How people use nonverbal behavior to communicate is something that needs to be understood if people desire to have a true feeling of connection with one another. For healthcare practitioners, the uncertainty and anxiety that patients and clients experience is manifested in both what they say and what they do. The chapter is designed to expose you to many different types of nonverbal behavior that are capable of sending meaningful messages should a person be mindful to them.

 This chapter contains the nonverbal behaviors that patients and providers commonly engage in that can often result in misinterpretation and problematic communication. **Errors** We make suggestions throughout the chapter as to how healthcare professionals can interpret and send nonverbal messages

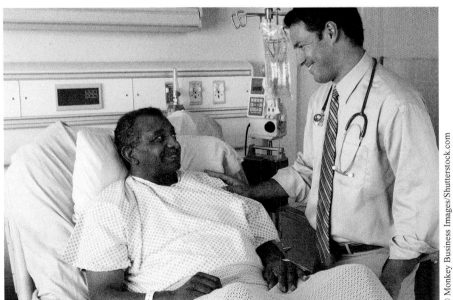

© Monkey Business Images/Shutterstock.com

key terms

autonomics	immediacy	physical stigma
ectomorph	kinesics	social stigma
endomorph	mesomorph	taste
formal time	paralanguage	

to better practice healthcare and develop more meaningful relationships with patients and clients.

Brief History of Nonverbal Communication

The study of nonverbal communication has received much attention from communication scholars since the 1960s. Although nonverbal behavior was investigated in other disciplines before the 1960s, it became an important area for communication scholars in part because of the cross-disciplinary work of James C. McCroskey. Working with graduate students, McCroskey developed seven categories for nonverbal behavior consisting of *face* (mimetics), *eye behavior* (occulesics), *vocal behavior* (vocalics), *space* (proxemics), *touch* (haptics), *scent and smell* (olifactics), and *time* (chronemics). Related disciplines such as psychology, linguistics, and anthropology provided the bases from which the study of *kinesics* (body movement) and *proxemics* were developed (Birdwhistell, 1970; Hall, 1966). The first book on nonverbal communication published within the field of communication studies was in 1972 by Mark Knapp; it was a relatively brief text by today's standards because there simply was not that much material on nonverbal behavior (Knapp, 1972; McCroskey, 2009).

How do your nonverbal signals add meaning to the words you speak?

© bikeriderlondon/Shutterstock.com

The development of nonverbal behavior theory and research began to proliferate with people such as Paul Ekman and Wallace Friesen. Ekman and Friesen (1975) wrote the first book on facial expressions: *Unmasking the Face: A Guide to Recognizing Emotions from Facial Expressions.* Edward Hall (1959, 1966) was an anthropologist who published a work on how cultures organize time in different ways and how people use space and physical distance to communicate. One other notable research development at this time was Albert Mehrabian's (1971) work on what comprises face-to-face communication. More specifically, using a mathematical approach he determined that 7% of communication comes through words, 38% is tone of voice, and 55% is facial expression. **Introduction to Nonverbal Communication** This equation of communication transmission is not to be applied to all communication situations, just when people are interested in determining what people are feeling, especially under conditions where the verbal and nonverbal messages are inconsistent with one another. **Inconsistent Messages** An example of this inconsistency would be a person who verbally says "I don't have a problem with you" while nonverbally they avoid eye contact, appear anxious, and display a closed body position. Although this entire body of work is distilled from many different scholars in different disciplines, they all have had a profound impact on the development of nonverbal communication as an independent field of study. **Nonverbal Communication**

Functions of Nonverbal Messages

Nonverbal behaviors and resulting messages serve many purposes for people. Several of these purposes are directly related to our verbal behavior. There are six **functions of nonverbal communication** consisting of *accentuating,*

What message does it send to others when you avoid eye contact?

Clearly explaining the directions while pointing to them on the prescription helps a patient better understand the dosage needed.

© Syda Productions/Shutterstock.com

complementing, contradicting, repeating, regulating, and *substituting.* The function of **accentuating** reflects the use of nonverbal behavior to emphasize particular points of a verbal message. This can take the form of raising or lowering the voice and using gestures, touch, and vocal cues to emphasize a particular point. For example, when explaining a medication regimen to a patient, a healthcare professional may point to the directions of the prescription bottle when explaining to the patient that they need to take two tablets twice daily.

The second function of nonverbal communication consists of **complementing** and refers to the use of nonverbal behavior to complement a verbal message. This type of behavior differs from accentuating in that accentuating *emphasizes* the verbal message, whereas complementing *reinforces* the message. An example of reinforcing a message would be telling a patient that they will be okay while simultaneously patting them on the back. In this case, the pat on the back reinforces the message of their well-being.

Contradicting is the function whereby the nonverbal behavior sends the opposite message that is being communicated verbally. For example, a colleague who is coming off a rotation may look tired and disheveled. Upon seeing this colleague, you say sarcastically, "Looking good." The paralanguage (e.g., tone, inflection) is used to communicate to the other person that they should take the opposite meaning that is inferred from the verbal message. Generally speaking, when verbal and nonverbal messages are in conflict with one another, people tend to attribute meaning to the nonverbal message. In contrast, Reilly and Muzarkara (1978) found that people who are emotionally disturbed tend to rely on the verbal message, as opposed to the nonverbal message, when interpreting contradicting messages.

The **repeating** function of nonverbal communication occurs when the nonverbal behavior is an actual replication of the verbal message. In the

© Monkey Business Images/Shutterstock.com

How does this doctor reinforce her message?

earlier example of the healthcare worker explaining the medication regimen to the patient, instead of pointing to the prescription, the healthcare worker holds up two fingers when informing the patient that he or she needs to take two tablets twice daily. The fifth function of **regulating** includes the use of nonverbal behavior to manage turn-taking behavior, start and stop conversations, and change topics. For example, we can use our voice inflection, turn our head, change our facial expression, or do any combination of these and use other nonverbal behaviors to signal to another communicator that the interaction is concluding. The final function of nonverbal communication is **substituting** and refers to when nonverbal messages are used in place of the verbal message. For example, a surgeon may point to a scalpel rather than verbally calling for it when a patient anesthetized (numbed) with Novocain is still awake. In pointing to the scalpel, the surgeon is asking for the instrument nonverbally, instead of having to verbalize "knife," the request that very may well result in great anxiety for the barely conscious (sedated) patient.

Components of Nonverbal Communication

Historically, nonverbal communication has been divided into many subcategories in order to more easily classify the enormous body of research. Keeping with this system, the following sections are separated into 24 distinct areas of nonverbal research and their implications for communication in general and healthcare professionals in particular.

Kinesics. **Kinesics** is the study of how body movements communicate. We will present seven different categories of body movement that comprise the study of kinesics. Although we will focus on the seven categories of *emblems,*

| kinesics

The study of nonverbal behavior that focuses on how people use body movements to communicate.

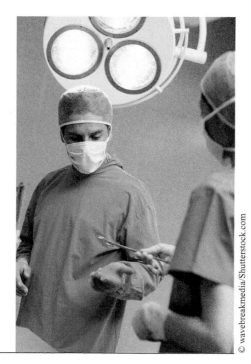

In some cases, substituting a nonverbal message is better than using a verbal message.

illustrators, regulators, affect displays, adapters, courtship readiness cues, and positional cues, scholars believe that there are approximately 700,000 possible physical signs that can be transmitted by body movements (Polack, Richmond, & McCroskey, 2008). **Emblems** are gestures that can be used instead of verbal messages. They have a direct verbal translation to them. Some of the most notable examples of emblems include the hitchhiking sign, okay sign, thumbs-up sign, and nodding your head in agreement. It should be noted that emblem use and the meanings that people attach to them are culture specific. For example, the thumbs-up sign indicates "good," "okay," or "approval" in American culture. In contrast, within the sport of scuba diving giving the thumbs-up sign indicates that the person has a problem that requires that person to resurface. **Illustrators** are body movements that are generally in the hands and serve to add meaning to a message. Illustrators allow us to add meaning to a message to help "capture the mood" of the message. For example, when a practitioner informs a patient that her computed tomography (CAT) scan result has come back negative (normal), the doctor may be moving his or her arms and hands more dramatically in excitement as the good news is being shared.

Regulators are movements that serve to coordinate turn-taking behavior during conversation. During a conversation there are four major turn-taking behaviors that must be regulated: (a) *turn taking* (signals when it is time for someone else to talk), (b) *turn maintaining* (signals when it is okay to continue speaking), (c) *turn requesting* (signals when a person wants to begin speaking), and (d) *turn denying* (signals when it is an inappropriate time for another person to begin speaking). If healthcare professionals are not aware

© Maridav/Shutterstock.com

Emblems have a direct verbal translation, so everyone knows what they mean.

of how they use regulators, they can easily use turn-denying behavior with a patient or colleague and be unaware that they are engaging in this behavior. This often results in the patient not revealing important symptoms or not fully elaborating on the symptoms that they present.

Affect displays refer to the voluntary or involuntary movements that reveal a person's emotional state. For example, if we are tired we may walk with a slower gait or slump in our chair. **Adaptors** are behaviors that people use to "cope" with different situations. An example of an adaptor would be when someone taps their foot, plays with their hair, or crosses their arms in front of their chest. These behaviors can send definite messages of impatience, being uncomfortable, and being closed to communication respectively. **Courtship readiness cues** are behaviors exhibited in courtship situations and may include behavior cues such as sucking in your stomach to appear thinner, flexing your biceps (males), or conducting preening behavior such as adjusting your tie (males) or touching up your makeup (females). The final kinesic type is **positional cues** and concerns how people position their body in relation to others. This behavior often communicates interest or disinterest in a conversation.

Hands.   The study of hands and nonverbal behavior has provided researchers with a wealth of information. Mensah (2000) divided hand gestures into five categories: *greeting gestures* (e.g., handshake, wave, high five); *identification gestures* (e.g., pointing or movement of the hand to illustrate a particular idea); *meaningless gesture* (e.g., casual waving); *hands still* (e.g., hands in pocket, arms crossed, hands on hips, fingers interlocked); and *angry gestures* (e.g., giving "the finger" or clenching fists). According to Pease and Pease (2004), our hands are constantly visible and easily controlled when communicating. The use of the hands as a means of communication is culture specific. For

What is this woman conveying by displaying this adaptor?

example, in the United States, it is usually insulting to point with the index finger, whereas in other cultures this is a perfectly acceptable behavior. In Britain, large hand and arm gestures are interpreted as an indication of high excitement and dominance. This interpretation is in contrast to Italian culture where flamboyant hand motions using the entire arm (from the shoulder down) when communicating are common (Gallois & Callan, 1997).

Although there are literally thousands of hand gestures, there are five generalizations about hand behavior that are believed to be cross-cultural (Pease & Pease, 2004). First, *open palms are generally considered a positive nonverbal message.* This assumption goes back to medieval times when a person would show open palms to indicate that they had no weapons or had nothing to hide. Second, *hands clasped behind the head indicate dominance or superiority.* Third, *hand-wringing indicates apprehensiveness, nervousness, and a lack of confidence.* Fourth, *steepling of the fingers* (touching the fingers of one hand to the matching fingers on the opposing hand) *shows dominance or control.* Finally, *self-touching gestures* (e.g., play with your hair) indicate nervousness and insecurity, whereas touching of the face may be indicative of deceit or deception.

Legs and Feet. One great misconception of nonverbal behavior is that when trying to detect deception, we should look into a person's eyes. In fact, many scholars argue that the feet are the most honest part of the body because we do not pay as much attention to these appendages as we do to other parts of the body (e.g., hands) when communicating. People generally do not consider the legs and feet as nonverbal communicators. The importance of accounting for lower extremities when communicating was first advocated by Paul Ekman (Pease & Pease, 2004). Before Ekman's work, the functions of the legs and feet were simply to move to acquire food and run away from danger.

© DW labs Incorporated/Shutterstock.com

Can you tell what kind of a conversation is occurring here?

The prevailing assumption as to why a person should look to the legs and feet when trying to detect deception is that most people are oblivious to movement in lower extremities when engaging in deceptive communication. For example, when a patient is answering questions about potential risk factors and behavior (e.g., drug or alcohol use), many people are reluctant to reveal the true degree to which they engage in these behaviors, and by positions such as crossed legs may be contrary to open communication. Perhaps healthcare professionals should be trained to look for patient leg and foot behavior, and if deception is suspected, follow-up questions about the behavior can be asked to create a supportive, nonjudgmental environment that is more conducive to more accurate and truthful patient disclosure. In the book *How to Read a Person Like a Book* (1971), Gerard Nierenberg and Henry Caleroh reported a study investigating the effectiveness of sales techniques. The analysis of 2,000 sales transactions indicated that salespeople who crossed their legs while attempting to sell did not make a single sale.

In a clinical situation, the most appropriate stance for a healthcare professional is facing the patient, having an open body position with palms exposed, and smiling modestly. These suggestions about appropriate body positioning do not mean that you should be standing at attention, but you should display a forward-facing, relaxed position. The open body position helps create a comfortable and accepting environment as opposed to one of judgment and intimidation. As a general rule, consider leg and foot behavior as strong indicators as to where the mind wants (and body hopes) to go.

Attractiveness and Physical Appearance.   When people generally think of attractiveness they immediately conjure up visions of some Hollywood actor or supermodel. **Attractiveness** is defined as the degree of appeal a person has regarding physical, task, and social qualities. The effect of appearance

© FXQuadro/Shutterstock.com

What message is she sending with her body language?

and attraction in communication is far more complex because the nonverbal signals they send can serve as an advantage or disadvantage for the sender of the message. There are three types of attractiveness (McCroskey & McCain, 1974). First is **physical attractiveness,** which refers to the degree to which a person's physical characteristics are desirable to others and is believed to be the most important during initial interactions. However, most experts agree that physical attractiveness is less important as relationships begin to develop into more meaningful interpersonal connections. This principle is evidenced thousands of times a day throughout the world when people who initially avoid those with some physical stigma (e.g., amputee, developmental deformity, burns), after having conversations with such people, form meaningful friendships that move well beyond the superficial physical stigma. **Social attractiveness** is defined as attraction based on a person's communication abilities and social networks (e.g., they know a lot of important people). **Task attractiveness** reflects attraction based on what someone does (e.g., cardiothoracic surgeon). Although all three types of attractiveness can have both positive and negative effects on relationships, if a person cannot form quality relationships with others, the benefits associated with attractiveness are minimized. Therefore, as a general rule, attraction is a factor that tends to dissipate over time in lieu of more important and meaningful characteristics such as strength of character and the ethical grounding of the person.

Somatypes. The type of body one possesses can serve as a powerful nonverbal communicator (Sheldon, Stevens, & Tucker, 1940). There are three main body types, also known as somatypes. A **somatype** is a classification of a person's body type and consists of endomorph, mesomorph, and ectomorph. The endomorph tends to have a rounded body with a large abdomen. People with this body type are considered slow, lazy, calm, soft-hearted, and kind. Examples of endomorphs include Sir Winston Churchill, Santa Claus, and Emeril Lagasse. The mesomorph is a somatype that reflects a triangular athletic body that is muscular and firm with good posture. People with the mesomorphic body type are perceived as being intelligent, outgoing, energetic, dominant, and determined. Some examples of the mesomorph body type include Governor Arnold Schwarzenegger, Derek Jeter, and LeBron James. The third somatype is the ectomorph and reflects a body that is tall and slender with poor muscle tone. People with these types of bodies are perceived as awkward, high strung, tense, and anxious. Examples of the ectomorph include Howard Stern, Abraham Lincoln, Barack Obama, Jackie Joyner- Kersee and Nicole Kidman. Of the three body types, people in Western cultures prefer the mesomorphic body type.

| **endomorph**
A somatype consisting of a round body with a large abdomen.

| **mesomorph**
A somatype that reflects a triangular athletic body that is muscular and fi rm with good posture.

| **ectomorph**
A somatype that refl ects a body that is tall and slender with poor muscle tone.

Clothing and Artifacts.   The main functions of clothing are to provide comfort, protection, and modesty (Morris, 1985). Social groups often use a form of clothing to set themselves apart from other social groups. Professional sports teams, sororities, and street gangs are but a few examples of the importance of clothing and the nonverbal messages that it sends. In particular professions, uniforms communicate rank and affiliation such as that found in the military. Within healthcare, the Occupational Safety and Health Administration (OSHA) requires the use of scrub suits for some healthcare professionals. In a study of professional dress and physician image, Rowland, Coe, Burchard, and Pricolo (2005) had people rate the clothing of male and female physicians. The findings indicate that a physician's appearance significantly affects perceptions of his or her professional image. Further, personal appearance can have both positive and negative effects on the physician's overall reputation and success. This finding is consistent with Hippocrates and others making reference to acceptable images for physicians. Therefore, the importance of appropriateness of physician dress dates back to antiquity. Considering the patient and clothing, one major issue for patients is the embarrassment experienced when required to wear the hospital gown that is provided before an examination. Patients, similar to any other person, desire to be treated with dignity and respect. Historically, these skimpy garments afford patients neither dignity nor respect. One little step toward this is to provide a gown that fits appropriately and the use of cover sheets where and when necessary.

Throughout human history, people have adorned themselves with jewelry and other artifacts. **Artifacts** are things that people wear that can communicate information to another person. In Western cultures, it is suggested that woman wear no more than five pieces of jewelry to include a watch, simple earrings, simple necklace, a ring, and a pin or bracelet. For men, two pieces of jewelry such as a watch and a wedding band are advised (Kaiser, 1999). Within the health care arena, both men and women should avoid

In addition to comfort and protection, some clothing is meant to send a clear nonverbal message.

© zoff/Shutterstock.com

wearing faith-based icons that can be seen by others. Frequently, the Christian cross and the Star of David are signs of religious beliefs that people wear with pride. Yet in the pluralistic society of America, we must recognize the religious mosaic (e.g., Christianity, Judaism, Muslim, Hindu, Shinto) within which healthcare is practiced and be aware that that particular religious branding may not be that of colleagues or patients, which can create unnecessary interpersonal tension; thus, such items should be worn with caution when in professional environments.

Body Hair.   The way in which people utilize hair on the body is another important impression-making nonverbal element. Facial, scalp, and body hair send messages to others. Culture, gender, race, profession, religion, and many other factors contribute to the determination of what is an appropriate display of hair. For example, it is rare to see someone in pharmaceutical sales wearing a full beard, yet contrast that to the less appearance-regulated university professor who regularly wears different styles of facial hair. In American culture, Kalick, Zebrowitz, Langlois, and Johnson (1998) found that men with beards are commonly perceived as being deceptive or having something to hide. This perception is so strong that jury selection experts recommend that defendants and witnesses be clean shaven because this lends to the overall credibility of the person. Overall, men who are clean shaven are perceived as more youthful and less tense than men with beards (Pease & Pease, 2004). Within healthcare, facial hair is not only an issue of aesthetics, but also one of safety. Hair, regardless of where on the body, can spread germs and contaminate sterile environments. It is for these reasons that the U.S. Food and Drug Administration regulations have strict guidelines for people who work in food service and other more sanitized-centric industries such as healthcare.

Changes in body hair can also bring about changes in social justice or the way a person is treated by others. For example, Malcolm Gladwell, author of the bestselling book *Blink* (2005), describes the time he decided to grow an "afro." Being the son of biracial parents (Jamaican mother and Caucasian father), he experienced a life change as a result of his hairstyle. He noted that he was receiving more speeding tickets, was frequently being pulled out of airport security lines for increased interrogation, and was once detained for being suspected of committing rape. In this case, a change in hairstyle meant a change in social status as perceived by others.

Mimetics.   The importance of facial expressions when communicating with other people and as a means of sensing the psychological, emotional, and behavioral experiences of another person has been advocated by everyone from our parents to our teachers. The study of **mimetics** is the study of how facial expressions are used, interpreted, or filtered during human interaction. A person's facial appearance provides a wealth of information about their race; gender; nationality; emotional state; and, for the more perceptive, the type and quality of the person's character.

The face is the most expressive part of the body. In fact, Charles Darwin (1872) argued that all mammals show emotion through their faces. In terms of human beings, the most significant pioneering work on facial expressions was conducted by Paul Ekman and associates. Part of this body of work resulted in the concept of microexpressions. **Microexpressions** are the brief involuntary facial expressions shown on the human face when people are trying to conceal or deceive. These involuntary expressions occur extremely quickly (about 1/25th of a second) and are thought to occur frequently when one is actively engaging in deception. **Deception** is the intentional act of distorting, altering, or omitting information from another person or person(s).

© lightpoet/Shutterstock.com

It's not unusual for a university professor to wear a beard, unlike many other professions.

Deception is a naturally occurring phenomenon in human relationships and is no different within hospital settings. Patients, coworkers, and others with whom we interact regularly deceive each other for a variety of reasons including self-preservation, esteem protection, acts of psychological aggression and abuse, and so on. Therefore, healthcare professionals should be aware of such tendencies and the types of behaviors that are associated with deception.

It is extremely difficult to detect deception; in fact, in a study of more than 20,000 people, only 50 were able to naturally detect lies (Camilleri, 2009). What this and dozens of other studies indicate is that detecting deception is extremely difficult to do, yet the research reviewed here indicates that most information about a person's deceptive intent centers on the study of mimetics. In fact, there are programs being implemented in airports throughout the United States based on facial microexpression profiles that may help security better detect people of interest through both video-imaging and interviewing techniques (Frank, Yarbrough, & Ekman, 2006; Pavlidis, Dowdall, Frank, & Ekman, 2006; Tarko, 2006).

According to Ekman and Friesen (1975), six basic emotions are communicated through the face. These emotional states are believed to be universal in that all humans, regardless of culture, gender, age, and the like, all communicate similarly. These emotions are *sadness, anger, disgust, fear, surprise,* and *happiness* (Fig. 5.1). To test the theory that certain facial expressions were a result of being human as opposed to being a function of our cultural surroundings, Ekman traveled to Papua, New Guinea (a place that, in the 1960s, was void of popular culture in the late 1960s). Ekman recorded the facial expressions with a movie camera with results indicating that even though the participants in the study had never met Westerners before the study, their facial expressions were almost identical to those found in the United States. Thus, it was concluded that facial expressions are more biologically driven behavior with regard to the six basic emotions than being a function of any particular outcome. With this information in hand, Ekman and Friesen studied the anatomy of the face and concluded that there are 43 muscles capable of creating 10,000 different facial configurations. Of these configurations, 3,000 are meaningful for the expression of the six universal emotions (Guthrie, 2002). The seventh universal emotion—*contempt*—was later added to the list (Matsumoto, 1992).

Of all the universal emotions, fear prompts a unique physiological reaction. Ekman and Friesen (1975) believe that the experience of fear, as displayed on the face, is pancultural. That is, facial expression and body tension are automatic responses that convey messages of being fearful or safe. According to Kalick et al. (1998), fear can be detected (67% of the time) by changes in the eyes and eyelid region of the face. Figure 5.2 illustrates this universal facial expression.

Because fear is connected to areas of the brain responsible for fight or flight responses (see Chapter 2), the **amygdala** is an important brain structure for identifying and reacting to emotion in the faces of others. In fact, the amygdala appears to be the most attuned for detecting and reacting to

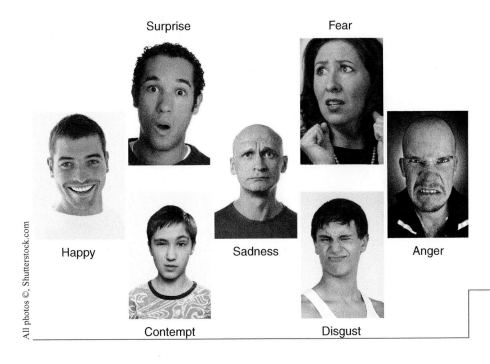

All photos ©, Shutterstock.com

figure 5.1

The Seven Universal Facial Expressions of Emotions

fear (Morris et al., 1996). Fear is a reaction that is based on socially derived stimuli (Hardee & Thompson, 2008). Seeing a fearful expression on another person's face will often shift our attention to see what the fearful person is reacting to, as opposed to staying focused on the face of the person.

The ability of healthcare professionals to identify a patient's fearful expression and react in ways to reduce that reaction is a mark of a communicatively competent professional. The reduction of patient uncertainty and fear is a central component of establishing quality interpersonal relationships between patients and providers.

Smile.   The human smile is a universal facial expression for happiness or friendliness. Pease and Pease (2004) provide a physiological distinction between the genuine expression of happiness and that of a fake expression. The fake smile is primarily restricted to the zygomaticus muscles only (i.e., the sides of the mouth turn up), whereas a true smile only occurs in the eye regions where the eyebrows and skin between the upper eyelid and the eyebrow come down slightly (Fig. 5.3). The muscles involved in the genuine smile consist of the orbicularis occuli (i.e., muscles surrounding the eye) and the pars lateralis (i.e., a forehead muscle) (Forman, 2003).

Occulesics.   The study of **occulesics** or eye behavior is the study of how people use the eyes to communicate and has received an incredible amount of attention from researchers in the Western world. Eye behavior is believed to regulate turn-taking behavior during conversation, assist in establishing relationships with other people, maintain existing relationships, express emotions, show respect for others, and express interest in what other people are saying (Kendon, 1967). Eye behavior and the meaning of eye behavior

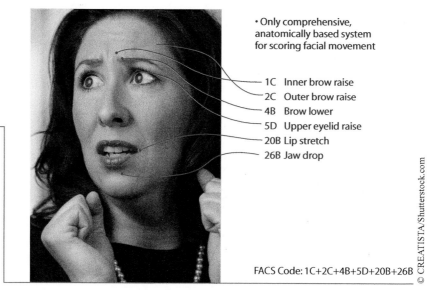

figure 5.2

Facial Action Coding of a Fear Expression

From: Morris, J. S., Frith, C. D., Perrett, D. I., Rowland, D., Young, A. W., Calder, A. J., et al. (1996). A differential response in the human amygdala to fearful and happy facial expression. Nature, 383, 812–815.

• Only comprehensive, anatomically based system for scoring facial movement

1C   Inner brow raise
2C   Outer brow raise
4B   Brow lower
5D   Upper eyelid raise
20B   Lip stretch
26B   Jaw drop

FACS Code: 1C+2C+4B+5D+20B+26B

© CREATISTA/Shutterstock.com

are bound by the culture within which it occurs. For example, in Western cultures, people engage in direct eye contact, whereas in Eastern cultures (specifically China) direct eye contact is viewed as rude and disrespectful behavior.

Within the clinical setting, Ruusuvouri (2001) investigated which non-verbal behaviors were most important to patients during the medical interview with their physician. Eye contact emerged as the most important. If a healthcare provider is distracted (e.g., looking at her notes or computer and not making adequate eye contact), a patient can interpret this as a lack of interest, which can result in inhibiting open communication exchange with the patient. This results in bad first impressions and violation of expectations for the patient. **Doctor Effectiveness**

Paralanguage.   When people consider the use of voice when communicating, they generally think of it as a simple means to transport words to another

Smile Example

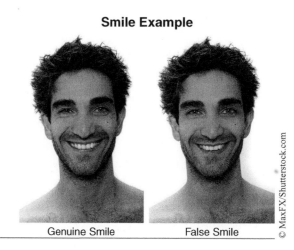

Genuine Smile   False Smile

© MaxFX/Shutterstock.com

figure 5.3

The Genuine and Fake Smile

person. In fact, vocal qualities or paralanguage are an integral part of effective communication; sometimes it is a powerful tool to infer meanings to messages without having to overtly state the meaning. Paralanguage, then, is defined as all the verbal communication behavior we use besides the actual words to send messages. According to McCroskey (2001), it is impossible to send a verbal message without voice inflection. It is important to understand that there are some vocalic messages that can exist without the use of verbal messages, yet these utterances, when sent by a patient or client, are extremely valuable to the perceptive healthcare professional. For example, sighs, laughs, groans, or moans all are expressed without the use of verbal messages. The many characteristics and qualities of the human voice that are considered paralanguage occur simultaneously with verbal messages. Linguists divide vocalics into the two major categories: **prosody,** which are vocal qualities that are easily measurable; and **paralinguistics,** which are vocalizations that are difficult to measure. Prosody includes vocal qualities such as pitch, loudness, rhythm control (duration and tempo), and lip control (intonation). Paralinguistics includes vocal qualities such as expression, voice quality (pitch height, intensity, loudness, softness), and stylistic variations such as vocal segregates (e.g., um, ah), emotion, and speech clarity.

Vocal inflection can deliver potent nonverbal messages and add information to the intended meaning. For example, consider the concept of sarcasm. **Sarcasm** is a creation brought about by paralanguage, not by literal language, and is defined as a paralinguistic device that communicates to the receiver that the meaning of the message being sent should be the opposite of the meaning inferred by the spoken word. Sarcasm and its ability to be produced effectively has been attributed to the regions in which people are raised (e.g., New York,

> **paralanguage**
>
> All the verbal communication behavior we use besides the actual words to send messages.

© michaeljung/Shutterstock.com

Why is eye contact important in the clinical setting?

Boston, New Jersey) or as a well-crafted ability that is honed with practice (e.g., use of comedy). The use and interpretation of sarcasm are not only dependent on the sender's abilities, but also on the capacity of the receiver to infer the hidden meaning in the message. For example, people from other countries, particularly non-Western countries, have great difficulty interpreting sarcasm and generally look to the literal meaning of the words. Therefore, we recommend that healthcare practitioners refrain from using sarcasm unless the relationship with the patient is one where there will be little chance for misinterpretation and there is a high probability that the sarcasm will be appreciated by the patient.

The human voice serves the following six functions: (1) *creates your image to others*; (2) *communicates emotional state*; (3) *indicates socio-economic level and status*; (4) *indicates background and home culture*; (5) *regulates the flow of conversation*; and (6) *shows interest or disinterest in the subject at hand* (Polack et al., 2008). In a study of physician—patient conversation, Levinson, Roter, Mullooly, Dull, and Frankel (1997) sought to determine if there was any connection to litigious behavior (i.e., tendency to sue) that could be associated with a physician's communication style. The linguistic differences between those who have been sued in the past and those who have not been sued were as follows.

Those that have never been sued:

1. Spend an average of 3 minutes longer with each patient.
2. Make orienting comments before beginning any procedure such as, "What I am going to do is give you some information, perform a physical exam, and then explain what we can or cannot do about this problem."
3. Engage in active listening (e.g., "Tell me more").
4. Tend to laugh and use humor with the patient during the visit.

Overall, a central determining factor distinguishing sued from nonsued physicians was based on how they talked to their patients. Simply put, it comes down to basic respect and courtesy. A dominant or condescending tone of voice used by a physician creates a significant barrier to the creation of a patient—provider relationship that is best based on mutuality or equal power between patient and provider.

Proxemics.   **Proxemics** is the study of how people use space to communicate (Hall, 1966). The use of space, and personal space in particular, varies among people but is influenced by gender and culture. For example, males tend to stand further away from other people than do females when communicating. Culturally, Latin Americans, Italians, Puerto Ricans, and people from the Middle East maintain an 18-inch intimate distance from one another, whereas Americans, Germans, Chinese, and Japanese maintain a 48-inch intimate distance. As you can see, these drastically different space orientations can make for some interesting interpersonal interactions if one is not aware of these special practices.

People in the United States use four distinct categories for defining personal space (Hall, 1966). These consist of (1) **intimate distance**—0 to 18 inches; (2) **personal distance**—18 inches to 4 feet; (3) **social distance**—4 to 8 feet; and (4) **public distance**—8 eight feet to the point where a person is beyond our vision and hearing. People are protective of their personal space and, when violated, people may react in interesting ways. People use four general strategies, including completely withdrawing from the situation (Hall, 1983), proactively avoiding situations where one expects their space to be violated, insulating oneself (e.g., with a desk or chair) to ensure that people do not violate personal space (Conigliaro, Cullerton, Flynn, & Roeder, 1989), and fighting to defend your space (which can include directly challenging anyone who violates your space communicatively or physically) (Lyman & Scott, 1967). How we manage our space is known as **territoriality.** Office space, our favorite chair, office supplies, and the like constitute things that we control to mark our territory. As a general rule, the person with the higher rank has the right to violate the space and possessions of the person who is subordinate. Some examples include a parent and child, boss and subordinate, and doctor and patient.

Within healthcare, the modern-day examination room is a place that is small in size and thus challenging to both the provider and patient because they must be able to maintain their personal space while reducing stress and uncertainty as much as possible. This delicate balance can be achieved through mindful behaviors on the part of the healthcare practitioner. For example, the provider can sit on a scooting stool and communicate at eye level with the patient while moving in and out of the patient's personal space while seated. Other ways to make the most of this situation include remembering to knock on the door before entering and close the door behind you. If the examination is to be performed in more public or open spaces, make sure to completely draw the curtains or privacy dividers. By ensuring that the patient has as much privacy as possible, this sends the nonverbal message to the patient that the provider is mindful and considerate of the patient's dignity and respect.

Haptics.   **Haptics,** or the study of touch, is perhaps one of the most central nonverbal elements for both psychological and physiological development and well-being. During the 19th and 20th centuries, each year a large percentage of children died from a disease called **marasmus.** The word *marasmus* is derived from a Greek word meaning "waste away." In orphanages, the mortality rate for children suffering from marasmus was nearly 100%. Children in homes, hospitals, and other types of institutions also suffered high mortality rates from this disease. When the causes of the disease were finally discovered, it was determined that infants who suffered from this disease lacked physical contact with parents or parent surrogates. The infant deaths were not from a lack of nutrition or inadequate medical care, but rather, they were from a lack of human touch. From this finding came the practice of "mothering" children, whether it be in the institution or the home. This mothering behavior included picking up a baby, carrying the child around, and handling it several times a day. Once this behavior was instituted in hospitals, the death rates from marasmus fell from between 30% and 35% to less than 10%. Simply put, we can die from a lack of touch.

Cultures differ in the way people use touch to communicate (Jones, 1999; Jourard, 1996). In the United States, people generally do not like to touch or be touched. However, in countries such as Latin America, Europe, and the Middle East touching is an essential part of communicating. **Culture and Touch** According to Polack, et al., (2008), there are five different types of touch consisting of (1) **professional touch,** which reflects the type of touch experienced when you visit a doctor, dentist, or a person who uses touch as a professional service; (2) **social touch,** which can take the form of greeting people and reflects the touch involved during routine social exchanges; (3) **friendship touch,** which reflects touch to indicate that the other person is a close friend such as giving them a hug instead of a handshake when you greet them; (4) **love or intimate touch,** which refers to touch that indicates a powerful bond with another person such as stroking a child's face; and (5) **sexual arousal touch,** which reflects touching others in a sexual way or for sexual gratification.

Earlier we mentioned that Americans are not as "touch friendly" as people from other cultures. In fact, it is estimated that approximately 15% of Americans are touch avoidant (Guerrero & Anderson, 1994). For a person who is touch avoidant, even innocent touching gestures may be interpreted as offensive. If a person is touch avoidant, any touch regardless of the type or intent is interpreted as a threatening event. For healthcare professionals, understanding that some patients are touch avoidant can assist in determining appropriate ways of going about practicing healthcare without increasing the anxiety of the patient. Whether or not to use touch is person specific and is partially influenced by the patient's culture.

| autonomics

A dimension of nonverbal behavior referring to how involuntary signs communicate a person's internal state.

Autonomics. **Autonomics** are the involuntary signs that people communicate that reflect their internal state (Pease & Pease, 2004). Some autonomics include tearing of the eyes, sweaty palms, or changes in respiration based on physiological reaction. Some respiratory changes can include hyperventilation, sighing, taking a deep breath, or shallow rapid breathing such as when someone is startled. Additionally, the pupils of the eye are easily recognizable autonomic indicators because they can dilate (when excited) or constrict (when fearful). Given that we are unable to control

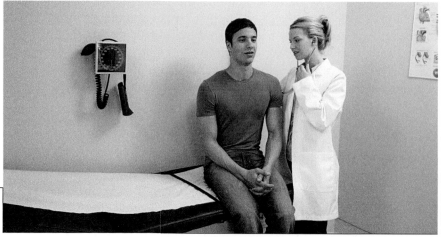

It's not easy to maintain your personal space in a small examination room.

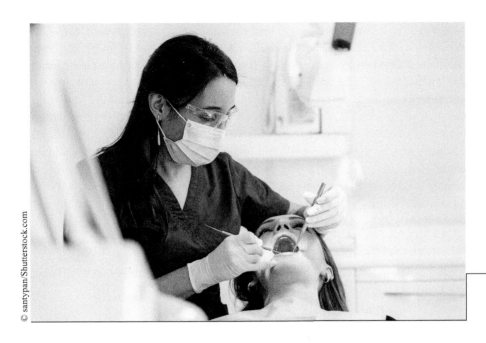

© santypan/Shutterstock.com

A patient receives the professional touch from her dentist.

this physiological response, a person who is mindful of autonomic indicators can use such signals to craft messages accordingly. If a patient is emitting autonomic signals indicating that they are nervous or scared, perhaps using supportive messages would be the most appropriate type of communication in an effort to reduce their physiological arousal.

Sizing. As discussed earlier, the body type that a person possesses is believed to be closely related to a person's general temperament and personality (Sheldon, 1954). More specifically, the endomorph is round shaped and friendly, the ectomorph is thin and anxious, and the mesomorph is triangular and calm. In human relationships, anthropologist Boguslaw Pawlowski (2003) found that in "ideal relationships" trust, money, and respect are actually less important than height differences between relational partners. More specifically, the study indicates that men need to be 1.09 times taller than the woman and that this height difference is a better predictor of relationship quality than other factors. For example, a woman who is 66 inches (5 feet 6 inches) tall would have a greater probability of experiencing an "ideal relationship" with a man who is 72 inches tall (6 feet). Although not something that can be altered, a person's size does communicate something because if a patient or provider deviates from the norm in terms of their size and communication expectations (too thin, too fat, too tall, too short compared to the norm), this may affect the flow of communication and as such should also be considered as important nonverbal information.

Olfactics. The nonverbal aspect of **olfactics** refers to how people use scent and smell as a means of communicating and interacting with others (Cain, 1981). Although scent and smell are an invisible part of nonverbal communication, scent may signal an increase in interpersonal attraction and evoke memories and meanings of things, people, and environments from past experiences. For example, the smell of a particular food or fragrance may result in a flood of memories for people because these sorts of nonverbal stimuli are stored in both long- and short-term memory.

Smell can also alert healthcare providers to the presence of particular diseases (Polack et al., 2008). The most common diagnostic determination based on smell is the presence of alcohol, with another being the odor of ketones (which smells sweet) on the breath of a patient who is in a diabetic coma. Some other scents that are extremely meaningful to healthcare professionals for accurate diagnosis and treatment include pemphigus (a skin disorder), which smells like dead rats; yellow fever, which smells like a butcher shop; scurvy and smallpox, which emit a putrid odor; Typhoid fever, which smells like freshly baked bread; *Pseudomonas* infection, which smells like fruit; diphtheria, which has a sweet odor; and the plague, which smells like apples. Smell is something that, when made mindful, can serve the healthcare practitioner with both relational and medical benefits.

| taste

A study of nonverbal behavior focusing on the role of taste in communication.

Taste. Taste is a vital life function that allows us to not only enjoy life, but also remain alive. Taste is also a valuable communicator of messages for people. The lack of taste has been linked to anorexia, weight loss, and depression (Padala, Hinners, & Padala, 2006). One of the most common causes of not being able to taste food is the normal aging process (Schiffman, 1997). Other common factors include medications such as lipid-lowering drugs, antihistamines, antibiotics, anti-inflammatory medications (e.g., aspirin, ibuprofen), asthma treatment, treatment for blood pressure, anticonvulsants (Dilantin-type drugs), antidepressants, muscle relaxants, and vasodilators. It is believed that more than 250 different medications may alter taste sensation (Feske & Samuels, 2003). These medications can cause a metallic taste; enhance the bitter flavors in things such as beef, pork, coffee, and chocolate; and reduce the taste of sweet flavors (*Oncology Encyclopedia,* 2010).

In terms of illness and the influence on taste and smell, several common illnesses including Alzheimer's disease, Parkinson's, Multiple Sclerosis, viral hepatitis, diabetes, kidney disease, liver disease, and thyroid disease have been identified as having adverse effects on a person's sense of taste and smell. Other causes include nutrient deficiency—more specifically, the lack of copper, niacin, vitamin B[12], nickel, vitamin A, and zinc (*Oncology Encyclopedia,* 2010). With zinc being a major element affecting taste, some supplemental food sources that are rich in zinc—such as oysters, crab, beef, pork, eggs, nuts, yogurt, and whole grains—can assist in restoring a more "normal" sense of taste.

Taste is both a physiological and psychological experience because it involves the tongue, back portion of the mouth (soft palate), and the back of the throat. The "taste buds" are on the tongue and are composed of taste cells with tiny hairs (microvilli) that take up microscopic particles of the food that come in contact with the tongue (Brand, 2000; Mann, 2002; Yasuda & Tomita, 2002). Taste buds have a life span of about 10 days and reveal four distinct taste qualities: *salty, sweet, sour,* and *bitter.* These tastes are detected in different areas of the tongue. The tip of the tongue is the most sensitive to salty and sweet substances, the sides of the tongue are most sensitive to sour substances, and the back of the tongue is most sensitive to bitter substances. There is a strong correlation between smell and taste. This relationship is so strong that any impairment in a person's sense of smell can bring about a dulled or impaired sense of taste. Alterations in the sense of taste often results in a "metallic taste." A 1994 survey indicated that 2.7 million American adults have difficulty in smelling, whereas 1.1 million report having difficulty with taste (Hoffman, Ishii, & Macturk, 1994).

Chronodynamics.   The effect of **chronodynamics** is extremely important in nonverbal communication. Within classroom settings, colors of blue and green tend to be calming, whereas orange, red, and yellow can be interpreted as aggressive (Richmond, 1997). The color of white, which is one of the most widely used colors in healthcare, is a symbol of purity and cleanliness but can be interpreted as cold, distant, and sterile. Despite this effect of white in healthcare settings, many patients expect their doctors to be in white coats and their nurses in white uniforms. These expectations of professional dress in healthcare can lead to a phenomenon known as the white-coat syndrome that results in an increase in blood pressure when a person is in a clinical situation (Jhalani, Goyal, Clemow, Schwartz, Pickering, & Gerin, 2005; Ruxer, Mozdzan, Baranski, Wozniak-Sosnowska, & Markuszewski, 2007).

Stigma.   A **stigma** is a mark of disgrace that people may attach to something they regard as unacceptable. The literature on interpersonal communication is almost nonexistent in terms of research investigating the effects of how people maintain distance from others who have stigmas (Hickson & Stacks, 1993). There are two general types of stigma: physical and social. The physical stigma is most relevant to healthcare and can be defined as any physical attribute that serves as a marker resulting in the marginalization of the person solely based on a physical attribute. For example, some people perceive they are stigmatized for using a wheelchair, crutches, cane, or walker. In the instance of someone who is in a wheelchair, how do we effectively and appropriately communicate with such a person? We advocate that the healthcare professional be seated and avoid touching the wheelchair because touching the chair can create a feeling of being entrapped for the patient.

| physical stigma
Any physical attribute that serves as a marker resulting in the marginalization of the person solely based on that physical attribute.

Other physical stigmas include being blind, being an amputee, or having a burn or severe scarring. Although it may be a "natural" initial reaction to step back from a person with any of these or other physical challenges, the healthcare practitioner must be mindful of their own behavior and tendencies to react. An example of this can be evidenced in a study conducted by Conigliaro and colleagues (1989) investigating how people accommodate people who are blind. Results indicated that people gave the person who was blind and using a cane on average 33 feet 8 inches of space, whereas people without a cane were given on average of 5 feet 6 inches of space.

© Volha_R/Shutterstock.com

What is the white coat syndrome?

| social stigma

Any social attribute that serves as a marker resulting in the marginalization of the person solely based on that social attribute.

The other general type of stigma, social stigma, is defined as any social attribute that serves as a marker resulting in the marginalization of the person solely based on that social attribute. Social stigma is often based on the type of job a person performs, what they look like, what they sound like, or where they live. Healthcare practitioners may also have a tendency to judge patients with certain conditions (e.g., sexually transmitted disease and hepatitis versus type 1 diabetes or Alzheimer's disease). We advocate that people avoid judging patients by any stigma or by any behavior that has brought them to you. Treating a patient in prison or who is homeless, for example, with the dignity and respect that any other patient would receive is the ethical and moral obligation of all healthcare practitioners.

Environment.   When we speak of **environment** we are referring to the natural and manmade surroundings that influence human behavior and communication. Research indicates that people placed in an unattractive environment colored in more aggressive colors such as red or orange, communicated less, were more fatigued, and were more irritable than people placed in an attractive environment containing soft colors such as blue or green (Maslow & Mintz, 1956). The overall findings of this study implicate the importance of environmental surroundings and that these surroundings influence the type of communication that transpires. Architects and other environmental designers are aware of such factors and are incorporating environments conducive to healing in newly constructed healthcare facilities.

In terms of existing healthcare facilities, there are things that we can control or change to make the environment more conducive to quality communication. For example, set the room temperature to approximately 68°F with a room humidity of about 50%. Mark Knapp (1980) described six perceptual frameworks from which people perceive and interpret an environment. First, the **formal environment** reflects surroundings that are sterile and formal such as a bank or traditional hospital. Second is the **warm environment,** which reflects surroundings where we feel comfortable sitting around and casually speaking with other people. Third are **private environments,** which reflect environments that are more intimate in nature such as a booth in a public restaurant. Fourth is the **familiar environment,** which reflects environments that we regularly inhibit such as our own living room. Fifth is the **constraining environment,** which reflects the surroundings that restrict physical and/or psychological space such as a jail or a small examination room. Finally, there are **distant environments,** reflecting surroundings that create physical and psychological distance and are impersonal in nature (e.g., a physician speaking to a patient from behind a large desk that is 10 feet away from the patient who is sitting in a straight-back chair on the other side of the room).

Chronemics.   The study of time and how people use time to communicate is known as the study of **chronemics**. Time and time use are believed to be culture specific. For example, American culture tends to be an **M-time** or **monochronic time** society (Hall & Hall, 1990). That is, Americans have a need to be on time and time is viewed as a commodity to be maximized. Any delay in time is considered "wasted time." Consider the amount of time people spend when waiting to see their physician. Most people consider such an experience wasted time. This feeling is so strong that many people will bring other tasks with them so as to not "waste" what precious little time they perceive they have available to them.

The other type of time is known as **P-time** or **polychronic time** and is most prevalent in Latin America and the Middle East. Polychronic time is an orientation where time is relative and is not a commodity to be consumed but something to mark the passing of days, years, and so on. In regions practicing polychronic time, a person scheduled for a meeting at noon may show up 30 minutes late or even on a completely different day. Further, the late person will not see their tardy behavior as inappropriate in any way (Hall, 1959). In monochronic cultures, people try to do one thing at a time and do that one thing well. It is in this sequential ordering of tasks that leads people from polychronic cultures to conclude that people from monochronic cultures are inflexible and insensitive to the needs of others. In contrast, people from polychronic cultures tend to do many things simultaneously. Therefore, people from monochronic cultures may perceive such "multitasking" as being easily distracted, uncommitted to the task, and convoluted.

People are believed to be oriented toward time in different ways that go beyond simply mono—poly distinctions. According to E. T. Hall (1983), there are three different time orientations that influence communication and consist of cultural, psychological, and biological time orientations. The **cultural time orientation** can be technical, formal, or informal in nature. **Technical time** reflects the scientific use of time as used by organizations such as NASA

Most people consider waiting as time wasted.

formal time

Reflects the keeping of time in a socially standardized way such as through days, months, years, etc.

(National Aeronautics and Space Administration). Formal time reflects how we keep track of days, months, and years via a calendar. **Informal time** is also known as casual time and is perhaps the most nuanced because it is defined by each individual person. For example, if a person informs you that they will have the report completed in the afternoon, does that mean 12:30 p.m., 1:30 p.m., 4:00 p.m., or 5:00 p.m.? Thus, this type of time use is specific to the person or people using it.

The second time orientation is **psychological time orientation** and reflects ordering events based on past, present, and future events (Hall, 1983). A **past-time ordering** focuses on reliving past events. These events can be both positive and negative experiences that are influenced by one's culture. For example, the Chinese culture and other cultures where the elders in the family or group are revered, focusing on the past is common and a well- respected practice. **Present-time ordering** reflects the here and now with little focus on the past or future. For example, people from Latino and Spanish cultures tend to be "in the moment" with less concern for future events in an effort to make the most of the present situation. **Future-time ordering** reflects being focused on what is coming tomorrow with less emphasis on the present or past. American culture is one such future-time ordering culture because Americans tend to be focused on things such as retirement, future professional opportunities, saving for college, and so on.

The third time orientation is **biological time orientation** and is based on our internal clock or **circadian rhythms.** These biological based times have been divided into *owls* (i.e., people who think and function best in the evening hours), *sparrows* (i.e., people who think or function best in the morning), and *sprowls* (i.e., people who think and function best in the late morning until early evening). Regardless of how we conceptualize or use time, it is a factor that affects us culturally and biologically. Further, being mindful of time and its effect on people can provide healthcare professionals with important information about their own preferences and biases and those of their patients.

Silence.   It has been argued that empathetic communication can positively affect the efficiency of communication with patients (Fogarty, Curbow, Wingard, McDonnel, & Somerfield, 1999). Part of empathetic communication can include attentive silence. Silence, when used competently and mindfully, can communicate concern, interest, and respect. For example, if a patient starts to make a comment and falls silent, allow this silence to continue for approximately 5 seconds, and then softly inquire, "What are you thinking?" Although our culture dictates that silence is a signal of awkwardness in conversation, the fact remains that silence can be an invaluable therapeutic tool for healthcare practitioners.

Ageism.   Age has long been an important factor in communication of all types (Klopf & McCroskey, 2007), and healthcare communication is no exception. For example, healthcare professionals must be sensitive to the needs of a child patient. More often than not, an adult will accompany the child into the healthcare interview. For this reason, it is important to make the conversation three-way in nature. If the child is of school age (at least 5 years old), it is important for healthcare professionals to first direct attention to the child and ask as to whether she would like to "tell her story" or if she prefers for the adult companion to tell her story.

In America it is readily acknowledged that there is or will be an elderly population explosion as baby boomers grow older. In fact, it is estimated that by the year 2030, 35% of the population of the Western world will be older than age 60 and beginning to experience a variety of age-specific psychological (e.g., decreased health literacy, depression, anxiety) and physical (e.g., diminished eyesight, hearing, motor coordination) challenges. As such, age requires an additional level of patience on the part of the healthcare provider.

Nonverbal Immediacy.   Albert Mehrabian (1971, 1981) defined immediacy as the degree of perceived physical and psychological closeness or distance between people in a relationship. The verbal and nonverbal messages we send will define the level of immediacy. For example, verbal immediacy is achieved through the use of "we" and "us" language as opposed to using "I" and "you" language. **Nonverbal immediacy** can be defined as the degree to which people use nonverbal communication to increase the physical and psychological closeness or distance among people in a relationship. This closeness can be achieved through using a relaxed, open body position; leaning forward when communicating; using gestures in a positive manner; and smiling where appropriate. Nonverbal immediacy also involves wearing appropriate clothes for the situation, speaking with vocal variety, engaging in turn-taking behavior, and acknowledging the contributions of the other person with utterances such as "Yes, I understand, tell me more."

| immediacy
The degree of perceived physical and psychological closeness or distance between people in a relationship.

Children should be given the opportunity to "tell their story" to the healthcare professional.

In summary, immediacy leads to an increase in the amount of communication among people, results in relaxed and open communication, increases attentiveness, and augments listening. Beck, Daughtridge, and Sloane (2002) found that doctors who established appropriate nonverbal behavior with their patients (e.g., eye contact, forward lean, open body position) have more satisfied patients.

In a study of nonverbal perceptiveness in the patient—provider dyad, Levinson et al. (1997) found that the provider's ability to accurately interpret and act on patient nonverbal cues resulted in shorter office visits (i.e., 17.6 minutes) as compared to visits where patient nonverbal cues were not attended to (i.e., 21.1 minutes). The conclusions of this study reveal that if the provider can detect nonverbal cues and respond in an appropriate manner, it becomes a critical component to creating a patient—provider relationship, thus improving the outcome of patient care. An example of such nonverbal detection and appropriate action on behalf of the physician would be when a physician detects a nonverbal cue being sent (e.g., clenching of the teeth or fists), the physician should reflect back to the patient to be sure the interpretation is correct. In this case, say, "You appear to be angry about this matter," and then let the patient respond. **Nonverbal Effectiveness**

Conclusion

This chapter synthesizes a vast body of research on nonverbal behavior and the meaning that people attach to such behavior. Dozens of different behaviors were analyzed and presented throughout this chapter including the functions that nonverbal behavior serve; our use of body movement and space; use of our extremities; the clothes and accessories we wear; and physiological indicators such as somatyping, autonomics, and stigma. Understanding how to properly interpret nonverbal communication cues from other people can result in a profoundly enhanced ability to communicate effectively. The ability to engage in competent nonverbal behavior is a macro-behavior or a behavior composed of understanding the dozens of micro-behaviors that comprise a nonverbal message. We believe that by understanding each of these micro-behaviors, a person can become not only a competent communicator with regards to interpreting nonverbal messages, but also a better healthcare practitioner. **Delivering Bad News**

Questions for Discussion/Review

1. Explain how the knowledge of nonverbal communication aids in the delivery of better quality healthcare.
2. List and define the six functions of nonverbal communication. Provide a healthcare example for each function.
3. What role does a person's legs and feet play in the communication process? Provide an example.
4. What suggestions would you make to a newly hired healthcare professional concerning the use of clothing and artifacts when on duty?
5. Explain the six universal emotions that are communicated through the face. How can the knowledge of these emotional expressions assist a healthcare practitioner?
6. Explain how knowledge of paralanguage can improve the delivery of healthcare. Provide two examples of the effectiveness that results from being mindful of such nonverbal communication.
7. Explain how the study of haptics can serve as both a positive and negative influence on the practice of healthcare.
8. Describe the various functions that taste and smell can serve in the practice of medicine and provide an example of how these senses can aid in the diagnosis of disease.
9. Describe the function of stigma and how stigma can affect the patient and how stigma can negatively influence the practice of medicine.
10. Explain how the concept of time and time orientation can affect job performance and how an understanding of how time is conceptualized can help a person become a more effective health practitioner.

References

Ambady, N., Laplante, D., Nguyen, T., Rosenthal, R., Chaumenton, N., & Levinson, W. (2002). Surgeons' tone of voice: A clue to malpractice history. *Surgery, 132,* 5–9.

Beck, R. S., Daughtridge, R., & Sloan, P. D. (2002). Physician/patient communication in the primary care office: A systematic review. *The Journal of the Board of Family Practice, 15,* 25–38.

Birdwhistell, R. L. (1970). *Kinesics and context.* Philadelphia: University of Pennsylvania Press.

Brand, J. G., (2000). Within reach of an end to unnecessary bitterness. *Lancet, 356,* 1371–1372.

Cain, W. S. (1981). Educating your nose. *Psychology Today, 15,* 45–56.

Camilleri, J. (2009, January 21). Truth wizard knows when you've been lying. *Chicago Sun-Times,* p. 25.

Conigliaro, L., Cullerton, K., Flynn, K., & Roeder, S. (1989). Stigmatizing artifacts and their effort on personal space. *Psychological Reports, 65,* 897–898.

Darwin, C. (1872). *The expression of the emotions in man and animals.* London: John Murray.

Ekman, P., & Friesen, W. (1975). *Unmasking the face: A guide to recognizing emotions from facial expression.* Englewood Cliffs, NJ: Prentice Hall.

Feske, S. K., & Samuels, M. A. (2003). *Office practice of neurology* (2nd ed.). Philadelphia: Elsevier Science.

Fogarty, L. A., Curbow, B. A., Wingard, J. R., McDonnel, K., & Somerfield, M. R. (1999). Can 40 seconds of compassion reduce patient anxiety. *Journal of Clinical Oncology, 1,* 371.

Forman, J. A. (2003, August 5). A conversation with Paul Ekman: The 43 facial muscles that reveal even the most fleeting emotions. *The New York Times,* p. F5.

Frank, M. G., Yarbrough, J. D., & Ekman, P. (2006). Improving interpersonal evaluations: Combining science and practical experience. In T. Williamson (Ed.), *Investigative interviewing: Rights, research, & regulation* (pp. 229–255). Portland, OR: Willan Publishing.

Gallois, C., & Callan, V. (1997). *Communication and culture: A guide for practice.* New York: John Wiley & Sons.

Gladwell, M. (2005). *Blink: The power of thinking without thinking.* Boston, MA. Little Brown and Company.

Guerrero, L. K., & Andersen, P. A. (1994). Patterns of matching and initiation: Touch behavior and touch avoidance across romantic relationship stages. *Journal of Nonverbal Behavior, 18,* 137–154.

Guthrie, J. (2002). The lie detective S. F. Psychologist has made a science of reading facial expressions. *San Francisco Chronicle,*

Hall, E. T. (1983). Proxemics. In A. M. Katz & V. T. Katz (Eds.), *Foundations of nonverbal communication: Readings, exercises, and commentary* (pp. 5–27). Carbondale, IL: Southern Illinois University Press.

Hall, E. T. (1966). *The hidden dimension.* Garden City, NY: Doubleday.

Hall, E. T. (1959). *The silent language.* Greenwich, CT: Fawcett.

Hall, E. T., & Hall, M. R. (1990). Monochronic and polychromic time. In L. Guerroro, J. A. DeVito, & M. L. Hecht (Eds.), *The nonverbal communication reader: Classic and contemporary readings* (2nd ed., pp. 237–240). Prospect Heights, IL: Waveland Press.

Hardee, J., Thompson, J. C. (2008). Neuroscience in human communication. In E. P. Polack, V. P. Richmond, & J. C. McCroskey (Eds.), *Applied communication for health professionals* (pp. 249–261). Dubuque, IA: Kendall-Hunt.

Hickson, M. L., & Stacks, D. W. (1993). *Nonverbal communication: Studies and applications* (3rd ed.). Madison, WI: Brown & Benchmark.

Hoffman, H. G., Ishii, E. K., & Macturk, R. H. (1998). Age-related changes in the prevalence of smell/taste problems among the United States adult population. Results of the 1994 disability supplement to the National Health Interview Survey (NHIS). *Annals of the New York Academy of Science, 855,* 716–722.

Jhalani, J., Goyal, T., Clemow, L. A., Schwartz, J. E., Pickering, T. G., & Gerin, W. (2005). Anxiety and outcome expectations predict the white-coat effect. *Blood Pressure Monitoring, 10,* 317–319.

Jones, S. E. (1999). Communicating with touch. In L. K. Guerrero, J. A. DeVito, & M. L. Hecht (Eds.), *The nonverbal communication reader: Classic and contemporary readings* (pp. 233–244). Prospect Heights, IL: Waveland Press.

Jourard, S. M. (1996). An exploratory study of body-accessibility. *British Journal of Social and Clinical Psychology, 5,* 221–231.

Kaiser, S. B. (1999). Women's appearance and clothing within organizations. In L. K. Guerrero, J. A. DeVito, & M. L. Hecht (Eds.), *The nonverbal communication reader: Classic and contemporary readings* (2nd ed., pp. 106–113). Prospect Heights, IL: Waveland Press.

Kalick, S. M., Zebrowitz, L. A., Langois, J. H., & Johnson, R. M. (1998). Does human facial attractiveness honestly advertise health? Longitudinal data on an evolutionary question. *Psychological Science, 9,* 8–13.

Kendon, A. (1967). Some functions of gaze-direction in social interaction. *Acta Psychologica, 26,* 22–63.

Klopf, D. W., & McCroskey, J. C. (2007). *Intercultural communication encounters.* Boston, MA: Allyn & Bacon.

Knapp, M. L. (1972). *Nonverbal communication in human interactions.* New York: Holt, Rinehart and Winston.

Knapp, M. L. (1980). *Essentials of nonverbal communication.* New York: Holt, Rinehart & Winston.

Levinson, W., Roter, D. L., Mullooly, J. P., Dull, V. T., & Frankel, R. M. (1997). Physician–patient communication: The relationship with malpractice claims among privacy care physicians and surgeons. *Journal of the American Medical Association, 277,* 553–559.

Lyman, S. M., & Scott, M. B. (1967). Territoriality: A neglected sociological dimension. *Social Problems, 15,* 236–249.

Mann, N. M. (2002). Management of smell and taste problems. *Cleveland Clinic Journal of Medicine, 69,* 329–336.

Maslow, A. H., & Mintz, N. L. (1956). Effects of esthetic surroundings: Initial effects of three esthetic conditions upon perceiving 'energy' and 'well being' in faces. *Journal of Psychology, 41,* 247–254.

Matsumoto, D. (1992). More evidence for the universality of a contempt expression. *Motivation and Emotion, 16,* 363–368.

McCroskey, J. C. (2001). *An introduction to rhetorical communication* (8th ed.). Englewood Cliffs, NJ: Prentice Hall.

McCroskey, J. C., & McCain, T. A. (1974). The measurement of interpersonal attraction. *Speech Monographs, 41,* 261–266.

Mehrabian, A. (1971). *Silent messages.* Belmont, CA: Wadsworth.

Morris, D. (1985). *Body watching.* New York: Crown.

Morris, J. S., Frith, C. D., Perrett, D. I., Rowland, D., Young, A. W., & Calder, A. J. (1996). A differential response in the human amygdala to fearful and happy facial expressions. *Nature, 383,* 812–815.

Nierenberg, G. I., & Caleroh, H. (1971). *How to read a person like a book.* New York: Pocket Books.

Oncology Encyclopedia. (2010). *Taste alteration.* Retrieved March 1, 2010, from http://www.answers.com/topics/taste-alteration.

Padala, K., Hinners, C. K., & Padala, P. (2006). Mirtazapine therapy for Dysguesia in the elderly. *The Primary Care Companion to the Journal of Clinical Psychiatry, 8,* 178.

Pavlidis, I., Dowdall, J., Frank, M. G., & Ekman, P. (2006). Imaging facial physiology for the detection of deceit. *International Journal of Computer Vision, 71,* 123– 253.

Pawlowski, B. (2003). Variable preferences for sexual dimorphism in height as a strategy for increasing the pool of potential patterns in humans. *Proceedings of the Royal Society of London Series, B, 270,* 709–712.

Pease, A., & Pease, B. (2004). *The definitive book of body language.* New York: Bantam Books.

Polack, E. P., Richmond, V. P., McCroskey, J. C. (2008). *Applied communication for health professionals.* Dubuque, IA: Kendall Hunt.

Reilly, S., & Muzarkara, B. (1978). *Mixed message resolution by disturbed adults and children.* Paper presented at the annual meeting of the International Communication Association, Chicago, IL.

Richmond, V. P. (1997). *Nonverbal communication in the classroom.* Acton, MA: Tapastry.

Rowland, P., Coe, N., Burchard, K. W., & Pricolo, V. E. (2005). Factors affecting professional physician images. *Current Surgery, 61,* 214–219.

Ruxer, J., Mozdzan, M., Baranski, M., Wozniak-Sosnowska, U., & Markuszewski, L. (2007). "White coat hypertension" in type 2 diabetic patients. *Polish Archives of Internal Medicine, 117,* 452–456.

Ruusuvouri, J. (2001). Looking means listening: Coordinating displays of engagement in doctor-patient interaction. *Social Science and Medicine, 52,* 1093–1108.

Schiffman, S. S. (1997). Taste and smell looses in normal aging and disease. *Journal of the American Medical Association, 278,* 1357–1362.

Sheldon, W. H. (1954). *Atlas of men: A guide for somatotyping the adult male of all ages.* New York: Harper and Brothers.

Sheldon, W. H., Stevens, S. S., & Tucker, W. B. (1940). *The varieties of the human physique.* New York: Harper and Brothers.

Tarko, V. (2006). Lying is exposed by micro facial expressions we can't control: The science of interpreting facial expression has reached a new level. *Science Technology News, 23,* 41.

Yasuda, M., & Tomita, H. (2002). Electron microscopic observations of glossal circumvallate papilli in dysguesic patients. *Acta Otolaryngol, 122,* 122–128.

chapter SIX

Intercultural Sensitivity and Behaviors

The study of culture and cultural practices transcends all categories and disciplines because the need to understand cultures, how they develop, and how they change is of utmost importance for all human beings. **Culture** is defined as the traditions, customs, norms, beliefs, values, and thought patterning passed down from generation to generation (Infante, Rancer, & Avtgis, 2010). Cultures can be based on factors such as ethnicity, race, socioeconomic status, sex, illness, social groups, vocations, religion, memberships, specialties, geographic location, or a combination of these and many other factors. This chapter will introduce the concept of culture and how cultural and group membership can serve as both a benefit and a detriment to healthcare practitioners. This chapter also will discuss the culture of medicine and the culture clashes that exist between and among healthcare professionals in everyday practice.

chapter objectives

Upon completion of the chapter, the student should be able to:

1. Compare and contrast intracultural and intercultural communication

2. Explain how future population projections of both patients and healthcare practitioners require intercultural communication competence

3. Explain the implications of ethnocentrism for the practice of medicine

4. Explain the two main models of stigmatization

5. Explain how the assumptions of both patients and healthcare practitioners can affect the quality of care

© didesign021/Shutterstock.com

129

| anchoring bias | culture shock | stereotyping |
| culture | prejudice | xenophobia |

© LightField Studios/Shutterstock.com

Does your family have traditions that have been passed down from generation to generation?

| culture

The traditions, customs, norms, beliefs, values, and thought patterning passed down from generation to generation.

Context and Culture

To fully understand the impact of culture on communication and human relationships, one must understand that all communication is bound by the context (environment) within which it occurs. When considering culture, six general contexts of cultural communication serve a sense-making function so we can better understand the meaning people attribute to the verbal and nonverbal messages of others and as a way for us to make sense of other people's behavior. These contexts of communication consist of (a) *intracultural*; (b) *intercultural*; (c) *cross-cultural*; (d) *international*; (e) *interethnic*; and (f) *interracial* communication (Klopf & McCroskey, 2007; Polack, Richmond, & McCroskey, 2008).

 Intracultural communication refers to communication between members of the same culture or subculture (Klopf & McCroskey, 2007). This is the most common context of communication where there is a high level of **synchrony** in the shared meanings of words and nonverbal behaviors. When we refer to synchrony, we are referring to the high level of commonality the communicators share as a result of being from the same culture. Within any given culture people learn through both the formal education process and the experience of everyday life the meanings of messages and beliefs about their healthcare (Chugh, Agger-Gupta, Dillman, Fisher, Gronnerud, Julig, 1994). Chugh and colleagues (1994) argued that beliefs about health *within* one culture can be just as diverse as those *between* two different cultures. For example, there may be just as many diverse perspectives on health and healthcare within the Hispanic community as there are between Hispanic and Asian communities.

In a survey of 1,816 adults who had recently visited a primary care practice, Cooper-Patrick (1999) found that African American patients rated their visit with the physician as less participatory in decision-making than white patients did. However, when an African American patient was reporting on a visit where the physician was also African American, the visit was rated as being higher in participatory decision-making. The increased levels of participatory decision-making resulted in higher levels of patient satisfaction and ultimately improved health outcomes. This study demonstrates the need for all healthcare practitioners to be versed in competent and mindful communication with diverse groups and illustrates that the concept of **homophily** is a powerful tool that can be effectively used for better health outcomes (Rogers, 1971). Homophily is the degree of closeness that a person feels with another person and can be based on things such as ethnicity, sex, place of origin, or socioeconomic status. However, if cultural homophily is not possible, the mindful healthcare practitioner can utilize other strategies to account for such cultural differences including education, practice, and experience with diverse patient populations.

Intercultural communication occurs between people who are members of different cultural groups. Intercultural communication can also refer to communication between members of two subcultures if there is a wide cultural gap between them. For example, if a person attends medical school at the University of Virginia and another person attends medical school at the University of Vermont, although both trained in medicine, they each have learned unique processes, practices, and traditions. As such, both medical schools can be considered different subcultures of the larger culture of "medical school" and thus can be considered intercultural in nature. Traditionally, when people expose healthcare practitioners to cultural training, the practitioner is taught at

© George Rudy/Shutterstock.com

Intercultural communication occurs between two people who are members of different cultural groups.

the intercultural level how to properly behave or greet someone of a different culture. Perhaps the two most significant barriers for effective communication consist of *language barriers* and *nonverbal barriers.*

The **language barrier** is the inability to relay effective and appropriate communication through verbal behavior. This can be problematic to the degree that a trained interpreter may be needed to facilitate an accurate and competent exchange of information between the patient and provider. In a study of Chinese and Vietnamese immigrants to the United States, Ngo-Metzger and colleagues (2003) found that when encountering Western health professionals, the Chinese and Vietnamese patients preferred the use of a *professional interpreter* of the same sex instead of a family member. Patients of both Chinese and Vietnamese descent report great levels of frustration with the Western healthcare providers' lack of information and awareness of traditional Asian medical beliefs and practices. It is assumed that such an understanding would allow the provider to tailor the verbal messages more effectively so as to consider the cultural aspects of the patient's health. Thus, the lack of cultural knowledge represents a level of disrespect for the patient. The **nonverbal barrier** reflects the inability to relay effective and appropriate communication through nonverbal behavior. It is important to note that nonverbal behavior is not *pancultural.* More specifically, gestures, touch, proxemics, and eye contact are all ways to convey relational communication but are specific to any given culture, not all cultures. An excellent example of this concept is illustrated in Nilda Chong's (2002) book *The Latino Patient: A Cultural Guide for Healthcare Providers.* Chong developed a translational

table 6.1	Intersection of Latino Cultural Value and Medical Care
Collectivism	Taking a friend and/or family member to the healthcare provider's office
Familism	Unwillingness to disclose pathology or dysfunction about the family in an attempt to protect the family and family secrets
Personalism/self-worth	Expressing interest in overcoming a health problem despite all odds
Machismo	Refusing to submit to a rectal examination or other such "invasive procedure"
Marianismo	Accepting the responsibility for the health of all members of the family
Power distance	The willingness to accept the healthcare practitioner's recommendations based on their medical expertise
Respect	The act of remaining in a standing position until asked to sit down when in the presence of a female healthcare practitioner
Religiosity	Telling the healthcare practitioner that a family member's good health has been a blessing from God
Simpatia	The act of bringing homemade food or a present for the healthcare provider on a subsequent visit
Time orientation	When late for an appointment, giving a full explanation as to the cause for the tardiness
Personal space	The appreciation of a handshake or other form of reassuring touch from the healthcare provider at the conclusion of the visit

taxonomy for the "culturally competent" healthcare of the Latino patient. For example, an American provider may say that meat has 200 grams of fat. However, the Latino translation to this is that meat has 12 tablespoons of grease. Similarly, an American provider may say that a serving of meat is a 4-ounce portion, whereas the translation may be that a piece of meat is the size of a deck of cards. Table 6.1 lists some examples of the Latino cultural values and how they may translate during a healthcare visit.

Cross-cultural communication is generally a synonym for intercultural communication but is subtly different in that it concerns communication behaviors across cultures from different nations. For example, with American doctors and doctors from Canada, although both trained in Western medicine, communication differs slightly because they are from different countries.

International communication refers to communication between governmental bodies of different cultures. The gaps between two such parties can be great. For example, consider the cultural gaps between England and China when engaged in international communication. However, the gap between the two parties can be barely distinguishable, such as interaction between members from the United States and Canada. Most international communication is bounded and greatly influenced by politics, which has the added dimensions of having an agenda and predefined goals to the already complex phenomenon of culturally bound communication.

Interethnic communication reflects the communication between members of different ethnic groups; not necessarily people from different countries, political systems, and the like. For example, communication between an Irish American and Italian American would be considered interethnic in nature. **Interracial communication** is interaction between members of different racial groups. Given this is based on race, not ethnicity, an African American interacting with a Korean American would constitute interracial

© Stuart Jenner/Shutterstock.com

The need for communication competence will increase as population demographics change.

communication, whereas the interaction between the Irish American and Italian American would not because the former are from two different races (i.e., the former is African American and the latter two are white). The study of communication between races is not a popular line of research because culture is by far the most significant influence on human interaction, with race being more of an anthropologic designation than a factor that influences social interaction. All of these distinctions and derivations of cultural differences among people are ways that researchers and practitioners seek to explain and understand the behavior of others.

Call for (Inter) Cultural Competence.   Compelling data suggest that by the year 2025, whites will make up 62% of the U.S. population. By 2050 only 50% of the U.S. population will be white (Neuliep, 2003). Contrast these statistics with the 1960 U.S. population where 90% of the people were white. The greatest increases in minority representation within the U.S. population are those of Hispanic descent. Between the years 1990 and 2000, the Hispanic population of the United States increased by 60% (predominately in the western and southwestern regions of the United States). By 2025 Hispanics will account for 18% of the total population of the United States. Contrast these statistics with the fact that in the first decade of the 21st century, Hispanics comprise about 12.5% of the population, whereas the African American population, the second largest non-white group, makes up just over 12% and is expected to remain relatively stable. That is, the African American population will increase by only one percentage point to 13% of the U.S. population by the year 2025. Figure 6.1 indicates the U.S. population of Hispanic and non-Hispanic population.

According to Michael Katz, ". . . healthcare is a cultural construct arising from beliefs about the nature of disease in the human body, cultural issues

figure 6.1

Hispanics and Non-Hispanics as Percentage of U.S. Population: 2000-2050

Source: CRS extraction from: U.S. Census Bureau, 2004. U.S. Interim Projections by Age, Sex, Race, and Hispanic Origin. at [http://www.census. gov/ipc/www/usinterimproj/] internet release date: Mar 18, 2004.

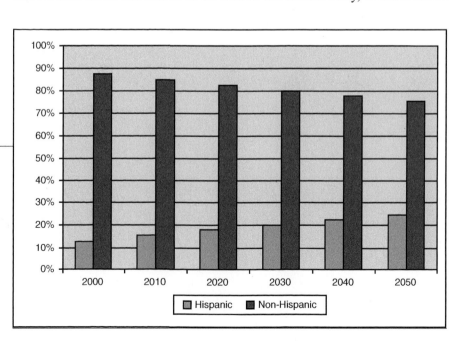

are actually central to the delivery of health services, treatment, and preventative interventions. By understanding, valuing, and incorporating the cultural differences of America's diverse population and examining one's own health related values and beliefs, healthcare organizations, practitioners, and others can support a healthcare system that responds appropriately to and directly serves the unique needs of the populations whose cultures may be different from the prevailing culture" (U.S. Department of Health and Human Services, Office of Minority Health, 2010). As this quote indicates, healthcare practitioners must consider the patient's attitudes toward, level of belief in, and level of confidence in the Western medical system.

Case in Point.   In the 1997 best-selling book *The Spirit Catches You and You Fall Down: A Hmong Child, Her American Doctors, and the Collision of Two Cultures,* author Anne Fadiman illustrates the degree of disparity in cultural practice that can exist between a doctor and patient. In the book, the Lee family are members of the Hmong culture, who were originally from Southern Laos but resettled—after the war in Vietnam (1959–1975) and spending a decade in a refugee camp in Thailand—in the United States. In 1982 the family took their daughter Lia, who had intractable seizures, to a hospital in Merced, California where there was a *clash of cultures* between the neuroscientific perspectives of her primary care doctors and neurologist (Western medical perspective) and the *spirit concept,* which is part of the Hmong culture. It was the anchoring bias (i.e., when a practitioner latches onto the features of a patient's presentation that suggest a specific diagnosis, thus "constraining" the practitioner to alternative explanations) of the primary care physicians, Neil Ernst and Peggy Philip (a married couple), who believed that because of the Lee's **animist culture** (a cultural belief in the existence of spirits that are separate from the body) and the Hmong concept that preventative medicine (as practiced in Western cultures) was culturally foreign, that Lia would not be given the proper dosage of her much-needed medication. The physicians' bias resulted in the projection that if the "big one" (an uncontrollable seizure) should occur, it would result in a dense coma. Furthermore, should the big one occur, it would be a result of noncompliance on the part of the parents to adhere to the medication regimen.

| anchoring bias
When a person latches onto the features of a patient's presentation that suggests a specific diagnosis.

The big one did occur and caused irreversible brain damage in Lia. A neurologist at a nearby hospital (where Lia was also treated) concluded that the uncontrollable seizure was brought about by septic shock (i.e., low blood pressure in reaction to bacteria in the bloodstream) and not the lack of compliance on the part of the parents to provide proper medication. In fact, the prescribed medication used to treat Lia's condition had immunosuppressant properties (i.e., depressing the immune system), which may have even created the conditions for an infection to occur. This neurologist recommended that the family should go back to Merced Medical Center and advise the doctors that it was not the Lee's noncompliance with the medication regimen that caused the big one, but rather the noncompliance of the doctors to consider the Hmong traditions and the doctors exclusive reliance on Western medical treatment that resulted in septic shock and irreversible brain damage. In summary, it was the physicians' commitment to the conclusion of *noncompliance* that kept them from considering any other possibilities including their own possible error in medication or treatment choice (i.e., there must have been a moral defect on the part of the parents based on culture; we are the good doctors, they are the bad parents; we are working to help their daughter and their noncompliance is making her condition worse).

As the story of the Lee family illustrates, medicine comprises a myriad of cultures, traditions, and customs that come together at the most inconvenient of times (i.e., emergencies and tragedies). Therefore, the lesson from this story is that culture matters and is ever present in all aspects of medical decision-making on the part of both the patient and the provider.

Culture and Interpersonal Communication

Many times when people speak of interpersonal relationships, they refer to them in terms of being static and stable. However, so many variables can affect the relationships between and among people. One major area of influence is that of culture. This section will present several aspects of culture that directly influence how relationships are created and maintained. These examples of cultural influences include *ethnocentrism, cultural encounter, stereotyping,* and *prejudice.* All of these are important within the healthcare environment because combinations of possible cultural influences between the healthcare provider and patient are virtually endless.

Ethnocentrism.   **Ethnocentrism** is the belief that the customs and practices of one's own culture are superior to those of other cultures (McCroskey & Richmond, 1996). The word *ethnocentrism* is a combination of two Greek words—*ethnos* meaning "nation" and *kentron* meaning "center." Positive and negative outcomes are associated with having high levels of ethnocentrism. For example, ethnocentrism can help maintain members of a culture, maintain the integrity of that culture against external threats, serve as a powerful source of cultural identity, and promote effective communication among all members of the culture. High levels of ethnocentrism, however, can also lead to the idea that one's culture is superior and thus more worthy than other cultures. This "more worthy" concept was demonstrated by the American doctors at Merced Medical Center in the story of Lia Lee. Ethnocentric behavior, when taken to an extreme, can lead to **xenophobia,** or the fear of strangers. This fear of outsiders can lead to isolation and prejudice. Taken as a whole, a moderate level of ethnocentrism serves to instill pride in its members without devaluing or feeling threatened by people of other cultures. Humans have a primary need to link to others of similar culture. For example, consider the various reunions, pride marches, and homecomings in which people regularly engage. This gives an idea as to the power of the innate human need for cultural identity.

According to Joseph DeVito (1994), ethnocentrism can be best thought of as a continuum containing five points: *equality, sensitivity, indifference, avoidance,* and *disparagement.* **Equality** reflects the lowest level of the ethnocentric spectrum. If both people have this level of ethnocentrism, the probability of

xenophobia

The fear of strangers.

effective communication is high. Unfortunately, when engaged in intercultural interaction, the probability of both communicators having an equal level of ethnocentrism is unlikely. **Sensitivity** is the second point on the ethnocentric spectrum and reflects the concept that one person is aware of the ethnocentrism of another person and, as such, the communication can be tailored to accommodate the ethnocentrism of the other person. The third point, **indifference,** reflects a tendency for a person to not pay attention to the culture or subcultures of other people because of a desire to communicate with people of their own culture. When people who are indifferent have to interact with people of other cultures, the indifferent person will display a greater level of ethnocentrism. **Avoidance,** the fourth point in the ethnocentrism spectrum, reflects a person who wants little or nothing to do with people of other cultures. If communicating with people from other cultures, the person practicing avoidance will attempt to evade the communication if at all possible. If the interaction occurs, the level of ethnocentrism displayed by the person will greatly interfere with competent communication. The final point on the ethnocentric spectrum is **disparagement** and reflects a person who displays a great deal of prejudice and intolerance for people of other cultures. Communication between this person and people of other cultures will most likely be aggressive and hostile. All these points of ethnocentrism are displayed in the book *The Spirit Catches You and You Fall Down: A Hmong Child, Her American Doctors, and the Collision of Cultures,* which was mentioned earlier in this chapter.

Cultural Encounter.   Sometimes when a person encounters a new culture, it can become overwhelming to the point where the newcomer to the culture has a hard time functioning within the new culture or having effective interactions with members of the new culture. **Culture shock** is the degree to which a person feels trauma related to the experience of a new culture. By the word *shock* we

culture shock
The degree to which a person feels trauma related to the experience of a new culture.

© tommaso79/Shutterstock.com

A person practicing avoidance will attempt to evade communication with people from other cultures.

The adjustment phase reflects a newcomer becoming more comfortable with his surroundings and feeling at ease.

mean a realization of an overwhelming experience as opposed to the medical term *shock*, which reflects the drop in blood pressure. According to Bellini, Baime, and Shea (2002), throughout the year of internship, doctors regularly experience moods such as depression, hostility, and fatigue. The process of encountering and becoming part of a new culture during a doctor's intern year is a four-phase process. First is the **honeymoon phase,** which reflects the first 3 months of the internship during which the person feels like a special guest that is there for a pleasant visit. Second is the **culture shock phase,** which is marked by feelings of despair and depression that occur between the third and sixth months of the intern year. Third is the **adjustment phase** and reflects the newcomer becoming more comfortable with his or her surroundings and feeling at ease with successfully navigating through the new environment and culture. This occurs between the sixth and ninth month. The final stage of the intern year is the **acculturation phase,** when the newcomer begins to become a member of the new culture and starts to reflect the verbal and nonverbal behaviors of the new culture, which, in this case, is the culture of being a physician. The acculturation phase occurs between 9 and 12 months. Bellini, Baime, and Shea (2002) caution that although the intern may experience emotions of depression, hostility, and fatigue during the initial encounter of the new culture, these negative emotions may contribute to a lack of empathy toward the patient later in the physician's career. This culture shock effect is so prominent during the medical specialty internship year that many physicians decide to change their medical specialty as a result.

Culture shock and the resulting emotional and professional impact on the physician can be of great cost to both the physician and the hospital, eventually adversely affecting patient care and safety. Such economic and safety concerns have led to the development of curricula to bring these issues to light for the newcomer before they experience such negative emotional states and for the institutions to become mindful of such an experience. More specifically, Andol-sek (2005) developed a training curriculum that addresses issues of resident fatigue, managing the disruptive physician, burnout, violations, impairment, stress, depression, substance abuse, and communication and cultural differences. Through such efforts, the effect of culture shock can be diagnosed and reduced.

Stereotyping. Through stereotyping people attempt to make sense of the people and cultures that exist around them (Neuliep, 2003). This sense-making behavior requires a person to make generalizations. When a person stereotypes, there is a tendency to make three different types of errors: *overestimating* the actual differences of the stereotyped group; *underestimating* the actual differences of the stereotyped group; and *expectancy validation,* which is when we find what we expect to find regarding differences of the stereotyped group. All people tend to stereotype, and this behavioral tendency is no different within healthcare. For example, healthcare professionals may use physical aspects of a patient to stereotype, such as with someone being obese, smelling of alcohol, being dressed in an unkempt way, or having a lack of personal hygiene. Patients also stereotype, such as assuming that the person wearing the white coat must be the most senior physician or the man is the one with the higher-level medical credentials or treating foreign-looking and -sounding healthcare providers with contempt or suspicion. No one is beyond this behavior because it serves a sense-making function. However, this same behavior can mask the truth regarding the other person's character, competence, and motivations.

| **stereotyping**
A sense-making behavior that requires people to make generalizations in order to make sense of the people and cultures that exist around them.

Prejudice. Prejudice refers to a prejudgment of people that is based on stereotyping. The judgments that people make are made long before the target person is encountered. Prejudice means that we prejudge a person or the behavior of the person based on very limited and insignificant information about the person's culture or subculture of origin. For example, "All football players have a high tolerance for pain" or "Women have a greater tolerance for pain than men." Evidence clearly indicates that pain and the tolerance of pain is an individual experience, and tolerance is based on the specific person, not a sport the patient plays or the patient's sex. Another popular stereotype is that "Surgeons love to cut." In fact, surgeons suggest surgery when they believe, based on their education, training, and experience, that surgery would be the most beneficial treatment for the patient.

| **prejudice**
A prejudgment of people based on stereotyping.

Cultural Empathy

Empathy is defined as an ability to show others that you have an understanding of how someone else is feeling or identify with their emotional experience (Wilmer, 1968). **Cultural empathy** refers to the ability to show other people that you have an understanding of how someone else is feeling in a way that reflects the specific cultural influences that comprise that person's experience. For example, how do patients of different cultures experience bad news? Experience pain? Experience impending death? In healthcare, the ability to express culturally appropriate empathy is always the recommended course. Learning

*How do you show empathy
to others?*

to understand how other people view and interpret things through different vantage points is far more of an accurate interpretation than interpreting the experience of another person through our own cultural filters. This concept is reflective of **cultural sensitivity,** or the ability to demonstrate an awareness of the cultural influence of another person. Intercultural communication can be improved through any of the 12 practices illustrated in Table 6.2.

By considering these 12 principles, we greatly enhance our chances of having an intercultural experience with the patient that is more positive, mindful, and competent.

table 6.2	**Twelve Behaviors of Cultural Sensitivity**

1. Recognize your own ethnocentrism; your patients are likely to have values different from yours.
2. Avoid derogating anyone else's culture.
3. Demonstrate respect for the other person and his or her culture.
4. Be empathetic.
5. Develop a higher tolerance for ambiguity.
6. Reduce the level of evaluation in your messages.
7. Be very careful when interacting with someone from another culture; it is the roles and rules of the patient's culture that must be adjusted to, not our own.
8. Be sensitive to relational/social needs of the patient as to whether or not they are from a culture that is high in context (heavy reliance on nonverbal cues such as Japanese and Hispanic cultures) or low context (heavy reliance on verbal messages such as the United States and Canada).
9. Do not assume that nonverbal messages, particularly gestures, are pancultural.
10. Be sensitive to both differences and similarities between and among cultures.
11. Work to build better more productive stereotypes not based on prejudgment.
12. Understand that meanings are in people, not in cultures. So much so that there can be as much diversity within a culture than between them.

Source: Neuliep, J. W. (2003). Intercultural communication: A contextual approach. Boston, MA: Houghton, Mifflin Company.

When we speak of cultural competence, especially within healthcare, we are referring to something that is inextricably linked to communication competence. Canales and Bowers (2001) argue that there should be little distinction made between competent healthcare and culturally competent care. Such "cultural" diversity includes gender, sexual orientation, age, racial or ethnic group, physical ability, physical challenge, religion, class, nationality, region, personal identities, and so on. These are but a few of the cultural factors involved in caring for "other." Therefore, when engaging in healthcare, we are caring for "other" and, as such, we are engaging in the practice of healing a patient as opposed to a person from a different culture. The concept of *patient* can be thought of as an umbrella term that includes any cultural distinctions that can be used to separate people from one another. Culture is not understanding a single story of a patient at a single time, but being able to recognize the complexity, diversity, and dynamic factors that affect those people we perceive as different. By understanding this process, healthcare professionals can become culturally competent and compassionate caregivers.

Interpreters and Translators.   In today's medical marketplace comprising patients and practitioners from a variety of cultures and traditions, practitioners must be both culturally and linguistically sensitive in their service to people who may be limited in their English proficiency or Western cultural traditions. Practitioners are aware of the most obvious of sensitivities such as treating patients with hearing impairment who, by federal mandate, require the availability of a signer. This ensures the ethically bound principle of having a linguistically competent interpreter for your patients (Ngo-Metzger et al., 2003). It should be noted that there is a marked difference between *interpretation* and *translation* in that **interpretation** refers to making sense of and relaying culturally sensitive oral communication, whereas **translation** refers to making sense of and relaying

© 2011, wavebreakmedia ltd, Shutterstock, Inc.

figure 6.2

Both the patient and the interpreter should face the healthcare provider in a meeting.

culturally sensitive written communication. The inclusion of an interpreter, although trained to be nothing more than the voice of the patient, makes the patient–provider dyad into somewhat of a triad (patient–patient interpreter–provider). A culturally sensitive interpreter is one who is trained in all aspects of ethics, impartiality, accuracy, and completeness. The interpreter must be able to relay with great accuracy not only the words of the patient, but also the feelings of the patient when sending the message. All of this must be done without interjecting any bias or opinion on the part of the interpreter.

It is extremely important to consider the unique dynamics that exist when using an interpreter. All interactions need to be performed at eye level. Furthermore, Herndon (2004) suggests that the interpreter should be seated beside the patient with both parties facing the healthcare practitioner. Figure 6.2 illustrates this concept.

The practitioner should initiate the interaction and clearly identify the role of the interpreter (Lee, 1997). Such behavior should keep the patient from developing a primary relationship with the interpreter and keep the relationship between the patient and provider. In fact, Lee advocates that two important aspects of interacting with a patient and interpreter must be considered by the healthcare provider before the interaction occurs. First, the practitioner should be aware of the age, gender, socioeconomic class, and any other ethnic and cultural differences that may exist between the patient and the interpreter. For example, it would be considered irreverent and disrespectful to use a young female interpreter with an older Asian male according to the Asiatic bias of patriarchy, which demands deference to the elderly. Second, prior to the clinician–patient encounter, if an interpreter is to be used, there should be a discussion beforehand that explains the medical terms and the condition that will be discussed (preconsultation education) before any interpretation begins. This process includes emphasizing that you and the interpreter are both part of the interdisciplinary clinical team. The interpreter serves as the "culturally sensitive" broker who will ultimately enhance or detract from the clinical interaction. As this indicates, the interpreter is a vital part of competent healthcare delivery.

According to Baker, Hayes, and Fortier (1998), patients who did not have an interpreter when they thought an interpreter was necessary reported being less satisfied with the patient–provider relationship. Similar negative outcomes as a result of language barriers were also observed by Sarver and Baker (2000) in emergency department visits. Patients who spoke the same language as their provider were given more follow-up appointments (83%). Also, 75% who communicated without an interpreter were given follow-up visits. Of the patients with a language barrier (i.e., speaking and understanding English), 76% reported that an interpreter should have been used but was not. This is of great concern given that there is a federal mandate requiring such assistance. Simply put, if the patient spoke English, he or she was given more follow-up appointments and if the patient did not, he or she was less likely to be given a follow-up appointment. It is important to note, however, that both fluent English-speaking patients and patients with language barriers were equally likely to comply with the follow-up instructions from the healthcare provider. Information regarding health information translation can be found at www.healthinformationtranslation.com. This site offers translation services in Arabic, Bosnian, Chinese (simplified), Chinese (traditional), English, French, Hindi, Japanese, Korean, Marshallese, Portuguese (Brazilian), Russian, Somali, Spanish, Tagalog, Ukrainian, and Vietnamese. This site is a collaborative effort facilitated by the Ohio State University Medical Center, Ohio Health, Mount Carmel Health System, Columbus Medical Association Foundation, American Medical Association Foundation, and the Mount Carmel Foundation.

Patient and Provider Assumptions

It is believed that within the patient–provider relationship, there is a disconnect between the perspective of the healthcare practitioner and the perspective of the patient. That is, the practitioner generally operates from a **disease framework.** The disease framework is primarily focused on obtaining the patient's history, performing the physical examination, and requesting the laboratory tests that contribute to a medical diagnosis in an effort to develop adequate treatment. The patient, however, operates from an **illness framework.** This framework has a primary focus on the affective state of the patient's fears, anxieties, expectations, feelings, and perceptions about illness in an effort to develop adequate treatment.

Murdock (1980) created two categories for how people from cultures throughout the world perceive illness. These categories consist of **natural causation** (i.e., infection, stress, organic deterioration, and accident or overt

Courtesy of Wheeling Hospital

figure 6.3

Hospital Visitor Policy Notice

human aggression) and **supernatural causation** (i.e., fate, contagion, and mystical retribution). Natural causation reflects **infections** such as sexually transmitted diseases, some of which include *HIV/AIDS*. Some of the most profound infections through human history included HIV/AIDS, which according to Mann (1987) is a disease in which the final stage of the disease is marked by stigma that wears down the victim, resulting in shame and isolation. *Leprosy* was a disease that was brought to Europe by Greek soldiers on their return from Asia in the century before Christ (Winkle, 1997). *Tuberculosis* and *polio* were both thought to be brought on by fatigue. More contemporary examples of natural causation include severe acute respiratory syndrome (*SARS,* a flu-like disease that can be fatal), which is believed to be related to chickens with most cases occurring in Hong Kong (Siu, 2008), and the recent global epidemic of *H1N1* (i.e., the Swine flu), which occurred in 2009 and 2010. In a direct response to the H1N1 outbreak, public health officials and hospital administrators throughout the country instituted policies in attempts to control the spread of the virus. Figure 6.3 illustrates one such attempt limiting the exposure hospital visitors have to the patient. **Stress** as a natural causation factor reflects disorders and diseases such as depression and burnout. There are also nonstress related organic deterioration of the brain such as *Alzheimer's* and *dementia*. The last type of natural causation is **accident or overt human aggression** and reflects trauma caused by automobile accidents, gunshot wounds, and stab wounds.

Supernatural Causation.   The first type of supernatural causation is **fate**, which is the belief in ominous sensations or feelings that something is going to happen and there is nothing that can done to stop it from occurring. The second type is **contagion** and reflects the rapid transmission or spread of disease from one person to another. The final type of supernatural causation is **mystical retribution**, which reflects the belief that a disease is caught or spread as a result of some deviant behavior or social practice. For example, some believe that *leprosy* was a disease that resulted from being unclean or being poor. Such a stigma perpetuated the imbalance of power and served as a barrier to social equality. During the Middle Ages, the *plague* was believed to be a punishment for misbehavior. In a more recent example, HIV/AIDS was viewed as a retribution for illegal drug use and the practice of homosexuality.

Stigma.   Despite the strong Judeo-Christian teachings of compassion, liberation, and hope (Messer, 2004), some Christian sects, notably the Evangelical church, believe that disease is a result of the "fall" of mankind and that redemption is reserved for the "chosen" or unaffected. The approach to disease susceptibility serves to either valorize or stigmatize people based on who either has or does not have a particular disease. Throughout the process of stigmatization, a person is considered either *sacred* or a *sinner, pure* or *impure, us* or *them*, resulting in creating an in-group and out-group membership. **Stigma** can be defined as a mark of disgrace that people can attach to something they regard as unacceptable.

Perhaps the most significant work on stigma has been conducted by Irving Goffman (1963), who indicated that stigma is an attitude that serves to significantly discredit the face of another person. According to Goffman, there are two main **models of the stigmatization process**. The first model is that of the **attribute as sufficient cause model** and reflects the qualities or traits that are seen as deficient or discrediting the moral being or moral character of the affected person. For example, if a person is of a different ethnic background than the larger group, the mere fact that the person belongs to that group may cause the people in the majority to project values and behavioral tendencies to the person in the minority such as was done to the European Jewish population during World War II. The second model is that of the **scapegoat model** and reflects the labeling of people who deviate from accepted social standards. For example, older men with earrings and various body piercings may be seen as "suspect" in character simply based on the attribute of being pierced and not on any other aspects of the person's character or behavior.

Healthcare: The Cultural Mosaic

The culture of medicine and healthcare in America is composed of an incredible number of subcultures contributing to an overall culture that is so pluralistic in nature it is extremely hard to define or agree on common attributes. Partly because of this multiculturalism, a crisis is developing in future projections of the number of physicians and nurses that will be practicing medicine. One of the governing agencies of postgraduate American medical education is the *Accreditation Council of Graduate Medical Education (ACGME)*, which notes that to meet the future needs for healthcare, medical schools will need to increase enrollment by 15%. However, at the current rate, American medical schools are predicted to grow only by 7.6% by the year 2020 (Aklea, Mustafa, Badair, & Schuneman, 2007). In light of this fact, the United States is making great effort to attract intelligence at the global level by "importing" qualified individuals from other countries to become providers in the American healthcare system. Currently, the largest international contributors to the American healthcare workforce are from India and the Philippines. This in part is because in both India and the Philippines, people are generally taught from texts written in English and the candidate's ability to write and comprehend English directly results in higher passage rates of the U.S. licensing examinations. This is illustrated in the fact that between the years 1995 and 2003, 14% of the newly licensed registered nurses in the United States were foreign educated. As the American population continues to become more diverse in culture and language, there is a greater demand for communicatively and culturally competent providers to accommodate such a demand.

As indicated earlier in this chapter, miscommunication can occur from people assigning different meanings to the words that others use to express and describe healthcare problems. For example, consider the particular set of symptoms that you would consider to be signs that you are coming down with a cold. Perhaps you would identify a headache, stuffy nose, and a cough. For someone of a different culture, symptoms could consist of a bad dream they experienced the night before or a particular occurrence from earlier in the day (e.g., a blackbird landed on their house). Culture can greatly influence which symptoms are seen as meaningful and how we express such symptoms to others. Therefore, culture can influence not only how people express themselves, but also how they see others. Davis and Flannery (2001) found that Puerto Rican women had greater trust in health information when the sources were similar in culture than sources of a different culture. These cultural differences are further cemented by a study comparing white, Japanese, and Pacific Islander patients who had cancer and their tendencies to obtain health information and what types of health sources were thought to be most reliable. The findings of this study indicated that ethnicity overrode any educational background in forming health choices. For Japanese and Pacific Islanders, the only credible source for health information is a physician of the same or similar ethnicity (Kakai, Maskarinec, Shumay, Tatsumura, & Tasaki, 2003). These findings mimic an earlier study by Cooper-Patrick (1999) indicating that African American patients reported greater satisfaction and participatory decision-making when their physician was also African American.

The Economics of Culture

Within the American healthcare system, perhaps one of the sharpest contrasts is that of patients who have insurance and patients who do not. According to U.S. government statistics, more than 45 million Americans lacked healthcare of any kind in fiscal year 2008 (U.S. Census Bureau, 2010). In 2006 more than 11 million immigrants in the United States were uninsured and accounted for 26.6% of all uninsured people in the country (Fronstin, 2007). Between the years 1996 and 2003, immigrants accounted for 86% of the growth in uninsured people (Fronstin, 2005). This growth in uninsured immigrants was a direct result of a U.S. immigration policy that barred any immigrant arriving in the U.S. after 1996 from participating in public health insurance programs such as Medicaid and the State Children's Health Insurance Program (SCHIP) for the first 5 years of residence in the United States (Rosenbaum, 2000). In 2007 the Robert Wood Johnson Foundation reported that 11.3% of children in the United States were uninsured. Of these, 37.8% were white, 17.5% were African American, 38.4% were Hispanic, and 6.3% were designated as "other." In total within the United States, 12.1% of the uninsured are white, 20.4% are African American, 33.5% are Hispanic, and 18% are listed as "other" (Population Survey Annual Social and Economic supplement, 2008). It is a common misconception that within this country it does not matter whether or not a person has health insurance. The reality is that 18,000 to 22,000 people in America die annually as a direct result of not having health coverage (Dom, 2004). Therefore, the culture of healthcare insurance, its reality, and its misconceptions all have to be revisited and reconceptualized based on these data alone.

Conclusion

This chapter introduced the concept of culture and how culture can serve as a profound influence on medicine including patient safety and satisfaction. The many subtle distinctions of communication between people of different backgrounds and the verbal and nonverbal barriers that are commonly encountered by healthcare professionals were discussed. The concepts of intercultural communication competence and cultural competence were introduced, highlighting the devastating effects that can occur when people cling to biases and faulty assumptions about others. The interpersonal relationships between patient and provider were introduced along with the possible benefits and pitfalls that accompany a person's level of ethnocentrism and their capacity to stereotype and engage in prejudices.

The need for cultural empathy was introduced as a core competency for delivering effective care. Such cultural empathy includes the proper use of verbal and nonverbal behavior, the appropriate use of interpreters, and awareness of the philosophical differences that exist between the physician and the patient. Further, how people interpret and are oriented to sickness and disease can be important pieces of information for the healthcare practitioner.

Finally, we introduced the internationalization of American medicine, the American patient, and the healthcare worker shortages that are projected. If we are to overcome these projected shortfalls, there will be a heavy reliance on healthcare workers from faraway cultures and places. The disparity of insured to uninsured has been demonstrated to not only be an alarming statistic, but also a direct reason for causes of death. The uninsured issue transcends race but is still predominately a "newer immigrant" issue. Healthcare providers must be aware of all barriers that can affect their pursuit of healing a patient, regardless of who, what, where, when, or why.

Questions for Discussion/Review

1. List and define the six contexts of communication and culture.
2. Define the concepts of synchrony and homophily and discuss how each of these can affect communication between a patient and a healthcare professional.
3. Discuss some of the implications of both verbal barriers and nonverbal barriers to effective communication within healthcare. Provide an example for both types of barriers.
4. Explain how changing ethnic and demographic trends in both patient and provider populations will affect the future of healthcare. Provide statistical data to support your answer.
5. Explain how the anchoring bias on the part of the healthcare provider can threaten patient safety and how the anchoring bias on the part of the patient can affect quality delivery of healthcare.
6. Explain the concept of ethnocentrism, its different levels, and its dynamic relationship to healthcare. Provide an example for your answer.
7. Define and provide an example of the cultural encounter process.
8. Explain the difference between empathy and cultural empathy. Why are both important to delivering quality healthcare?
9. Distinguish between interpretation and translation. Discuss when and how interpreters should be used. Provide an example for your answer.
10. Distinguish between natural causation and supernatural causation. Provide an example for each.
11. Discuss the two main models of stigmatization. Provide an example for each.

References

Aklea, E., Mustafa, R., Badair, F., & Schuneman, H. J. (2007). The United States physician workforce and international medical graduates: Trends and characteristics. *Journal of General Internal Medicine, 22,* 264–268.

Andolsek, K. M. (2005). *Life curriculum.* Retrieved March 23, 2010, from http://www.lifecurriculum.info

Baker, D. W., Hayes, R., & Fortier, J. P. (1998). Interpreter use and satisfaction with interpersonal aspects of care for Spanish-speaking patients. *Medical Care, 36,* 1461–1470.

Bellini, L. M., Baime, M., & Shea, J. A. (2002). Variation of mood and empathy during internship. *Journal of the American Medical Association, 287,* 3143–3146.

Canales, M. K., & Bowers, B. J. (2001). Issues and innovations in nursing education: Expanding conceptualizations of culturally competent care. *Journal of Advanced Nursing, 36,* 102–111.

Chong, N. (2002). *The Latino patient: A culturally competent guide for health care providers.* Boston, MA: Nicholas Brealey Publishing Company.

Cooper-Patrick, L., Gallo, J. J., Gonzales, J. J., Vu, H. T., Powe, N. R., & Nelson, C. (1999). Race, gender, and partnership in the patient–physician relationship. *Journal of the American Medical Association, 282,* 583–589.

Chugh, U., Agger-Gupta, N., Dillman, N. E., Fisher, D., Gronneru, D. P., & Julig, J. C. (1994). The case for culturally sensitive health care: A comparative study of health beliefs related to culture in six North-East Calgary communities. Calgary, Alberta, Canada: Citizenship and Heritage Secretariat.

Davis, R. E., & Flannery, D. D. (2001). Designing health information delivery systems for Puerto Rican women. *Health Education and Behavior, 28,* 680–695.

DeVito, J. (1992). *The interpersonal communication handbook* (6th ed.). New York: Harper Collins.

Dom, S. (January, 2004). *Uninsured and dying because of it: Updating the institute of medicine analysis on the impact of uninsurance on mortality.* Paper presented at the Urban Institute 2008 and final report release event, Insuring America's health: Principles and recommendations. Institute of Medicine.

Fadiman, A. (1997). *The spirit catches you and you fall down: A Hmong child, her American doctors, and the collision of two cultures.* New York: Straus and Giroux.

Fronstin, P. (2005). The impact of immigration of health insurance coverage in the United States. *EBRI Notes, 26.*

Fronstin, P. (2007). Sources of health insurance and characteristics of the uninsured: Analysis of the March 2002 current population survey. *EBRI, 310.*

Goffman, E. (1963). Stigma: Notes on the management of spoiled identity. Inglewood Cliffs, NJ: Prentice Hall.

Herndon, E., & Joyce, L. (2004). Getting the most from language interpreters. *Family Practice Management, 11,* 37–40.

Infante, D. A., Rancer, A. S., & Avtgis, T. A. (2010). *Contemporary communication theory.* Dubuque, IA: Kendall-Hunt.

Kakai, H., Maskarinec, G., Shumay, D. M., Tatsumura, Y., & Tasaki, K. (2003). Ethnic differences in choices of health information by cancer patients using complimentary and alternative medicine: An exploratory study with correspondence analysis. *Social Science and Medicine, 56,* 851–862.

Katz, M. (1998). *What is cultural competency?* Washington, DC: Department of Health and Human Services, Office of Minority Health. Retrieved December 26, 2010, from http://minorityhealth.hhs.gov/templates/browse.aspx?lvl=1&lvlid=3.

Klopf, D. W., & McCroskey, J. C. (2007). *Intercultural communication encounters.* Boston, MA: Allyn & Bacon.

Lee, E. (1997). Cross-cultural communication: Therapeutic use of interpreters. In E. Lee (Ed.), *Working with Asian Americans: A guide for clinicians* (pp. 477–489). New York: Guilford.

Mann, J. (October, 1987). *Statement at an informal briefing on AIDS.* Paper presented at the 42nd session of the United Nations General Assembly. New York.

McCroskey, J. C., & Richmond, V. P. (1996). *Fundamentals of human communication: An interpersonal perspective.* Prospect Heights, IL: Waveland Press.

Messer, D. E. (2004). *Breaking the conspiracy of silence: Christian churches and the global AIDS crisis.* Minneapolis, MN: Fortress.

Murdock, J. P. (1980). *Theories of illness: World survey.* Pittsburgh, PA: University of Pittsburgh Press.

Neuliep, J. W. (2003). *Intercultural communication: A contextual approach.* Boston, MA: Houghton Mifflin Company.

Ngo-Metzger, Q., Massagli, P., Clarridge, B. R., Manocchia, M., Davis, R. B., Iezzoni, et al. (2003). Linguistic and cultural barriers to health care. *The Journal of General Internal Medicine, 18,* 44–52.

Polack, E. P., Richmond, V. P., & McCroskey, J. C. (2008). *Applied communication for health professionals.* Dubuque, IA: Kendall Hunt.

Rogers, E. M., & Bhowmik, D. K. (1971). Homophily-heterophily: Relational concepts for communication research. *Public Opinion Quarterly, 34,* 523–538.

Sarver, J., & Baker, D. W. (2000). Effective language barriers on follow-up appointments after emergency department visits. *Journal of General Internal Medicine, 15,* 256–264.

Siu, J. Y. (2008). The SARS associated stigma of SARS victims in the post-SARS era of Hong Kong. *Qualitative Health Research, 8,* 729–738.

Wilmer, H. A. (1968). The doctor–patient relationship and issues of pity, sympathy and empathy. *British Journal of Medical Psychology, 41,* 243–248.

Winkle, S. (1997). *Cultural history of plagues.* Dusseldorf/Zurich: Artemis and Winkler.

chapter seven

Health Literacy:
The Not So Silent Epidemic

chapter objectives

Upon completion of the chapter, the student should be able to:

Literacy throughout the United States and the world is beginning to be considered a fundamental human right. The National Literacy Act of 1991 defines **literacy** as "an individual's ability to read, write, and speak in English, and compute and solve problems at levels of proficiency necessary to function on the job and in society, to achieve one's goals and develop one's knowledge and potential" (p. 7). Literacy pervades all aspects of a person's life. Poor literacy can significantly affect simple everyday tasks such as shopping, paying bills, and holding down a job. Some consider poor literacy as an epidemic resulting in a lower quality of life and a decreased life expectancy (Baker, Wolf, Feinglass, Thomas, Gazmararian, & Huang, 2007). This chapter will present information and data indicating the impact that literacy has on society in general and on health care in particular. As will be demonstrated throughout this chapter, literacy is quickly becoming one of the most expensive burdens of the U.S. system.

1. Compare and contrast the specialized vocabulary of terms associated with literacy

2. Explain the four areas of health literacy

3. Compare and contrast the assessment tools used to measure general literacy and health literacy

4. Explain the concept of e-health and its implication for health literacy

5. Explain the four-dimensional approach to helping patients with low literacy

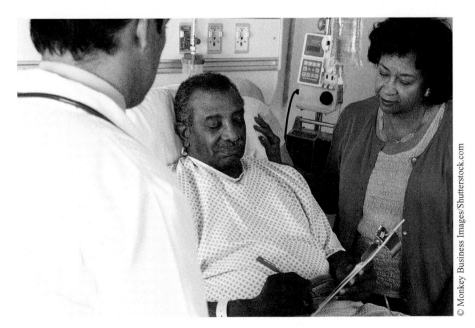

© Monkey Business Images/Shutterstock.com

key terms

cognitive chunking	literacy	rapid estimate of adult literacy
health literacy	newest vital sign (NVS)	in medicine (REALM)

literacy

An individual's ability to read, write, and speak English and compute and solve problems at levels of proficiency necessary to function on the job and in society; to achieve one's goals and develop one's knowledge and potential.

Illiteracy and Its Ubiquity

In a 1992 survey, 40 million American adults had a literacy rate at the 5th grade level or lower, whereas another 50 million had a literacy rate at the 7th or 8th grade level (Kirsch, Jungeblut, Jankins, & Kolstad, 2002). Taken as a whole, 90 million adults in this country have problems finding information, integrating information, and performing basic calculations. Low literacy levels serve to hobble a person in the most basic and fundamental ways. For example, performing day-to-day tasks and finding gainful employment are severely limited by low literacy levels.

Literacy is composed of three dimensions: *prose, document,* and *quantitative ability*. **Prose** is the ability to find information and have the skills necessary to follow instructions (e.g., the ability of a person who is scheduled for an x-ray in the morning to follow written instructions stating that they are not to eat or drink after midnight). **Document** refers to the ability to integrate or make sense of information. This requires a person to be able to read and synthesize information so as to be able to follow instructions. For example, a person is given written instructions to check

We use our literacy skills every day to perform a multitude of tasks.

© Iakov Filimonov/Shutterstock.com

their temperature every eight hours. If the temperature is greater than 101.7 °F, the patient should call the practitioner immediately. The third dimension of literacy is **quantitative ability** and reflects the ability to find numbers and be able to perform basic calculations, which require an understanding of numeracy and the skills necessary to perform as directed by the calculation. For example, on a prescription label a patient is instructed to take two pills every eight hours three times a day (six pills per day total). The ability to take the correct number of pills at the correct time reflects quantitative ability.

A follow-up study in 2005 comparing data to that of the 1992 study of Kirsch et al. (2002) indicated little to no improvement in the three dimensions of literacy. Only the dimension of quantitative ability increased slightly (Nielsen-Bohlman, Pranzer, & Kindig, 2004). The major findings of this study indicate that 89 million American people cannot read complex text or have difficulty in understanding complex instruction. Putting this in perspective, approximately one half of the U.S. adult population has limited literacy (Nielsen-Bohlman et al.). This limited literacy costs the U.S. healthcare system between $106 and $238 billion annually (Vernon, Trujillo & Rosenbaum, 2007).). In summary, this represents between 7 and 17% of all personal expenditures for health care and putting it into perspective, it would be enough to insure all of the more than 40+ million people who lacked healthcare insurance stimulating the development of the Affordable Care Act in 2010 (National Network of Libraries of Medicine). All of these data beg the basic question: *What is the impact of low literacy on healthcare and healthcare professionals?* Low levels of patient literacy severely impair the functioning of the healthcare environment and negatively affect the patient-healthcare professional dynamics, resulting in substandard care (American Medical Association, 1999; Schillinger, Piette, Grumbach, Wang, Wilson, Daher, 2003). In an Institutes of Medicine report titled A Prescription to End Confusion, the authors opine that efforts to improve quality, reduce cost/disparity cannot succeed without simultaneous improvement in health literacy (Institute of Medicine, 2004; Nielsen-Bohlman et al., 2004). Furthermore, the Agency for Health Care Research and Quality in two more recent reviews provided evidence as to the need to improve health literacy (Agency for Health Care Research and Quality, 2011).

Most patients, regardless of their level of literacy, seek the answers to four basic questions:

1. *What is my main problem (i.e., what is wrong with me)?*
2. *What do I need to do to alleviate this problem?*
3. *What can be done to make me better (i.e., what is the treatment plan)?*
4. *Why is this important for me to do (i.e., what is going to happen to me if I do not follow instructions)?*

It is in the answering of these questions where literacy significantly affects patient understanding and compliance.

Correctly reading a prescription requires quantitative ability.

Basic Terminology of Literacy

In attempting to understand the concept of literacy and its impact on society and health care, one must understand the unique vocabulary necessary to critically assess such impact (McKinney & Kurtz-Rossi, 2000). The language of literacy includes terms such as:

- **Adult education**—any education that is targeted toward adult populations *(androgogy)*.
- **Adult basic education (ABE)**—adult education that primarily targets reading, writing, and math skills that are at high school level or below.
- **Plain language (simple language and easy-to-read language)**—writing that is comprehensible at an 8th grade level or below and often contains large font size.
- **English as a second language (ESL)**—teaching efforts targeted at people whose first language is something other than English. Generally speaking, these efforts are focused on speaking, reading, and writing.
- **Grade level** (reading level)—average literacy skill associated with each grade in the K–12 American public school system. Grade level is commonly used as the standard way to describe the level of reading (e.g., ranging from easy to difficult) for a particular text.
- **Low literacy** (limited literacy)—having a reading level at or below 7th grade level or having deficiencies in both reading and writing such that necessary personal and work-related tasks suffer.
- **Participatory education**—education that fosters a team concept between the teacher and the learner such that the student becomes an active agent in acquiring necessary skills as opposed to being a passive receptacle for knowledge deposit.

Adult education is any education that is targeted toward adult populations.

- **Primary language**—the first acquired language and the language that is most used within one's home. With these terms defined, we can now present the implications of literacy specific to health care.

Defining Health Literacy

Although literacy affects all aspects of a person's life, there is no other area where literacy can mean the difference between life and death than that within the healthcare context. The American Medical Association (1999) defines health literacy as a constellation of skills that constitutes the ability to perform basic reading and numeric tasks for functioning in the healthcare environment and acting on healthcare information. Other scholars have argued that health literacy should include a working knowledge of the disease process (Nutbeam, 2000).

There is an incongruity between what is known about health literacy and what is practiced in the development of written health materials for patients. Most patient materials are written at a level that ranges from 11th grade to sophomore year in college. The fact remains that people have a reading level that is below this range, and those with a higher reading level often prefer material written at a 7th grade level (Davis, Crouch, Wills, Miller, & Adbehou, 1990; Kirsch et al., 2002). Therefore, healthcare professionals are designing and disseminating health information that is well above the target audience and quite likely contributing to increased uncertainty and anxiety on the part of the patient (i.e., healthcare consumer). Clearly there is a distinction between *literacy* and *health literacy*. Literacy refers to a general ability to read and write (Oxford-English Dictionary, 2003). It can be contextual in nature, however. For example, people can vary in their level of literacy in subject areas

health literacy
A constellation of skills that constitutes the ability to perform basic reading and numerical tasks for functioning in the healthcare environment and acting on healthcare information.

such as science, mathematics, engineering, music, and sports. Health literacy goes far beyond other contexts, in that regardless of a person's formal education or reading ability, people are motivated and have a high need for knowledge about their health. The American Medical Association (1999) identified four areas of health literacy that need to be addressed by researchers. These consist of *methods of health literacy screening* (i.e., the ways in which health literacy is assessed), *efforts to improve communication with patients with low literacy* (i.e., communication strategies to be used by the healthcare practitioner to increase patient understanding), *reductions in the cost and outcomes associated with poor health literacy, and the negative impact that poor health literacy has on the entire healthcare system*. Health literacy is such a major factor in current healthcare effort that it is considered the "currency for success" (Carmona, 2003).

Demographics of Health Literacy

As mentioned earlier in this chapter, approximately 90 million American adults have low levels of literacy. However, there are two particular demographic groups that are disproportionately affected: the poor and the elderly (Kirsch et al., 2002). This finding is made clear by a study investigating the cost differences between high literate (above 3rd grade level) and low literate (at or below 3rd grade level) Medicaid recipients (Weiss & Palmer, 2004). Results indicated that the patients with low literacy skills had significantly greater overall healthcare costs than patients with high literacy skills ($10,688 versus $2,891) and much greater impatient costs ($7,038 versus $824). In fact, when controlling for other factors that could contribute to these findings such as age, ethnic group, and health status, literacy level was the strongest predictor of cost. Overall, the findings of this and other studies indicate that patients with poor literacy skills have an overall poorer health status, are hospitalized more often, and make more visits to the emergency room than patients with high literacy skills (Baker, Gazmararian, Williams, Scott, Parker, & Green, 2002; Baker, Parker, Williams, Clark, & Nurss, 1997). In 1999, the Institutes of Medicine was requested to review the extent of disparity in health care based on race, ethnicity, and socioeconomic status. In this study, Unequal Treatment: Confronting Racial and Ethnic Disparities, the authors uncovered significant disparities particularly based on race even when insurance status, income, age, and severity of condition was comparable. Individuals that are in the minority are less likely to receive routine medical procedures and generally experienced a lower quality of services. For example, they are less likely to be given appropriate cardiac medications or undergo bypass surgery, they are less likely to receive dialysis or kidney transplant. In contrast, they are more likely to receive lower limb amputations for diabetes and other conditions. This study emphasizes that the healthcare community must be vigilant so that such disparity does not occur.

As people age their cognitive ability begins to diminish (Baker, Gazmararian, & Sudano, 2000). There is a direct relationship between the decline in cognitive abilities and declines in literacy levels. In fact, the majority of patients 60 years and older display low levels of literacy (5th grade or lower) (U.S. Department of Education, 1996). Further, 80% of elderly adults have difficulty completing the intake forms presented in the physician's office or hospital waiting rooms. In the year 2000, approximately 7% of U.S. adults did not speak English (U.S. Census, 2000). However, a 1999 study indicated that 34% of elderly who did speak English and 54% of the Spanish-speaking elderly had inadequate or marginal health literacy (Gazmararian, Baker, Williams, Parker, Scott, & Green, 1999).

Other factors that accompany the aging process include the prevalence of chronic conditions. It is logical that the impact of chronic conditions such as decreased vision, hearing loss, and cognitive impairment affects a person's level of health literacy (Wolf, Gazmararian, & Baker, 2005). Other chronic conditions that have been linked to poor health literacy include hypertension, diabetes, heart failure, and arthritis. Further evidence of the low health literacy–healthcare cost relationship was found in a study of Medicare patients indicating that elderly patients with low health literacy have overall higher medical costs and are less efficient in medical decision-making, resulting in fewer appropriate choices of medical services (e.g., emergency room versus doctor office visits) (Baker et al., 2002). Ultimately, poor literacy has been linked to higher levels of mortality. More specifically, in a longitudinal study of 3000 senior citizens, it was observed that over a six-year period seniors with low health literacy had a mortality rate of 39% compared to 29% for seniors with marginal literacy and 19% for seniors with high levels of literacy (Baker, Wolf, Feinglass, Thomas, Gazmararian, & Huang, 2007).

Race and ethnicity are strongly correlated with health literacy. The National Adult Literacy Survey (1992) reported that white populations scored between 25 and 80 points higher on literacy tests than nonwhite

© Syda Productions/Shutterstock.com

How can the aging process affect a person's literacy level?

populations (Raudenbush & Kasim, 1998). This discrepancy in literacy scores translates into different health outcomes. This finding is supported in hospital research indicating that 35% of English-speaking patients and 62% of Spanish-speaking patients have fair to poor literacy (Williams, Parker, Baker, Parikh, Pitkin, & Coates, 1995). How is the provider to overcome such barriers to literacy? What most patients look for in a clinician is someone who uses plain English and simple expression and is able to break down information (chunk) into small segments (e.g., not more than three items at a time, ensuring that the most important elements of the information are first stressed). If the patient does not understand, a communicatively competent practitioner will ask the patient to repeat the information just presented, take extra time to ensure the patient understands, and treat the patient with dignity and respect. Regardless of a person's cognitive capacities, the complexities of the healthcare system can overwhelm anyone, regardless of their literacy or education level (*Wall Street Journal,* 2004). Therefore, it is imperative for clinicians to be able to adapt their communication to the literacy level of each patient. Such adaptation is not only ethical and the right thing to do, but it is also a good medicine and business.

Healthcare practitioners can use several other strategies when communicating with patients with low health literacy. The National Patient Safety Foundation outlined a list of historically problematic words/phrases for patients with low literacy divided into four categories: *medical words, concept words, value judgment words*, and *category words*. The list also offers more easily understandable alternatives for each problematic words/phrases. Figure 7.1 illustrates these concepts.

Some things that occur in health care may transcend the specific medical context (environment) within which they occur. Communicating with patients with low health literacy is one such cross-contextual practice. Regardless of the context, when communicating with patients with low health literacy, providers should (a) use pictures or visual aids, (b) be repetitive and redundant, and (c) use reflective or active listening techniques. The use of visual aids will improve information retention by 20% (Michielutte, Bahnson, Dignan, & Schroeder, 1992; Murphy, A. Chesson, Walker, Arnold, & L. Chesson, 2000; Sepucha & Mulley, 2003; Wydra, 2001). To help with understanding, repeat the information and say it in a different way. However, be careful to limit the information to no greater than three points (information chunking; Figure. 7.2). Also, be sure to use reflective or active listening techniques such as having the patient "teach back" what they have just been told. Such techniques, along with demonstrating respect, caring, and sensitivity toward the patient, serve to reduce uncertainty and internal noise that can create stress in the patient–provider relationship.

figure 7.1

Problematic Words/Phrases and Suggested Alternatives

Medical Word Examples: Words frequently used by doctors and in health care institutions

PROBLEM WORD	ACCEPTABLE ALTERNATIVE
Ailment	Sickness; Illness; problem with your health
Benign	Will not cause harm; is not cancer
Condition	How you feel; health problem
Dysfunction	Problem
Inhibitor	Drug that stops something that is bad for you
Intermittent	Off and on
Lesion	Wound; sore; infected patch of skin
Oral	By mouth
Procedure	Something done to treat your problem; operation
Vertigo	Dizziness

Concept Word Examples: Words frequently used to describe an idea, metaphor, or notion

PROBLEM WORD	ACCEPTABLE ALTERNATIVE
Active role	Taking part in
Avoid	Stay away from; do not use (or eat)
Collaborate	Work together
Factor	Other thing
Gauge	Measure; get a better idea of; test (dependent on context)
Intake	What you eat or drink; what goes into your body
Landmark	Very important (adj.) Important event; turning point (n)
Option	Choice
Referral	Ask you to see another doctor; get a second opinion
Wellness	Good health; feeling good

The Words to Watch Fact Sheet is reprinted courtesy of National Patient Safety Foundation.

Continued

figure 7.1 (*continued*)

Category Word Examples: Words frequently used to describe a group or subset that may be unfamiliar to the patient

PROBLEM WORD	ACCEPTABLE ALTERNATIVE
Activity	Something you do; something you do often, like driving a car
Adverse (reaction)	Bad
Cognitive	Learning; thinking
Hazardous	Not safe; dangerous
High-Intensity Exercise	Use an example, such as running
Generic	Product sold without a brand name, like ibuprofen (Advil is brand name)
Noncancerous	Not cancer
Poultry	Chicken, turkey, etc.
Prosthesis	Replacement for a body part, such as manmade arm
Support	Help with your needs—for money, friendship, or care

Value Judgment Word Examples: Words that may need an example or visual to convey their meaning with clarity

PROBLEM WORD	ACCEPTABLE ALTERNATIVE
Adequate	Enough *Example (adequate water): 6–8 glasses a day*
Adjust	Fine-tune; change
Cautiously	With care; slowly *Example: making sure to hold on to handrails*
Excessive	Too much *Example (bleeding): if blood soaks through the bandage*
Increase gradually	Add to *Example (exercise): add 5 minutes a week*
Moderately	Not too much *Example (exercise): so you don't get out of breath*
Progressive	Gets worse (or better)
Routinely	Often *Example: every week; every other day*
Significantly	Enough to make a difference *Example (smoking/heart disease): 2 times the chance of having heart disease*
Temporary	For a limited time; for about (an hour, day…) *Example: for less than a week*

figure 7.2

Steps of Information Chunking

Before:

Instructions for Use of a Metered-Dose Inhaler

1. Remove the mouthpiece from the inhaler.
2. Insert the inhaler into the spacer.
3. Shake the inhaler four to five times.
4. Breathe out.
5. Place the mouthpiece of the spacer between your teeth, above your tongue.
6. Close your lips around it.
7. Press down on the inhaler once.
8. Take a slow, deep breath.
9. Hold your breath for 5 to 10 seconds after inhaling.
10. Remove the spacer from your mouth and exhale.

With Chunking:

Get Ready	Get Set	Go
1. Take the cap off the inhaler. 2. Insert the inhaler into the spacer. 3. Shake the inhaler 4 to 5 times.	1. Breathe out. 2. Put the open end of the spacer between your teeth, above your tongue. 3. Close your lips around the spacer.	1. Press down on the inhaler. 2. Take a slow deep breath. 3. Hold your breath for 5 to 10 seconds, then breathe out.

Source: Wolf, M. S., Lindquist, L., & Skripkauskas, S. (2008). Health literacy from epidemiology to intervention. In E. P. Polack, V. P. Richmond, & J. C. McCroskey (Eds.), Applied communication for health professionals (pp. 93–108). Dubuque, IA: Kendall-Hunt.

Assessing Health Literacy

Given that health literacy is a major factor in patient safety and the quality of medical care, how do we go about assessing health literacy? Literacy, unlike blood pressure, cholesterol, or any host of other biological assessments, is much more complex because low literacy is seen as a stigma. In fact, it is common for people to develop elaborate strategies to hide their lack of literacy from others. Health literacy is no different. Many patients will nod their heads in agreement (engage in literate-like behaviors) with a healthcare professional whose messages they do not understand or they will bring a family member with them to explain information that was presented by the healthcare professional.

These *literate-like* behaviors may suggest that patients are higher in health literacy than they actually are. For example, in a study conducted by Bass, Wilson, Griffith, and Barnett (2002) medical students were asked to identify patients who they believed were low in health literacy. This process resulted in 10% of the sample of patients being identified as low in health literacy. In fact, after being tested using established literacy measures, 33% of the sample were low in health literacy; thus patient literacy results in an additional $75 billion annual cost for the healthcare system (Friedland, 1998). According to the Center for Health Care Strategy, the cost of low health literacy is greater than the amount Medicare pays for physician services, dental services, home health care, drugs, and nursing home care combined (IOM, 2004).

Most physicians attempt to measure the literacy of their patients by making the mistake of asking the patient the highest grade or level of education they have completed. As indicated earlier, the final grade that patients report completing is often higher than their literacy level (Kirsch et al., 2002). For example, patients may report completing high school yet have an 8th grade reading comprehension level. Many high school graduates are illiterate. This level of illiteracy is exacerbated by aging (i.e., increased time since formal education; decreased sensory abilities [hearing and seeing]), thus making the difference between formal education and actual literacy level notable. Many patients who have low health literacy will tell you that they read "well." Therefore, there is a high degree of self-protection and image maintenance on the part of the patient. This willingness to capitulate to the physician and "act literate" is doing more harm than good. In an effort to circumvent such patient behavior, healthcare professionals are advised to look to other patient behaviors to determine a more accurate health literacy level. For example, Saffer and Keenan (American Medical Association, 1999) developed a typology of behaviors that are possible indicators of low health literacy: (a) asking staff for help with paperwork; (b) bringing along a family member or friend who reads documents to them; (c) failing to keep appointments (i.e., avoidance behavior); (d) making excuses (e.g., I forgot my glasses); (e) not complying with directives (e.g., do not take proper dose, timely dose, or any dose); or (f) having poor adherence to recommended interventions. For example, in Medicare populations, women with inadequate literacy are less likely than women with adequate literacy skills to have a Pap test performed (Scott, Gazmararian, Williams, & Baker, 2002).

Assessment Tools

Several instruments are available to assess a person's general literacy and health literacy. One widely used general literacy assessment tool is the **Wide Range Achievement Test (WRAT)**, which is a general literacy measure that assesses a person's ability to read words, comprehend sentences, spell, and compute solutions to math problems. The WRAT was originally developed in 1941 and is now in its fourth edition (Reynolds & Fletcher-Janzen, 2007). Focusing specifically on health literacy, the Rapid Estimate of Adult Literacy in Medicine (REALM) is a measure designed to accurately assess a patient's level of health literacy. The REALM lists several dozen commonly used medical terms. The patient is instructed to read aloud the list of terms to the best of their ability. The more words the patient is able to pronounce correctly, the greater the level of health literacy. Figure 7.3 presents the REALM measure.

rapid estimate of adult literacy in medicine (REALM)

A measure designed to accurately assess a patient's level of health literacy.

Figure 7.3

The Rapid Estimate of Adult Literacy in Medicine (REALM)

Rapid Estimate of Adult Literacy in Medicine

Patient name _____ Date of birth _____ Reading level _____

Date _____ Clinic _____ Examiner _____ Grade completed _____

List 1		List 2		List 3	
Fat	☐	Fatigue	☐	Allergic	☐
Flu	☐	Pelvic	☐	Menstrual	☐
Pill	☐	Jaundice	☐	Testicle	☐
Dose	☐	Infection	☐	Colitis	☐
Eye	☐	Exercise	☐	Emergency	☐
Stress	☐	Behavior	☐	Medication	☐
Smear	☐	Prescription	☐	Occupation	☐
Nerves	☐	Notify	☐	Sexuality	☐
Germs	☐	Gallbladder	☐	Alcoholism	☐
Meals	☐	Calories	☐	Irritation	☐
Disease	☐	Depression	☐	Constipation	☐
Cancer	☐	Miscarriage	☐	Gonorrhea	☐
Caffeine	☐	Pregnancy	☐	Inflammatory	☐
Attack	☐	Arthritis	☐	Diabetes	☐
Kidney	☐	Nutrition	☐	Hepatitis	☐
Hormones	☐	Menopause	☐	Antibiotics	☐
Herpes	☐	Appendix	☐	Diagnosis	☐
Seizure	☐	Abnormal	☐	Potassium	☐
Bowel	☐	Syphilis	☐	Anemia	☐
Asthma	☐	Hemorrhoids	☐	Obesity	☐
Rectal	☐	Nausea	☐	Osteoporosis	☐
Incest	☐	Directed	☐	Impetigo	☐

List 1 score _____   List 2 score _____   List 3 score _____

Raw score _____

Directions:
1. Give the patient a laminated copy of the REALM form and score answers on an unlaminated copy that is attached to a clipboard. Hold the clipboard at an angle so that the patient is not distracted by your scoring. Say: "I want to hear you read as many words as you can from this list. Begin with the first word in List 1 and read aloud. When you come to a word you cannot read, do the best you can or say, 'blank' and go onto the next word."
2. If the patient takes more than five seconds on a word, say "blank" and point to the next word, if necessary, to move the patient along. If the patient begins to miss everyword, have him or her pronounce only known words.
3. Count as an error any word not attempted or mispronounced. Score by marking a plus (+) after each correct word, a check (√) after each mispronounced word, and a minus (−) after words not attempted. Count as correct any self-corrected words.
4. Count the number of correct words for each list, and record the numbers on the "Score" line. Total the numbers, and match the score with its grade equivalent in the table below.

Scores and Grade Equivalents for the REALM Questionnaire

Grade equivalent

Raw score	Grade range
0 to 18	Third grade and below; will not be able to read most low-literacy materials; will need repeated oral instructions, materials composed primarily of illustrations, or audio or video tapes
19 to 44	Fourth to sixth grade; will need low-literacy materials, may not be able to read prescription lables
45 to 60	Seventh to eighth grade; will struggle with most patient education materials; will not be offended by low-literacy materials
61 to 66	High school; will be able to read most patient education materials

Source: Davis, T. C., Long, S. W., Jackson, R. H., Mayeaux, E. J., George, R. B., Murphy, P. W. (1993). Rapid estimate of adult literacy in medicine: A shortened screening instrument: Family Medicine, 25, 391–395. Reprinted with permission from the Society of Teachers of Family Medicine, www.stfm.org.

A third measure of health literacy is the **Test of Functional Health Literacy in Adults (TOFHLA)** (Parker, Baker, Williams, & Nurss, 1995). The WRAT and REALM measures are both word recognition tests. The TOFHLA, however, is a bit different in that it asks the patient to read passages in which every fifth to seventh word is deleted and the patient must insert the correct word from a choice of four words. In addition, the TOFHLA may ask the subject to respond to a prompt such as information found on pill bottle instructions and appointment slips. This process serves to assess both the reading and numerical comprehension of the patient rather than just the ability to recognize and pronounce words. One of the drawbacks of all three measures reviewed thus far is that they are all developed and written in English (Baker et al., 2003). Weiss, Mays, Martz, Castro, DeWalt, Pignone, Mockbee, and Hale (2005) developed a bilingual instrument known as the Newest Vital Sign (NVS). The NVS is applicable in both Spanish and English and involves reading a nutrition label and a label on a container of ice cream. The patients are then asked six questions regarding what they have read. The entire test takes approximately three minutes to complete (Weiss et al.). Figure 7.4 displays the NVS measure. Wolfe, Williams, Parker, Parikh, Nowlan and Baker (2007) caution against using patient assessment tools in clinical practice because by using these instruments, you may create patient shame instead these authors caution that communication must be improved so as to foster a culture that emphasizes mutual understanding in communication. Going back to our original definition of communication, the process of a source creating meaning in the mind of a receiver through verbal and nonverbal messages.

newest vital sign (NVS)

A bilingual measure of health literacy (in both Spanish and English) that involves having a patient read a nutrition label on a container of ice cream and then they are asked six questions about what they have read.

E-Literacy

Globally, healthcare systems remain provider based and all too often patients and their families are not as engaged as they should be (Fowler, Gerstein, & Barry 2013). According to Workman, deBronkart, Quinlan, and Pinder (2014) patients want reciprocal communication, emotional support, empathy, and personalization of coordinated services and continuity of care. They desire information and education that is easy to understand, reliable, pertinent, and they would like to be involved in decision-making as well as to be treated with privacy, confidentiality, and dignity. Carman, Maurer, Mallery, Wang, Garfinkel, Richmond, and Windham (2013) also report that patients want more education about evidenced-based medicine and what healthcare costs. Patients also advocate that the patient should have involvement in the organizational structure and the policies that govern health care. One major factor changing the healthcare landscape from a provider model to a collaborative model was the Affordable Care Act of 2010 which created several innovations that include the **Accountable Care Organization (ACO)**, which is a network of healthcare providers that will provide for total care of the patient including primary care and specialty care. The network will receive a payment for all care provided to the patient, and the organization will be held accountable for quality and cost of care. In return, Medicare and Medicaid would provide financial incentives for these organizations to improve the quality of care and reduce costs by allowing the providers to participate in this risk sharing agreement (Kaiser Family Foundation 2014), and The **Medical Home** (PCMH Patient-Centered Medical Home) generally led by a primary care physician for patients of all ages is designed to provide a comprehensive package of medical care, and also designed to increase satisfaction and improve health (American Academy of Family Physicians, 2015). A paradigm shift from the provider-centered model to a model of mutuality.

The Internet is an increasingly accessible communication channel for a growing segment of the population that will eventually lead to significant changes in consumer behavior (National Academy of Sciences, 2000). The use of the Internet, email, and other mediated technologies in the healthcare arena is known as e-health (Eng, 2001). According to Cline and Haynes (2001), e-health is defined as "reflecting a paradigm shift by offering interactivity and reciprocal influence, pointing toward *transactional* rather than a one-way process and blending interpersonal and mass communication processes" (p. 676). The use of technology allows for patients, contingent on the fact that they are willing to do so, to become a partner in their care alongside the healthcare provider. Traditionally, many patient experiences with health care have been one of simple compliance with the wishes of the healthcare practitioner where there was little to no opportunity to participate in their own care (Connecting for Health, 2004). The use of communication technology has drastically altered the patient–provider relationship—it was once one of paternalism and is now one of mutuality.

The Internet is a technology medium that, although ubiquitous throughout the United States, is not evenly distributed among all Americans. It is estimated that 63% of American adults use the Internet, with an ever-increasing amount of people using it to specifically look for health-related information. Women are more likely to seek out health information not only for themselves, but also for members of their family (Madden & Rainie, 2003). Although the degree of increase in Internet use is difficult to determine (Baker, Wagner, Singer, & Bundorf, 2003), in 2004, approximately 17% of people of age 69 or older have used the Internet, 46% between ages 59 and 68 have access to the Internet, whereas 62% of people 50 to 58 years of age were actually online (Fox, 2004). There is an education factor that influences Internet use for health information. The largest percentage of health-information seekers on the Web have at least a 2-year college degree (*Health Care News,* 2003), with elderly populations in rural areas with fewer than 12 years of education rarely using the Internet (Licciardore, Smith-Barbato, & Coleridge, 2001).

Noblin, Wan, Fottler (2014) thought to prove a hypothesis that patients who were younger, more educated, and had a higher income would be more willing to adopt the personal health record (PHR). This hypothesis was refuted because none of the factors (age, education, and income) were statistically significant as to one's willingness to adopt a personal health record.

figure 7.4

The Newest Vital Sign

Nutrition Facts

Serving Size	½ cup
Servings per container	4

Amount per serving

Calories	250	Fat Cal	120

	%DV
Total Fat 13g	20%
Sat Fat 9g	40%
Cholesterol 28mg	12%
Sodium 55mg	2%
Total Carbohydrate 30g	12%
Dietary Fiber 2g	
Sugars 23g	
Protein 4g	8%

*Percentage Daily Values (DV) are based on a 2,000 calorie diet. Your daily values may be higher or lower depending on your calorie needs.

Ingredients: Cream, Skim Milk, Liquid Sugar, Water, Egg Yolks, Brown Sugar, Milkfat, Peanut Oil, Sugar, Butter, Salt, Carrageenan, Vanilla Extract.

Source: http://www.pfizerhealthliteracy.com/physicians-providers/newest-vital-sign.html.

Continued

Score Sheet for the Newest Vital Sign Questions and Answers

READ TO SUBJECT: This information is on the back of a container of a pint of ice cream.

	ANSWER CORRECT?	
	yes	**no**

1. If you eat the entire container, how many calories will you eat?

   Answer: 1,000 is the only correct answer

2. If you are allowed to eat 60 grams of carbohydrates as a snack, how much ice cream could you have?

   Answer: Any of the following is correct: 1 cup (or any amount up to 1 cup), Half the container Note: If patient answers "two servings," ask "How much ice cream would that be if you were to measure it into a bowl."

3. Your doctor advises you to reduce the amount of saturated fat in your diet. You usually have 42 g of saturated fat each day, which includes one serving of ice cream. If you stop eating ice cream, how many grams of saturated fat would you be consuming each day?

   Answer: 33 is the only correct answer

4. If you usually eat 2500 calories in a day, what percentage of your daily value of calories will you be eating if you eat one serving?

   Answer: 10% is the only correct answer

READ TO SUBJECT: Pretend that you are allergic to the following substances: Penicillin, peanuts, latex gloves, and bee stings.

5. Is it safe for you to eat this ice cream?

   Answer: No

6. (Ask only if the patient responds "no" to question 5): Why not?

   Answer: Because it has peanut oil.

Interpretation

Number of correct answers:

Score of 0-1 suggests high likelihood (50% or more) of limited literacy
Score of 2-3 indicates the possibility of limited literacy.
Score of 4-6 almost always indicates adequate literacy.

Do you use the Internet to access health information?

A generation gap has been documented regarding Internet use for health-care information. More specifically, 31% of seniors age 65 and older reported accessing health information online. This number is dwarfed by 70% of the baby-boom generation (ages 50–64) reporting Internet use for health information (Kaiser-Permanente, 2005). In just four short years, Internet use for healthcare information has exploded. Compare this to the fact that in 2001, Licciardone, Smith-Barbado and Coleridge (2001) reported that the Internet is one of the least used media channels (32%) when compared to 69% of health information coming from newspapers and magazines, 56% from television, and 30% from the radio.

Internet Information Credibility

The IOM (2001) cautions that the Internet, when it comes to healthcare information, is an unregulated territory where no person or organization is responsible for the content and quality. In fact, 86% of people who access information via the Web are concerned with the reliability and validity of the information (Fox & Rain, 2000). Interestingly enough, although people report having concerns over the quality of information on the Web, research indicates that those same people rarely check website information and ignore disclaimers and/or disclosure statements (Eysenbach & Kohler, 2002; Jadada, 2002). In all due fairness to Internet-based information, other media sources for health information such as newspapers, magazines, books, and television programs are also sources whose information accuracy is unregulated. Therefore, the sheer amount of information pertaining to a specific disease and the varying perspectives pertaining to that disease are left to the consumer to sift through and assess for quality (Delamote, 2000). It has been suggested that to assist the consumer in filtering through the available information, health-related information should be customized for specific socio-demographic factors such as culture, health beliefs, health-specific behaviors, and level of ethnocentrism (Kreuter, Lukwango, Bucholtz, Clarke, & Sanders Thompson, 2002). Such targeted information is believed to be more relevant to the patient, results in higher levels of patient satisfaction, and results in greater intention to comply with the advocated behavior (e.g., exercise, periodic checkups) than does generic health information (Oenema, Brug, & Lechner, 2001).

Identifying and Adapting to Low Health Literacy

Over the past decade, many attempts have been made to improve health literacy levels on behalf of both the patient and provider. However, few of these efforts are ever evaluated for validity and actual impact on patient outcomes. Outcomes can reflect anything from patient perceptions of quality and perceptions of satisfaction, to compliance with medical directives and lower morbidity. The writing of health-related materials has been an area of improvement; literacy advocates have attempted to rewrite health materials at a simpler level or target them to a microsegment of the population (e.g., culture-specific or age-specific materials) to enhance reading comprehension (Pignone, DeWalt, Sheridan, Berkman, & Lohr, 2005). It should be noted that some of these efforts have been met with little to no success (Davis, Fredrickson, Arnold, Murphy, Herbst, & Bocchini, 1998). As with most print-based materials, health literacy advocates believe that the integration of multimedia and multimodal presentations may reveal greater patient understanding and retention. Unlike print material, multimedia presentations can be easily adapted to microsegments of patients to achieve maximum message effectiveness. To this point, there is no conclusive information determining whether there are differences in effectiveness between print and multimedia presentations of health information.

A few promising interventions have proved effective initially in combating low health literacy. For example, efforts directed at improving clinicians abilities to recognize and adapt communication to accommodate the patient with low literacy has resulted in promising results (Ferreira, Dolan, Fitzgibbon, Davis, Gorby, & Ladewski, 2005). Further, ongoing education efforts between the primary caregiver and patients with chronic illness such as diabetes have also proved beneficial (Rothman, DeWalt, Malone, Bryant, Shintani, & Crigler, 2004).

Simplifying the Link between Health Literacy and Outcomes

Perhaps one of the most effective and simplest ways to conceptualize the link between health literacy and outcomes was proposed by Wolf et al. (2008). It is predicated on the concept that health literacy is one of the strongest socio-demographic indicators of health outcomes such as age, race, ethnicity, cognitive ability, education, culture, and occupation—the known socio-demographic variables that have been linked to negative health outcomes (Figure. 7.5). All of these contribute to the level of health literacy, which then, in turn, regulates the health outcome including the level of information accessed (e.g., simple versus complex), level of self-efficacy, disease preventive behavior, and self-care.

The American Medical Association advocates that practitioners utilize a four-dimensional approach to helping patients with low literacy, which includes *identifying patients with limited health literacy, adopting universal precautions, integrating the "teach-back" method,* and *enhancing print materials.* The approach of identifying patients with low health literacy is primarily based on socio-demographic characteristics of the patient. More specifically, patients who are older, less educated, poor, and of minority status tend to have lower levels of health literacy than others. Therefore, it is advocated that healthcare professionals inquire/observe how their patients obtain health information and implement suggested health-related behaviors. For example, if an elderly patient is instructed on how to use a glucose monitoring device, how well does that patient implement the suggested behaviors? Did they seek out any information about their condition before coming in? Did they bring a family member on whom they are relying to assist them in interpreting the instructions? Any of these can be an indicator of poor health literacy. Unfortunately, routine screening for health literacy is only advocated after conclusive evidence supports it. Conclusive evidence in this case would be only the most obvious or extreme forms of illiteracy. Being mindful to patient behaviors can be a powerful tool in early diagnosis and intervention for the patient with low health literacy. A valuable website for practitioners to gauge literacy estimates for their practice is www.casas.org/lit/litcode/Search.cfm (CASAS, 2007).

figure 7.5

Model of Health Literacy and Health Outcomes.

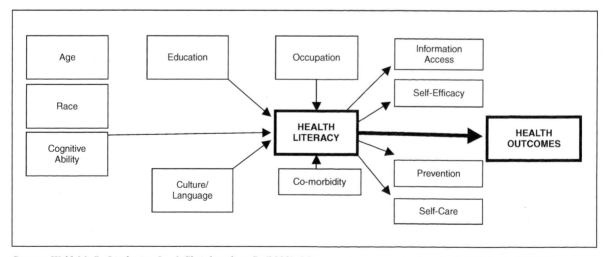

Source: Wolf, M. S., Lindquist, L., & Skripkauskas, S. (2008). Messages in communication. In E. P. Polack, V. P. Richmond, J. C. McCroskey (Eds.). Applied communication for health professional (pp. 93–108). Dubuque, IA: Kendall-Hunt.

What can a healthcare professional do when he or she suspects a patient has low health literacy? According to Wolf et al. (2008), "[S]imple, direct, and respectful questions can alleviate much of the shame and stigma a patient may feel with regard to any such limitations. For instance, a provider may simply and politely ask, 'Do you have any trouble reading print forms?' or, 'How often do you have someone help you read your health materials?', or 'Do you have any problems learning about your medical condition?'" (p. 100). Other devices to combat low literacy include streamlining clinical practices such that forms and questioning routes are kept as simple and as brief as possible and instituting uniform policies as to mandatory health literacy assessment for all patients seeking care. Such a uniform policy will assist in early detection in a nonstigmatizing way (as opposed to picking the "suspected" patient out for literacy assessment).

The second dimension in combating low health literacy is the adoption of universal precautions. Although there are vast differences in communication based on the type of medicine practiced, medical specialty, patient demographics, and so on, there are universal practices that can and should be used regarding health literacy, such as standardizing language use and questioning routes. For example, speak simply and only use medical jargon when necessary, ensuring that all terms are clearly defined. The use of universal clinical interview techniques should also be implemented in efforts to create a "health literate" environment. As mentioned earlier in this chapter, patients want to know what is wrong with them, what will be done to get them better, and how the proposed treatment will improve the problem.

The third dimension in combating low health literacy is the utilization of the "teach-back" technique when consulting with a patient. This technique is a way to cement the patients' understanding of material. Simply put, after the practitioner has presented the diagnosis and proposed treatment, the patient is then asked to educate the practitioner on the information that was just presented to them. This process allows for the patient to communicate the diagnosis and proposed treatment in his or her own words. According to Wolf et al. (2008), "[U]se of the teach-back technique will aid in identifying and correcting misinformation, allow for teachable moments, and further solidify understanding among patients" (p. 101). Methods such as the teach-back technique have been shown to improve understanding of glycemic control in patients with diabetes (Schillinger, Grumbach, Piette, Wang, Osmond, & Daher, 2002).

The final dimension in combating health literacy is the enhancement of print materials. The simplification of print materials entails avoiding the use of complicated medical terminology unless absolutely necessary. This includes writing information at a comprehension level of 8th grade or lower, clearly stating objectives, effectively packaging information, using multimedia channels, and utilizing cognitive chunking. Cognitive chunking refers to the grouping of related information in a way that is easy for a person to commit to both short-term and long-term memory. Figure 7.2 illustrates the cognitive chunking procedure. Some researchers argue that four to seven pieces of new information should be given at a time (Chandler & Sweller, 1991). Even in

cognitive chunking
The grouping of related information in a way that is easy for a person to commit to both short-term and long-term memory.

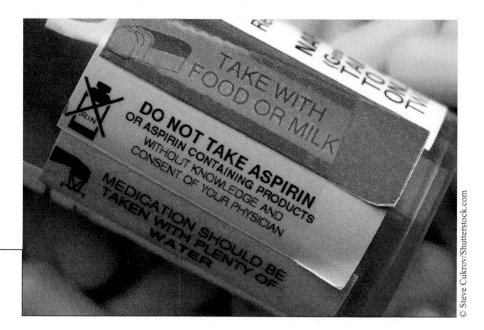

© Steve Cukrov/Shutterstock.com

Common drug warnings placed on prescription labels are often misunderstood.

light of compelling evidence, the majority of healthcare information developed in the United States fails to follow these simple guidelines. The results of noncompliance with the guidelines for the development of accessible health information are materials that are too difficult to understand for the average person and, as such, are frequently discarded.

A study applying the cognitive chunking technique to warning labels on medication bottles was conducted in reaction to the fact that more than half of adults misunderstand common drug warnings placed on prescription labels. Shrank, Agnew-Blaise, Choudhry, Wolf, Kesselheim, and Avorn (2007) advocate that there should be no more than two warning labels on any one prescription bottle. In a study investigating prescription-label comprehension, people who were given prescriptions with standard labeling comprehended 80% of the information, people who were given instructions written in simplified language comprehended 91% of information, and people who were given labels with simplified text and icons comprehended 92% of information. Clearly, the way in which printed information is relayed has a measurable effect on patient awareness, recall, and behavior and overall patient safety.

Conclusion

This chapter presented the concept of literacy and how literacy affects the healthcare system. The lack of literacy in the United States is at epidemic proportions, and this inability to comprehend information, follow basic instructions, and perform basic calculations has been shown to decrease the quality of life and decrease life expectancy. The various factors that contribute to low health literacy were presented with evidence indicating poor literacy levels being prevalent in elderly, poor, and minority populations.

Various approaches to combating low health literacy were presented and discussed. Some of these efforts ranged from the simplification of health information materials to the early detection of patients with limited literacy skills. These approaches for assessing and combating low health literacy represent just some of the efforts being conducted by researchers. Finally, the concept of e-health was discussed and relevant data were presented. User tendencies and factors influencing the credibility of online information were discussed, along with ways that healthcare practitioners can be proactive and mindful in addressing the patients' literacy needs. The ability to adapt one's communication based on a patients' literacy level is crucial to the delivery of quality health care.

Questions for Discussion/Review

1. Why is literacy an important factor in the delivery of quality health care?
2. Compare and contrast the concepts of literacy, health literacy, and e-literacy.
3. Based on your own experience, are the statistics on national trends presented in the chapter accurate? Provide an example.
4. Describe a situation in which you encountered a patient who was low in health literacy. What did you do to overcome this? Would you do anything differently after reading the information contained in this chapter?
5. Do you agree with the concept that all patients should be screened for literacy levels? Why or why not?
6. Describe the differences among the WRAT, REALM, TOFHLA, and NVS measures of literacy. Which one do you think would be most effective?
7. If asked by a patient, how would you respond to the following question: *How do I know if the information on the Internet is accurate?*
8. In this chapter, we highlight several ways that a healthcare practitioner can identify a patient with low levels of health literacy. Develop and describe another way that low literacy can be detected.
9. The American Medical Association proposed a four-dimensional approach to combating illiteracy. Develop a pneumonic device to assist healthcare professionals in remembering the four dimensions.
10. Provide two suggestions, as presented in the chapter, for a healthcare provider who needs immediate help making an encounter with a patient with a low level of health literacy more productive and satisfying.

References

Agency for Health Care Research and Quality (AHRQ.2011), Health Literacy Interventions and Outcomes: An Update of the literacy and health outcomes systematic review of the literature, 2011. Retrieved from http://www.ahrq.gov/research/findings/evidence-based-reports/er199-abstract.html.

American Academy of Family Physicians (2015). *Patient-centered medical home, definition of.* Retrieved from http://www.aafp.org/practice-management/transformation/pcmh.html.

American Medical Association (1999). Ad hoc committee on health literacy for the council on scientific affairs. *Journal of the American Medical Association, 281,* 552–557.

Baker, D. W., Gazmararian, J. A., & Sudano, J. (2000). The association between age and health literacy among elderly persons. *Journal of Gerontology, series B, Psychological Scientific Social Science, 55,* S368–374.

Baker, D. W., Gazmararian, J. A., Williams, M. V., Scott, T., Parker, R. M., Green, D. (2002). Health literacy and use of outpatient physician services by Medicare managed care enrollees. *Journal of General Internal Medicine, 19,* 215–220.

Baker, D. W., Parker, R. M., Williams, M. V., Clark, W. S., & Nurss, J. (1997). The relationship of patient reading ability to self-reported health and use of health services. *American Journal of Public Health, 87,* 1027–1030.

Baker, L., Wagner, T. H., Singer, S., & Bundorf, M. K. (2003). Use of the internet and e-mail for health care information: Results from a national survey. *Journal of the American Medical Association, 289,* 2400–2406.

Baker, D. W., Wolf, M. S., Feinglass, J., Thomas, H., Gazmararian, J., & Huang, J. (2007). Health literacy and mortality among elderly patients. *Archives of Internal Medicine, 167,* 1503–1509.

Bass, P. F. III., Wilson, J. F., Griffith, C. H., & Barnett, D. R. (2002). Resident's ability to identify patients with poor literacy skills. *Academic Medicine, 77,* 1039–1041.

Carman, K. L., Maurer, M., Mallery, C., Wang, G., Garfinkel, S., Richmond, J., & Windham, A. (2013). Community forum delivered its methods demonstration: Evaluating effectiveness and eliciting public views on use of evidence. Executive Summary. Washington, D.C.: American Institutes of Research.

Carmona, R. H. (2003). *Health literacy in America: The role of health care professionals.* American Medical Association House of Delegates Meeting, June 14, 2003. Retrieved from http://www.surgeongeneral.gov/news/speeches/ama061403.htm.

Census 2000 Brief C2KBR-29. (2000). *Language use and English speaking ability.* Retrieved from http://www.census.gov.prod/2003pubs/c2kbr-29.pdf.

Chandler, P., & Sweller, J. (1991). Cognitive load theory and the format of instruction. *Cognition and Instruction, 8,* 293–332.

Cline, R. J., & Haynes, K. M. (2001). Consumer health information seeking on the internet: The state of the art. *Health Education Research, 16,* 671–692.

Connecting for Health. (2004). *Achieving electronic connectivity in health care: A preliminary road map for the nation's public and private-sector health care leaders.* Retrieved from http://www.connectingforhealth.org/resources/cfh_aech_roadmap_072004.pdf.

Davis, T. C., Crouch, M. A., Wills, G., Miller, S., & Adbehou, D. M. (1990). The gap between patient reading comprehension and the readability of patient education materials. *Journal of Family Practice, 31,* 533–538.

Davis, T. C., Frederick, D. D., Arnold, C., Murphy, P. W., Herbst, M., & Bocchini, J. A. (1998). A polio immunization pamphlet with increased appeal and simplified language does not improve comprehension to an acceptable level. *Patient Education and Counseling, 33,* 25–33.

Davis, T. C., Long, S. W., Jackson, R. H., Mayeaux, E. J., George, R. B., & Murphy, P. W. (1993). Rapid estimate of adult literacy in medicine: A shortened screening instrument. *Family Medicine, 25,* 391–395.

Delamote, T. (2000). Quality of web sites: Kite marking the west wind. *British Medical Journal, 321,* 843–844.

Eng, T. R. (2001). *The e-health landscape: A Touraine map of emerging information and communication technologies in health and health care.* Princeton, NJ: The Robert Wood Johnson Foundation.

Eysenbach, G., & Kohler, C. (2002). How do consumers search and appraise health information on the World Wide Web? Qualitative study using focus groups, usability test, and in-depth interviews. *British Medical Journal, 324,* 573–577.

Ferreira, M. R., Dolan, N. C., Fitzgibbon, M. L., Davis, T. C., Gorby, N., & Ladewski, L. (2005). A health care provider-directed intervention to increase colorectal cancer screening among veterans: Results of a randomized controlled trial. *Journal of Clinical Oncology, 23,* 1548–1554.

Fowler, F. J., Jr., Gerstein, B. S., & Barry, M. J. (2013), How patients centered our medical decisions?: Results of a national survey. JAMA, 173, *13,* 1215–1221.

Fox, S. (2004). *Older Americans and the internet. Internet in American Life Project.* Retrieved from http://www.pewinternet.org/Reports/2004/Older-Americans-and-the-internet.aspx.

Fox, S., & Rain, E. (2000). The on-line health care revolution: How the web helps Americans take better care of themselves. *Pew internet in American life project.* Retrieved from http://www.pewinternet.org/Reports/2000/The-Online-Health-Care-Revolution.aspx.

Friedland, R. B. (1998). *Understanding health literacy: New estimates of the costs of inadequate health literacy.* Washington, DC: National Academy of Aging Society.

Gazmararian, J. A., Baker, D. W., Williams, M. V., Parker, R. M., Scott, T. L., & Green, D. C. (1999). Health literacy among Medicare enrollees in managed care organizations. *The Journal of the American Medical Association, 281,* 545–551.

Health Care News. (2003). *No significant change in number of "Cyberchondriacs," those who go on-line for health care information.* Retrieved from
http://www.harrisinteractive.com/news/newsletters/healthnews/HI_HealthCareNews2003Vol3_Iss04.pdf.

Institute of Medicine. (2004). *Health literacy: A prescription to end confusion.* Retrieved from http://iom.edu/Reports/2004/Health-Literacy-A-Prescription-to-End-Confusion.aspx.

Institutes of Medicine of the National Academies. (2002). Unequal treatment: Confronting racial and ethnic disparities. Retrieved from http://www.iom.edu/Reports/2002/Unequal-Treatment-Confronting-Racial-and-ethnic-disparities-in-Health-Care.aspx.

Jadada, R. (2002). Examination of instruments used to rate quality of health information on the internet: Chronicle of a voyage with an unclear destination. *British Medical Journal, 324,* 569–573.

Health Reform Glossary. The Henry J. Kaiser Foundation retrieved from http://kff.org/glossary/health-reform-glossary/.

Kaiser-Permanente (2005). E-health and the elderly: How seniors use the internet for health survey. *Kaiser-Permanente family foundation publication* 72–23.

Kirsch, H., Jungeblut, A., Jenkins, L., & Kolstad, A. (2002). *Adult literacy in America: A first look at the findings of the National Adult Literacy Survey* (3rd ed.). *Vol(201).* Washington, DC: U.S. Department of Education, Office of Educational Research and Improvement.

Kreuter, M. W., Lukwango, S. N., Bucholtz, R. D., Clarke, M., & Sanders-Thompson, V. (2002). Achieving cultural appropriateness in health promotion programs: Targeted and tailored approaches. *Health Education Behavior, 30,* 133–146.

Licciardone, J. C., Smith-Barbaro, P., & Coleridge, S. T. (2001). Use of the internet as a source for consumer health information: Results of the second Osteopathic survey of health care in America (OSTEO-Surv-2). *Journal of Medical Internet Research, 3,* e31.

Madden, M., & Rainie, L. (Eds.). (2003). America's on-line pursuits: The changing picture of who's on-line and what they do. *Internet and American Life Project.* Retrieved from http://www.pewinternet.org/~/media/Files/Reports/2003/PIP_Online_pursuits_Final.PDF.

McKinney, J., & Kurtz-Rossi, S. (2000). *Culture health and literacy: A guide to health education materials for adults with limited English skills. World Education.* Retrieved from http://healthliteracy.world.org/docs/culture_Health_Literacy.pdf.

Michielutte, R., Bahnson, J., Dignan, M. D., & Schroeder, E. M. (1992). The use of illustrations and narrative text style to improve readability of a health education brochure. *Journal of Cancer Education, 7,* 251–260.

Murphy, P. W., Chesson, A. L., Walker, L., Arnold, C. L., & Chesson, L. M. (2000). Comparing the effectiveness of video and written material for improving knowledge among sleep disorders, clinic patients with limited literacy skills. *Southern Medical Journal, 93,* 297–304.

National Academy of Sciences. (2000). *Networking health: Prescriptions for the Internet.* Washington, DC: National Academic Press.

National Literacy Act of 1991. (1991). *Publication L.* No. 102–173, 105STAT.333. National Network of Libraries of Medicine. Nlm.gov. Retrieved from http://nlmn.gov/outreach/consumer/hlthlit.html.

Nielsen-Bohlman, L., Pranzer, A. M., & Kindig, D. A. (Eds.) (2004). *Health literacy: A prescription to end confusion.* Washington, D.C.: National Academic Press.

Noblin, A. M., Wan, T. H., & Fottler, M., (2014). The impact of health literacy on a patient's decision to adopt a personal health record, *Perspectives in Health Information Management, 9.*

Nutbeam, D. (2000). Health literacy as a public health goal: A challenge for contemporary health education and communication strategies in the 21st century. *Health Promotion International, 15,* 259–267.

Oenema, A., Brug, J., & Lechner, L. (2001). Web-based tailored nutrition education: Results of a randomized controlled trial. *Health Education Research, 16,* 647–660.

Oxford-English Dictionary OED On-Line. (2003). *OED on-line.* Retrieved from http://dictionary.oed.com.

Parker, R. M., Baker, D. W., Williams, M. V., & Nurss, J. R. (1995). The test of functionalhealth literacy in adults: A new instrument for measuring patients literacy skills. *Journal of General Internal Medicine, 10,* 537–541.

Pignone, M., DeWalt, D. A., Sheridan, S., Berkman, N., & Lohr, K. N. (2005). Interventions to improve health outcomes for patients with low literacy: A systematic review. *Journal of General Internal Medicine, 20,* 185–192.

Raudenbush, S. W., & Kasim, R. M. (1998). Cognitive skill and economic inequality: Findings from the National Adult Literacy Survey. *Harvard Educational Review, 68,* 33–80.

Reynolds, C. R., & Fletcher-Janzen, E. (2007). *Encyclopedia of special education.* Hoboken, NJ: John Wiley & Sons.

Rothman, R. L., DeWalt, D. A., Malone, R., Bryant, B., Shintani, A., Crigler, B., Weinberger, M., & Pignone, M. (2004). Influence of patient literacy on the effectiveness of a primary care-based diabetes disease management program. *Journal of the American Medical Association, 292,* 1711–1716.

Schillinger, D., Grumbach, K., Piette, J., Wang, F., Osmond, D., & Daher, C., et al. (2002). Association of health literacy with diabetes outcomes. *Journal of the American Medical Association, 288,* 475–482.

Schillinger, D., Piette, J., Grumbach, K., Wang, F., Wilson, C., Daher, C. (2003). Closing the loop: Physician communication with diabetic patients who have low health literacy. *Archives of Internal Medicine, 163,* 1745–1746.

Scott, T. L., Gazmararian, J. A., Williams, M. V., & Baker, D. W. (2002). Health literacy and preventative health care used among Medicare enrollees in managed care organization. *Medical Care, 40,* 395–404.

Sepucha, K. R., & Mulley, A. J. (2003). Extending decision support: Preparation and implementation. *Patient Education and Counseling, 50,* 269–271.

Shrank, W. H., Agnew-Blais, J., Choudhry, N. K., Wolf, M. S., Kesselheim, A. S., & Avorn, J. (2007). The variability and quality of medication container labels. *Archives of Internal Medicine, 167,* 1760–1765.

U.S. Department of Education. (1996). *Literacy of older adults in America.* Washington, DC: National Center for Educational Statistics. Retrieved on April 8, 2010 from http://nces.ed.gov/pubs97/97576.pdf.

Vernon, J. A., Trujillo, A., & Rosenbaum, S. (2007). Low health literacy: Implications for national health policy. Washington, DC: Department of Health Policy, School of Public Health and Health Services, George Washington University.

Wall Street Journal. (2004). *On-line Harris interactive health care poll.* Retrieved from www .harrisonline.com.

Weiss, B. D., Mays, M. Z., Martz, W., Castro, K. M., DeWalt, D. A., Pignone, M. P., Mockbee, J., & Hale, F. A. (2005). Quick assessment of literacy in primary care: The newest vital sign. *Annals of Family Medicine, 3,* 514–521.

Weiss, B. D., & Palmer, R. (2004). Relationship between health care costs and very low literacy skills in medically needy and indigent Medicaid populations. *Journal of the American Board of Family Practice, 17,* 44–46.

Williams, M. V., Parker, R. M., Baker, D. W., Parikh, N. S., Pitkin, K., Coates, W. C., & Nurss, J. R. (1995). Inadequate functional health literacy among patients at two public hospitals. *Journal of the American Medical Association, 274,* 1677–1682.

Wolf, M. S., Gazmararian, J. A., & Baker, D. W. (2005). Health literacy and functional health status among older adults. *Archives of Internal Medicine, 165,* 1946–1952.

Wolf, M. S., Lindquist, L., & Skripkauskas, S. (2008). Health literacy from epidemiology tointervention. In E. P. Polack, V. P. Richmond, & J. C. McCroskey (Eds.). *Applied communication for health professionals* (pp. 93–108). Dubuque, IA: Kendall Hunt.

Wolf, M. S., Williams, M. V., Parker, R. M., Parikh, N. S., Nowlan, A. W. & Baker, D. W. (2007), Patients' shame and attitudes toward discussing the results of literacy screening. *Journal of Health Communications*, 12, 721–732.

Workman, T.A., de Bronkart, D., Quinlan, C. & Pinder, J. (2014), What do patients and families want from patient engagement?, Washington, D.C.

Wydra, E. W. (2001). The effectiveness of a self-care management interactive multi-media module. *Oncologic Nursing Forum, 28,* 1399–1407.

Practice of Medical Communication

chapter eight

Humor and Aggressive Communication in Health Care

As anyone who is employed within health care can attest to, it can be quite an emotional experience when treating the sick and servicing the needy. Two aspects of communication that have a profound impact on the organization's culture, the patient's experience, and the provider's experience are that of humor communication and aggressive communication. Both humor communication and aggressive communication are two emerging areas with scores of studies revealing the benefits as well as the deleterious effects of these two types of communication (DiCioccio, 2012; Rancer & Avtgis, 2015). This chapter will discuss these two types of communication and the profound impact that they have on relationships, the healing process, professionalism, and civility within perhaps one of the most uncertain environments; the healthcare system.

1. Explain the psychology of humor

2. Explain the role of humor in the patient-provider relationship

3. Explain the six guidelines for healthcare professional humor use with patients

4. Explain the prevalence of aggressive communication in healthcare

5. Compare and contrast the different explanations for verbal aggressiveness

6. Explain affirming communication and its implications for healthcare

7. Explain the doctor-nurse game

© Halfpoint/Shutterstock.com

Key Terms

Humor	Verbal aggressiveness	Affirming communication
Laughter	Argumentativeness	Conflict

Humor Communication in Health Care

The multitude of functions that humor serves in relation to the human condition have long been acknowledged and researched. Throughout human history there are examples of humor and humorous communication regardless of culture, language, or other factors that serve to differentiate people from one another. Given this, it is safe to say that humor is a part of the human experience and worthy of investigation. Such investigations will enable us to better explain the benefits and drawbacks of humor use. So what exactly is humor? According to Vera Robinson (1991), humor is "any communication which is perceived by any of the interacting parties as humorous and leads to laughing, smiling, and a feeling of amusement" (p. 10). Humor requires spontaneity and an element of surprise. However, humor is a receiver-focused concept as opposed to sender focused as all humor is subjective and unique to each individual (Fry, 1963). It is important to distinguish humor from laughter; the former is a cognitive or thought requiring process while the latter is a physical response that results in a physiological experience that is considered a behavior (Robinson).

The process of humor is linear and starts with a **cognitive response,** which can take the form of our interpretation and thought process about the incoming stimuli. By stimuli we are referring to any verbal and nonverbal information. For example, have you ever witnessed someone trip on the sidewalk, resulting in your uncontrollable laughter? This laughter reaction is based on your choice to interpret this event as something humorous as opposed to something threatening. The second step in this linear progression is the **emotional response,** which reflects the affective reaction to amusement and pleasure. This reaction can range from something mildly humorous to feeling overcome with amusement. The **physical response** (i.e., smile or laughter) is the final element in the process of humor consisting of the behaviors that we engage in to physiologically express our amusement. This too can range from a small smile to "doubling over" in laughter.

The vast majority of humor that occurs within the healthcare setting is **spontaneous humor.** Spontaneous humor arises out of "ordinary situations and is usually a witty remark or ludicrous action inspired by the circumstances at hand" (Robinson, 1991, p. 10). The three types of spontaneous humor consist of **pleasantry, witticism,** and **unintentional humor.** A pleasantry is considered a milder form of humor that may or may not elicit laughter but results in a smile. However, the witticism is deliberately designed to entertain through clever and original spontaneity (Robinson). Unintentional humor results from when the person has no intention of making another person laugh—it just occurs (Ziv, 1983). The use of humor in the practice of health care should be

---

humor

Any communication perceived by any of the interacting parties as humorous and leads to laughing, smiling, and a feeling of amusement.

laughter

A physiological experience that is considered a behavior.

Humor requires spontaneity and an element of surprise, and laughter is the physical response.

viewed as a therapeutic tool that health clinicians should cultivate and use when developing the entire approach of care for the patient. It should also be noted that similar to pharmaceuticals, humor should be used judiciously because too much of it is not necessarily better (Robinson).

Can humor serve in a therapeutic capacity? Perhaps the first scientific evidence of humor as an effective therapy was suggested by Norman Cousins (1976). Cousins was confined to bed after being diagnosed with *ankylosing spondylitis* (a crippling degenerative disease). After experiencing the depressing atmosphere of the hospital setting, Cousins checked himself out of the hospital and into a hotel room where he could be comfortable and watch funny movies. He also treated himself with high doses of vitamin C. The self-reported results were astounding in that he experienced a miraculous recovery that was attributed to both humor and high doses of vitamin C (Cousins, 1976, 1979). The results of this study set the stage to consider humor as a meaningful and significant tool for healing patients.

The Psychology of Humor

Until the late 20th century, the psychological perspective of humor was entirely based on the psychoanalytic theories of Sigmund Freud (1928). His theory of humor contended that humans developed humor to protect the ego from being distressed or to free it from suffering from reality. According to Goldstein and McGhee (1972), although psychoanalytic theory has made a significant contribution to the field of psychology, it is limited in its capacity to explain the complexities of the humor process and experience. Other theories include Berlyne's (1969) **theory of arousal and cognitive factors,** which assumes that humor is not just a present stimulus, but also a recollection of past experiences, the reality of the present, and the anticipation of the future, which are all collated into generating and arousing pleasure. Other researchers believe that humor and laughter play a major role in the maintenance of both psychological and physical health in the face of the stresses that people encounter on a daily basis (Lefcourt & Martin, 1986).

One of the reasons there is a paucity of research on humor and laughter is partly because the field of psychology, since its inception, has primarily focused on the study of negative emotional states, with the focus on positive emotional states being a relatively new endeavor (Burgdorf & Panksepp, 2006). According to Frederickson's (1998) **broaden-and-build theory of positive emotions,** "Experiences of positive emotions broaden people's momentary thought-action repertoires, which in turn serves to build their enduring personal resources, ranging from physical and intellectual resources to social and psychological resources" (Fredrickson, 2001, p. 218). It is also assumed that positive emotions have their roots in evolution, whereby spontaneous smiling and laughing have been documented in primate behavior. For example, Gervais and Wilson (2005) developed the concept of **nonserious social incongruity,** which is the common factor of safe surprise or being surprised in a good or nonthreatening kind of way. Such surprise may elicit laughter or a smile such as that witnessed in infants, tickling and physical play (witnessed in both apes and human children), and the incongruity-based humor of human adults and signing apes (Taber, Redden, & Hurley, 2007). This approach to humor assumes that laughter and humor benefit both sender and receiver to spread positive emotion, promote stability, decrease negativity, moderate stress, and strengthen group identity and cohesion (Gervais & Wilson). It is in these prosocial benefits that humor is seen as aiding in the survival of the group.

Humor in the Patient–Provider Relationship

Humor has been an important part of human existence and is believed to serve survival functions (Darwin, 1872). In the Middle Ages, humor was referred to as an "energy" thought to be a direct determinant of a person's health and disposition (Wooten, Hodkin, Connors, & Bell, 1993). In fact, renaissance scholars believe that **sanguine humor** is a cheerful type of humor associated with the blood, **choleric humor** is an angry humor associated with bile, **phlegmatic humor** is an apathetic humor associated with mucous, and **melancholy humor** is a depressing humor associated with black bile. Although there are many humors, only the sanguine humor is the one of cheer (Moody, 1978). In the 1300s, Henri de Mondville, a surgeon, was quoted as saying, "Let the surgeon take care to regulate the whole regimen of the patient's life for joy and happiness, allowing his relatives and special friends to cheer him, and by having someone tell him jokes" (Walsh, 1911, p. 270). It is clear that humor and medicine have been inextricably linked for centuries.

In contemporary medicine, Dr. Vera Robinson (1991) argues that "opening up yourself to humor, looking for the absurdities of life and becoming more playful and less serious about life, is a broad perspective from which we might increase our use of humor in healthcare" (p. 185).

A more contemporary use of humor in health care can be seen in the 1998 film based on the true life and times of Hunter Campbell. The film "Patch Adams" features an American physician who founded the **Gesundheit Institute** in 1971, which was based on the principles of the complementary and alternative (holistic) effects of humor. Some popular books also extol humor for its virtues and include *Love, Medicine, and Miracles (2011)* by surgeon Dr. Bernie Siegal and *Quantum Healing (1990)* by Dr. Deepak Chopra. According to Hampes (2001), "Both humor and empathetic concerns are associated with people who have emotional intelligence and use humor to interact effectively with other individuals" (p. 241). Developing empathy, like humor, as a part of emotional self-awareness when comforting a sick or distressed person makes it easier for the other individual to trust you. In fact, Provine (2000) believes that the evolution of humor and laughter results from the effect that it has on others and not on the self.

Therapeutic humor in medicine, given that it relies on mindfulness, is also influenced by empathy and compassion (Berger, Coulehan, & Belling, 2004). The concept of therapeutic medicine can be considered any intervention that promotes health and wellness by stimulating a discovery, expression, or appreciation for the absurdity or incongruity of life and life situations (Fultanoff, 2010). Many scholars believe that the appropriate use of humor can facilitate communication, promote bonding, and enhance a patient's satisfaction (Francis, Monahan, & Berger, 1999). In fact, regardless of the patient's level of frustration with the bureaucracy associated with managed care, a caregiver's appropriate use of humor can dramatically alter the

© Tyler Olson/Shutterstock.com

How can therapeutic humor promote health and wellness?

patient–provider relationship for the better, which may equate to a higher level of satisfaction and patient adherence to therapy. Given that all communication, including humor is contextual, humor should be avoided during emergency situations in lieu of more sober behavior such as holding the patient's hand, listening, reassuring, and feeling empathy (Berger et al., 2004). Although some believe that humor is a way of sense making, emergency medical situations must be free of extraneous communication and rely exclusively on effective information exchange.

Although humor can prove to be an effective segue into more personal or sensitive patient disclosure, all healthcare providers should be aware of destructive elements. Humor use can be counterproductive when it magnifies the distance between the patient and provider or somehow belittles the patient by unintentionally using it at an inappropriate time or in an inappropriate way. For example, consider a provider who, when consulting with a patient who is obese, suggests that "perhaps there should be a prescription written for tap dancing lessons." This insensitive attempt at humor is clearly based on the sole enjoyment of the provider without regard to the detrimental effects it can have on the patient.

Just as a provider needs to consider many factors when communicating humor to a patient, a patient is also bound by the patient–provider relationship when communicating and, as such, is bound by social norms according to the context. A patient is, by the structure of the healthcare system, in a one-down position by virtue of the **authority gradient.** In some cases, humor may function as a means of empowerment that serves to humanize the patient in the eyes of the provider (Francis et al., 1999). Similar to the healthcare provider, patient-generated humor can also be either constructive or destructive in nature. An example of a constructive use of humor would be a patient who has waited a long time to see a physician and greets the physician by saying, "Doc, I was just about to send out a search party to find you." A more destructive form could be based on stereotype, such as "Look who just came in from the golf course! How about doing some work for a change?" Of these two examples, the former is based on a mutual beneficial way to reduce uncertainty yet address the fact that the patient has been waiting an extended period of time to see the physician. It also allows for the physician to acknowledge the patient's waiting time in a way that is not threatening or aggressive to the physician or patient. In the latter example, the comment has a rude, hostile, one-upmanship quality to it and is most likely to bring about an equally hostile and aggressive response from the healthcare provider (Berger et al., 2004). Such aggressive exchanges are extremely detrimental for the healing process and the relationship between the patient and provider.

There are some cultural differences in the way in which patients' view both healthcare practitioners and the healthcare system in general. These perceptions can make appropriate humor use especially challenging. For example, African-American patients tend to have a general distrust of the health establishment regarding both quality of and access to care. Such distrust can serve to filter the interpretation of any humor use as being disrespectful or not genuinely directed toward the patient's well-being (Dula, 1994; Murry, 1992).

Another example of cultural influence is that of Asian cultures who hold great respect for physician authority. Patients display deference and nonassertiveness, which are considered virtues in Asian cultures. Should a physician engage in self-deprecating and self-effacing humor, he or she may be seen as lacking medical competence in the eyes of a patient of Asian cultural descent (Cumura, 1992).

Given there are so many contextual variables that can affect the use of humor, should a healthcare practitioner even attempt to engage in humorous communication? Berger et al. (2004) offer several guidelines for humor use that can be applied across situations:

1. Be conservative in selecting both content and the manner of humor. It may serve as a wedge between you and the power-disadvantaged patient.
2. The least risky type of humor is gentle self-deprecating humor that is externally focused (e.g., discussing how difficult it was to park due to the snow that has recently accumulated).
3. Avoid facetious or flippant humor. Patients generally expect healthcare providers to have a respectful and optimistic outlook. Such flippancy can come across as negative and mean spirited.
4. Any humor used by the provider should be grounded in an accurate understanding of the patient's values, limits, predispositions, and receptivity to such communication (i.e., a general empathetic consideration of the patient).
5. If the patient initiates humor, respond in kind (e.g., similar topic or an extension of their humorous message) with constructive humor.
6. If the patient engages in destructive humor (e.g., "Were you out playing golf again?"), it is appropriate to confront the patient in an effort to diffuse the aggressive form of humor and discuss the exact issue that is leading to the displaced hostility (e.g., waiting too long, not receiving enough information about their illness).

In general, a dialectical tension exists with humor use in medical care. According to Robinson (1991), "[I]llness is a serious business…. [I]t is not a laughing matter," (p. XIV) yet when one is constantly dealing with "stress, illness, naked bodies, blood, guts, excrement, trauma, and death" (p. XIV), the humor is generally dark, aggressive, sexual and/or aggressive in nature. This indicates that humor, in terms of healthcare personnel, serves as a sense making and coping function for psychological well-being.

Aggressive Communication

It is common knowledge that employees within healthcare experience more intense verbal and physical aggression than in almost any other profession (Lanza, 2006). According to Avtgis and Polack (2010), there is a misconception that when people consider the concept of health care and violence, they generally think of episodes that occur within a traditional hospital setting. However, when considering the concept of aggression in health care, we should broaden this definition to include all varieties of healthcare facilities. Therefore, a **healthcare facility** is defined as any place where there is a regular practice of medicine and healing regarding the treatment of physical and psychological illness.

Although the data have only been actively tracked since 1983, the presence of aggressive communication has been present in health care for a much longer time and includes behaviors such as threats, name calling, and yelling, (Gates, 2004; Gerberich, Church, McGovern, Hansen, Nachreiner, & Geisser, 2004; Henderson, 2003; Kingma, 2001; Lanza, 2006). Healthcare education is replete with research and anecdotal evidence concerning the benefits of communication in the healing process. However, there can also be detrimental effects on the healing process as a result of communication and human relationships. The duality of communication in health care is that communication is considered an imperative to the healing process, yet it also can be considered an impediment to that very same healing process (Avtgis & Polack, 2010).

The study of aggressive communication within healthcare encompasses several other related terms that can be considered as specific types of verbal and physical aggression. Therefore, we are including all of these when we refer to aggressive communication. Table 8.1 highlights these definitions.

Given the variety of terms encompassing aggressive communication, one can see how such behavior, regardless of the label we choose to use, is ubiquitous throughout all of health care. **Aggressive communication** is defined as any interpersonal behavior that "applies force physically or symbolically in order, minimally, to dominate and perhaps damage or, maximally, to defeat and perhaps destroy the locus of attack" (Infante, 1987, p. 158). Who then is more susceptible or has a greater probability of experiencing (i.e., being the target of) or engaging in (i.e., being the perpetrator of) aggressive communication? In a study conducted in Great Britain, nurses and healthcare personnel are second to police and security staff in the probability that there will be violent episodes at work (Budd, 1999). This means that British healthcare workers are two times more susceptible to physical and verbal aggression than the national average for the entire population of the United Kingdom. Specifically focusing on healthcare organizations within the United States, the Bureau of Labor Statistics reports that American healthcare workers are 16 times more likely to experience assault during a typical work shift than workers within any other industry.

According to Avtgis and Polack (2010), there is an increased risk of experiencing an aggressive episode associated with age (younger), gender (women), work hours (overnight shift), and occupational status (nurse). Given that all of these factors are likely to be present within healthcare facilities, the potential for aggressive communication and behavior becomes intrinsic to healthcare professions. It is not in these risk factors alone that the potential for an aggressive encounter exists, but when these risk factors are present and combined with patients who are experiencing pain, frustration, uncertainty about their illness/survival, and quite often under the influence of alcohol and drugs, the potential for an aggressive episode increases exponentially. In fact,

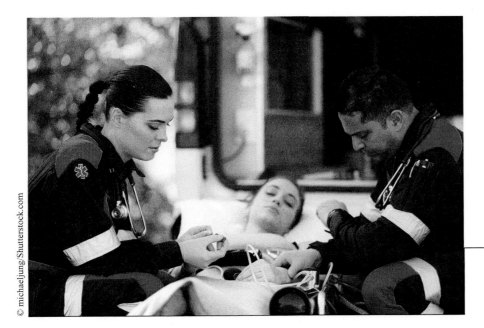

Some of the most risky healthcare positions include EMS or ambulance personnel.

violence is believed to be part of the working milieu for all healthcare workers regardless of position (Beech & Leather, 2006). Some of the most risky healthcare positions include emergency medical services (EMS) or ambulance personnel, student nurses, emergency room personnel, those working with the elderly and patients with disabilities, and mental health workers. In fact, mental healthcare personnel are 2.5 times more likely to experience verbal and physical aggression than even the most susceptible of positions in health care.

Because of the unique factors involved in health care, aggressiveness can be exacerbated by a multitude of factors, including interpersonal dynamics (i.e., the relationship between the provider and patient), social roles (i.e., the

table 8.1	Various Definitions of Behavior Encompassed by Aggressive Communication
Psychological Violence	The intentional use of power that may include the threat of physical force against another person or group of people.
Abuse	Behavior that results in humiliation or degradation or shows a lack of dignity or respect for another person.
Bullying	Activity that occurs repeatedly and is considered offensive to the receiver. These behaviors are intentional, vindictive, malicious, or undermine a person or a group of people.
Discrimination	Undesired or unreciprocated behavior degrading a person's dignity and based on demographic categories such as race, gender, and social status.
Sexual Harassment	Unreciprocated or unwanted behavior of a sexual nature that offends the victim or makes the victim feel threatened, embarrassed, or humiliated.
Threat	The overt or implied promise of physical or psychological force resulting in the person fearing psychological or physical harm or other perceived retribution.

At times, hospitals may need to limit the number of visitors.

status the parties play in the community at large), organizational roles (i.e., the specific power and control associated with the various roles), the process and procedure protocols associated with each setting (e.g., psychiatric inpatient versus outpatient care), degree of control or lack of control that a patient experiences, and the level of provocation from visitors and other patients (Beech & Leather, 2006; Powell, Caan, & Crowe, 1994). Other factors include the enforcement of rules or implementation of policies that take away control and choice from the patient. For example, in the H1N1 flu outbreak in fall 2009, many hospitals altered their visitation policies to better protect the patient and hospital employees from possible infection from contact with nonessential personnel (e.g., people visiting patients). Such measures included limiting the number of visitors a patient can have at any one time and allowing only adults to visit patients. Putting additional control over the behavior of people, especially in times of uncertainty such as when visiting an ill relative or friend, can trigger an aggressive reaction. Overcrowding, provocation, inexperienced healthcare staff, stringent management practices, structural factors, and environmental factors all can contribute to aggressive episodes (Davis, 1991; Whittington, 1994).

"One bad apple spoils the bunch" is a commonplace expression; however, this expression has a scientific basis in the construct of emotional contagion. **Emotional contagion** can be defined as the process of a person's emotive state influencing the emotive state of another person or persons in a similar way (Barsade, 2002; Hatfield, Cacioppo, & Rapson, 1993). For example, smiling or exhibiting a positive attitude can bring about similar smiling or positive attitudes from those around you. This is also true for negative emotions. Several studies indicate that 10% to 60% of patients exhibit aggressive verbal and physical behavior (Erb, 2001; Hahn, 2001). Such patient emotional expression can include anxiety, guilt, frustration, and dislike, which is usually expressed

How does employee burn-out affect the healthcare system?

through aggressive communication such as profanity and threats of litigation. Further, exposure to prolonged negative behavior can have negative psychological and emotional impact on healthcare workers. Employee burnout is a common outcome of long periods of abuse exposure and negative work environments. **Employee burnout** can be defined as feelings of overwhelming exhaustion, frustration, anger, and cynicism associated with work (Maslach, 2003; Maslach & Goldberg, 1998). Among those who suffer the most from burnout are elementary through high school teachers and healthcare workers (Avtgis & Rancer, 2010; Snyder, 2009). Given that turnover costs associated with replacing a registered nurse costs the healthcare system 9.75 billion dollars annually (Altergroup, 2015), burnout and contributing factors can place a large financial burden on the healthcare system. A myriad of factors can exacerbate aggressive situations. Most of these situations that escalate into physical aggression begin with, and are compounded by, aggressive communication.

The Origins of Aggressive Communication

To gain a complete understanding of aggressive communication, one must understand its origins and reasons for use. As will be demonstrated throughout this chapter, aggressive communication can serve a myriad of functions for the user with varying effects on the receiver. This type of communication, depending on its form, can have either devastating or beneficial effects on relationships at all levels of healthcare (Avtgis & Polack, 2010). The factors that determine whether or not the effects will be prosocial or antisocial will be reviewed and discussed in this section.

The foundations of aggressive communication lie in the larger personality traits of hostility and assertiveness. **Hostility** is a globally destructive trait expressed in interpersonal communication as irritability, negativity, resentment, and suspicion (Rancer & Avtgis, 2006, p. 19). Assertiveness, however, is a global trait where a person tends to be interpersonally dominant and forceful to achieve personal goals in socially appropriate ways (Rancer & Avtgis, 2015). **Verbal aggressiveness** is a subset of the larger personality trait of hostility in that it is a predisposition to "attack the self-concepts of individuals instead of, or in addition to, their positions on topics of communication" (Infante & Wigley, 1986, p. 61). **Argumentativeness,** however, is a subset of the larger personality trait of assertiveness in that it is "a generally stable trait which predisposes the individual in communication situations to advocate positions on controversial issues, and to attack verbally the positions which other people take on these issues" (Infante & Rancer, 1982, p. 72). For example, consider that a patient is told by an office receptionist that a physician will be meeting with them within five minutes; the assertive patient will probably wait the five minutes then, upon waiting more than five minutes, will remind the receptionist of the delay and inquire as to a more accurate time assessment. This reminder to the receptionist does not necessarily have to involve argument but it still is deemed to be assertive in nature. Contrast this with the patient saying to the receptionist, "You are rude and obviously cannot tell time." This type of response is considered verbally aggressive and likely counterproductive. Let us now take a closer look at verbal aggressiveness.

The development of verbal aggressiveness has been conceptualized from the five different perspectives of **psychopathology** (repressed hostility), **disdain** (intense dislike toward someone), genetics (inherited traits), **social learning** (modeling our behavior after the behavior of other people), and **argument skills deficiency** (communication abilities need to be developed). Regardless of how

---

verbal aggressiveness

A predisposition to attack the self-concept of individuals instead of, or in addition to, their positions on topics of communication.

argumentativeness

A generally stable trait that predisposes an individual in communication situations to advocate positions on controversial issues and to attack verbally the positions other people take on these issues.

How would you ask about an appointment delay in an assertive manner?

© Iakov Filimonov/Shutterstock.com

one chooses to conceptualize verbal aggressiveness, it is universally seen as a destructive force that can be exacerbated by particular circumstances. These circumstances can be idiosyncratic in nature or more systematic across people and are known as verbal trigger events. Recently, Avtgis and Madlock (2008) believed that verbal aggression can be exacerbated by factors unique to the healthcare setting. More specifically, they identified possible **verbal trigger events** or factors that, when present, result in an onset of verbal and potentially physical aggression (Wigley, 2010). These triggers include exhaustion and stress, patient distrust, managed care programs, and patient consumerism.

Exhaustion and stress reflect the "physical and psychological response to overwhelming stimuli that has long been associated with elevated heart rate and blood pressure" (Avtgis & Madlock, 2008, p. 173). Patients entering a healthcare facility are experiencing an incredible amount of uncertainty, which serves to increase stress. Patient stress has been linked to an inability to fight disease, increased depression, and sometimes violent episodes (Goodkin, Fletcher & Cohen, 1995; Herbert, 1997). Stress and exhaustion are not only issues for the patient; healthcare providers can also experience exhaustion and stress. The long hours associated with medical education and residency requirements sometimes render the practitioner a willing accomplice in the escalation of aggressive encounters (Bonsteel, 1997).

The development of the **managed care industry** has created a type of gatekeeping in terms of determining appropriate care through the paying of efficient patient care incentives. This moderating role between healthcare provider and patient has been shown to undermine the trust between the patient and physician (Annas, 1997; Mechanic & Schlesinger, 1996). Figure 8.1 shows the flow of this process.

© michaeljung/Shutterstock.com

What factors contribute to exhaustion and stress?

Another moderating function of managed care is increased demands on physician time to see more patients in less time. The decrease in consultation visit fees, along with the increase in patient volume, creates a business model resulting in physicians reducing face-to-face time with patients. According to Avtgis and Madlock (2008), "This decrease in interaction between patient and physician results in the appearance of being rushed and impatient" (2008, p. 174). The reduction in time between the physician and patient is believed to restrict the communication to the point where it is disease centered (i.e., diagnosis centered) rather than illness centered (i.e., patient narrative centered) (Ben-Sira, 1990). The decrease in face-to-face interaction has been linked to patient dissatisfaction, more frequent follow-up visits, and diminished health outcomes (Roter, 1989).

Patient distrust has become a potent verbal trigger event causing patients to doubt the effectiveness of their medical treatment resulting in underutilizing available healthcare services (Ferguson et al., 1998). This distrust can be a powerful force resulting in increased malpractice claims (Boehm, 2003). Beyond the provider–patient relationship there are some system-wide mandates on how physician's practice (e.g., Medicare, only reimburses for inpatient IV [intravenous] antibiotic treatment when the patient would be more comfortable at home). This type of regulation can directly result in patient skepticism and a deterioration of the patient–provider relationship. Further, intervention can compromise the integrity that exists between the physician and patient (Morreim, 1989; Rodwin, 1995). In fact, even greater distrust can be realized through the introduction of mediated communication (e.g., email and other interactive media) into the physician–patient consultation (Avtgis, Polack, Staggers, & Wieczorek, 2011).

The societal shift from "patient as reactive agent" in the healing process to "patient as proactive agent" has introduced a consumerism mentality that may trigger aggressive episodes. **Consumerism** as a verbal trigger event reflects a shift in healthcare-seeking behavior in that patients will seek out the "best fit" for their healthcare needs. This best fit principle goes beyond the physician–patient relationship and includes competition for services based on a patient's wealth or willingness to pay for such services. According to Avtgis and Polack (2010), this shopping for best fit medical services is partly a result of federal and state legislation and partly from the formation of tax savings vehicles such as flexible savings accounts (FSAs) that allow patients to shop and compare services. Further, also, the relative cost of best fit services is often considerably cheaper when a patient is willing to pay in cash as opposed to grinding through the bureaucratic process of an insurance company. In fact, this consumerism has led to an influx of American patients opting for medical services outside of the United States also known as **medical tourism**.

The proactive nature of the patient role also is reflected in the reduction of the power dynamic traditionally associated with the physician–patient relationship. In the past, when a physician spoke, the patient complied. In today's

figure 8.1

Patient - - - - - - - - - - ➔ Managed Care Programs - - - - - - - - - - ➔ Physician medical marketplace, patients regularly challenge or ignore recommendations from physicians and may seek out other healthcare professionals who will advocate a medical regimen more congruent to the wishes of the patient. This lack of patient compliance, depending on the temperament of the physician, can lead to an aggressive exchange (Turk & Meichenbaum, 1991).

Nursing and Verbal Aggressiveness

By far, the nursing profession is the most violent job within the healthcare profession due to the fact that nurses have greater frequency and depth of contact with patients (Avtgis & Polack, 2010; Lanza, 2006). Of all staff nurses, 90% experience at least one episode of abusive anger, condescension, or being globally rejected by a physician every 60 to 90 days. This is further complicated by 30% of nurses reported having suffered some form of sexual abuse ranging from inappropriate sexual communication to inappropriate touch every two to three months (Steadman, Mulvey, Monohan, Robbins, Applebaum, & Grisso, 1998). According to the National Veterans Administration, in the routine performance of their job, 48% of nurses have been verbally and/or physically assaulted within the last year (Lanza, Zeiss, & Rierdan, 2005) with other estimates being as high as 85% (Coombs, 1998).

Although these statistics are alarming and show that both verbal and physical aggressions are at epidemic levels, they are believed to be somewhat underreported. In a study by Gerberich, Church, McGovern, Hansen, Nachreiner, and Geisser (2004), nurses reported that they frequently avoided reporting nonphysically aggressive incidents, with 44% of nurses considering such verbally aggressive episodes to be part of the job, 30% believing that any complaints made would fall on deaf ears or not be taken seriously by supervisors and administrators, 17% believing such incidents were not worth reporting, and 8% viewing such verbal aggression as being a rare event and not worthy of being reported. The remaining nurses said they were too busy to report the incident or indicated that the process of registering such a complaint would require a lengthy filing/administrative process. Of verbal aggression experienced by nurses, 90% is through face-to-face interactions with patients and only 5% is verbal abuse via email and other media forms. However, because of the introduction of various kinds of media being integrated into health care and medical practice (i.e., implementation of SMART technology), the number of verbally aggressive incidents via media channels is likely to increase (Avtgis et al., 2011).

Argumentativeness

The ability to argue effectively has been generally viewed as a "gift," partly because Western societies are founded on concepts such as individual freedom and expression. This value of argument also pervades the scientific and legal communities (Rancer & Avtgis, 2015). Can effective arguing save lives?

figure 8.2

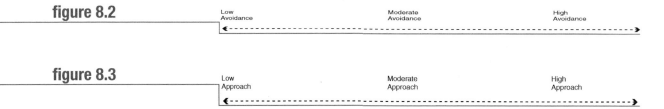

Low   Moderate   High
Avoidance   Avoidance   Avoidance

figure 8.3

Low   Moderate   High
Approach   Approach   Approach

The answer overwhelmingly is yes. Argument training is commonplace in professions where volatility and violence are commonplace. For example, law enforcement personnel at all levels have attended some form of argument training. In the volatile and violent world of health care, however, no such training is required. This section is dedicated to argumentativeness because it is a vital skill that should be developed by all healthcare personnel.

Argumentativeness, as defined earlier in the chapter, assumes that people have a trait or tendency to want to engage others in argument. This is not to say that you either are or are not argumentative; it is saying that people have two competing motivations to argue. The first motivation is called **argument avoidance** and reflects the degree to which we avoid argumentative situations. Figure 8.2 illustrates this range of motivation.

The second motivation is called **argument approach** and reflects the degree to which we approach argumentative situations. Therefore, a person's general tendency to argue can be determined by subtracting your motivation to avoid arguments by your motivation to approach argumentative situations. Figure 8.3 illustrates this motivation.

The overwhelming majority of research indicates that as people develop their trait of argumentativeness, they experience an abundance of positive personal and organizational satisfaction (see, for example, Rancer & Avtgis, 2015). In fact, the use of argumentative communication is believed to be one of the most effective strategies for diffusing potentially aggressive situations. Why would developing a person's argumentative behavior be important in health care? Consider the concept of health literacy, which is a major issue for practitioners. For both healthcare professionals and patients alike, the ability to argue also equates to an increased ability to describe more accurately their symptoms when meeting with a healthcare professional. For the healthcare practitioner, there is an increase in their ability to probe for accurate information when taking a patient's history. In the next section, we will discuss some of the efforts identified as effective strategies at reducing aggressive situations within health care and in society in general.

Fighting Against Aggressive Communication

An important question becomes: What factors can serve to diffuse or escalate verbal and physical aggression? What can be done to defuse such situations before the situation becomes uncontrollable? Effective interventions and proactive circumvention strategies are being taught and implemented in healthcare organizations throughout the United States. The Occupational Safety and Health Administration (2008), the regulatory division of the U.S. Department of Labor, has identified particular factors that exacerbate the use of verbal and physical abuse within healthcare facilities. A few of these factors include: (1) the presence of handguns (upward of 25% of patients, their families, and friends are believed to possess a firearm when in healthcare facilities); (2) the increased use of hospital police and security guards; (3) decreased use of larger psychiatric hospital facilities to care for patients with acute or chronic mental illness. Psychiatric patients are discharged from the hospital without concern for follow-up care. These same psychiatric patients are exercising their rights to refuse medication and can no longer be involuntarily committed unless they are a threat to themselves or others around them; (4) issues involving the general (nonpsychiatry) hospital community include availability of both drugs and money in hospital clinics and pharmacies (which are common motivations for theft and robbery), unrestricted access of the public to these general healthcare facilities (e.g., 24 hours a day/7 days a week); and (5) long waits for treatment in emergency rooms and clinics.

Contexts that increase risk exposure for healthcare professionals include, but are not limited to: (1) times of low-staffing (e.g., this may include meal-time and night shifts); (2) healthcare worker isolation during examination and treatment (e.g., the healthcare worker and patient in a room with the door closed for privacy); (3) an additional risk to healthcare workers (especially in remote locations) may be that they have little backup or means of calling for assistance when an aggressive encounter is experienced (Avtgis & Polack, 2010). Yet when we consider all of the risks in variable contexts it is not uncommon for healthcare personnel to be unaware or unable to adhere to any specific safety protocol regarding violent behavior (both physical and verbal), although most are vaguely aware that their facility has such policies/training.

Although the factors listed here represent some of the elements ubiquitous throughout the United States across all healthcare facilities, there are subtle differences in culture, structure, and practice. Therefore, it is difficult to set national safety standards or reforms. Although efforts are being made to reduce hostility and aggressive communication in the workplace, there remains a paucity of quality efforts. According to the Occupational Safety and Health Promotion Management Guidelines for Workplace Violence and Prevention Programs (Federal Register 54, pp. 3904–3916), four main components should be targeted when implementing education programs for the reduction of verbal and physical violence: (1) management consisting of the active containment of situations where aggression is about to take place or has just started to occur; (2) commitment and employee involvement, which reflects having all healthcare members committed to a mission of creating and maintaining a safe and violence-free workplace and a culture that reflects a willingness to actively aid and assist others in pursuing such a mission; (3) worksite analysis, which involves conducting a comprehensive review of all aspects and procedures of health care, including the physical, psychological, and social factors present in the delivery of health care; and (4) safety and health training, which calls for the adoption of aggression diffusion techniques and the knowledge of the detrimental effects of aggressive communication.

According to Lanza (2006), training to reduce the escalation of verbal and physical aggression may significantly reduce the need to train personnel in actual physical restraint techniques. This assumption is consistent with the argument skills deficiency model of verbal aggression that assumes people resort to aggressive communication because they lack arguing skills and effective arguing behavior (Infante et al., 1989). Given this, training in the de-escalation of verbal aggression should target a person's ability to combat, deflect, or dissolve a verbal attack, thus rendering the situation less volatile and less likely to develop into an aggressive encounter (Avtgis & Polack, 2010). Such communication skills training has been advocated by both communication scholars and health professionals and is believed to be core training that all healthcare personnel should partake (Avtgis & Madlock, 2008; Avtgis & Polack, 2010; Rossi et al., 2009a, 2009b).

The Lanza (2006) approach to training for diffusing aggressive situations is based on the assumptions that potential perpetrators often feel helpless, fear losing control, or are frightened by their own capacity to become aggressive. Given this, healthcare practitioners are encouraged to establish a rapport with the patient through the use of empathy and affirming communication. The concept of **affirming communication** (i.e., verbally and nonverbally validating the self-concept of another person) is a proven technique for creating a positive relationship and environment that has less probability of becoming verbally and physically violent (see Rancer & Avtgis, 2006, 2015). Affirming communication training has been successfully implemented in healthcare systems and healthcare education (Polack, Avtgis, Rossi, & Shaffer, 2009; Rossi et al., 2009a, Kappel et al., 2011).

Appropriate timing is the key to any successful intervention. Successful timing for an intervention can make the difference between a violent and nonviolent episode (Avtgis & Polack 2010). Lanza (2006), in her training targeted at nursing personnel, argues that nurses should look for a **preassaultive tension state,** which is a point in a situation where verbal and physical aggression is about to be triggered and is marked by anxiety, a rigid or stiff body posture, clenching of the teeth and/or fists, and other signs of physiological arousal (e.g., increased breathing rate and visible temporal artery pulsation). These noticeable nonverbal signs represent the presence of factors from which an aggressive episode will occur and needs to be diffused (Avtgis & Polack, 2010). One proven way to diffuse such a situation is to adopt an affirming communication style (both verbally and nonverbally) (Rancer & Avtgis, 2015).

Effective programs for diffusing verbal and physically aggressive situations must focus on communication skills and basic physical restraint techniques (e.g., Judo, Aikido). Further, we advocate that any intervention training must be based on statistical and scientific evidence, be applicable to the entire healthcare system (not just for one position such as nurses), emphasize the concept of affirming communication and communication competence, and

affirming communication

Communicating in a way that verbally and nonverbally validates the self-concept of another person.

create a culture where personnel at all levels of the healthcare facility value communication and the practice of effective communication. Perhaps the most representative effort, in terms of incorporating all of these recommendations, was suggested by Briles (2003). This approach advocates that healthcare personnel at all levels be taught to embrace and value "soft skills." For example, soft skills can include communication competency training and conflict resolution. This valuation of soft skills has to occur at all levels of the organization through a "culture of communication." It is only through creating a culture that values communication that the second recommendation can occur. The second recommendation is the effective teaching of communication. Those employees who do not greet such training efforts with motivation and positivity should be deemed "marginal employees" and targeted for transfer or termination. Finally, institutionalizing policies that affirm the healthcare organization's commitment to reducing aggressive communication and enhancing the practice of competent communication should be developed and strictly reinforced. For example, no-tolerance policies regarding aggressive interpersonal behavior would illustrate such an institutional value.

Conflict

Now that we have discussed the implications of aggressive communication in the practice of health care, it is important to discuss the interpersonal concept of conflict. Arrogant Conflict can be defined as an intrapersonal (i.e., something experienced within one's own mind) and an interpersonal (i.e., something experienced between two people) state where people perceive that they are in an opposing position, or are actually in an opposing position, from another person in a particular situation or on a particular issue. To discuss conflict in a clear and concise way, it is important to distinguish it from conflict behavior. **Conflict behavior** reflects the ways that people engage in proactive and reactive behavior when in a state of conflict. Such behaviors include **sabotage,** which is indirect interpersonal aggression when someone consciously or unconsciously undermines or destroys another person's personal property, personal integrity, professional integrity, credibility, and/or self-esteem. **Front-stabbing** is a conflict behavior that is overt, direct, and leaves no ambiguity as to the person's intent but is intended to cause personal and/or professional harm to you. This type of conflict behavior, because it is overt, can be dealt with via interpersonal negotiation, mediation, or damage control on the part of the recipient of the behavior. Front-stabbing behavior tends to be utilized more by males and people in higher-power positions because it creates an overtly uncomfortable social situation for all involved and is more utilized by people of higher status or those who are use to overt conflict. **Back-stabbing,** however, is a type of indirect interpersonal aggression and reflects covert and indirect conflict behavior where the destructive properties are difficult to measure or control (e.g., a surgical nurse spreads a rumor about a fellow nurse indicating that this nurse is having a romantic affair with a surgeon and this affair is one of the main reasons that she remains employed).

conflict

An intrapersonal and interpersonal state where people perceive that they are in an opposing position or are actually in an opposing position from another person in a particular situation or on a particular issue.

How does the victim of this rumor combat such a story? This is especially difficult when one considers that the victim of this rumor has little knowledge as to what exactly was said and to whom it was said. It is extremely difficult to measure the personal and professional damage this type of back-stabbing behavior can cause. This type of behavior has been associated with the conflict behavior of women and those who are in lower-power positions within an organization. Although it avoids the overtly uncomfortable social situation associated with overt conflict, this behavior creates a chilling effect or situation where the conflict is known to exist but is not overtly acknowledged by the affected parties.

In a survey of 1200 nurses, physicians, and hospital executives within the Voluntary Hospital Association of America (VHA), a network that includes 26% of the community hospitals within the United States, almost 93% of respondents report having observed disruptive behavior by physicians toward nurses and 31% of nurses report knowing at least one nurse actually leaving her or his position because of disruptive behavior associated with conflict (Rosenstein, 2002). This type of healthcare personnel turnover is a considerable financial burden for healthcare facilities. Terminations and quitting associated with conflict and problematic communication cost the healthcare system billions of dollars annually.

Physician–Nurse Power

The power dynamic and any perceived power imbalance that exists between a physician and nurse serve as a powerful precursor to ill feelings and potential conflict. It is common knowledge that the physician–nurse relationship is frequently filled with animosity and a lack of personal and professional respect. In an article entitled "The Doctor–Nurse Game," Leonard Stein (1967) observed several differences in power common between physician and nurses. First, overt disagreement is something that is to be avoided because it goes against the existing power structure (i.e., physician is the superior and the nurse is the subordinate). Thus, nurses are expected to relay recommendations without appearing to make the recommendations themselves as to the proper course of treatment. In this case, there is a respect for power but not to the point where the nurse is seen as powerless. Nurses are not given this institutional power over the medical treatment processes, but as the nursing profession has developed to include many subdiscipline and specialties (e.g., nurse practitioner), a degree of control is afforded to the nurse that in earlier times was not available or acceptable. Nurses who have more experience tend to be more of the opinion that nurses should be an extension of the physician and nothing more.

This traditional perspective focuses on the physician being given utmost power and the nurse being given very little. Such a perspective can have negative effects on decision-making. Second, physicians exert overt power over the medical treatment process in that they control who will be admitted and what type of treatment they will receive. Third, physicians and nurses take different approaches to medical care. Physicians tend to be diagnosis oriented or only

How does a team atmosphere contribute to beneficial outcomes in medical units?

concerned with the symptoms and signs as opposed to how the patient feels about having those symptoms and signs. This disease orientation is based on deductive (algorithmic) logic developed in the scientific method and serves as the foundation of medical care. However, nurses tend to be more holistic in their approach to health care and understand the larger social networks and contexts in which patients are embedded and that these networks can directly influence decision-making processes (e.g., understanding the influence that family and friends exert over patient health decisions and how to recognize such influences and use them for the benefit of the patient).

In a follow-up article 23 years later, Stein and his colleagues argued that some improvements have been made regarding the traditional physician–nurse power dynamic but that some practices remain unchanged and still reflect a maximum power imbalance (Stein, Watts, & Howell, 1990). Some of the most significant improvements were evidenced in medical units where teamwork is essential to beneficial outcomes. Intensive care units and operating rooms are two such areas where overt power use is subordinate to the more critical tasks at hand, such as patient survival and treatment coordination. Some of this improvement can be attributed to encouraging both physicians and nurses to gain an understanding of each other and their unique professional cultures (i.e., what it means to be a physician and what it means to be a nurse) and encouraging nurses to expect to have arguments with physicians and other healthcare personnel, be assertive but not aggressive, and avoid overqualifying when asking a question. **Overqualifying questions** are asked in a way that makes the person who asks the question appear unsure and powerless (e.g., "Doctor, I know I am probably wrong and that I am just a nurse, but do you think the dosage that you suggested is correct?").

The four major types of physician–nurse interactions range from total asymmetrical power dynamics (i.e., physician has all of the power and the

table 8.2

Statement	Response Difference
Communication between nurses and physicians regarding patient care is open and effective	Physicians rated this statement as more positive than nurses did
In the documentation of patient care, there is frequent duplication of effort between physicians and nurses	Both physicians and nurses rated this statement positively
Formal disciplinary action is more likely to be sought by physicians against nurses than against other physicians	Although both physicians and nurses agreed to this statement, nurses endorsed this statement as being much more true than physicians did
The role of the nurse in patient care should not go beyond following the physician's orders	Physicians believed that nurses should do more in terms of going beyond their responsibilities. Nurses reported not wanting to take the risk of getting into trouble
Physicians use nursing evaluations and documentation of the patient to plan patient care	Nurses viewed this statement more negatively than did physicians
The time nurses spend in chart documentation would be better invested in patient care	Both physicians and nurses agreed with this statement with nurses responding with a high level of frustration about the required documentation resulting in frequent overtime
The communication between male nurses and male physicians is more collegial than communication between female nurses and female physicians	This statement was supported more so by nurses than by physicians
The best nurses practice in specialized areas such as intensive care	Staff nurses took great exception to this question, finding it to be inappropriate and presumptuous
Based on their professional preparation (e.g., hospital-based diploma, associate degree, or baccalaureate degree), there is a direct correlation between formal education and competency	The most notable response to this statement was made by nursing administrators because it was of major importance to them and of less importance to others in the study
The major responsibility of the nurse is to serve as the patient's advocate	This was a polarizing question with physicians opposing this statement and nurses supporting this statement
Nurses do a better job than physicians in the management of the dying patient	Nurses agreed more with this statement than physicians because nurses view physicians as intervening to prolong life in a sometimes futile attempt that often results in discomfort for the dying patient
Physicians lack an understanding in the science and scope associated with the practice of nursing	There was high agreement on the part of both nurses and physicians on the physician's lack of familiarity with nursing practice
Because of nurses' perceived lack of respect and power, there is a justification for the formation of a nursing union	This statement received very little support from physicians; nurses were not asked this question
The education and training of nurses and physicians should be coordinated to allow for more professional interaction	Although both physicians and nurses agreed to this statement, nurses rated the statement as much more favorable
The quality of nursing care has improved significantly during the past 20 years	Physicians reported no significant improvement with nursing care performance and nurses cited excessive workloads as a justification for not endorsing the statement

Adapted from Greenfield, L. J. (1999). Doctors and nurses: A troubled partnership. *Annals of Surgery, 230 (3)*, 279–288.

nurse has none) to total symmetrical power balance (i.e., both the physician and nurse share power). Interactions reflective of symmetrical power dynamics consist of **unproblematic subordination,** which is when the nurse carries out the physician's orders without question in a subordinate fashion, yet is still considered asymmetrical. **Informal covert decision-making** is when the nurse carries out the orders from the physician but with open disagreement. This type of interaction reflects more symmetry than unproblematic subordination. **Informal overt decision-making** (symmetrical) reflects the nurse being invited to offer opinions about treatment but does so on an informal basis. **Formal overt decision-making** is the highest level of symmetrical power and reflects the nurse making the decisions in a spirit of shared power. These types of interactions reflect the most shared power among healthcare personnel.

In a study to investigate the different perceptions of physicians and nurses regarding the practice of medicine, procedure, communication, credentialing, and power, Greenfield (1999) found interesting differences between physicians and nurses and their perceptions of how they relate to each other and to patients (Table 8.2). The findings of this study clearly endorse the concept that physicians and nurses, although they work within the same institutions and units, live and perceive very different professional lives. As evidenced throughout this chapter, becoming mindful of our communication can bring about positive relational outcomes so that many of these differing perceptions might become minimized. Although the information presented in this section reflects power dynamics specific to the physician–nurse dyad, these principles can be generalized to any healthcare situation where power differences are based on professional status and require coordinated effort on behalf of the more powerful and less powerful.

Conclusion

This chapter surveyed the influence that humor communication and aggressive communication have on various relationships within healthcare. Research clearly demonstrates that both of these types of communication can serve in both positive and negative ways. The competent communicator understands how to implement each type of communication basing it on situational factors and the nature of the relationship with the receiver. In perhaps one of the most uncertain contexts conceivable, both humor and aggressive communication can help in providing a sense-making process for both the patient and the provider.

Questions for Discussion/Review

1. Distinguish among the cognitive, emotional, and physical responses to humor.
2. Discuss the broaden-and-build theory of positive emotions.
3. Explain why humor research in medicine has been primarily restricted to complementary and alternative medicine.
4. Explain the concept of "therapeutic humor" and how such humor can be of benefit to both the patient and provider.
5. Explain how culture can affect a provider's use of humor. Provide two examples of situations where culture has negatively affected the use of humor.
6. Why is it important for healthcare professionals to understand aggressive communication with regard to the practice of medicine?
7. What is meant when we say that a culture of aggressive communication can be spread through emotional contagion? Provide an example for your answer.
8. How would teaching argumentation and critical thinking skills aid in healthcare practitioners' ability to diffuse aggressive situations? Provide an example.
9. List and describe the verbal trigger events (VTEs) of aggressive communication that are unique to health care. Can you think of any other VTE that is unique to your specific facility or your past experience in health care? Explain your answer.
10. Explain the physician–nurse game and how those power dynamics can be present in any superior–subordinate relationship within health care.

References

Altergroup (2015). *Turnover costs.* Retrieved from http://www.altergroup.com/alter-care-blog/index.php/healthcare/rn-turnover-costs.

Annas, G. J. (1997). Patients' rights in managed care—Exit, voice, and choice. *New England Journal of Medicine, 33*(3), 210–215.

Avtgis, T. A., & Madlock, P. (2008). Implications of the verbally aggressive patient: Creating a constructive environment in destructive situations. In E. P. Polack, V. P. Richmond, & J. C. McCroskey (Eds.), *Applied communication for health professionals* (pp. 169–183). Dubuque, IA: Kendall Hunt.

Avtgis, T. A., & Polack, E. P. (2010). Aggressive communication within medical care: Mapping the domain. In T. A. Avtgis & A. S. Rancer (Eds.), *Arguments, aggression, and conflict: Theory and research.* New York: Routledge.

Avtgis, T. A., Polack, E. P., Staggers, S. M., & Wiecorek, S. M. (2011). Healthcare provider–recipient interactions: Is "on-line" interaction the next best thing to being there. In K. B. Wright & L. Webb (Eds.), *Computer mediated communication in personal relationships* (pp. 266–284). Cresskill, NJ: Hampton Press.

Avtgis, T. A., & Rancer, A. S. (2010). Burnout and aggressive communication in educational institutions: An emic or etic phenomena? In M. B. Hinner (Ed.), *Freiberger beitrage zur interkutuellen und wirtshaftskommunication: A general forum for general and intercultural business communication. 59,* 282–293. Frankfurt, Germany: Peter Lang.

Barsade, S. G. (2002). The ripple effect: Emotional contagion and its influence on group behavior. *Administrative Quarterly, 47,* 644–675.

Beech, B., & Leather, P. (2006). Workplace violence in the healthcare sector: A review of staff training and integration of evaluation models. *Aggression and Violent Behavior, 11,* 27–43.

Ben-Sira, Z. (1990). Primary care practitioners' likelihood to engage in a biopsycho-social approach: An additional perspective on the doctor-patient relationship. *Social Science and Medicine, 154,* 1365–1370.

Berger, J. P., Coulehan, J., & Belling, C. (2004). Humor in the physician–patient encounter. *Archives of Internal Medicine, 164,* 825–830.

Berlyne, D. E. (1969). Laughter, humor, and play. *Handbook of Social Psychology, 3,* 795–813.

Boehm, F. H. (2003). Building trust, *Family Practice News, 33,* 12.

Bonsteel, A. (1997). Behind the white coat, *The Humanist, 57,* 15–19.

Briles, J. (2003). Zapping conflict in the health care workplace. Retrieved from www.briles.com/articles/ZappingConflict.pdf.

Budd, T. (1999). *Violence at work: Findings from the British crime survey.* London: Health and Safety Executive.

Burgdorf, J., & Panksepp, J. (2006). The neurobiology of positive emotions. *Neuroscience Biobehavioral Review, 30,* 173–187.

Chopra, D. (1990). *Quantum healing: Exploring frontiers of mind/body medicine.* New York: Bantam Books.

Cousins, N. (1976). Anatomy of an illness (as perceived by the patient). *New England Journal of Medicine, 295,* 1458–1463.

Cousins, N. (1979). *Anatomy of an illness as perceived by the patient: Reflections on healing and recovery.* New York: Norton.

Cumura, R. (1992). Conflict and harmony in Japanese medicine: A challenge to traditional culture in neonatal care. In E. Pellagrino, P. Mazzarella, & P. Corsi (Eds.), *Transcultural dimensions of medical ethics* (pp. 145–153). Frederick, MD: University Publishing Group.

Darwin, C. (1872). *The expressions of emotions in man and animals.* London: John Murray.

Davis, S. (1991). Violence by psychiatric patients: A review. *Hospitals and Community Psychiatry, 42,* 585–590.

DiCioccio, R. (2012). *Humor communication: Theory, impact, and outcomes.* Dubuque, IA: Kendall Hunt.

Dula, A. (1994). African-American's suspicion of the health care system is justified: What do we do about it? *Cambridge Quarterly Health Care Ethics, 3,* 347–357.

Erb, J. (2001). Assessment and management of the violent patient. In J. L. Jacobson & A. M. Jacobson (Eds.), *Psychiatric secrets* (2nd ed., pp. 440–447). Philadelphia, PA: Hanley and Belfus.

Francis, L., Monahan, K., & Berger, C. (1999). A laughing matter? The use of humor in medical interactions. *Motti's Emotion, 23,* 155–174.

Fredrickson, B. L. (1998). What good are positive emotions? *The Review of General Psychology, 2,* 300–319.

Ferguson, J. A., Weinberger, M., Westmorland, G. R., Mamlin, L. A., Segar, D. S., & Green, J. Y. (1988). Racial disparity in cardiac decision making: Results from patient focus groups. *Archives of Internal Medicine, 158, 13,* 1450–1453.

Fredrickson, B. L. (2001). The role of positive emotions in positive psychology: The broaden-and-build theory of positive emotion. *American Psychologist, 56,* 218–226.

Freud, S. (1928). Humour. *The International Journal of Psychoanalysis, 9,* 1–6.

Fry, W. F. (1963). *Sweet madness: A study of humor.* Palo Alto, CA: Pacific Books.

Gates, D. M. (2004). The epidemic of violence against healthcare workers. *Occupational Environmental Medicine, 61,* 649-650.

Gerberich, S., Church, T., McGovern, P., Hansen, H., Nachreiner, N., & Geisser, M. S. (2004). An epidemiological study of the magnitude and consequences of work related violence: The Minnesota Nurses' study. *Occupational Environmental Medicine, 61,* 495–503.

Gervais, M., & Wilson, D. S. (2005). The evolution and functions of laughter and humor: A synthetic approach. *Quarterly Review of Biology, 80,* 395–430.

Goldstein, J. H., & McGhee, T. E. (1972). *The psychology of humor: Theoretical perspectives and empirical issues.* New York: Academic Press.

Goodkin, K., Fletcher, M. A., & Cohen, N. (1995). Clinical aspects of psychoneuro-immunology. *Lancet, 345* (8952), 183–185.

Greenfield, L. J. (1999). Doctors and nurses: A troubled partnership. *Annals of Surgery, 230, 3,* 279–288.

Hahn, S. R. (2001). Physical symptoms and physician-experienced difficulty in the physician–patient relationship. *Annals of Internal Medicine, 134,* 897–904.

Hampes, W. P. (2001). Relation between humor and empathetic concern. *Psychological Reports, 88,* 241–244.

Hatfield, E., Cacioppo, J. T., & Rapson, R. L. (1993). Emotional contagion. *Current Directions in Psychological Science, 2,* 96–99.

Henderson, A. (2003). Nurses and workplace violence: Nurses' experiences of verbal and physical abuse at work. *Canadian Journal of Nursing Leadership, 16,* 82-98.

Herbert, J. (1997). Stress, the brain, and mental illness. *British Medical Journal, 315* (7105), 530–536.

Infante, D. A. (1987). Aggressiveness. In J. C. McCroskey & J. A. Daly (Eds.), *Personality and interpersonal communication* (pp. 157–192). Newbury Park, CA: Sage.

Infante, D. A., & Rancer, A. S. (1982). A conceptualization and measure of argumentativeness. *Journal of Personality Assessment, 46,* 72–80.

Infante, D. A., & Wigley, C. J. (1986). Verbal aggressiveness: An interpersonal model and measure. *Communication Monographs, 53,* 61–69.

Kappel, D. A., Rossi, D. C., Polack, E. P., Avtgis, T. A., & Martin, M. M. (2011). Does the RTTDC© (rural trauma team development course©) shorten the interval from trauma patient arrival to decision to transfer? *Journal of Trauma, Injury, Infection, and Critical Care, 70(2), 315–319.*

Kingma, M. (2001). Workplace violence in the health sector: A problem of epidemic proportion. *International Nursing Review, 48,* 129–130.

Lanza, M. L. (2006). Violence in nursing. In E. K. Kelloway, J. Barling, & J. J. Hurrell (Eds.), *Handbook of workplace violence* (pp. 147–168). Thousand Oaks, CA: Sage.

Lanza, M. L., Zeiss, R., & Rierdan, J. (2005, November). *Violence assessment, medication, and prevention: Factors related to staff violence and implications.* Paper presented at the annual meeting of the American Nurses Conference, Washington, DC.

Lefcourt, H. M., & Martin, R. A. (1986). *Humor and life stress: Antidote to adversity.* New York: Springer-Verlag.

Maslach, C. (2003). Job burnout: New directions in research and intervention. *Current Directions in Psychological Science, 12*, 189–192.

Maslach, C., & Goldberg, J. (1998). Prevention and burnout: New perspectives. *Applied and Preventive Psychology, 7,* 63–74.

Mechanic, D., & Schlesinger, M. (1996). The impact of managed care on patients' trust in medical care and their physicians. *Journal of the American Medical Association, 275* (21), 1693–1697.

Moody, R. (1978). *Laugh after laugh.* Jacksonville, FL: Head Waters Press.

Morreim, E. H. (1989). Conflicts of interest: Profits and problems in physician referrals. *Journal of the American Medical Association, 262* (3), 385–389.

Murry, R. F. (1992). Minority perspectives in biomedical ethics. In E. Pellagrino, P. Mazzarella, & P. Corsi (Eds.), *Transcultural dimensions of medical ethics* (pp. 35–42). Frederick, MD: University Publishing Group.

OSHA Statistics. Retrieved June 12, 2008, from www.osha.gov/oshstats/index.html.

Powell, G., Caan, W., & Crowe, M. (1994). What events precede violent incidents in psychiatric hospitals? *British Journal of Psychiatry, 165,* 107–112.

Provine, R. R. (2000). *Laughter, a scientific investigation.* New York: Viking Penguin.

Rancer, A. S., & Avtgis, T. A. (2006). *Argumentative and aggressive communication: Theory, research, and application.* Thousand Oaks, CA: Sage.

Rancer, A. S., & Avtgis, T. A. (2015). *Argumentative and aggressive communication: Theory, research, and application* (2nd ed.). Thousand Oaks, CA: Sage.

Robinson, V. M. (1991). *Humor and the health professions, the therapeutic use of humor in health care* (2nd ed.). Thorofare, NJ: Slack.

Rodwin, M. A. (1995). Strains in the fiduciary metaphor: Divided physician loyalties and obligations in a changing health care system. *American Journal of Law & Medicine, 21,* 241–257.

Rosenstein, A. H. (2002). Nurse–physician relationships: Impact of nurse satisfaction and retention. *American Journal of Nursing, 102* (6), 26–34.

Rossi, D., Polack, E. P., Kappel, D., Avtgis, T. A., & Martin, M. M. (2009). It is not about being nice; It's about being a better doctor: The investigation into problematic communication and delays in trauma patient transfers. *Medical Encounter, 23,* 5–6.

Roter, D. L. (1989). Which facets of communication have strong effects on outcome—A meta analysis. In M. Stewart & D. Roter (Eds.), *Communicating with medical patients: Vol. 9. Interpersonal communication* (pp. 183–196). Newbury Park, CA: Sage.

Siegal, B. (1998). *Love, medicine, and miricles.* New York: Harper Row.

Snyder, J. (2009). The role of coworker and supervisor social support in alleviating the experience of burnout for caregivers in the human-services industry. *Southern Communication Journal, 74,* 373–389.

Steadman, H., Mulvey, E., Monohan, J., Robbins, P., Applebaum, P., & Grisso, T. (1998). Violence by people discharged from active psychiatric in-patient facilities and by others in the same neighborhoods. *Archives of General Psychiatry*, 55, 393–401.

Stein, L. I. (1967). The doctor–nurse game. *Archives of General Psychiatry, 16* (6), 699–703.

Stein, L. I., Watts, D. T., & Howell, T. (1990). The doctor–nurse game revisited. *New England Journal of Medicine, 322* (8), 546–549.

Sultanoff, S.M., Humor Matters. Retrieved on August 19, 2010 from: http://www.humormatters.com

Taber, K. H., Redden, M., & Hurley, R. A. (2007). Functional anatomy of humor: Positive affect and chronic mental illness. *The Journal of Neuropsychiatry and Clinical Neurosciences, 19,* 358–362.

Turk, D., & Meichenbaum, D. (1991). Adherence to self-care regimens—The patient's perspective. In J. J. Sweet, R. H. Rozensky & S. M. Tovian (Eds.), *Handbook of clinical psychology in medical settings* (pp. 249–267). New York: Plenum Press.

Walsh, J. J. (1911). *Old-time makers of medicine*. Retrived from http://www.todayinsci.com/M/ Mondeville_Henri/MondevilleHenri-Quotations.htm.

Whittington, R. (1994). Violence in psychiatric hospitals. In N. T. Wykes (Ed.), *Violence and healthcare professionals* (pp. 23–44). London: Chapman and Hall.

Wigley, C. J. (2010). Verbal trigger events—Other catalysts and precursors of aggression. In T. A. Avtgis & A. S. Rancer (Eds.), *Arguments, aggression, and conflict: New directions in theory and research* (pp. 388–399). New York: Routledge.

Wooten, P., Hodgkin, J., Connors, G., & Bell, C. (editors) (1993). Laughter as therapy for patient and caregiver. *Pulmonary Rehabilitation,* Philadelphia, PA: Lippincott.

Ziv, A. (1983). The influence of humor's atmosphere on divergent thinking. *Contemporary Educational Psychology, 8,* 413–421.

chapter nine

Medical and Relational Information Processing

chapter objectives

Upon completion of the chapter, the student should be able to:

1. Explain the physiology of hearing

2. Explain the concept of mindfulness

3. Explain the importance of narrative medicine

4. Compare and contrast the different types of listening

5. Explain the process of therapeutic writing and its potential impact on the healthcare practitioner

K nowing what constitutes information, processing that information, and listening are three skills vital to the effective treatment of patients, yet they are overlooked and devalued by medical personnel. As has been evidenced in the seven previous chapters of this book, communication involves not only the effective and appropriate encoding, sending, receiving, and decoding of messages, but also having the proper information on which to draw when engaging in communication exchanges. For example, Leape and colleagues (1991) reviewed more than 30,000 randomly selected hospital records outlining any incidences of *adverse events* and *negligence* resulting in injuries to hospital patients. An adverse event is any injury caused by medical **error.** It does not imply negligence or poor-quality care. Rather, it is an undesirable outcome resulting from some aspect of diagnosis or therapy

© Pressmaster/Shutterstock.com

key terms

adverse event	listening apprehension	sentinel events
burnout syndrome	mindfulness	therapeutic listening
closed-ended question	narrative medicine	therapeutic writing
discriminative listening	open-ended question	witnessing

adverse event

Any injury caused by medical care. It does not imply negligence or poor quality of care; rather, it is an undesirable outcome resulting from some aspect of diagnosis or therapy; not an underlying disease process.

that is not attributable to an underlying disease process. **Negligence** is an unanticipated event caused by the lack of using reasonable care or an error in the performance of duty. The results of the Leape et al. (1991) study indicate that 3.7% of the patients were being injured in hospitals and, of those, two thirds of the injuries were preventable. The most prevalent factor in these preventable injuries was adverse drug events resulting directly from poor communication. More specifically, double dosing (e.g., one nurse not knowing what the other nurse had already administered) and poor hand-off communication (e.g., the necessary information had not been transferred or incorrectly transferred from one nurse to another regarding the patient's medication needs).

Communication-related findings in such events were further highlighted by the Institute of Medicine reporting that medical error causes between 44,000 and 98,000 deaths per year in our healthcare system (National Institutes of Health, 1999). The resulting policy changes to reduce medical error consisted of a 5-year plan that was to be fully implemented by 2005. As of 2011, however, few of these changes have occurred. Overall, the concepts of communication, information transfer, and listening skills and their influence on error have been shown to be a result of human relationships—not pure science—and thus can be improved with communication training. This

How does poor communication contribute to hospital errors?

© Barabasa/Shutterstock.com

chapter will focus specifically on how people gather information, process information, and engage in effective listening to deliver better healthcare and increase patient safety.

The Physiology of Hearing

Before a thorough discussion of information processing and listening can occur, we must make a clear distinction between the concepts of *listening* and *hearing*. **Listening** is the process of receiving, constructing, deriving meaning from, and responding to spoken and/or nonverbal messages, whereas **hearing** is a physiological process that occurs when sound waves enter the ear canal and vibrations are converted to electrical signals sent to the brain (Avtgis, Rancer, & Madlock, 2010). The human ear is a sensitive yet extraordinary organ. Unlike smell, taste, and vision, which involve chemical reactions, hearing is a system based solely on physical movements and includes the concepts of *sound, matter,* and *amplitude*. **Sound** is created when an object vibrates in matter. **Matter** can be either a solid (e.g., the Earth), a liquid (e.g., water), or gas (e.g., air) in nature. Therefore, sound is vibration in the air and the resulting movement of air particles. People can hear different sounds from different vibrating objects. The greater the frequency of the vibration, the higher the pitch; the lesser the frequency of the vibration, the lower the pitch.

The ear is comprised of three basic sections. The **pinna** or external ear is a series of folds that serve to harness the external sound waves and assist in harnessing the sound into the ear canal. The **ear canal** is also known as the external auditory canal, which funnels the sound into the eardrum that

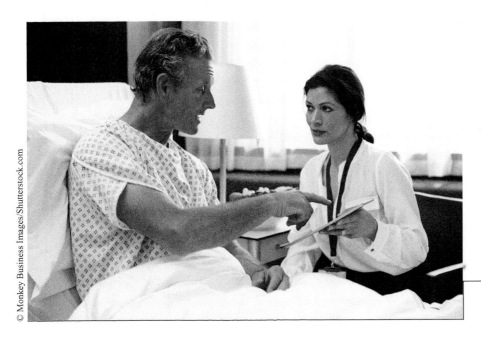

© Monkey Business Images/Shutterstock.com

What is listening as opposed to hearing?

then vibrates the three bones of the middle ear; the **malleus** (the hammer) is a lever that vibrates the **incus** (the anvil), which is the middle bone; and the **stapes** (stirrup) is an oval window against which the sound is amplified.

As indicated in Figure 9.1, the **Eustachian tube,** which connects the throat and mouth area, equalizes pressure on both sides of the eardrum. The external ear is exposed to the environment; the middle ear pressure is equalized through air from the mouth coming through the Eustachian tube into the middle ear. To give an idea as to how dynamic the process of hearing is, the eardrum is approximately 55 square millimeters, yet the sound is transferred through the three bones to the face plate of the stapes, which is approximately 3.2 millimeters in size. The stapes communicates with the oval window, which then vibrates the fluid-based environment of the **cochlea** (i.e., a snail-like structure containing three connected fluid-filled areas). These transmitted vibrations of fluid matter are then electrically transferred to the temporal lobe of the brain by the **cochlear nerve** (i.e., part of the auditory nerve that transmits impulses to the portion of the brain responsible for sound processing).

Information Processing

Within any discipline there comes a unique vocabulary and way of looking at the world that demands all who engage in that discipline to be competent in identifying and valuing particular pieces of information. Healthcare is no different. What constitutes information? According to Avtgis et al. (2010), information is defined as "bits of data that are created when people assign them significance" (p. 234). Given this definition, medical personnel generally seek out information from the patient such as their history of symptoms, test results, specific nonverbal aspects of the patient's presentation, and so

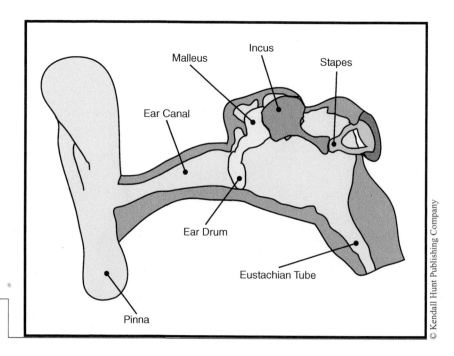

figure 9.1

Anatomy of the Human Ear

on. These bits of data, along with many others, are recognized as important information by medical science and learned during the medical education process. The way in which people identify and attribute significance to bits of information in the environment is known as **information scanning**. The environment, in the case of healthcare, can take the form of the patient's verbal and nonverbal presentation and things not related to the symptoms of the patient such as cultural background, assumptions about healthcare, and a host of other idiosyncratic attributes specific to the patient. This scanning of the environment for information can be either proactive or reactive in nature.

Proactive scanning is a person's tendency to identify and assign significance to data that may be or will be used in future decision-making, whereas **reactive scanning** reflects the tendency to identify and assign significance to data only after a problem or situation requiring a decision presents itself (Avtgis et al., 2010). Healthcare professionals can use several practices to create an environment of proactive scanning: (a) keep in contact with other members of the global organization (hospital/office/clinic) including people from other shifts and other units, if appropriate (b) develop, maintain, and regularly access information databases on patients, unit performance, and hospital performance as a whole (CQI—continuous quality improvement); (c) openly discuss both internal and external influences on patient safety and outcomes and recognize the importance of multiple perspectives of the same information; and (d) develop practices to improve proactive scanning such as manipulating the environment (e.g., changing the position of a piece of office furniture or adding a new analysis to a report to distinguish between those who recognize the new data and those who ignore or overlook them) (Choo, 2006). The development of proactive scanning behavior is necessary for mindful communication because it affords the communicator a level of awareness that can provide invaluable information that would otherwise go undetected by the less aware communicator.

Some major hurdles to effective information processing may result in a threat to patient safety. One of the more significant factors is a communication trait known as **informational reception apprehension (IRA)**. IRA is a tendency to process information reflecting "a pattern of anxiety and antipathy that filters informational reception, perception, and processing, and/or adjustment (psychologically, verbally, physically) associated with complexity, abstractness, and flexibility" (Wheeless, Preiss, & Gayle, 1997, p. 166). The degree a person experiences apprehension is based on the complexity, abstractness, and flexibility of both the *information* and the *person*. **Complexity** reflects the amount of detail in the information and the capacity of the person to process that information. **Abstractness** refers to the level of concreteness of the information and the capacity of the person to think in abstract terms. **Flexibility** refers to the demands of the external environment, which includes the level of openness, adaptability, and change, and a person's ability to select, receive, and process such information.

Informational reception apprehension contains the three separate dimensions of listening apprehension (i.e., fear associated with either anticipated or real listening situations), **reading anxiety** (i.e., the degree of anxiety a person experiences when reading information), and **intellectual inflexibility**

listening apprehension
Fear associated with either anticipated or real listening situations.

(i.e., the degree to which people are unwilling to consider different points of view). Many patients and healthcare professionals suffer from IRA. The way that people cognitively and emotionally respond to information directly determines the type of information they seek and how accurately that information is recalled. Such a lack of information processing abilities can drastically reduce patient safety on the part of the healthcare providers and contribute to low levels of health literacy on the part of the patient.

The Hand-Off Process

Healthcare is by nature a human relationship business that in most cases occurs on a 24-hour, 7-day-a-week basis. As a result of the constant service nature of healthcare, there are many transitions of patient care including from provider-to-provider, nurse-to-nurse, nurse-to-provider, inpatient-to-outpatient, hospital-to-chronic care, or hospital-to-skilled care facility. Given this constant "hand-off" process, there are many mistakes that can and do occur. Recall that between 44,000 and 98,000 deaths occur annually due to medical error and that a large number of these deaths can be attributed to communication problems associated with the patient hand-off process (Leape et al., 1991; National Institutes of Health, 1999). This is further complicated by the fact that in July 2003, all postgraduate residency programs in medicine were required to adhere to a new 80-hour work week to maintain their accreditation. This reduced work schedule resulted in more information needing to be transferred from one healthcare practitioner to the next because of the increase in shift change frequency. Before the 80-hour mandated work week, continuity of care was generally ensured by long work hours rather than transferring responsibility to other providers. Therefore, there have been several attempts at streamlining the hand-off process so as to make the transfer of patient information one that is concise, efficient, and ideally free of error.

One promising way in which the hand-off process is being made more efficient is through the use of pneumonic devices developed specifically for quick and efficient information transfer (SBAR). Hand-off Exchange One other effort was developed by Van Eaton, Horvath, Lober, and Pellegrini (2004) involving a computer system specifically designed to improve hand-off communication by creating a computerized resident sign-out system. The system, known as UWCores, centralizes patient information and creates checklists for transfer of care duties. For example, vital signs (including blood pressure, pulse, and respirations) and intake/output of fluids (intake of fluids includes those taken either by mouth, feeding tube, or by IV and output of fluids can be either by urine or loss of fluids from stomach, wound, or stool). Van Eaton et al. (2004) found that the system improved accuracy, was portable enough to be utilized in a variety of healthcare facilities, and was easily adaptable. Other successful attempts at computer hand-off communication efficiency include systems that have not only personnel shift sign-out, but also patient medication information (Frank, Wallace, & Steinberg, 2005) and physician-focused systems that track patient sign-out and include summaries for all discharges (Kanney & Moore, 1999).

© ESB Basic/Shutterstock.com

The hand-off process needs to be communicated accurately to increase patient safety.

Despite all of the efforts to increase the efficiency of the hand-off process (through elimination of redundancy, message construction, and standardization of information), an incredible amount of inaccurate and omitted information is transferred on a daily basis during the hand-off process. This fact is illustrated in a 2010 study looking at interns and the hand-off process (Chang, Arora, Lev-Ari, D'Arcy, & Keysar, 2010). Chang et al. (2010) concluded that the most important information about a patient and the patient's condition was not successfully communicated to receiving personnel 60% of the time. This finding is especially problematic in light of these same interns rating their communication during the hand-off process as being very high. The interns' overestimation of their own communication competence when compared to the actual understanding on the part of the receiver is a gap that needs to be reduced to properly align what is being assumed about one's communication efficacy and the actual efficacy of that communication. The fact that 65% to 70% of the sentinel events (i.e., an event causing or risking serious injury or death to the patient) are related to communication (Leonard, Graham, & Bonacum, 2004), standardized educational efforts regarding the hand-off process must be undertaken and properly assessed to maximize accuracy and increase patient safety.

Mindfulness

The concept of mindfulness has recently received an abundance of attention from both scholars and practitioners from many disciplines. However, this movement of being fully aware of one's surroundings is not a new phenomenon; it has been of concern for more than a century. According to the

sentinel event

An event causing or risking serious injury or death to the patient.

mindfulness

The process of being aware of your behavior and basing your behavior on a specific situation as opposed to simply enacting a generic script used for a variety of situations.

world-renowned psychologist William James (1924), "[C]ompared to what we ought to be, we are only half awake" (p. 237). **Mindfulness** is defined as "being aware of your behavior and basing your behavior on a specific situation as opposed to simply enacting a generic script that is used for a variety of situations" (Avtgis et al., 2010, p. 76). Mindfulness has its roots in the Eastern religions of Zen, Buddhism, and other contemplative traditions where *consciousness, attentiveness,* and *awareness* are actively cultivated (Gazzela, 2005; Kapileau, 1965). **Consciousness** is a state of existence that requires both attention to and awareness of outside sources of energy. According to Weston (1999), **awareness** serves as the "radar" for consciousness and is defined as the continuous monitoring of the inner and outer environment such that stimuli may be registered in the consciousness without being the center of focus. For example, emergency room personnel may be exposed to, and have an awareness of, a variety of stimuli such as patient cries, screams, or commotion yet not let any of these stimuli overtake their focus on their immediate duty of patient care. **Attention** is a focused type of consciousness resulting in a heightened sensitivity to stimuli. Both awareness and attention are interactive concepts in that we are constantly pulling stimuli out of our awareness in order to focus attention on any given area of importance.

Given the popularity of the mindfulness construct and the concept of intertwining other disciplines such as psychology, communication, and the humanities with medicine (**integrative medicine**), scholars argue that the practice of mindfulness in medicine should take the form of a compassionate and nonjudgmental awareness of the present moment (Shapiro & Schwartz, 2000; Shapiro, Schwartz, & Bonner, 1998). Some of the challenges to the practice of mindfulness in medicine are summed up by Julie Connelly (1999), who states that "medical practice is beset by interruptions, contests for attention, and urgent demands that diminish the attentiveness required for humanistic care of patients" (p. 420). The concept of integrative medicine was met with skepticism by the traditional scientific-based medical community. Now, schools of nursing, medicine, physical therapy, dentistry, and the like have recognized the merging of social sciences, humanities, and the hard sciences as a valuable attribute in the development of a hybrid skill set necessary for the practice of medicine in the 21st century.

One of the most prominent scholars of mindfulness is Ellen Langer (1989), who describes interpersonal self-awareness or social intelligence as a state of "could be" whereby a person welcomes uncertainty. In the fast pace of medicine, uncertainty can be seen as an opportunity rather than something to be avoided or reduced. Throughout human history, the state of mindfulness has resulted in the creation of many discoveries. For example, when a person encounters a problem or a situation that needs to be altered or resolved, the solving of that problem becomes a very mindful process. The fields of science and medicine are no different. Some mindful discoveries include penicillin, radiation, and the benzene ring. All of these were developed by someone paying attention to what seemed to be an anomaly or chance reaction (i.e., what would not normally garner attention). Finding out why such odd reactions occur has resulted in a myriad of discoveries in both industry and science. This mindful human curiosity is central to both caring for patients and solving problems. It is only through the practice of mindfulness that we can fully develop compassionate action toward others, use a wide assortment of data to better make decisions, and understand the patient in order to optimally relieve suffering.

A recent study by Krasen and colleagues (2009) found that education in mindful communication is associated with both short- and long-term sustained improvement in one's professional sense of well-being and improved attitude about patient care. However, even in light of this finding, 60% of practicing physicians report symptoms of psychological distress related to work, which is also known as *burnout syndrome* (Shanafelt, Bradley, Wipf, & Back, 2002). **Burnout syndrome** is a general malaise with increased feelings of emotional exhaustion, of detachment from both colleagues and patients, and of professional failure (Maslach, Schaufli, & Leiter, 2001). Burnout syndrome among healthcare professionals has been linked to poor-quality healthcare including patient dissatisfaction, increase in medical errors and medical litigation, and a decreased ability to express empathy (Shanafelt, Sloan, & Habermann, 2003).

One of the most effective ways to foster mindfulness and decrease the symptoms of burnout syndrome is to practice **mindfulness meditation,** which emphasizes the quality of being fully present and attentive to the moment during everyday activities (Epstein, 1999). More specifically, mindfulness meditation is a contemplative practice designed to cultivate a person's attention and awareness to surrounding stimuli. Such an educational effort is focused on two general concepts of *appreciative inquiry* and *narrative medicine* (discussed later in this chapter). **Appreciative inquiry (AI)** is a newer

| burnout syndrome

A general malaise with increased feelings of being emotionally exhausted, of detachment from both colleagues and patients, and of professional failure.

© pathdoc/Shutterstock.com

What is burnout syndrome?

approach to organizational development that "rejects the problem-solving or deficit-based approach...and focuses on doing things right and using those things to build the future of the organization" (Avtgis et al., 2010, p. 294). For example, the concept of wellness or preventative medicine is to put the focus on what humans can do in wellness to prevent disease and infection. Such an approach is in sharp contrast to the more traditional focus on healing only after disease or infection is present. The focus that AI puts on both listening to the patient's story and reflecting on these stories and how this reflection can aid in the healing process are some of the main components believed to be especially beneficial to quality patient care (Cooperrider & Srivastva, 1987; Cooperrider, Whitney, & Stavros, 2008). By using both appreciative inquiry and narrative medicine, the healthcare provider is more invested in mindful perspective-taking that can lead to interesting discovery of the patient and/or an increased sense of self-worth for the provider. The implementation of such an educational effort requires two phases and a total of 52 hours of participation. Phase one is the *intensive phase,* which requires 8 weekly sessions at 2.5 hours per session with a final session lasting 7 hours. The second phase is the *maintenance phase,* which requires 10 monthly sessions at 2.5 hours per session. Much of the time spent in the maintenance phase is done in silent practice of meditation. Overall, such efforts have been found to offer both short- and long-term positive effects on the healthcare provider's sense of well-being and attitudes, particularly when associated with patient care.

Narratives in Healthcare

| **narrative medicine**

The utilization of the patient's story regarding illness in the development and application of medical treatment.

Narrative medicine is the utilization of the patient's story regarding illness in the development and application of medical treatment. This type of storytelling is based on the concept that they contain something powerful, informative, and useful that can aid in the practice of medicine (Charon, 2006). The patient's story allows for the patient to have a voice during the medical encounter and a vehicle through which the healthcare practitioner can better relate to and ultimately heal the patient. Charon identified five basic characteristics of narrative medicine: *time, individuality, the cause or reason, personal relationships,* and *ethics.*

Time.   The concept of time in narrative medicine is compelling in that so many stories throughout one's life are based on some form or concept of time. In childhood, we encounter stories and fairy tales that start with "Once upon a time..." Such narratives teach us where we come from and where we are going and allow us to understand the meaning of our own lives by respecting time— simply put, the beginning, the middle, and the end of human events. Time also influences the interpretation of narrative. For example, consider reading a story today that you had read 10 years earlier. The story will probably have an entirely different meaning than it once did. For healthcare practitioners, listening to the narrative of a patient with HIV/AIDS 20 years ago will probably reveal a different interpretation than if the same narrative was told today.

© Tyler Olson/Shutterstock.com

Do you get frustrated when waiting for an appointment?

Disease is also a time-oriented concept. Consider the ailments associated with growing old. Most patients die of some pathology associated with chronic disease such as diabetes, heart disease, cancer, dementia, or disabling conditions such as arthritis. All of these chronic diseases are associated with older people. However, if the patient is a child with one of these ailments, the narrative is drastically changed from one that is routine in nature (elderly patient) to one that is tragic (young patient). For healthcare practitioners, how time is used is also of great importance for the patient. Healthcare practitioners are historically known for being late for appointments. This is evidenced in the waiting rooms in most clinics, hospitals, and medical offices. Many practitioners make the faulty assumption that the waiting experience for the patient is not overly adverse and therefore is not a significant issue. However, patients garner powerful meaning with regard to waiting and directly attribute differences of human worth to such an event—they may see it as the time of the healthcare practitioner is of great value, whereas the time of the patient is of little value.

When considering time as a major component of a person's life story, we cannot forget the rather recent popularity of end-of-life documents (e.g., advanced directives). From a narrative perspective, these types of instruments serve as a level of autonomy for the patient where the patient is actually engaged in the "end narrative" of their life. In other words, these end-of-life documents give control to a person as to how their "story" will conclude or directs other people as to how they should "act" at the end of the story.

Individuality.   The concept of individuality reflects the fact that every person's story is different from one another. Consider how a healthcare practitioner would describe a rash. Perhaps they will name the rash and describe the pathology and probabilities of treatment. This approach is representative of the *disease perspective.* Contrast this with the description of a rash given by the patient. The patient's description may be based on symptoms related to the rash such as the appearance of it and how it affects their everyday life (e.g., itchy, ugly, painful). This type of approach is representative of the *illness perspective.* This sharp contrast in perspective can lead the patient to feel devalued and as if they are being treated as an object. This devaluation has become such a major source of frustration for patients that the field of **concierge medicine** has emerged. Concierge medicine is the practice of medicine whereby a physician takes care (for a retainer fee) of a small panel of patients, making house calls, and being available around the clock. According to participants in such practices, this style of medicine results in the merging of disease and illness perspectives and science and art. This type of medicine is believed to be more mindful in nature than the more traditional patient–provider models of care because of its structure and intimacy between the patient and provider.

Reason.   All stories have a **plot.** The plot is the organizing line or the thread that makes the narrative possible. Depending on how well it is articulated, some narratives are easy to understand, whereas others are more difficult. One of the ways in which we make sense of a story is to focus directly on the plot. It is only when human beings frame these events with the beginning, middle, and end can sense be made or meaning be attributed. This idea of sense making is important, especially in light of the fact that healthcare practitioners tend to be reductive and parsimonious in their communication with patients. Practitioners give little time to the concepts of a narrative that is long, fragmented, and full of metaphor. However, the stories of patient's are often full of metaphors and quite often exaggeration. Therefore, it is important for practitioners to be mindful of both the science and humanity involved in the practice of medicine and how the narrative of their patients can be valuable information in medical care.

Personal Relationships.   The narrative is also a way in which the patient can connect with the healthcare provider. As mentioned earlier, the differing perspectives of the patient (i.e., illness perspective) and the provider (i.e., disease perspective) can be merged through the mindful application of the "common narrative" created between the patient and provider. The Patient's Story Thus, "my story" becomes "our story." This phenomenon can be seen in a patient recovering from cancer, who, when discussing their story, refers to the doctor as a team member or someone who is fighting the cancer alongside them.

Ethics.   Stories are a form of *witnessing* and, as such, are considered sacred. Witnessing is defined as being in the presence of an event that is significant to one or all of the parties involved. There are responsibilities for the healthcare practitioner in possessing, knowing, and grasping the narrative of another person. This responsibility is synonymous with power because it carries with it a daunting ethical responsibility. This ethical responsibility is different from that associated with clinical competency such as taking a present or

witnessing

Being in the presence of an event that is significant to one or all of the parties involved.

How healthcare providers become part of the patient's recovery team?

past medical history, and so on. When a practitioner has heard a narrative or has to "bear witness" to a patient's very sacred and confidential information, the information revealed may be information that has not been revealed to anyone before. This very fact alone makes that information sacred.

These five characteristics of narrative medicine, if considered in the everyday practice of medicine, provide the healthcare practitioner with a valuable source of information from which to better treat the patient's body, mind, and soul.

Information Gathering: The Ultimate Storyteller

Information comes in all forms and through all five human senses. Therefore, healthcare professionals should seek to be mindful of their presence, the presence of the patients, and the presence of the patient–provider dyad. Translational science requires a person to use multiple logics; the concept is best articulated in Daniel Pink's 2005 book, *A Whole New Mind.* Pink argues that for any system to survive, there needs to be not only the use of logical and critical processes (such as those found in the left side of the human brain) for thinking about information, but also use of processes such as inventiveness, empathy, joyfulness, and meaning (such as those associated with the right side of the human brain). Such combinations are believed to directly translate into mindfulness or the creation of a "whole new mind." Such a synthesis is considered essential in the practice of contemporary medicine. This is especially important because medicine, being greatly steeped in science, sees anecdote (i.e., use of personal experience or storytelling) as one of the lowest forms of scientific inquiry and thus of little value at best and contemptible at worst.

The practice of mindful medicine has been shown to have bottom-line effects for practitioners. For example, Hampton, Harrison, Mitchell, Prichard, and Seymour (1975) argue that if the healthcare practitioner actively listens to the history (story) of the patient, the information contained in the patient's initial presentation is sufficient to make a diagnosis in 82% of the patients. Of the remaining 18%, 9% of diagnoses were made by physical examination and the remaining 9% were diagnosed by laboratory findings. A similar finding indicates that between 60% and 82% of data needed to make a diagnosis comes from listening to the patient's history (Peterson, Holbrook, Von Hales, Smith, & Staker, 1992). Contrast this with common medical practices approximately 30 years ago where during the doctor–patient interview process, the provider interrupted the patient within the first 18 to 21 seconds of telling their story (Beckman & Frankel, 1984). The reality is that if the healthcare practitioner allows the patient to complete his or her story, it will take on average approximately 90 seconds (Langewitz, Denz, Keller, Kiss, Ruttimann, & Wossmer, 2002). Generally speaking, the patient is aware of the time constraints on the healthcare provider and has developed a scripted and rehearsed presentation before they even enter the provider's office.

Information exchanged between the patient and the practitioner does not occur in a vacuum. It is constrained and guided by the context within which it occurs. Very often the provider's demeanor sets the context for information exchange. If open and honest information is desired, a study by Makoul, Zick, and Green (2007) provides some prescriptive behaviors that a practitioner can use to facilitate such information. In terms of what patients desire when the healthcare practitioner enters the room, 78% want a handshake, 56% want the practitioner to introduce himself or herself by first and last name (i.e., "I'm Margaret Johnson and I practice primary care"), and 32% prefer the use of a title then the surname (i.e., "I'm Dr. Johnson). With this said, it is believed

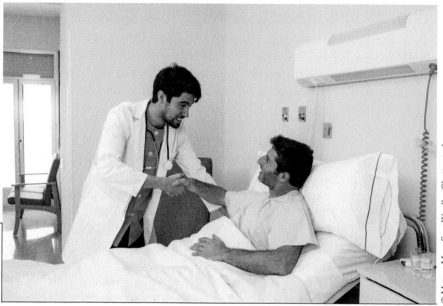

Patients prefer practitioners to shake hands and introduce themselves using first and last names.

best practice to use both first and last name when introducing yourself while also referring to the patient by his or her name. For example, "Good afternoon, Mr. Smith [while offering a handshake]. I'm Margaret Johnson, a primary care physician."

To maximize effective information gathering, the healthcare practitioner should begin with open-ended questions (Silverman, Kurtz, & Draper, 2005). An open-ended question is one that gives the opportunity for the patient to answer in ways that allow for more elaborate and extensive explanations. For example, when first encountering a patient, the provider may begin with a question such as "Why are you here?" This type of approach is in contrast to beginning with the provider looking at the printed history form or a computer screen, then saying to the patient: "So you are coming in for abdominal pain, is that correct?" In the first part of this example the practitioner allows the patient, via the open-ended question, to present a narrative. In the second part of this example the practitioner uses a closed-ended question (i.e., a question that forces the patient into a fixed response with little or no opportunity for elaboration), which results in the patient not having or feeling the opportunity to engage in their narrative, thus increasing the probability of missing important information.

The most effective technique for beginning the patient interview is obtained through open-ended questions. Figure 9.2 illustrates this deductive questioning technique, which starts at the macro narrative level, then moves to a more focused questioning route that concludes with diagnosis and treatment (funnel technique).

One of the key factors to successfully eliciting a narrative from the patient lies in the initial behaviors displayed by the provider. If the pro-

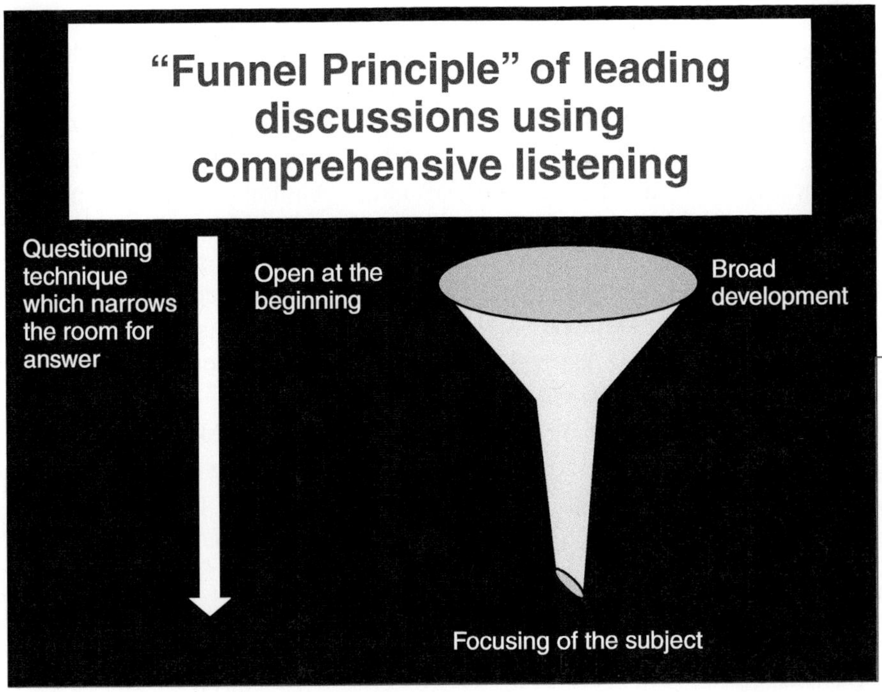

open-ended question

A question that gives the opportunity for the patient to answer in ways, that allow for more elaborate and extensive explanations.

closed-ended question

A question that forces the patient into a fixed response with little or no opportunity for elaboration.

"Funnel Principle" of leading discussions using comprehensive listening

Questioning technique which narrows the room for answer

Open at the beginning

Broad development

Focusing of the subject

figure 9.2

Funnel Method of Patient Information Gathering

From Polack, E.P. Surgeons as effective communicators: Sharpening skills for critical moments. 96th Annual Clinical Congress, American College of Surgeons, Tuesday, October 5, 2010. Washington, D.C.

vider "takes the floor," talks too much, or interrupts the patient, the flow of the narrative will be disrupted and an inaccurate history often results (Beckman & Frankel, 1984). Although this process of allowing the patient to express his or her story may take time, this extra time can reap incredible benefits for both the patient and provider. According to Bylund and Makoul (2005), the more empathy-filled the response is from the practitioner, the lower the practitioner's exposure to liability and the lower the levels of stress and burnout experienced by the practitioner.

Listening

The concept of listening reflects a dynamic process that has to be understood if one wants to maximize efficiency and accuracy of information exchange. The need to be listened to is fundamental to the health and well-being of any individual (Rogers, 1980). Throughout this chapter, we have eluded to the fact that to effectively gather, process, and be mindful to the needs and narrative of the patient, effective listening skills are requisite. Listening is believed to take several different forms (Wolvin & Coakley, 1992). Discriminative listening reflects when we listen in order to distinguish between different elements of a message or when we are in a "learning state." When a patient is presenting symptoms, the healthcare practitioner is primarily engaged in this type of listening. **Appreciative listening** is when we listen in order to form a connection to the other person or object. Appreciative listening can be seen when we listen to music, poetry, or a good story told by someone else. **Comprehensive listening** is listening for the totality of a message (e.g., when we listen to a patient's complete narrative). **Critical listening** is associated with the evaluation of the message or information. By "critical" we are not referring to being negative as much as scrutinizing the information in hopes of greater clarity. For example, critical listening is evident when a healthcare practitioner probes the patient to elaborate on a particular part of the narrative. This request for elaboration comes from the practitioner critically listening to the patient. Therapeutic listening is the ability to listen to both the message and all of the emotional and psychological information that accompanies it. This type of listening is also known as *empathetic listening*. Although all types of listening are important, the patient perceives support, empathy, and connectedness to the practitioner through therapeutic listening.

How does one improve listening skills? Listening is a psychological construct, so it can be learned. Figure 9.3 offers nine tips for improving listening skills when engaged in face-to-face interaction.

Just as careful listening and information-gathering skills can enhance patient care, constant interruption and a lack of listening can result in dire outcomes. Levinson, Roter, Mulloony, Dull, and Frankel (1997) found that among the negative consequences associated with such behavior is an increase in medical malpractice litigation. By using open-ended questions and encouraging patients to expand their stories, a practitioner can actually lower incidences of medical liability. Other research has further validated this finding specifically to surgeons (Adamson, Bunch, Baldwin, & Oppenberg, 2000).

discriminative listening

When we listen in order to distinguish between different elements of a message or when we are in a "learning state."

therapeutic listening

The ability to listen to both the message and all of the emotional and psychological information that accompanies it.

1.	Concentrate fully on the person who is speaking.
2.	Avoid trying to think of an answer until the other person is completely finished with his or her thought.
3.	Eliminate the noise or distractions occurring around you.
4.	Practice basic manners via being polite and respectful with regard to turn taking, eye contact, head nodding, etc.
5.	Pay attention to the vocal inflection and other paralanguage being used by the patient. Avoid being distracted by speech impediments, stuttering, accents, etc.
6.	Be an active or reflective listener. Paraphrase what the patient has just said to you. For example, "What I understood you to have said is that you have tenderness near your belly button. Is this correct?
7.	When introducing yourself to patients, repeat their name after they have given it to you, and if you did not hear it the first time, ask them to repeat it. This type of behavior indicates to the patient that you are showing concern for them as an individual and also puts you in a mental state to be an effective listener.
8.	If you did not hear something, understand something, or simply were not listening, do not hesitate to ask the patient to repeat themselves. For example, "I'm sorry, would you mind repeating that for me?"
9.	Understand that listening is indeed a learned skill. It is something that can be improved if a person wishes to do so.

figure 9.3

Tips for Effective Listening

figure 9.4

1.	Build a relationship.
2.	Open the discussion.
3.	Gather information.
4.	Understand the patient's perspective.
5.	Share information.
6.	Reach agreement on problems and places.
7.	Provide closure.

Kalamazoo Consensus Statement

Source: Makoul, G. (2001). Essential elements of communication in medical encounters: The Kalamazoo consensus statement. Academic Medicine, 75, 390–393.

In light of the evidence provided thus far and scores of other evidence linking quality patient–provider interactions with beneficial outcomes, several approaches and methods have been developed to guide practitioners through the patient consultation. Perhaps the most comprehensive and effective is that of the Kalamazoo Consensus Statement (KCS) (Makoul, 2001), which consists of seven separate phases of the patient consultation. Figure 9.4 lists these phases.

Therapeuic Writing

The emergence of therapeutic writing in medicine serves many of the same functions for the provider as it does for the patient. Therapeutic writing is an exercise designed to allow the practitioner to fully express his or her

therapeutic writing
An exercise designed to allow the practitioner to fully express his or her experience with a patient.

experience with a patient. One of the first articles to bring attention to this "literary" exercise was published by Scheetz and Frye (2000). Although these writings can take many forms, one particular form emerged that constrained the writer to a specific word count; Moss (1998) suggested "to tell—preferably in 55 words exactly—a story that helps to understand or to appreciate something about a patient or about the practice of medicine" (p. 1934). This quote is consistent with the thinking of Socrates, who once said at his heresy trial in 403 B.C., "[T]he unexamined life is not worth living" (Allen, 1989). The mindful consciousness of the body, mind, and spirit of the patient serves as a constant reminder as to the dignity of each person. The 55-word format for the therapeutic exercise serves as an ideal creative endeavor for practitioners for whom time is a vital and scarce resource. Further, such a format serves as an intellectual exercise that requires not only emotion and experience, but also intellect and creativity. The sum effect of such an exercise is an abbreviated journal or diary that allows a provider to take pause or perspective.

Therapeutic writing and the rules for doing so serve to be consistent with the everyday provider's acts of writing personal notes and in patients' charts. Scheetz and Frye (2000) believe that the topics of such writings should be interesting and focus on some characteristic of the patient that weighs heavy on the provider's conscience and experience. The process starts with the provider writing down everything that comes to mind regarding the patient. One way to generate such a list is to take multiple perspectives: the provider's, the patient's, one of empathy, one of disgust, and one where we have no understanding of the patient. It does not matter if the list is composed of a mix of fantasy, fact, or opinion. Once this "long list" is comprised, then edit, deleting less interesting and unnecessary words and substituting one word to take the place of several words. Remember that all stories occur within a time frame, have a plot, and occur within a relationship. This process should result in a 55-word story.

Conclusion

This chapter presented the variety of factors involved in the successful gathering, processing, and exchange of information. We began with distinguishing between hearing and listening, with the former being a physiologic concept and the latter being a psychological one. The processing of information was presented so as to introduce the reader to the variety of ways in which people are able to garner information for the environment—more specifically, the difference between proactive and reactive scanning and how these different types of scanning influence how we process information and act on that information.

The communication trait of information reception apprehension was discussed to indicate how our very personalities can affect our ability to gather and process information. Being apprehensive when receiving different types of information can adversely affect a variety of healthcare processes, none of which is more important than hand-off communication. Problems during this process result in thousands of deaths annually and, as such, have been the focus of much attention from researchers.

The act of mindfulness and appreciative inquiry are both concepts of presence and positivity with distinct benefits for both the patient and the provider. In the fast-paced world of medicine, it is easy to become blinded to the day-to-day humanity that occurs within the healthcare setting. Therefore, approaches to assist the healthcare practitioner to be "present" psychologically to the patient and their own experience are crucial. The story of the patient or the practice of narrative medicine is a relatively modern concept yet simultaneously one that has been practiced for thousands of years. The patient narrative has been shown to be a great source for information gathering.

The act of listening and its different facets were presented and discussed. The necessary skills and ways to improve listening were presented along with evidence that indicates the benefits of appropriate listening for healthcare provider competence and patient safety. Finally, we discussed the concept of therapeutic writing for the healthcare practitioner, which helps make sense of the daily experiences of the practice of medicine and serves as a catharsis for the practitioner.

Questions for Discussion/Review

1. Distinguish between an adverse event and negligence and provide an example of each in terms of patient safety.
2. Explain the physiological process of hearing while providing explanations for each component of the hearing process.
3. Discuss the concept of information scanning and how the different types of scanning behavior result in different types of information being processed.
4. Define the communication trait known as informational reception apprehension and discuss the different facets of this trait.
5. Explain why the hand-off process is a part of healthcare that is ripe for human error. Explain some of the ways that researchers are trying to improve this process.
6. Discuss the concept of mindfulness and distinguish among consciousness, awareness, and attention.
7. Explain how the concept of mindfulness can improve the way healthcare is delivered. Provide an example.
8. What are the basic assumptions of mindful meditation and appreciative inquiry regarding healthcare? How can each of these be used to increase patient safety?
9. Describe the basic assumptions behind the use of narrative medicine and what benefits it has for the patient and practitioner.
10. Discuss the five basic characteristics of narrative medicine as proposed by Charon.
11. Explain why the funnel technique is believed to be the optimal way to solicit information from a patient.
12. List and define the different types of listening and which types are especially beneficial for the practice of healthcare.
13. Explain how therapeutic writing can assist a healthcare practitioner in coping with the day-to-day struggles with patient care and disease.

References

Adamson, T., Bunch, W., Baldwin, D., & Oppenberg, A. (2000). Does the virtuous orthopedist have fewer malpractice suits? *Clinical Orthopedics and Related Research, 378,* 104–109.

Allen, R. F. (translator) (1989). *The dialogues of Plato, Volume 1: Euthyphro, apology, citro, mengo, gorgias, menexenus.* New Haven and London: Yale University Press.

Avtgis, T. A., Rancer, A. S., & Madlock, P. E. (2010). *Organizational communication: Strategies for success.* Dubuque, IA: Kendall-Hunt.

Beckman, H. B., & Frankel, R. M. (1984). The effect of physician behavior on the collection of data. *Annals of Internal Medicine, 101,* 692–696.

Bylund, C. L., & Makoul, G. (2005). Examining empathy in medical encounters: An observational study using the empathetic communication coding system. *Health Communication, 18,* 123–140.

Chang, V. Y., Arora, V. M., Lev-Ari, S., D'Arcy, M., & Keysar, B. (2010). Interns over-estimate the effectiveness of their hand-off communication. *Pediatrics, 125,* 491–496.

Charon, R. *Narrative medicine: Honoring the stories of illness.* (2006). Oxford, UK: Oxford University Press.

Choo, C. W. (2006). *The knowing organizations: How organizations use information to construct meaning, create knowledge, and make decisions* (2nd ed.). New York: Oxford University Press.

Connelly, J. (1999). Being in the present moment: Developing the capacity for mindfulness in medicine. *Academic Medicine, 74,* 420–424.

Cooperrider, D. L., Whitney, D., & Stavros, J. M. (2008). *Appreciative inquiry handbook* (2nd ed.). Brunswick, OH: Crown Custom Publishing.

Cooperrider, D. L., & Srivastva, S. (1987). Appreciative inquiry in organizational life. In R. W. Woodman & W. A. Pasmore (Eds.). *Research in organizational change and development* (Vol. 1, pp. 129–169). Greenwich, CT: JAI Press.

Epstein, R. M. (1999). Mindful practice. *Journal of the American Medical Association, 282,* 833–839.

Frank, G., Wallace, S. P., & Steinberg, T. H. (2005). Improving physician communication through an automated, integrated sign out system. *Journal of Health Care Information Management, 19,* 68–74.

Gazzela, C. A. (2005). Conversations with Jon Kabat-Zinn. *Alternative Therapies, 2,* 3.

Hampton, J. R., Harrison, J. J. G., Mitchell, J. R., Prichard, J. S., & Seymour, C. (1975). Relative contributions of history taking, physical examination and laboratory investigation to diagnosis and management of medical outpatients. *British Medical Journal, 2,* 486–489.

James, W. (1924). *Memories and studies.* New York: Longmans, Green, and Company.

Kapileau, P. (1965). *The three pillars of Zen.* Tokyo: John Weatherhill, Inc.

Kanney, J., & Moore, C. (1999). MediSign: Using a web based sign out system to improve provider identification. *AHIA Annual Symposium Proceedings,* 550–554.

Krasner, M. S., Epstein, R. M., Beckman, H., Suchman, A. L., Chapman, B., & Mooney, C. J. (2009). Association of an educational program in mindful communication with burnout, empathy, and attitudes among primary care physicians. *Journal of the American Medical Association, 302,* 1284–1293.

Langer, E. G. (1989). *Mindfulness.* Reading, MA: Addison-Wesley Publishing Company.

Langewitz, W., Denz, M., Keller, A., Kiss, A., Ruttimann, S., & Wossmer, B. (2002). Spontaneous talking time at start of consultation in outpatient clinic: Cohort study. *British Medical Journal, 325,* 682–683.

Leape, L. L., Brennan, T. A., Laird, N., Lawthers, A. G., Localio, A. R., & Barnes, B. A. (1991). The nature of adverse events in hospitalized patients. Results of the Harvard medical practice study II. *New England Journal of Medicine, 324,* 377–384.

Leonard, M., Graham, S., & Bonacum, D. (2004). The human factor: The critical importance of effective teamwork and communication in providing safe care. *Quality and Safety in Health Care, 13,* 85–90.

Levinson, W., Gorawara-Bhat, R., & Lamb, J. (2000). A study of patient clues and physician responses in primary care and surgical settings. *Journal of the American Medical Association, 284,* 1021–1027.

Makoul, G. (2001). Essential elements of communication in medical encounters: The Kalamazoo consensus statement. *Academic Medicine, 75,* 390–393.

Makoul, G., Zick, A., & Green, M. (2007). An evidence-based perspective on greetings in medical encounters. *Archives of Internal Medicine, 167,* 1172–1176.

Maslach, C., Schaufli, W. B., & Leiter, M. P. (2001). Job burnout. In St. Fiske, D. L. Schacter, & C. Zahn-Waxler (Eds.), *Annual Review of Psychology, 52,* 397–422.

Moss, S. (1998). *The world's shortest stories.* Philadelphia, PA: Running Press Book Publishers.

National Institutes of Health. (1999). *To err is human: Building a safer health system.* Publication Number 97-4051. Bethesda, MD: National Institutes of Health.

Peterson, M. C., Holbrook, J., Von Hales, D., Smith, N. L., & Staker, L. V. (1992). Contributions of the history, physical examination and laboratory investigation in making medical diagnoses. *West Virginia Medical Journal, 156,* 163–165.

Pink, D. (2005). *A whole new mind: Moving from the information age to the conceptual age.* New York: Riverhead Books.

Rogers, C. R. (1980). *A way of being.* Boston, MA: Houghton Mifflin.

Scheetz, A., & Frye, M. E. (2000). The stories. *Journal of the American Medical Association, 283,* 1934.

Shanafelt, T. D., Bradley, K. A., Wipf, J. E., & Back, A. L. (2002). Burnout and self-reported patient care in an internal medicine residency program. *Annals of Internal Medicine, 136,* 358–367.

Shanafelt, T. D., Sloan, J. A., & Habermann, T. M. (2003). The well-being of physicians. *American Journal of Medicine, 114,* 513–519.

Shapiro, S. L., & Schwartz, G. E. (2000). Intentional systematic mindfulness: An integrative model for self-regulation and health. *Advances, 16,* 128–134.

Shapiro, S. L., Schwartz, G. E., & Bonner, G. (1998). Effects of mindfulness-based stress reduction on medical and pre-medical students. *The Journal of Behavioral Medicine, 21,* 581–599.

Silverman, J., Kurtz, S., & Draper, J. (2005). *Skills for communication with patients* (2nd ed.). Oxford, UK: Radcliffe Publishing.

Van Eaton, G. E., Horvath, K. D., Lober, W. B., & Pellegrini, C. A. (2004). Organizing the transfer of patient care information: The development of a computerized resident sign-out system. *Surgery, 246,* 5–13.

Weston, D. (1999). *Psychology: Mind, brain, and culture* (2nd ed.), New York: Wiley.

Wheeless, L. R., Preiss, R. W., & Gayle, B. (1997). Receiver apprehension, information receptivity, and cognitive processing. In J. A. Daly, J. C. McCroskey, J. Ayres, T. Hopf, & D. M. Ayres (Eds.). *Avoiding communication: Shyness, reticence, and communication apprehension* (pp. 151–187). Cresskill, NJ: Hampton Press.

Wolvin, A., & Coakley, C. G. (1992). *Listening.* Dubuque, IA: William C. Brown.

chapter ten

Theories of Health Communication

chapter objectives

Upon completion of the chapter, the student should be able to:

1. Explain the functions of communication in the health context

2. Discuss communication contexts within health communication

3. Explain the health belief model

4. Explain Uncertainty Management Theory

5. Explain the Transtheoretical Model

Over the last several decades, the field of Communication Studies has experienced incredible growth in both scholarly attention and legitimization as an invaluable discipline that is becoming ever increasingly problem focused. Perhaps one of the most influential factors for this growth can be traced to the proliferation of health communication theory and research. In the first edition of *Contemporary Communication Research*, we relegated the health communication context to a chapter titled *Tributary Contexts*. The sheer mass of published data and theory building within health communication simply demands its own chapter. Further, as health care becomes a focal point of national debate whether it is the Affordable Care Act or changes to Medicare and Medicaid to reflect the quality of the patient experience in calculating reimbursement rates, the focus on communication and interpersonal relationships has never been greater. Theresa Thompson (2006) conducted a meta-analysis of

© ESB Professional/Shutterstock.com

key terms

communication channel	external locus of control	power
cooperation	innovation	redundancy
counsel	internal locus of control	social system
diagnosis	locus of control	time
dominance	mutuality model	transtheoretical model
education	paternalistic model	uncertainty management theory

articles published in *Health Communication* between the years of 1989 and 2003. Results indicated that 20.7 percent focused on patient–physician interaction, 13.4 percent focused on health campaigns, 11.8 percent risky health behavior, 8.4 percent on aging, 7 percent on language or the creation of shared meaning, and 5.9 percent on issues related to the media.

The U.S. Department of Health and Human Services' Agency for Health Care Research and Quality (AHRQ) (2007) reported that communication errors accounted for more than 42,000 deaths annually. Further, Leonard, Graham, and Bonacum (2004) reported that 70 percent of sentinel events (i.e., events causing serious injury or death to the patient) were directly related to communication and relational issues among members of the medical team (Polack & Avtgis, 2011). These data are startling, especially when considering the fact that they are communication based, not medically based. It is data such as these that make the undeniable and compelling case for the development of quality health communication theory and research.

When discussing any concept, we need to have a clear conceptual definition. Similar to most any communication construct, definitions will differ depending on the particular scholar. A few examples include Linda Lederman (2009) defining health communication as "the study of the impact of communication on health and health care delivery, with attention to the role that communication plays in the definition of health and wellness, illness and disease, as well as in developing strategies for addressing ways to deal with those issues" (p. 236); Donohew and Ray (1990) define health communication as "the dissemination and interpretation of health-related messages" (p. 4); Ratzan, Stearns, Payne, Amato, Libergott, and Madoff (1994) define health communication as "…the art and technique of informing, influencing, and motivating individual, institutional, and public audiences about important health issues. Its scope includes disease prevention, health promotion, health-care policy, business, as well as enhancement of the quality of life and health of individuals within the community" (p. 362). These definitions are but a few of the many definitions available within the field of Communication Studies.

Kreps, Bonaguro, and Query (1998) attribute the explosion of interest in health communication to the fact that health communication, unlike many other communication contexts, went outside of the academy and into the "real world" to help solve everyday health issues. The Kreps *et al.* call for having research be socially relevant is still advocated today (see, for example, Thompson, Dorsey, Miller, & Parrot, 2003).   At one point, there were two primary journals within which health communication scholars published their research. In 1989, *Health Communication* was the first journal within the field of Communication Studies dedicated to publishing high quality health communication research. This was followed by the 1996 creation of the *Journal of Health Communication*. These journals are not only prospering today, but there are literally dozens of interdisciplinary journals dedicated to publishing health communication theory and research.

Health communication theorists and researchers often focus their efforts on identifying, examining, and offering insights into how to improve health care and to promote taking responsibility for one's health. Communication has been associated with numerous health-related factors including physical and psychological well-being, patient satisfaction, patient confidence in the physician, malpractice rates, and patient-provider nonverbal communication to name but a few (Arntson & Droge, 1988; Street & Buller, 1988). Further, research has spanned well beyond the practice of health care to include the development of AIDS prevention (Brown, 1991), organ donation (Morgan & Miller, 2002), and bullying campaigns (Roberto & Eden, 2014).

Before presenting theories of health communication it is important to consider the different ways that people define health. Traditionally, people consumed health care from a sickness perspective in that people would seek out health care when they were ill. Further, when the healthcare practitioner gave a recommendation, the patient would follow those directions to the letter and not question any of the practitioner's orders. This is known as the paternalistic model. In contemporary health care, especially since the Vietnam War when people began to question authority, healthcare consumers are much more likely to educate themselves before the encounter with the healthcare provider and engage in a collaboration of joint input resulting in a mutually agreeable treatment protocols. This is known as the mutuality model (Polack & Avtgis, 2011).

Functions of Communication in the Health Context

Costello (1977) identified four functions of communication interaction regarding patient–provider communication. These functions include elements of interpersonal and persuasive communication (see Figure 10.1).

Four functions of health communication
- Diagnosis—the data-gathering, data-interpretation, and problem-solving skills used by the healthcare provider.
- Cooperation—communication concerning the nature of one's illness and the implication of measures prescribed for care.
- Counsel—involves the role of the provider as "therapist." DeVito (2002) included therapeutic communication as one of the major purposes of interpersonal communication. The healthcare provider engaged in the therapeutic function deals with the patient's "symbolic" symptoms.

paternalistic model

A patient following a health care practitioner's recommendation to the letter, not questioning any of the practitioner's orders

mutuality model

Health care consumer engaging in a collaboration of joint input with the health care provider resulting in a mutually agreeable treatment protocol

diagnosis

A function of health communication that involves data gathering, data interpretation, and problem-solving skills used by the health care provider

cooperation

A function of health communication that involves communication concerning the nature of one's illness and the implication of measures prescribed for care

counsel

A function of health communication that involves the role of the provider as "therapist"

figure 10.1

Four functions of health communication.

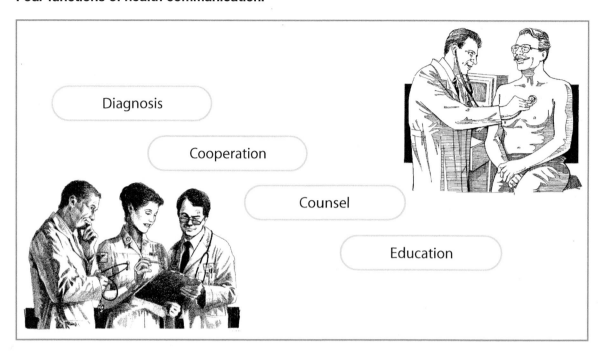

- **Education**—health education is the process of disseminating information to individuals to attempt to reduce health risks and to increase the effectiveness of health care. Health education proceeds through channels ranging from informal patient–provider interaction to more formal mass-mediated campaigns designed to achieve clear and planned objectives. The Act Against Aids campaign is one such example.

Communication Contexts within Health Communication

Researchers have attempted to provide some structure for studying health communication. Some believe it is helpful to categorize and define the study of health communication according to communication contexts (Ratzan, Payne, & Bishop, 1996). Much of the research in health communication has examined the interpersonal communication relationship between patient and healthcare provider. Other heavily research contexts within health communication include mass and mediated communication, which "focuses on effective message dissemination for health promotion, disease prevention, and health-related messages transmitted through mediated channels, including health marketing and policy-making" (Ratzen et al., 1996, p. 28).

For most people, the term "health communication" refers to the interpersonal context. In fact, in recent years, communication training has been part

A healthcare provider must be able to communicate instructions accurately.

of many medical education curricula (see, for example, Polack, Avtgis, Rossi, & Shaffer, 2010). The Accreditation Counsel for Graduate Medical Education (ACGME), accrediting body for post-MD education programs, has made communication one of the six core competencies that all physicians are required to demonstrate. Given that communication between patient and provider generally assumes that both parties are competent communicators, such an assumption is far from reality. When a patient presents to a provider, the episode requires the patient to communicate their symptoms to the provider as accurately as possible. Similarly, the provider must be able to communicate instructions accurately and competently on how to relieve, eliminate, or manage healthcare problems.

Ineffective communication is costly and concerted efforts are being put forth to increase health literacy at many levels. Such costs are not just financial but misdiagnosis and incorrect treatment are also outcomes related to communication. Even if the instructions are delivered clearly, if the interaction between the healthcare provider and the patient is abrupt, hurried, and impersonal, the patient may not be satisfied, and compliance with provider recommendations may not result. At a minimum, effective interpersonal communication between patients and providers is a necessary prerequisite for the development of the open and trusting relationships which are critical factors within health communication contexts. Once established, diagnosis and treatment are much more accurate and effective. Further, quality relationships between patient and provider result in fewer malpractice suits.

While much of the theory-building research efforts have been developed focusing on interpersonal communication, several specific aspects of interpersonal interaction are especially important in the health communication context.

Relational Control/Compliance

Many people feel that healthcare providers dominate most interactions. Providers can engage in control tactics before they even see patients by making them wait for an appointment and treatment. Healthcare providers control the interaction and conversation when they engage in one-way communication: asking questions but not encouraging others to do the same; interrupting; changing topics abruptly; or ignoring patients completely (Cline & Cardosi, 1983).

A model of relational interaction by Millar and Rogers (1976, 1987) assumes that message exchanges have patterns of control, trust, and intimacy. Recall that the model includes the message exchange patterns of control, trust, and intimacy. The control dimension refers to the process by which individuals establish the defining and directing actions of the relationship. Relational control is measured by redundancy, dominance, and power. Redundancy refers to the amount of change in the dyads negotiations over rights. Dominance describes how much one individual commands the interaction. Power is the potential to influence or restrict another person's behaviors. Given the status differences that are inherent in the health context, the relational control approach is particularly useful.

Although the model was conceptualized and developed as a way to examine marital dyads, O'Hair (1989) applied the relational control component of the model to the study of the patient–provider relationship. He argued that the model is especially appropriate for researching patient–provider communication in general and control in particular. Patients are no longer passive participants in the healthcare relationship (i.e., paternalistic model). Patients regularly challenge the authority and control of the provider. The relational control model allows us to observe and examine the control strategies attempted by patients. Patients dissatisfied with the control exercised by the provider generally engage in fewer compliance behaviors. Thus, identifying relational control patterns of both the patient and provider have direct influence on treatment outcomes.

To examine the issue of relational control in patient–provider communication, O'Hair (1989) recorded actual interactions and looked for indications of redundancy, dominance, and power. His findings indicated that patients attempted control almost as often as the provider. O'Hair calls this *competitive symmetry*. The following conversation illustrates this:

> **Physician:** "I would continue on the antibiotics until your throat clears."
> **Patient:** "They haven't helped. I would prefer a new medication."

Complimentarity emerged as the second most frequently used control sequence. Messages are complementary if one speaker attempts control of the exchange, while the other yields, or if one speaker yields control while the other assumes control. O'Hair (1989) found that patients were twice as willing to yield control of the interaction after the physician sought control. For example:

> **Physician:** "If you are going to travel long distances, be sure to stop periodically to empty your bladder."
> **Patient:** "I'll schedule stops to make sure I do that."

| redundancy

Refers to the amount of change in interactant's negotiations over rights

| dominance

Degree to which one partner is said to dominate a dyad's interaction

| power

The potential to influence or restrict another person's behaviors

The results of this application of interpersonal theory in the healthcare context show the benefits of extending an existing theory of communication. O'Hair (1989) suggested that relational control analyses could be used to examine incidences of patient noncompliance. For example, relational control analyses could help us determine which patients are willing to challenge the authority and competence of physicians; two factors that may predict noncompliance with physician recommendations.

Compliance is a critical dimension in the patient–provider relationship. Within healthcare, compliance can be defined as the degree to which the patient engages in the provider's suggested lifestyle changes, treatment procedure, or other health-related behaviors (e.g., adhering to a particular medication regimen). Providers engage in many messages with their patients in an effort to guide them on a road to wellness. Kreps (1988) argued that from a relational perspective the responsibility for "getting well" is a joint function of both the patient and provider. Compliance is influenced by strategic messages used by both parties.

Research into compliance in the health context has taken two distinct directions consisting of determining what kinds of compliance gaining strategies providers use effectively and the relationship between the use of specific strategies and outcomes such as patient satisfaction with healthcare quality and individual health status. Michael and Judee Burgoon (1990) explored the use of both verbal and nonverbal physician compliance gaining strategies and concluded that physicians tend to use nonthreatening verbal strategies when attempting to convince their patients to follow suggested treatment regimens. Physicians emphasize their expertise as an incentive to comply. For example, "If you comply with my recommendations to lose weight and exercise, your blood pressure should go down." When there is resistance from the patient, the physician adopts more aggressive compliance gaining strategies such as "If you do not follow my instructions, you may very well have another and more severe heart attack!" Physicians rarely rely on the use of positive reinforcing compliance gaining strategies with their patients (e.g., "if you lose weight, you will feel better about yourself.").

Providers employ a range of nonverbal communication behaviors which can serve to enhance or deter patient compliance. As discussed in Chapter 5, nonverbal immediacy is the use of behaviors that create liking and a psychological closeness (e.g., eye contact, little physical distance between patient and provider, and smiling) whereas nonimmediate behaviors include excessive distance between patient and provider, frowning, lack of eye contact, etc.). In fact, J. Burgoon, Pfau, Parrott, Birk, Coker, and M. Burgoon (1987) found that patient compliance was greatly enhanced when physicians exhibited greater similarity to the patient, communicated greater receptivity, composure, immediacy/affection, and were moderately formal. Further, patient satisfaction was also found to be related to the use of an affiliative nonverbal style and less dominant behaviors by the physician (Street & Buller, 1987).

There is a plethora of applied research indicating the importance of compliance at both the interpersonal and public health campaign levels. Some of these include using strategies to get patients with border-line personality disorders to comply with general healthcare suggestions (Sansone, Bohinc, &

Wiederman, 2015), as a means of persuading minority, low income, and under-insured patients to participate in colon cancer screening (Hunleth, Steinmetz, McQueen, & James, 2016), to increase hand hygiene behavior in the clinical context (King, Vlaev, Everett-Thomas, Fitzpatrick, Darzi, & Birnbach, 2016), and as a means to optimize treatment adherence for low health literacy patients living with HIV (Pellowski, Kalichman, & Grebler, 2016).

Communication Traits and Health Behavior

As with most other communication contexts, health communication has also utilized certain communication traits to explain and predict both patient and provider behavior. Such research continues as the need to account for predispositions toward communication in the health context has proved fruitful in improving the quality of healthcare delivery.

| **locus of control**

A personality trait that concerns how people interpret outcomes in their life

| **internal locus of control**

A perception that the person has direct control over their lives and behaviors

| **external locus of control**

A perception that the person perceives that their lives and behavior are controlled by others

Locus of Control.   The construct of locus of control was originally applied to health communication by Brenders (1989). He argued that perceptions of personal control have been linked to such health-related factors such as life stress, coping with illness, and the success of preventative practices. Individuals with internal locus of control expectancies perceive that outcomes in their lives are due to their own purposive behavior and that they are in control of their destiny. Individuals with external locus of control expectancies perceive that outcomes in their lives are controlled by outside forces such as luck, chance, and fate (Lefcourt, 1982). The major assumption of this work is that "persons are likely to evaluate information and advice from within the context of their perceived control orientation" (Brenders, 1989, p. 119). People with internal control expectancies are more assertive, proactive, and autonomous in interpersonal situations. After reviewing the array of research on locus of control in the health communication context, Brenders (1989) concluded: (a) internals are more receptive to healthcare information and advice; (b) internals may respond poorly to treatment unless provided with specific information about procedures and a rationale; (c) congruent control messages. For example, providing an internal control-oriented patient with information that is relayed in a way that is consistent with specific recommendations for the patient to control his or her own destiny regarding the specific health concern; (d) the interaction among control beliefs, communication, and health care is likely to yield promising theory building and practical results in health communication.

This has been evidenced in more recent research. Avtgis and Polack (2007) found that patients with an internal health locus of control also reported greater quality of health information exchange with their provider and higher levels of perceived physician communication competence than patients reporting an external locus of control. Further, Avtgis, Brann, and Staggers (2006) reported that patients who report high internal control expectancies, low chance control expectancies (e.g., belief in chance or fate controlling outcomes), and low powerful other control expectancies (e.g., people who believe that practitioners or religious figures control outcomes) reported

How do you create an affirming communicator style?

high levels of provider information giving. However, when separated between scheduled healthcare visits and emergency room visits, Patients who report high chance control expectancies reported engaging in information-verifying (e.g., clarifying messages for accuracy) when in an emergency visit situation yet report little information giving (i.e., patient providing information to the provider) in the scheduled visit condition. Avtgis et al. (2006) concluded "the medical situation influences the relationship between information exchange and socio-emotional support. The influence of the medical situation is so great, that it confounds the simple linear notion that the relationship between information exchange and locus of control is static in all medical exchange situations" (p. 236).

Communicator Style.   Recall that communicator style (Chapter 3) may be viewed as an overall impression of a number of different styles: contentious, open, dramatic, dominant, precise, relaxed, friendly, attentive, and animated with the overall impression comprising the communicator image. For example, a person can create an affirming communicator style (e.g., relaxed, friendly, and attentive styles) or a non-affirming style (e.g., contentious and dominant styles) when interacting with others.

Communicator style has been used to study how patients' perceptions of their healthcare provider's style and the link to patient satisfaction. Buller and Buller (1987) have identified communicator styles such as affiliation (i.e., friendly, open, attentive, and relaxed styles) and control (i.e., dominant and contentious styles) finding that physician used an affiliative communicator style and the less they used the control style the more satisfied the patient experience. Cardello, Ray, and Pettey (1995) reported that physicians who were perceived as being more attentive, animated and less dominant and contentious were perceived as more empathetic. In a study of physician-executives, Garko

(1994) reported that when trying to influence their superiors, physician-executives use different styles based on the communicator style of their superior. More specifically, when the superior was perceived as having an attractive communicator style the physician-executive reported using the attentive, dramatic, friendly, open, and relaxed style when exerting upward influence. Superiors who were perceived as having an unattractive communication style resulted in the physician-executive using animated, contentious, dominant, and precise style when trying to influence their superior. Physician communicator style was also found to influence nurses' well-being. More specifically, V. Wheeless, L. Wheeless, and Riffle (1989) reported that physician responsiveness was positively related to nurses' compliance decision style, as opposed to an avoidance decision style, and negatively related to decision quickness. Finally, in a study looking at predictors of empathy in health science students, the friendly and relaxed communicator styles were significant predictors of the students' level of empathy (Brown, Boyle, Williams, A. Molloy, Palermo, McKenna, & L. Molloy, 2011). Overall, the communicator style construct does influence relational tactics and outcomes within health care.

Verbal Aggressiveness.   Verbal aggressiveness within the health context is extremely prevalent. According to Steadman, Mulvey, Monohan, Robbins, Applebaum, and Grisso (1998), 90 percent of all staff nurses experience at least one episode of abusive anger, condescension, or being globally rejected by a physician every 60–90 days. Further, 48 percent of nurses have been verbally and/or physically assaulted within the last year (Lanza, Zeiss, & Reardan, 2005). What contributes to this verbally aggressive culture? Nurses reported avoidance in reporting verbally aggressive incidence with 44 percent considering verbal aggression to be part of the job (Lanza et al.). Structurally, there are verbal trigger events that lead to the onset of patient verbal aggressiveness. Wigley (2009) defines verbal trigger events as factors that, when present, result in an onset of verbal and potentially physical aggression. Utilizing this framework, Avtgis and Madlock (2008) identified the following verbal trigger events/situations specific to health care; patient exhaustion and stress, frustration with the managed care industry, patient distrust in the provider and health care in general, and the culture of patient-oriented consumerism with regard to health care. Each of these trigger situations suggest that the uncertainty latent environment that exists within the health context has a great influence on health communication behavior on behalf of both the patient and the provider.

Health Beliefs Model

Developed in the early 1950s, the health belief model (HBM) is considered one of the first systematic, theory-based research effort in health communication and one of the most accepted models of behavioral change specific to health and safety issues. The first research effort on the HBM attempted to identify factors that underlie decisions to get a chest x-ray for the early

A person may make a change in lifestyle if it might prevent disease.

detection of tuberculosis. The health belief model permits researchers to explain and predict complaint behavior and thereby allow people to control their behavior. One of the originators of the theory stated: "The early researchers concerned with the health belief model would work cooperatively, build on each other's work, develop a theory that would include a heavy component of motivation and the perceptional world of the behaving individual...toward developing a theory not only useful in explaining a particular program problem, but also adaptable to other problems" (Rosenstock, 1974, p. 329).

The HBM is composed of five components that may influence a person to take some type of action (e.g., to lessen the chances of getting a disease or suffering a health-related malady). These components are *perceived susceptibility, perceived seriousness or severity, perceived benefits, perceived barriers to taking action,* and *Cues to action.*

Perceived susceptibility refers to the perceived subjective risks of contracting a disease or health-related condition (Rosenstock, 1974). Some people (low susceptibles) believe it is very unlikely that they would contract a particular disease or health-related condition. Other people (high susceptibles) perceive that it is very likely or inevitable that they will experience a disease or health condition. In between high and low susceptibles are the moderate susceptibles who operate on statistical probabilities when assessing their perception of susceptibility (e.g., "my mother and grandmother had Alzheimer's disease, therefore it is quite probable that I, too, will likely develop this condition").

Perceived seriousness or severity refers to an evaluation of the types of impact that potential health and safety conditions would have on our lives, emotional states, and the lives of families. Such assessment of severity includes physical, emotional, and even financial assessments. This may include asking questions such as, "How much pain, suffering, and discomfort would I experience if I experience this condition?" "How will I cope with the loss of income due to loss of work or costly medical bills?" and "What emotional effects will the condition have on the rest of my family?"

Perceived benefits of taking action involve the assessment of the possible benefits of performing the recommended behaviors to lessen the chances of being affected by the health or safety threat. If the susceptibility of getting the condition is perceived to be high, the individual assesses the benefits of taking some type of action to prevent the disease. In essence, the individual performs a cost–benefit analysis. Decisions are often influenced by norms and group pressure, as well as recommendations by health professionals and physicians (Rosenstock, 1974). If the perceived benefits of taking action outweigh the perceived barriers, the likelihood of adopting the recommended preventative actions increase.

Perceived barriers to taking action refers to the assessment as to whether the suggested recommendations or preventative action will be expensive, painful, upsetting, time consuming, or inconvenient. If the individual perceives a high probability of encountering these conditions, then he or she may not adopt the recommended behaviors that could lead to better health and safety outcomes. If the perceived barriers of taking action outweigh the perceived benefits, the likelihood of adopting the recommended preventative actions decreases. Consider the options for the treatment of an opioid addiction. The patient in this case will have to weigh options of in-patient versus out-patient treatment, the types of psychological counseling options (individual versus group), pharmaceutical interventions (whether or not you are going to use medications and if so, which ones (e.g., naltrexone, methadone, and buprenorphine), as well as the cost associated with each of these choices.

Cues to action are persuasive devices intended to motivate people to adopt or incorporate behaviors that could lead to a desired goal, such as better health or an increase in safety. The assumption is that in addition to the individual's beliefs, certain health-related actions might need to be prompted or triggered. These cues to action are "the specific stimuli necessary to trigger appropriate health behavior" (Mattson, 1999, p. 243). Cues to action within the health context can be internal or external in nature. Internal cues are more intrapersonal. That is, they are messages one sends to oneself about health-related concerns. For example, a person who chronically drives while legally drunk may have a close call in terms of an accident with another vehicle. Upon reflecting on this potentially life altering experience, the person decides that they will no longer drive after drinking. External cues to action are communicated by someone or something outside of the person. For example, a conversation with a physician, friends, parents, media messages, post cards from practitioners etc. all can serve to trigger changes in behaviors such as smoking cessation, breast cancer screening, sexually transmitted infection testing to name just but a few (Chew, Palmer, & Kim, 1998; Rosenstock, 1974; Witte, Stokols, Ituarte, & Schneider, 1993).

The HBM has been one of the most utilized frameworks in health communication research. For example, researchers have used it in a study designed to promote the use of bicycle safety helmets. The goal of the study was to investigate how the HBM's perceived threat factor and cues to action influenced bicycle safety helmet practices (Witte et al., 1993). In interviews with parents, researchers asked, "How often do you worry about your child being involved in a bicycle accident?" and "Do you believe that most head injuries resulting from bicycle accidents are (serious/not serious)?" to measure perceived susceptibility and perceived severity. In addition, the researchers used several external cues to action, including a community event that demonstrated bicycle safety, public service announcements on the radio about bicycle safety, direct mail brochures designed to increase perceptions of susceptibility and severity of head injury when not wearing a helmet, phone messages that presented similar information, and bicycle helmet coupons redeemable for $10 off the price of a helmet distributed through the mail.

The results of the study generally supported the HBM. Those individuals receiving the external cues to action (e.g., the community event, mass media announcements, and the telephone message) perceived bicycling injuries to be more serious and more likely to occur to their children than those not receiving the cues to action (Witte et al., 1993). Parents who perceived greater threat of bicycle injury had more favorable attitudes toward using bicycle helmets, were more likely to buy helmets for their children, and were more likely to insist that their children wear the bicycle helmet. In addition, the more cues to action received, the greater the perception of threat.

The HBM has also been used to guide research efforts designed to develop interpersonal communication strategies to prevent drug abuse by healthcare professionals and the elderly. The problems of impaired healthcare professionals are quite significant, with the incidence of healthcare professionals suffering from addiction to drugs and alcohol greatly exceeding that of the general population (Beisecker, 1991). The elderly are considered another at-risk group particularly susceptible to abuses of prescription and nonprescription medications. Beisecker (1991) recommended using the HBM to develop appropriate prevention strategies for both healthcare professionals and the elderly because the model focuses on two major needs of those groups, "education regarding the seriousness of substance abuse and a feeling of vulnerability and susceptibility to addiction" (p. 247). More specifically, it is recommended that the HBM cues to action in the form of interpersonal contact cues for at-risk healthcare professionals and healthcare counselors providing the interpersonal contact cues for the elderly. The impact of another important HBM cue to action, a television program, was tested to determine its influence on healthy eating practices. A one-hour television program, *Eat Smart*, was used in a naturalistic setting to determine its impact on health eating habits (Chew et al., 1998). The results of the study suggested that those individuals who watched the program perceived increased health benefits and reduced health barriers to healthy eating habits. Further, participants who viewed the program became more concerned about food fitness, had more confidence in the recommendations about healthy eating, and reduced their consumption of unhealthy foods after exposure to the program.

Marifran Mattson (1999) focused on interpersonal communication itself as a critical cue to action. The study explored the influence of a counseling session during HIV testing. It was thought that this interpersonal interaction would be especially useful in influencing individuals to change risky sexual behaviors and to comply with the recommendations for engaging in safer sex practices. Participants received an interpersonal counseling session designed to increase their awareness of the severity and their susceptibility to HIV/AIDS. Mattson measured several HBM factors, including risk appraisal (perceived severity of HIV/AIDS and perceived susceptibility to the disease), perceived benefits and barriers to taking action (employing safer sex practices such as using condoms), and perceived self-efficacy (perceptions of their ability to perform the safer sex recommendations). The results supported the HBM. Participant perceptions of their susceptibility to HIV/AIDS after participation in the interpersonal counseling session were moderately related to their decisions to comply with the safer sex recommendations (primarily using condoms). In addition, after the counseling session, participants also perceived that the benefits of engaging in safer sex practices outweighed the barriers to engaging in safer sex practices. This research suggests that we move toward "reconceptualizing the HBM in favor of centralizing the role of communication cues to action" (p. 258). Thus, it is recommended that the cues to action, originally located on the periphery of the HBM, be moved to a more central position in the model given its major influence on behavior change.

Uncertainty Management

Uncertainty manage-ment theory

Explains how people react to health-related uncertainty

Uncertainty management theory (UMT) was developed by Dale Brashers (2001a) as a reaction to the simplistic way that the term uncertainty has been conceptualized in communication theory. He believed that uncertainty is a multifaceted concept that can be more valuable and serve many more functions if not treated as an aversive state that needs to be reduced (see uncertainty reduction theory in Chapter 9). Instead, Brashers believes that although UMT was developed to predict people's experience with uncertainty (i.e., post-positivist perspective), he readily acknowledges that the experience of uncertainty is also a situation-based phenomenon (Brashers, Goldsmith, & Hsieh, 2002).

UMT was originally conceptualized to explain how people react to health-related uncertainty (Brashers, 2001b; Brashers, Hsieh, Neidig, & Reynolds, 2006). According to Afifi and Matsunaga (2008), the three features of UMT consist of: (a) the meaning and the experience of uncertainty, (b) the role of an individual's response to uncertainty, and (c) the psychological and communicative strategies used to manage uncertainty. Unlike other theories that conceptualize uncertainty, a key term with UMT is "management of uncertainty" as opposed to "reduction of uncertainty." In fact, Brashers (2001a) argued that the equation of more "information = less uncertainty" is false. He argued that information and uncertainty are not unidimensional constructs, but that both are separate constructs. The key question is, "How much information is enough?" The concept of "enough" varies from person to person. Therefore, Brashers (2001a, 2001b) believed that when people feel insecure about the amount of knowledge they possess or the amount of knowledge available, uncertainty is present. Simply put, "abandon the assumption that uncertainty will produce anxiety" (Brashers, 2001a, p. 477). A person, when experiencing uncertainty, can experience a plethora of other emotions. For example, consider a student who is on the border between receiving a course grade of C− or D+. After the final exam the student's lack of effort in contacting the instructor about the course grade (i.e., little information about the final grade) may in fact serve as a comforting feeling, and that the uncertainty may give the student "hope" of a better grade. This can also be seen in a person who sends out a resume for a position, then after one or two weeks does not follow up with a phone call to the employer to determine if they are still being considered for the position.

Uncertainty is ever present in health-related issues as well. In a study investigating the effects of illness on uncertainty, Brashers (2001b) investigated how HIV patients experience and manage uncertainty. Today, due to modern medicine and the reduced stigma associated with the disease, the diagnosis of being HIV positive is not to be thought of as the death sentence that is once was in the 1980s and 1990s. In terms of UMT, patients may actively seek out medical practitioners who provide them with uncertainty in an effort to give patients a sense of hope and a chance of some other outcome (e.g., controlling disease progression or cure). This provides an alternative to the certainty that the disease will eventually progress. Thus, uncertainty, in this case, can provide a sense of control and optimism (see Seligman, 1990). It has been revealed in a variety of medical studies that hope can prolong life and slow down the progression of the disease (Frank & Frank, 1991).

Another key component of UMT is that our reaction to uncertainty directly affects the influence or uncertainty and our psychological well-being. For instance, if a person interprets uncertainty in a negative way (i.e., negative emotional response) uncertainty is seen as a dangerous state that should be avoided whenever possible. On the other hand, when uncertainty is perceived as a positive experience (i.e., positive emotional response) uncertainty becomes beneficial to our physiological and psychological well-being. Figure 10.2 illustrates this process.

figure 10.2

A model of uncertainty management theory (UMT).

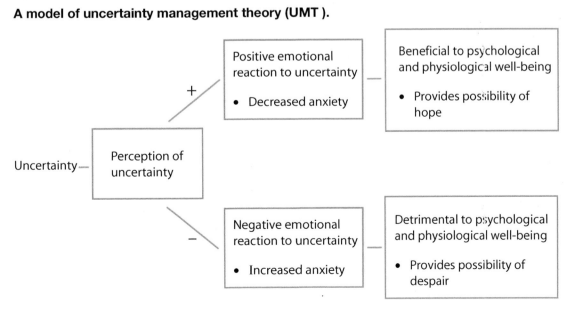

Research on information seeking has provided scholars with an abundance of findings that primarily focus on the premise that the more information we seek, the more control it provides us. This process has been described from a skill development perspective as a way to gain control over a particular situation (Cegala & Lenzmeir-Broz, 2003) as well as a personality characteristic that predisposes people to seek information (Lefcourt, 1981). However, UMT holds that our perceptions of uncertainty (positive versus negative) directly affect the strategies and types of communication that we engage in and expose ourselves to. The following experiment will illustrate this point. Ask ten people you know, if they had a choice, would they want to know the types of diseases that they will develop in the future? Chances are that some people will respond "yes." In this case, uncertainty is perceived as a negative state that needs to be reduced to be effectively maintained. By "maintained," we mean that every person has a level of uncertainty that they feel comfortable managing. Some people can only effectively manage uncertainty if it is totally reduced, whereas others can effectively manage some levels of uncertainty. Still others feel comfortable in managing high levels of uncertainty. For these people, uncertainty is seen as a positive state that needs to be maintained, as it generates less anxiety to the person rather than knowing about the specific disease they might develop.

In the healthcare context, people do not simply either seek information or not, and Brashers (2001a) provided three additional ways in which people can interpret information regarding illness. First, some people who live with chronic disease or chronic states of uncertainty adapt to the state of chronic uncertainty (e.g., it is something that I have to deal with, so I must get use to it). Second, social networks consisting of family and friends as well as social role models, such as people acting in prosocial ways may serve to aid in the management of high uncertainty. For example, a person with a spinal cord injury can rely on family and friends but may also rely on other people who have suffered a spinal cord injury. This experience is reflected by the late actor Christopher Reeve, who dedicated his life to helping people with spinal cord injuries, as well as by Michael J. Fox, who helps people cope with Parkinson's disease, and the late Princess Diana, who worked for land mine extraction throughout the world. Third, we engage in uncertainty management at a meta-level. That is, we manage our uncertainty in other areas. This is not to suggest that there is only so much management that we have to spread around (i.e., zero-sum game approach). Rather, our psychological efforts, in a proactive way, naturally determine where our uncertainty management efforts are needed (i.e., vital for effective management) and which are discretionary (i.e., desired but not vital). Second, through time and experience, people develop the flexibility to discern what information is trustworthy and relevant and what information is not in the management of uncertainty.

Diffusion of Innovation

Diffusion of innovation theory (DIT) was forwarded by Everett Rogers (1983). DIT was concerned with how innovations, primarily new technology, are adopted and implemented by people. This theory is especially well-suited for the field of health communication because it provides a comprehensive theoretical framework through which to explain and predict the effectiveness of any given health campaign and the adoption of health technologies. In fact, dozens of studies have utilized DIT to explain a variety of health-related campaigns (see, for example, Kreps, 2009).

There are four main elements of DIT consisting of the innovation, the channel through which the innovation is communicated, over a particular time period, and include members of a social system (Rogers, 1983). Now let's look more in depth at each of these elements.

Innovation.   Innovations are believed to contain five attributes; relative advantage (i.e., the degree to which the new innovation is superior to existing options), compatibility (i.e., the degree of ease to which the new innovation is integrated within existing products or processes), complexity (i.e., the degree to which the new innovation is understandable and usable), reliability (i.e., the degree to which the new innovation can consistently perform over time), and observability (i.e., the degree to which the new innovation performs as promised with measurable outcomes).

| innovation

Innovations contain five attributes: relative advantage, compatibility, complexity, reliability, and observability

Communication channel.   According to Rogers (1983), communication channel reflects the means through which messages about the innovation travels from one person to another. According to DIT theory, mass communication channels are believed to be most effective in bringing awareness and knowledge about a new innovation with interpersonal channels being more influential in forming, changing, or reinforcing attitudes toward the innovation. It is believed that most people evaluate new innovations through discussion with peers or respected others; not on empirical data or scientific evidence.

| communication channel

Reflects the means through which messages about the innovation travel from one person to another

Time.   The element of time involved in the new innovation adoption process involves adoption decisiveness, timeliness of the decision (e.g., some people adopt new innovations sooner than others), and the rate of adoption or the time it takes to make its way through any given social system (Rogers, 1983). This time-based decision-making process involves the following steps; knowledge (i.e., becoming aware that the new innovation exists), persuasion (i.e., attitudes toward the new innovation), decision (i.e., whether or not the new innovation will be acquired), implementation (i.e., degree to which the new innovation is easily integrated into existing processes or procedures), and confirmation (i.e., evidence that the new innovation is as effective as anticipated).

| time

the element of time involved in the new innovation adoption process involves adoption decisiveness, timeliness of the decision, and the rate of adoption or the time it takes to make its way through any given social system

Social system.   The social system element is "a set of interrelated units that are engaged in joint problem-solving to accomplish a goal" (Rogers, 1983, p. 120). The composition of the system can either accelerate or hinder the diffusion of the new innovation. Similar to the two-step flow theory discussed in Chapter 12, there are particular individuals who serve as opinion leaders or those people who can influence others to either accept or reject the new innovation.

| social systeml

a set of interrelated units that are engaged in joint problem-solving to accomplish a goal

In terms of DIT and health communication applications to public health campaigns and new technology. For example, the integration of electronic health records and personal health records has significantly changed the patient-provider dynamic. Research indicates that this new type of record keeping can serve to undermine the quality of relationship between the patient and the provider (Avtgis, Polack, & Liberman, 2015; Avtgis, Polack, Staggers, & Wiecorek, 2011). For example, generating the electronic health records require the provider to enter information into the computer during the patients presentation of their symptoms. This change in verbal and nonverbal behavior (e.g., the provider faces the computer screen and is focused on inputting data as opposed to facing the patient and being entirely attentive to the needs of the patient). In terms of public health, examples of applying DOI have successfully been applied to engaging students in school-wellness initiatives (Harringer, Lu, McKyer, E., Lisako, Pruitt, & Goodson, 2014) and to reduce the research-practice gap in autism intervention. That is, making sure that cutting edge research on autism is quickly integrated into practitioners treatment approaches (Dingfelder & Mandell, 2011).

Transtheoretical Model

transtheoretical model

Consists of five stages including the pre-contemplation stage, the contemplation stage, the preparation stage, the action stage, and the maintenance stage

The **transtheoretical model** (TTM) was developed utilizing the stages of change framework regarding health-related issues (DiClemente, Prochaska, Fairhurst, Velicer, Rossi, & Velasquez, 1991; Prochaska, 2013; Prochaska & Velicer, 1997; Prochaska, Wright, & Velicer, 2008). These five stages consist of: the pre-contemplation stage (i.e., people who are not intending to change behavior in the next six months), the contemplation stage (i.e., people who are intending to change their behavior within the next six months), the preparation stage (i.e., people who intend to change their behaviors within the next 30 days), the action stage (i.e., people who have actually made changes to the behavior), and the maintenance stage (i.e., people who continue engaging in the altered behavior). According to DiClemente *et al.* (1991), these stages have relationships with other measures of TTM such as processes of change, decisional balance, and self-efficacy (Fava, Velicer, & Abrams, 1995).

Processes of change reflect actual strategies that people engage in and contain both experiential and behavioral dimensions. Experiential processes consist of "consciousness raising, dramatic relief, environmental reevaluation, self-reevaluation, and social liberation" (Prochaska et al., 2008, p. 563). Behavioral processes consist of "stimulus control, counter conditioning, reinforcement management, self-liberation, and helping relationships" (Prochaska et al., 2008, p. 563). Decisional balance refers to the pro's and con's reflecting cognitive and motivational factors in the decision-making process (i.e., instrumental benefits to self, instrumental benefits to others, approval from self, approval from others, instrumental costs to self, instrumental costs to others, disapproval from self, and disapproval from others) (Janis & Mann, 1977). More specifically, people move from perceiving more con's than pro's to behavioral change before engaging in the behavioral change whereas people who have engaged in actual behavior change processes switch that perception to perceiving more pro's than con's to such change. Similar patterns across stages where observed regarding self-efficacy. That is, self-efficacy increases as people move through actual behavioral change (Janis & Mann, 1977).

The transtheoretical model has been utilized in many interventions for at-risk behaviors that include success for a variety of addictive behaviors (DiClemente & Prochaska, 1998) including alcohol abstinence (Carbonari & DiClemente, 2000), smoking cessation (Fava, Velicer, & Abrahms, 1995; Ham & Lee, 2007; Velicer, Prochaska, Fava, Norman, & Redding, 1998), weight management (Johnson, Paiva, Cummins, Johnson, Dyment, Wright, Prochaska, Prochaska, & Sherman, 2008), exercise (Marcus & Simkin, 1994), organ donation (Morgan & Miller, 2002), and HIV prevention (Prochaska, Redding, Harlow, Rossi, & Veliver, 1994). However, similar to most theories, the transtheoretical model is not without its detractors. More specifically, the TTM has been criticized for its lack of empirical evidence (West, 2005) and lack of predictive validity (Sutton, 2001).

Conclusion

The health communication context continues to be one of the fastest growing areas of research in the field of communication studies. This chapter discusses the various ways in which health communication has been conceptualized. Whether it be interpersonal, organization, or mass and mediated approaches (to name but a few), the vast landscape of health within society and globally continues to intrigue researchers and practitioners alike. We covered the functions that communication serves within the patient–provider dyad and discussed the various influences on that relationship. Whether it concern issues of relational control, mutual influence, communication traits, power status, or nonverbal behavior, there are myriad factors that have to be accounted for in efforts to improve health care and the patient–provider relationship.

Several models were presented regarding perceptions of health-related risks in ways to create effective health-related campaigns to inform and persuade publics to engage in wellness behavior. Some of these approaches include the health belief model, uncertainty management, and diffusion of innovation, all of which try to explain, describe, predict and control health-related behavior. Regardless of the approach or theory we choose to focus on, researchers will continue theory-building efforts with the goal of improving communication and quality of life regarding health-related outcomes.

Questions for Discussion/Review

1. What are the functions of communication in the health context?
2. Discuss communication contexts within health communication.
3. What is the health belief model?
4. Explain Uncertainty Management Theory.
5. What is the Transtheoretical Model?

References

Afifi, W. A., & Matsunaga, M. (2008). Uncertainty management theories: Three approaches to a multifarious process. In L. A. Baxter & D. O. Braithwaite (Eds.), *Engaging theories in interpersonal communication: Multiple perspectives* (pp. 117–132). Thousand Oaks, CA: Sage.

Arntson, P., & Droge, D. (1988). Addressing the value dimension of health communication: A social science perspective. *Journal of Applied Communication Research. 16,* 1–15. doi: 10.1080/00909888809365267

Avtgis, T. A., Brann, M., & Staggers, S. (2006). Information exchange and health control expectancies as influenced by a patient's medical interview situation. *Communication Research Reports, 23,* 231-237. doi: 10.1080/08824090600962284

Avtgis, T. A., & Madlock, P. E. (2008). Implications of the verbally patient: Creating a constructive environment in destructive situations. In E. P. Polack, V. P. Richmond, & J. C. McCroskey (Eds.), Applied communication for health professions (pp. 169–183). Dubuque, IA: Kendall Hunt.

Avtgis, T. A., & Polack, E. P. (2007). Predicting physician communication competence by patient perceived information exchange and health locus of control. *Human Communication, 10,* 136–144.

Avtgis, T. A., Polack, E. P., & Liberman, C. J. (2015). The impact of communication technology on healthcare organizations and patient-provider interactions. In K. B. Wright & L. Webb (Eds.), *Computer mediated communication in personal relationships* (2nd ed.). Cresskill, NJ: Hampton Press.

Avtgis, T. A., Polack, E. P., Staggers, S. M., & Wiecorek, S. M. (2011). Healthcare provider – recipient interactions: Is "online" interaction the next best thing to being there. In K. B. Wright & L. Webb (Eds.), *Computer mediated communication in personal relationships* (pp. 266–284). Cresskill, NJ: Hampton Press.

Beisecker, A. E. (1991). Interpersonal communication strategies to prevent drug abuse by health professionals and the elderly: Contribution of the health belief mode. *Health Communication, 3,* 241–250. doi: 10.1207/s15327027hc0304_6

Brashers, D. E. (2001a). Communication and uncertainty management. *Journal of Communication, 51,* 477–497. doi: 10.1111/j.1460-2466.2001.tb02892.x

Brashers, D. E. (2001b). HIV and uncertainty: Managing treatment decision making. *Focus: A guide to AIDS research, 16,* 5–6.

Brashers, D. E., Goldsmith, D. J., & Hsieh, E. (2002). Information seeking and avoiding in health contexts. *Human Communication Research, 28,* 258–271. doi: 10.1111/j.1468-2958.2002.tb0887.x

Brashers, D. E., Hsieh, E., Neidig, J. L., & Reynolds, N. R. (2006). Managing uncertainty about illness: Health care providers as credible authorities. In B. LePoire & R. M. Dailey (Eds.), *Applied interpersonal communication matters: Family, health, and community relations* (pp. 219–240). New York: Peter Lang.

Brenders, D. A. (1989). Perceived control and the interpersonal dimension of health care. *Health Communication, 1,* 117–135. doi: 10.1207/s15327027hc0102_3

Brown, W. J. (1991). A AIDS prevention campaign: Effects on attitudes, beliefs, and communication behavior. *American Behavioral Scientist, 34,* 666–678.

Brown, T., Boyle, M., Williams, B., Molloy, A., Palermo, C., McKenna, L., & Molloy, L. (2011). Predictors of empathy in health science students. *Journal of Allied Health, 40,* 143–149. doi: 10.1037/t01093-000

Buller, M. K., & Buller, D. B. (1987). Physicians' communication style and patient satisfaction. *Journal of Health and Social Behavior, 28,* 375–388.

Burgoon, J. K., Pfau, M.. Parrott, R., Birk, T., Coker, R., & Burgoon, M. (1987). Relational communication, satisfaction, compliance-gaining strategies, and compliance communication between physicians and patients. *Communication Monographs, 54,* 307–324. doi: 10.1080/03637758709390235

Burgoon, M. H., & Burgoon, J. K. (1990). Compliance-gaining and health care. In J. P. Dillard (Ed.), *Seeking compliance* (pp. 161–188). Scottsdale, AZ: Gorsuch Scarisbrick.

Carbonari, J. P., & DiClemente, C. C. (2000). Using transtheoretical model profiles to differentiate levels of alcohol abstinence success. *Journal of Consulting and Clinical Psychology, 68,* 810. doi: 10.1037/0022-D06x.68.5.810

Cardello, L. L., Ray, E. B., & Pettey, G. R. (1995). The relationship of perceived physician communicator style to patient satisfaction. *Communication Reports, 8,* 27–37. doi: 10.1080/08934219509367604

Cegala, D. J., & Lenzmeier-Broz, S. (2003). Provider and patient communication skills training. In A. M. Dorsey, T. L. Thompson, K. I. Miller, & R. Parrot (Eds.), *Handbook of health communication* (pp. 95–120). Mahwah, NJ: Erlbaum.

Chew, F., Palmer, S., & Kim. S. (1998). Testing the influence of the health belief model and a television program on nutrition behavior. *Health Communication, 10,* 227–245. doi: 10.1207/s15327027hc/003_3

Cline, R. J., & Cardosi, J. B. (1983). Interpersonal communication skills for physicians: A rationale for training. *Journal of Communication Therapy, 2,* 137–156.

Costello, D. E. (1977). Health communication theory and research: An overview. In B. Ruben (Ed.). *Communication Yearbook 1* (pp. 557–567). New Brunswick, NJ: Transaction Books.

DeVito, J. A. (2002). *Human communication: The basic course* (9th ed.). Boston: Allyn & Bacon.

DiClemente, C. C., & Prochaska, J. O. (1998). Toward a comprehensive, transtheoretical model of change. Stages of change and addictive behaviors. In W. R. Miller & N. Heather (Eds.), *Treating addictive behaviors: Applied clinical psychology* (pp. 3–24). New York: Plenum Press. doi: 10.1007/978-1-4899-1934-2.1

DiClemente, C. C., Prochaska, J. O., Fairhurst, S., Velicer, W. F., Rossi, J. S., & Velasquez, M. (1991). The process of smoking cessation. *Journal of Consulting and Clinical Psychology, 59,* 295-304. doi: 10.1037/0022-D06x.59.2.295

Dingfelder, H. E., & Mandell, D. S. (2011). Bridging the research-to-practice gap in autism intervention: An application of diffusion of innovation theory. *Journal of Autism & Developmental Disorders, 41,* 597–609. doi: 10.1007/s10803-010

Donohew, L., & Ray, E. B. (1990). Introduction: Systems perspectives on health communication. In E. B. Ray & L. Donohew (Eds.), *Communication and health* (pp. 3–8). Hillsdale, NJ: Lawrence Erlbaum.

Fava, J. L., Velicer, W. F., & Abrahms, D. B. (1995). *Two methods of assessing stages of change for smoking cessation.* Paper presented at the Ninth World Conference on Tobacco and Health, Paris, France.

Fava, J. L., Velicer, W. F., & Prochaska, J. O. (1985). Applying the transtheoretical model to a representative sample of smokers. *Addictive Behaviors, 20,* 189–203. doi: 10.1016/0306-4603(94)00062-x

Frank, J. D., & Frank, J. B. (1991). *Persuasion and healing: A comparative study of psychotherapy.* Baltimore: The Johns Hopkins University Press.

Garko, M. (1994). Communicator styles of powerful physician-executives in upward-influence situations. *Health Communication, 6,* 159–172. doi: 10.1207/s15327027hc0602_5

Ham, O. K., & Lee, Y. J. (2007). Use of the transtheoretical model to predict stages of smoking cessation in Korean adolescents. *Journal of School Health, 77,* 319–326. doi: 10.1111/j.1746-1561.2007.00213.x

Hunleth, J. M., Steinmetz, E. K., McQueen, A., & James, A. S. (2016). Beyond adherence: Health care disparities and the struggle to get screened for colon cancer. *Qualitative Health Research, 26,* 17–31. doi: 10.1177/1049732315593549

Harringer, D., Lu, W., McKyer, E. Lisako, J., Pruitt, B. E., & Goodson, P. (2014). Assessment of school wellness policies implementation by benchmarking against diffusion of innovation. *Journal of School Health, 84,* 275–283. doi: 10.1111/josh.12145

Janis, I. L., & Mann, L. (1977). *Decision making.* London: Cassel & Collier Macmillan.

Johnson, S. S., Paiva, A. L., Cummins, C. O., Johnson, J. L., Dyment, S. J., Wright, J. A., Prochaska, J. O., Prochaska, J. M., & Sherman, K. (2008). Transtheoretical model-based multiple behavior intervention for weight management: Effectiveness on a population basis. *Preventative Medicine, 46,* 238–246. doi: 10.1016/j.ypmed.2007.09.010

King, D., Vlaev, I., Everett-Thomas, R., Fitzpatrick, M., Darzi, A., & Birnbach, D. J. (2016). 'Priming' hand hygiene compliance in clinical environments. *Health Psychology, 35,* 96–101. doi: 10.1037/hea0000239

Kreps, G. L. (2009). Health communication theories. In S. Littlejohn (Ed.), *Encyclopedia of communication theory* (pp. 465–469). Thousand Oaks, CA: Sage. doi: 10.4135/978141295938.n172

Kreps, G. L. (1988). The pervasive role of information in health care: Implications for health communication policy. In J. Anderson (Ed.). *Communication Yearbook 11* (pp. 238–276). Newbury Park, CA: Sage.

Kreps, G. L., Bonaguro, E., & Query, J. L. (1998). The history and development of the field of health communication. In L. Jackson & B. Duffy (Eds.), *Health communication research* (pp. 1–15). Westport, CT: Greenwood Press.

Lanza, M. L., Zeiss, R., & Rierdan, J. (2005, November). *Violence assessment, medication, and prevention.* Paper presented at the annual meeting of the American Nurses Conference, Washington, DC.

Lederman, L. C. (2009). Health communication: The first twenty-five years. In J. W. Chesebro (Ed.), *From 20th century beginnings to 21st century advances: Developing and evolving from a century of transformation: Studies in honor of the 100th anniversary of the eastern communication association* (pp. 236–254). Los Angeles, CA: Roxbury.

Lefcourt, H. M. (1982). *Locus of control: Current trends in theory and research.* Mahwah, NJ: Erlbaum.

Leonard, M., Graham, S., & Bonacum, D. (2004). The human factor: The critical importance of effective teamwork in communication and providing safe care. *Quality and Safety in Healthcare, 13,* 185–190. doi: 10.1136/qshc.2004.D10033

Marcus, B. H., & Simkin, L. R. (1994). The transtheoretical model: Applications to exercise behavior. *Medicine & Science in Sports & Exercise, 26,* 1400–1404. doi: 10.1249100005768-199411000-00016

Mattson, M. (1999). Toward a reconceptualization of communication cues to action in the health belief model: HIV test counseling. *Communication Monographs, 66,* 240–265. doi: 10.1080/03637759909376476

Millar, F. E., & Rogers, L. E (1976). A relational approach to interpersonal communication. In G. R. Miller (Ed.), *Explorations in interpersonal communication* (pp. 87–103). Beverly Hills: Sage.

Millar, F. E., & Rogers, L. E. (1987). Relational dimensions of interpersonal dynamics. In M. E. Roloff & G. R. Miller (Eds.), *Interpersonal processes: New directions in communication research* (pp. 117–139). Newbury Park, CA: Sage.

Morgan, S. E., & Miller, J. K. (2002). Beyond the organ donor card: The effect of knowledge, attitudes, and values on willingness to communicate about organ donation to family members. *Health Communication, 14,* 122–134. New York: Springer. doi: 10.1207/S15327027HC1401_6

O'Hair, D. (1989). Dimensions of relational communication and control during physician-patient interactions. *Health Communication, 1,* 97–115. doi: 10.1207/s/5327027/hc0102_2

Pellowski, J. A., Kalichman, S. C., & Grebler, T. (2016). Optimal treatment adherence counseling outcomes for people living with HIV and limited health literacy. *Behavioral Medicine, 42,* 39–47. doi: 10.1080/08964289.2014.963006

Polack, E. P., & Avtgis, T. A. (2011). *Medical communication: Defining the discipline.* Dubuque, IA: Kendall Hunt.

Polack, E. P., Avtgis, T. A., Rossi, D., & Shaffer, L. (2010). A team approach in communication instruction: A qualitative approach. *Journal of Surgical Education, 67,* 125–128. doi: 10.1016/jsurg.2010.02.004

Prochaska, J. O. (2013). Transtheoretical model of behavior change. *Encyclopedia of Behavioral Medicine.* (pp. 1997–2000). New York: Springer.

Prochaska, J. O., & Redding, C. A., Harlow, L. L., Rossi, J. S., & Velicer, W. F. (1994). The transtheoretical model of change and HIV prevention: A review. *Health Education & Behavior, 21,* 471–486. doi: 10.1177/109019815402100410

Prochaska, J. O., & Velicer, W. F. (1997). The transtheoretical model of health behavior change. *American Journal of Health Promotion, 12,* 38–48. doi: 10.4278/0890-1171-12_1.38

Prochaska, J. O., Wright, J. A., & Velicer (2008). Evaluating theories of health behavior change: A hierarchy of criteria applied to the transtheoretical model. *Applied Psychology: An International Review, 57,* 561–588. doi: 10.1111/j.464-0597.2008.00345.x

Ratzan, S. C., Stearns, N. S., Payne, J. G., Amato, P. P., Libergott, J., & Madoff, M. A. (1994). Education for the health professional. *American Behavioral Scientist. 38,* 361–380. doi: 10.1177/0002764294038002015

Ratzan, S. C., Payne, J. G., & Bishop, C. (1996). The status and scope of health communication. *Journal of Health Communication, 1,* 25–41. doi: 10.1080/108107396128211

Roberto, A. J., & Eden, J. (2014). Prevalence and predictors of cyberbullying perpetration by high school seniors. *Communication Quarterly, 62,* 97–114. doi: 10.1080/01463373.860906

Rogers, E. M. (1983). *Communication technology: The new media in society.* New York: The Free Press.

Rosenstock, I. M. (1974). Historical origins of the health belief model. *Health Education Monographs, 2,* 354–385. doi: 10.1177/109019817400200403

Sansone, R. A., Bohinc, R., & Wiederman, M. W. (2015). Borderline personality symptomatology and compliance with general health care among internal medicine outpatients. *International Journal of Psychiatry in Clinical Practice, 19,* 132–136. doi: 10.3109/13651501.2014.988269

Seligman, M. E. P. (1990). *Learned optimism: How to change your mind and your life.* New York: Pocket Books.

Steadman, H., Mulvey, E., Monohan, J., Robbins, P., Applebaum, P., & Grisso, T. (1998). Violence by people discharged from active psychiatric in-patient facilities and by others in the same neighborhoods. *Archives of General Psychiatry, 55,* 393–401. doi: 10.1001/archpsyc.55.5.393

Street, R. L., Jr., & Buller, D. B. (1987). Nonverbal response patterns in physician-patient interactions: A functional analysis. *Journal of Nonverbal Behavior, 11,* 234–253. doi: 10.1007/BF00987255

Street, R. L., Jr., & Buller, D. B. (1988). Patients' characteristics affecting physician-patient nonverbal communication. *Human Communication Research, 15,* 60–90. doi: 10.1111/j.1468-2958.1988.tb00171.x

Sutton, S. (2001). Back to the drawing board? A review of Applications of the transtheoretical model to substance abuse. *Addiction, 96,* 175–186. doi: 10.1046/j.1360-0443.2001.96117513.x

Thompson, T. L. (2006). Seventy-five (count 'em – 75!) issues in health communication: An analysis of emerging themes. *Health Communication, 20,* 117–122. doi: 10.1207/s15327027hc2002_2

Thompson, T. L., Dorsey, A. M., Miller, K. I., & Parrott, R. (Eds.). (2003). *Handbook of health communication.* Mahwah, NJ: Erlbaum.

Velicer, W. F., Prochaska, J. O., Fava, J. L., Norman, G. J., & Redding, C. A. (1998). Smoking cessation and stress management. Application of the transtheoretical model of behavior change. *Homeostasis in Health and Disease: International Journal Devoted to Integrative Brain Functions and Homeostatic Systems,* 216–233.

West, R. (2005). Time for a change: Putting the transtheoretical (stages of change) model to test. *Addiction, 100,* 1036–1039. doi: 10.1111/j.1360-0443.2005.01139.x

Wheeless, V. E., Wheeless, L. R., & Riffle, S. (1989). The role of situation, physician communicator style, and hospital rules climate on nurses' decision styles and communication satisfaction. *Health Communication, 1,* 189–206. 10.1207/s15327027hc0104_1

Wigley, C. J. (2009, November). *Verbal trigger events (VTEs) and the measurement of reactive verbal aggression (RVA).* Paper presented at the annual meeting of the National Communication Association, Chicago, IL.

Witte, K., Stokols, D., Ituarte, P., & Schneider, M. (1993). Testing the health belief model in a field study to promote bicycle safety helmets. *Communication Research, 20,* 564–586. doi: 10.1177/005365093020004004

Assessment and Training within Healthcare: Training the Trainers

chapter objectives

Upon completion of the chapter, the student should be able to:

1. Explain the importance of training within healthcare

2. Understand the essential skills needed for effective training

3. Explain the various audience needs regarding training and approaches to training

4. Compare and contrast the various training delivery methods and vehicles available to trainers

5. Explain the concept of feedback and how such feedback can be applied effectively to enhance performance

T hroughout this book we have presented and discussed dozens of different professions and their roles in the everyday delivery of healthcare. Each of these roles are vital to delivering essential medical care efficiently and safely. How does a person learn to perform their professional duties efficiently and safely? How does one come to learn and navigate the different sets of rules and procedures unique to their chosen profession and to the culture of their facility? Although some of this knowledge comes from formal higher education, much of it is provided by peers and colleagues who train us (both officially and unofficially) so that we can understand and perform our required tasks, which results in the *organization* of *healthcare* running smoothly. This chapter will focus on training and the processes that are involved in the development, delivery, and assessment of training content within healthcare.

© wavebreakmedia/Shutterstock.com

Reasons for Training

Although the field of training and development is something applicable to all professions, when it is applied to healthcare it becomes an extremely valuable asset that can directly affect patient safety. In 1999 the Institute of Medicine (IOM) reported that as many as 98,000 people die annually from medical errors. This led to the establishment of the Quality Interagency Coordination (QuIC) task force, which concluded that training must be implemented to prevent such events from occurring. For example, one of the recommendations of QuIC was for **crew resource management (CRM)** training to be adapted to medicine (see Chapter 1 for a discussion of CRM). As such, standardized training is targeted at the reduction (and hopeful elimination) of healthcare personnel (human) error.

Given that healthcare professions are becoming increasingly specialized and of greater complexity, there becomes a great need for not only generalized training (e.g., training targeted at basic knowledge of an entire profession such as HIPAA training), but also training in specific processes within a discipline (e.g., training of micro-processes such as insurance approval processes or emergency contingency plans). Because of these needs, varied and effective training is essential. **Training** is defined as "the acquisition of knowledge and skills necessary for individuals to perform effectively on the job" (Avtgis, Rancer, & Madlock, 2010). **Knowledge acquisition** focuses on what people need to know about a particular policy or procedure, whereas **skills acquisition** focuses on the behaviors that people need to perform in accordance with policy or procedure, and such skills can be measured (Polack, Richmond, & McCroskey, 2008).

When applying training principles in the context of healthcare, we must define those general concepts that are specific to healthcare. Therefore, **healthcare training** can be defined as the process of acquiring the necessary knowledge and skill required to function in any given healthcare role effectively. It is important to distinguish between **healthcare knowledge acquisition** and **healthcare skill acquisition.** Healthcare knowledge acquisition refers to the adoption and integration of new (cognitive) knowledge in order to perform a function, whereas healthcare skill acquisition refers to the adoption or refinement of behavioral skills and processes associated with quality healthcare delivery.

Thousands of different types of training are pertinent to healthcare personnel, allied healthcare personnel, equipment suppliers, pharmaceutical representatives, and so on. For example, consider some of the major healthcare physician member normative organizations and the types of training they provide. For example, the *American Medical Association (AMA), American College of Surgeons (ACS), American Society for Surgery of the Hand (ASSH),* and the *American Association of Orthopedic Surgeons (AAO)* are organizations that range in scope and involve people from all specialties, disciplines, interests, and backgrounds.

When it comes to specific courses, a vast variety are available. A sampling of these include Advanced Trauma Life Support (ATLS), the Rural Training Team Development Course (RTTDC) for the rural trauma setting, Pediatric Advanced Life Support (PALS) training, Advanced Cardiac Life Support (ACLS) training, and Advanced Burn Life Support (ABLS) training, to name but a few. The end results of trainings such as these are based on both organizational and professional standards. To ensure such standards are adhered to requires effective communicators and training methods that are lasting and effective because the bottom line in healthcare is patient safety.

Considerations for Effective Training

Training and the ability to train others are uniquely communicative in nature. Thus, to effectively develop, deliver, and assess training success, a person should be versed in *educational approaches, communication competency,* and *effective assessment.* **Educational approaches** involve knowledge of the various pedagogical tools and theories that are available to the trainer for designing the most appropriate and effective training. Communication competency reflects the ability to relay information in an effective and socially appropriate way. **Effective assessment** reflects the ability to develop, implement, analyze,

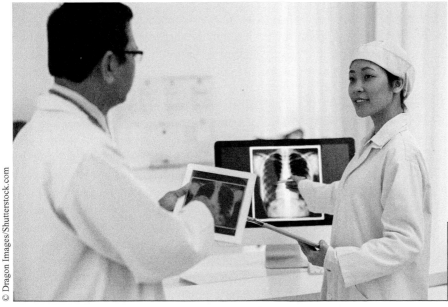

© Dragon Images/Shutterstock.com

Adapted from Avtgis et al. (2010). Organizational communication: Strategies for success. Dubuque, IA: Kendall Hunt.

and interpret the outcomes from measures given to the trainees. The following sections will review some of the basic elements of training and development targeted specifically for the demands of the healthcare industry.

One of the most fundamental concepts that must be understood and considered when training any adult population concerns the learning process. Adult learning is vastly different from the learning that children engage in. More specifically, when we seek to educate children we engage in pedagogy, or the art and science of child learning. The education of adults is known as andragogy and refers to the art and science of adult learning. When teaching adults, two main assumptions must be considered. The learning orientation of adults tends to focus on problem-solving and task completion. The trainees must see relevance in all material being presented and how the presented material can assist the learner in effective problem-solving. Simply put, the material has to have both immediate appeal and immediate use. The second assumption concerns the role the adult learner plays in the learning process. More specifically, adult learners need to be both **cognitively involved** (i.e., getting the learner to think about the information) and **behaviorally involved** (i.e., having the learner engage in activities that concretize the lessons). Therefore, it is always advised to incorporate activities, role play, and a variety of other training vehicles to keep the attention of, and involvement of, all participants. Such training vehicles will be discussed later in this chapter.

| **pedagogy**

The art and science of child learning.

| **andragogy**

The art and science of adultlearning.

Role of the Trainer

The trainer serves as the source through which all information filters. Training is generally broken down into two major areas: **instructional design** (i.e., the development of content lessons and modules that will be presented) and **course delivery** (i.e., the actual presentation of the instructional content).

Skill Sets of the Trainer.   There are many ways in which to effectively train others in policy and procedures. Although the methods may vary, the abilities for a person to do so effectively are not so varied. According to Avtgis et al. (2010), effective trainers possess nine different skills (Table 11.1).

Trainer Behavioral Characteristics.   As you probably can determine from your own training experiences, not all trainers are built the same. The personality and communication characteristics of an effective trainer can, to a certain degree, be acquired and developed. Perhaps the most important characteristic is eye contact (i.e., occulesics), body motion and movement (i.e., kinesics), and dynamic use of the voice (i.e., paralanguage) (Avtgis et al., 2010). Eye contact is considered a key ingredient in keeping the trainees engaged and is the most effective way to establish nonverbal immediacy. Nonverbal immediacy is the degree to which people use nonverbal communication to increase the physical and psychological closeness or distance between people in a relationship (Mehrabian, 1971). By displaying these immediacy behaviors, we create a positive link to the trainee; this is

table 11.1	Essential Skills of Effective Trainers
Skill	**Behavior**
Presentational Skills	The ability to be dynamic and energetic and channel the proper communication behaviors in an effort to create an atmosphere conducive to learning and enhancing trainer credibility.
Written Communication Skills	The ability to create relevant objectives, persuasively arrange content, and provide concise and interesting documents (e.g., trainees manual, PowerPoint slides and handouts).
Active Listening Skills	The ability to interact and listen to many different types of people at different levels of expertise and organizational status. Such skills include listening for comprehension and paraphrasing the input of others into the overall theme of the training module.
Facilitation Skills	The ability to guide discussion and topic direction of the group while also making sure that those who wish to contribute are recognized and their contribution is valued and synthesized into the overall theme of the training module.
Interpersonal Communication Skills	The ability to demonstrate appropriate and effective interpersonal behavior that facilitates open and honest communication between you and the trainees. This requires an appreciation of diversity in thought and perspective and the ability to show empathy.
Data-Gathering Skills	The ability to assess the needs of the trainees, the trainees' progress, and both the quality and effectiveness of the overall training. This can include knowledge of basic statistics and measurement development.
Data-Analysis Skills	The ability to evaluate and properly interpret the data obtained from the trainees. This type of data may include being able to interpret both quantitative data (e.g., On a scale of 1 to 5 tell me how you feel about the following) and qualitative data (e.g., Please write a brief paragraph of a time where a co-worker).
Political Skills	The ability to determine potential personality and relational difficulties among trainees given that most groups that require training have members with relational histories.
Skill of Understanding the Adult Learner	The ability to apply the basic concepts of andragogy and the learning tripartite of cognitive, affective, and behavioral components.

Adapted from Avtgis et al. (2010). Organizational communication: Strategies for success. Dubuque, IA: Kendall Hunt.

found to be effective regardless of how large the audience. By establishing this psychological link with the trainees, they will be much more receptive to the training material being presented. Kinesics can also be effective in keeping the trainees' attention. Imagine attending a training session where the trainer stands behind a computer or desk, rarely moves, and remains statuesque. Such a delivery style will probably result in the trainees becoming quickly bored and uninterested. Instead, imagine a trainer who utilizes dynamic movements that exude both energy and confidence. Such a presentation style will greatly enhance the learning experience for the trainees. The final important skill is the use of voice. A lot goes into presenting good and effective vocalic behavior, including volume, sound, inflection, accent, rate, and pitch. Can the person in the back row hear what you are saying? Is your vocal style too rhythmic (e.g., similar to how a teenager would speak)? Among the many characteristics that influence a trainer's effectiveness, how one looks, sounds, and behaves does not guarantee successful training. It is only a success when these behaviors are coupled with well-planned and developed training materials. However, failing to look, sound, and behave in professional and effective ways will keep the trainer from achieving their desired training goals.

Audience Needs

One of the more important characteristics of the audience refers to their level of interest and willingness to learn. We have all been to training where people either dismiss the information being presented or lack the level of understanding needed to acquire the new information. A common approach to leadership [and we believe also to training] that considers characteristics of the trainee, is the **situational leadership perspective** (Hersey & Blanchard, 1977). A trainer must focus the content of the material based on the employee's *psychological maturity* and *job maturity*. Psychological maturity is a person's degree of self-efficacy and willingness to accept the responsibility of acquiring and implementing the new information and skills that are being taught in the training. Job maturity is a person's level of both knowledge and skill needed to perform a task (Avtgis et al., 2010). For trainees with low levels of both psychological and job maturity, the trainer should take the approach of a *tell style*. The tell style of training is very task specific with little focus on relationship building. This style is advocated for trainees who are low in self-efficacy and are unmotivated. For example, this type of

| **psychological maturity**

A person's degree of self-efficacy and willingness to accept the responsibility of acquiring and implementing the new information and skills being taught in the training.

| **job maturity**

A person's level of both knowledge and skill needed to perform a task.

A successful trainer keeps the session participants interested with a dynamic delivery style.

© Rawpixel.com/Shutterstock.com

situation may occur when conducting communication training with medical students. They think that communication is common sense and a natural ability—not something that can and must be practiced—thus they tend to devalue the information. Yet another example may be seen in teaching a group of second-year surgical residents who scoff at the importance of understanding cultural differences when communicating with a patient from another culture. The next style would be the **sell style,** which consists of trainees who have some level of maturity but do not want to be told what to do yet are not motivated to take initiative on their own. Therefore, the trainer should be focused on both the task and the relationship. For example, the trainer should focus on not only explaining the content of the training, but also advising them in how acquiring the new skills will benefit them in their job. The **participative style** assumes that trainees have high levels of job maturity and low levels of psychological maturity. Therefore, this requires that the trainer diminish the focus on task training and emphasize the relationship among trainees. For example, a training consisting of enhancing teamwork would consist of every person in the training (e.g., physician, nurse, technicians) knowing their role and what is expected of them, even though they are reluctant to engage in the teamwork concept. This reluctance can result from a variety of factors including having relational difficulties, being unsatisfied with work, and experiencing burnout. The final level is the **delegating style** and reflects high levels of both job maturity and psychological maturity. Such trainees are capable of performing the tasks and are motivated to do so. Therefore, for the trainer, this is the optimal group of trainees because it consists of capable and motivated personnel who see themselves as having a stake in the successful implementation of the skills being taught.

Although understanding the maturity of the trainee is a critical component for the trainer in effectively designing goals and approaches for training content, it is also important to assess the trainees' level of self-awareness regarding their strengths and deficiencies. What we think we know and how we view our performance are controversial in terms of being accurate measures. The concept of self-assessment is defined as "the involvement of learners in judging whether or not learner-identified standards have been met" (Eva & Regehr, 2005, p. S46). In a study of orthopedic surgical residents and their ability to engage in accurate self-assessment, it was found that self-assessment was a poor tool for accurate measurement of quality performance (Harrington, Murnaghan, & Regehr, 1997). This finding was validated by similar studies involving a variety of healthcare professionals (Davis, Mazmanian, Fordis, Van Harrison, Thorpe, & Perrier, 2006). However, when there is a "benchmark" or a standard from which to compare a self-assessment, the accuracy of the self-assessment improves greatly. In a study utilizing videotaped performance, Ward and colleagues (2003) had senior surgical residents view a videotape of a resident performing a procedure followed up by viewing a series of "benchmark" procedures ranging in quality of performance. The providing of a quality benchmark assessment was found to improve the surgical residents' ability to accurately assess their own

tell style

A style of training where the trainees are low in both psychological and job maturity.

sell style

A style of training where the trainees have some level of psychological and job maturity and are reluctant to be told what to do, yet they are not motivated to take initiative on their own.

participative style

A style of training where trainees have high levels of job maturity and low levels of psychological maturity.

delegating style

A style of training where trainees have high levels of both job and psychological maturity.

performance. Such a process serves to "dial in" a person's thinking about what is good versus bad and to be more consistent with the accepted professional definitions.

It should be noted that not all self-assessments are equally flawed. In fact, the concept of self-assessment can be considered to be multidimensional in nature. That is, if we choose to use self-assessment for an evaluation tool, several characteristics of the trainee need to be considered. First, the level of **self-efficacy** of the trainee must be considered. Self-efficacy is the degree to which the trainee believes that he or she has the capacity to accomplish a particular act or achieve a particular goal. In this case, the trainee should be able to perform a self-assessment of his or her performance objectively and reflects their ability to improve performance. The second dimension is **self-concept,** or the level of general self-worth the trainee holds. If a trainee should have a bad or negative self-concept, he or she may be extremely negative or extremely positive in the self-evaluation to make up for insecurities associated with the performance. Third, cognitive and meta-cognitive ability reflects the ability of the trainee to learn new information and the ability to retrieve that information accurately and quickly from memory. If a person has a difficult time either learning a process or retrieving information from previously learned material, the self-assessment will be adversely affected. The final dimension is that of **social cognition** and reflects the trainee's ability to accurately compare his or her own thoughts and behaviors to those of others. There

cognitive and meta-cognitive ability

A dimension of self-assessment concerning the ability of the trainee to learn new information and the ability to retrieve that information accurately and quickly from their memory.

© wavebreakmedia/Shutterstock.com

What characteristics of the trainee need to be considered in self-assessments?

is a general tendency for self-assessments to be inflated or interpreted in the best possible light. Whether this rating inflation results from a conscious or unconscious process, most people tend to see themselves as being better than the norm. If it were true that most people are better than the norm, then the performance level of the norm would increase. Simply put, people think they are better than they really are and, as such, this tendency can negatively skew the self-assessment (Eva & Regehr, 2005).

Considering these potential problems with self-assessment, how can we use this self-assessment procedure in the best and most effective way? The answer is in the form of a four-point process developed by Hodges, Regehr, and Martin (2001). This process begins with obtaining a measure of the trainee's ability to actually engage in assessment. Such a measurement of assessment should occur before the trainee receives any training. Second is the constant attention to teaching self-assessment techniques at multiple times during medical school and residency. The third process consists of modeling the self-assessment. The fourth and final process concerns teaching the trainee the importance of the pursuit of continuing lifelong education, which includes the need to develop quality self-assessment skills at all levels of professional development (e.g., undergraduate and postgraduate levels).

Training Objectives

The use of objectives in the development of educational and occupational training serves as a roadmap that shapes and guides the training effort (Ittner & Douds, 1988). As with any endeavor, people need to clearly define what they want to achieve and then develop a plan to best go about achieving those goals. For example, when a patient is beginning physical therapy for a shoulder injury, the therapist may refer to standardized protocols for advancing the patient to the ultimate objective of regaining as much shoulder function as possible. This protocol contains several goals (e.g., by the first month the patient should be able to…by the second month the patient should be able to…) that are necessary in order to reach to fulfill an objective. **Training goals** are general statements as to what the trainee is expected to learn or do, whereas **training objectives** are "easily measurable and often include specific skills that are demonstrable. Goals serve as the 'target' for achievement of a given module or program and often serve as the basis for writing objectives" (Avtgis et al., 2010).

The main functions served through the development of objectives include aiding in the selection of training material that best suits the purpose of the training, guiding the general educational approach the trainer will take toward participants, and providing clear markers for measurement to determine if the goals of the training have been reached or behavior has improved.

The two main objectives used in the development of most professional training include both *instructional* and *behavioral objectives*. **Instructional objectives** consist of those things the learners or trainees are expected to know at the conclusion of the training, whereas **behavioral objectives** reflect those things that the learners or trainees are expected to do or perform at the conclusion of the training. To repeat, adhering to such objectives will provide expectations for both what should be known and what should be done. For example, if you were to conduct training on the efficient and effective care of a rural trauma patient, the instructional objectives (IO) and behavioral objectives (BO) may be as follows (see Rural Trauma Team Development Course, 2010):

At the conclusion of this training:

- IO#1: Understand the three components of the SIR acronym (i.e., **S**igns, **I**njury, **R**esponse) when treating a trauma patient.
- IO#2: Understand why using an affirming communication style (i.e., relaying information in a way that validates the self-concept of the other person) can improve patient safety.
- BO#1: Be able to relay medical information using the SIR acronym.
- BO#2: Be able to use affirming communication when communicating with trauma team members.

These clearly stated objectives are the schematic from which the content of the training will be derived. Now that we have the basic road map for our training and most important goals, how do we go about achieving them? The next section will address the different types of delivery vehicles commonly associated with any education.

Types of Training Delivery and Vehicles

Although there are many different ways to present content in a training session, the most effective and most commonly used vehicles are *lecture, role play, case studies,* and *games.* **Lecture** is perhaps the most common form of training vehicle because it is the most familiar. The lecture is "a method of delivery that allows for a great deal of content to be delivered in a short amount of time and affords the trainer a great amount of control over what occurs in the training session" (Avtgis et al., 2010, p. 270). Also, a great level of flexibility is afforded by the lecture in that it can be used in any size group of people (e.g., 2 to 200).

The **role play** is a training vehicle that affords the trainees the opportunity to apply the skills they have acquired during the training. For example, it is common in medical education to use a **simulated patient technique** to reinforce training content. The simulated patient is a type of role play where a person acts as a patient in ways that are consistent with a given directive. For example, a simulated patient scenario of a person experiencing myocardial infarction (i.e., heart attack) may be shortness of breath and pain in the left arm and radiating into the neck. The "patient" would tell the interviewer about these symptoms with the end result being a test of the interviewer's (e.g., medical or nursing student's) diagnostic skills and knowledge of medicine. Such role-play scenarios are invaluable as an educational tool because they provide a fairly accurate facsimile of "real-world" situations. Role-play

© Halfpoint/Shutterstock.com

What advantages does the lecture format have for training?

techniques are also being integrated into second-life experiences. Second-life experiences refer to people who are trained in computer simulated or virtual health environments in which they are embedded within a complete milieu where the choices they make result in differing consequences. For example, a medical student may be in a computer simulation where they have to deliver bad news to the family of a patient who is dying. The communication strategies the student chooses to use when delivering the bad news will have different consequences. When choosing a more stoic and distant communication strategy, the family may react with outrage and anger, whereas if a more empathetic and caring strategy is chosen, the family may react in a more nonjudgmental and less angry way.

According to Salas and Burke (2009), simulations are a crucial part of medical education and should be based on a theory, use standardized and structured exercises, and be able to be assessed (i.e., provide feedback for the trainee). The lack of quality control with simulated situations can result in many negative outcomes. Some examples may include trainees learning the wrong thing or learning the right thing incorrectly; they might not focus on the correct way to perform the behavior(s), may spend too much time on one specific part as a result of the training at the expense of other parts, and may have difficulty transferring the skills taught in the training to actual on the job behavior.

The **case study** is a training vehicle allowing the application of knowledge presented earlier in the training. This usually takes the form of some sort of problem-solving sequence or analysis technique. The case study is a scenario presented to the trainee and requires sifting through the facts to make a "best practices" conclusion. Case studies are often used in the "grand rounds" format of medical education. It is cost effective, and an abundance of case studies are readily available to the trainer. The keys to a good case study are a

second-life experience

A type of role play where people are trained in the use of computer-simulated or virtual health environments in which they are embedded within a complete milieu of a healthcare environment where the choices they make bring about differing consequences.

comprehensive description of the situation, the characters involved and the relationship among the characters involved followed by a set of questions that probe into the many different aspects of the case. For example, questions may include the behavioral (e.g., What should the nurse have said before the surgeon made the incision?), affective (e.g., What do you think the surgeon was feeling after being told by the nurse about the situation?), and cognitive (e.g., What do you think went through the minds of both the nurse and the surgeon when the problem occurred?).

The use of **instruments** provides insight for both the trainer and the trainee concerning their attitudes, beliefs, behaviors, and retention of knowledge. Instruments are measures of behaviors, thoughts, and feelings that can be used to determine the effectiveness of the training or information gathering to develop training content. For example, consider a person teaching a module on *empathic behavior in healthcare*. An effective approach to beginning the module would be to have the trainees complete an assessment of their own empathy. Once scored, the trainees can reflect back to this score as they are presented with the new material. The trainee's empathy score serves as a benchmark on which the training content can be compared and contrasted. Such testing can also be used to determine the degree to which a trainee has progressed (i.e., pre- and post-testing) or to see if the trainee learned something about empathetic behavior in healthcare via an inventory designed to assess the concepts presented during the training.

Instructional Aids

Of the different factors that have to be addressed by the trainer, determining the most effective visual aids can make the difference between success and failure. Presentational aids are "training devices that are designed to get the attention of the trainee, reinforce key points of the presentation, and aid in the retention of information presented" (Avtgis et al., 2010, p. 274). By far, the two most frequently used instructional aids are **presentation software** (i.e., **PowerPoint**) and the **flip chart**. PowerPoint allows for the use of text, pictures, sounds, video, and animation in the delivery of training content. Although the proper use of PowerPoint depends on the situation, there are a few "lawlike" rules one should follow when constructing PowerPoint presentations. First is the rule of 16, which is a principle that holds that there should be no more than 16 words on any given slide because any more can result in sensory overload for the trainees. If given a choice, it is better to have many slides with fewer words than fewer slides with many words. The same principle is true for the use of sound, animation, and video. Too much of any of these can serve as a distraction to the trainees and come across as less professional and more sophomoric than slides that limit such "bells and whistles."

The flip chart is historically the "go to" instructional aid that is low tech and effective for any trainer or training content. In today's world, flip charts serve two basic functions. First, if access to presentational software or

| **rule of 16**

A principle for Power-Point slides which holds that there should be no more than 16 words on any given slide because any more can result in sensory overload for the trainees.

technology is unavailable, the training content can easily be put on flip charts. Second, flips charts can be used as a means of recording ideas and responses that emerge throughout a training session. For example, when soliciting experiences that healthcare professionals have had regarding the patient hand-off process (i.e., information exchanged between the outgoing party and the incoming party regarding health and general information pertaining to patients and patient care), the trainer can record each response on the flip chart so that all of the trainees can see all responses given. Similar applications of recording responses can be used for problem-solving (e.g., the nominal group technique) and idea generation. Earlier in this chapter we addressed the issues surrounding self-assessment techniques and what is needed to make those measures of one's own performance a valid measure. In this section we will address the four levels of training effectiveness.

Assessing the Efficacy of Training

The outcome of any training can rest squarely on the way in which the outcomes are assessed. For example, imagine giving a patient a diet that has been proven to result in the reduction of both pounds and body fat. After 3 months, the patient returns to the office for an assessment as to how effective the diet has been. Instead of using a calibrated scale that weighs overall mass in pounds (e.g., an objective office scale), you proceed to use the method of simply asking the person and his or her family whether they notice any change in the way they feel or act. Such an objective outcome measure for a diet designed to bring about reduction in weight and body fat could be grossly

Flip charts can be used as a means of recording ideas that emerge throughout a training session.

distorted. In this example, we have good training being subverted by bad measurement. Any training can only be as good as the measurement used to assess the training.

In 1994, Kirkpatrick proposed four dimensions of training assessment that yield different information about the training and whether or not the training was effective in meeting the proposed objectives. Level 1 of the model is **reaction,** which consists of the more primitive aspects of evaluation concerning perceptions and feelings about the training. For example, if a person conducts training on a Friday afternoon where refreshments are served and the trainees fully enjoy the role play and games introduced during the training, they likely will report high levels of satisfaction and feeling "good" about the training. This perception as to how people feel about the training is what makes it the most basic of information types. Level 2 of the model is **learning** and refers to the degree to which trainees learned from the training. This level of assessment, unlike Level 1, is much more objective in nature in that one can derive whether or not the knowledge gained was learned correctly or incorrectly. According to Kirkpatrick and Kirkpatrick (2006), for a person to have learned something new during the training, attitudes must have been changed or knowledge must have been gained. The third level of assessment is **behavior** and reflects the degree to which the behavior of the trainee has actually changed as a result of having attended the training. Such data generally are a reflective observation of the trainee's behavior, self-assessment of behavior, and overall satisfaction scores. For example, implementing a new protocol for a procedure that uses a newly developed instrument will require training. The evaluation of the training can be seen in the learning curve of the trainees when using the instrument, report of the trainee's supervisor regarding their performance with the instrument, and the patient's perspective as to their level of satisfaction with the new procedure performed with the new instrument. If there is a problem with behavioral change after a person has attended a training session, the first two levels of training should be analyzed to determine if either (a) the trainee had negative feelings toward the training content or the trainer, or (b) the trainee did not learn, or incorrectly learned, the required knowledge and skill. The final level of assessment is that of **results.** Results consist of determining the degree to which the training assisted the individual or organization to achieve the larger goal/objective and/or to accomplish the mission of the organization. For example, is there an improvement in patient satisfaction? Is the instrument user friendly to the trainee? Is there a reduction in the turnover rate of the specialty nurses who work with the instrument? The assessment of training is a difficult process but one that should be approached with the utmost care. The information garnered from the assessment will eventually need to be condensed and presented to people at all levels of the healthcare hierarchy.

A frequent question in healthcare is how to present information that can be less than flattering to our peers who are passionately involved in their work. The next section presents the complex task of providing feedback in an effort to improve performance.

Feedback

Perhaps one of the most misunderstood concepts in communication and performance evaluation is that of feedback. Feedback is defined as the sharing of information regarding performance that is designed to serve as a road map toward achieving a desired standard of performance. Although most people would probably tell you that they would rather avoid receiving feedback, the lack of feedback as a corrective mechanism for behavior serves as a great source of frustration for healthcare professionals. In fact, according to Westberg and Jason (1991), feedback is highly desired with most people reporting that they receive too little feedback as opposed to too much. This in turn leads to the inability to fix the problematic behavior. Feedback should be considered part of the performance process where a person's performance is compared to an explicitly defined standard of behavior. Generally speaking, there are two types of feedback. **Formative feedback** is targeted at performance improvement and occurs before or during job performance. **Summative feedback** reflects a post-behavioral assessment where feedback takes the form of an evaluation or judgment of an already-performed behavior (Wood, 2000). As patient care evolves into a more relational-based practice, patient feedback is crucial in determining the quality of care and in revealing problematic issues with current standards of care. Not all feedback is considered equal. In fact, several different types of feedback processes are advocated by researchers. For example, Mariana Hewson and Margaret Little (1998) believe that the act of providing feedback is best approached through a six-stage process. First, the **orientation and climate stage** for the feedback session must be prepared. This can be achieved through giving advanced notice to all parties who are to receive feedback, providing an affirming atmosphere that is conducive to learning, and providing a full explanation as to exactly what will be covered. Second is the **elicitation stage** and reflects asking the person being evaluated not only how they view their performance or behavior, but also their thoughts and feelings during this performance. Such introspection can lead to **generative learning** (i.e., a type of learning that entails not only learning the process, but also how the process contributes to the function of the entire organization). The **diagnosis and feedback stage** reflects the identification of deficiencies where the person is in need of improvement. Such feedback should be corrective in nature and intertwined with the overall reason for having the feedback evaluation. It is also important to seek out the perspective of the person being evaluated to make sure that they are defining "proper" or "good" behavior from that which is "improper" or "bad" behavior. The fourth stage in this feedback process concerns the development of an improvement plan. The **improvement plan stage** is the creation of a document containing specific strategies as to how to improve performance. Again, the seeking of input from the person being evaluated is critical because ownership in the development of the plan has to be the responsibility of all people involved (i.e., the evaluator and the person being evaluated). Fifth is the **application stage** reflecting the actual implementation of the improvement plan into the everyday practice of healthcare. This is where the constant application of the newly acquired techniques and approaches can be implemented. The **review stage** is the sixth and final aspect of this process and consists of making sure that the person understands and agrees with all that has been presented and developed during the previous five stages. Such a systematic plan serves not only the employee, but also the organization and the patient. In a similar approach, Beverly Wood (2000) believes that the feedback process is best achieved by the following eight guidelines:

- Comments should be behavioral based as opposed to our perception of another person's intentions (e.g., "I liked the way you smiled and looked at the patient" rather than "You seemed friendly").
- Provide positive and affirming comments in an effort to create a more open environment before focusing on areas of deficiency.
- Feedback should emphasize an open exchange and sharing of both positive and negative information.
- The interpretation of feedback is time based and therefore should be offered in both a timely manner and at a time when all parties are not distracted by other demands on their time.
- Feedback should be objective and specific so as to provide an unambiguous identification of areas and behaviors that need to be improved.
- Feedback should focus on developing those aspects of the person's performance that are under their control. By focusing on controllable aspects, a person comes to understand that it is up to their own effort as to whether or not the behavior will improve.
- Utilize the teach-back method where the person receiving the feedback repeats back to the evaluator what they heard or experienced regarding the evaluation of their behavior. By doing so, any misinterpretation or incorrect meaning can be clarified in a way that all parties are sharing the same reality regarding what was said and what is expected in the future.
- The feedback process can be threatening to a person's self-esteem. As such, great preparation and the ability to tolerate criticism are important. People can vary greatly in their ability to tolerate criticism with some being hypersensitive and others simply not caring what others think about their performance. Therefore, seek the healthy balance between the two. By doing so, one cares enough to work on problematic behavior yet is not threatened by criticism to the degree that it becomes debilitating.

Although we only highlighted two different approaches to the feedback process, many others are available (e.g., Medina, 2007). Most approaches to giving feedback will reflect the concepts of using an affirming communication style, providing objective information that is based on some form of data, and letting the person who is being evaluated become an architect in the creation of his or her own plan of self-improvement.

Conclusion

The concept of assessment and training within healthcare is an important facet of the overall quality of medical care and the functioning of the healthcare system as a whole. This chapter presented a brief overview of training, assessment, and the considerations that should be addressed when undertaking such projects. The reasons for the systematic need for training were presented along with the different types of elements involved in the education of adults (as opposed to children). The essential skills needed to be an effective trainer were also presented and discussed.

The need to appropriately assess and understand the audience was shown to be a critical element for the development of training material and to the overall success of the training. The level of maturity and the psychosocial characteristics of the trainee, if not assessed before the training, can have detrimental effects on training outcomes. The development of training goals and objectives were presented and examples were provided. The most popular vehicles for training delivery were presented along with a discussion of the strengths and weaknesses of each. The complicated concept of feedback was discussed and focused on a few of the more successful ways in which to provide performance feedback to people at all levels of the healthcare hierarchy.

Questions for Discussion/Review

1. Explain how being versed in training methods can improve the quality of healthcare.
2. Compare and contrast healthcare knowledge acquisition and healthcare skills acquisition.
3. Discuss the essential skills effective trainers possess and why such a skill set is important.
4. Explain the different training approaches as influenced by the level of psychological and job maturity of the trainees.
5. What are some central concerns affecting the validity of self-assessment? How can such concerns be overcome?
6. Compare and contrast training goals and training objectives.
7. Describe the four training delivery vehicles discussed in the chapter.
8. Explain Kirkpatrick's four dimensions of training assessment.
9. Explain the importance of performance feedback for the healthcare professional.
10. What should be considered when providing performance feedback to a trainee?

References

Avtgis, T. A., Rancer, A. S., & Madlock, P. E. (2010). *Organizational communication: Strategies for success.* Dubuque, IA: Kendall Hunt.

Davis, D., Mazmanian, P., Fordis, M., Van Harrison, R., Thorpe, K., & Perrier, L. (2006). Accuracy of physician self-assessment compared with observed measures of competence—A systematic review. *Journal of the American Medical Association, 296,* 1094–1102.

Eva, K. W., & Regehr, G. (2005). Self assessment in the health professions: A reformulation and research agenda. *Academic Medicine, 80,* S46–S54.

Harrington, J., Murnaghan, J., & Regehr, G. (1997). Applying a relative ranking model to the self-assessment of extended performances. *Advances in Health Science Education, 2,* 17–25.

Hersey, P., & Blanchard, K. H. (1977). *Management of organizational behavior: Utilizing human resources* (3rd ed.). Englewood, NJ: Prentice Hall.

Hewson, M. G., & Little, M. L. (1998). Giving feedback in medical education. *Journal of General Internal Medicine, 13,* 111–116.

Ittner, P. L., & Douds, A. F. (1988). *Train the trainer: Practical skills that work.* Amherst, MA: HRD Press.

Kappel, D. A., Polack, E. P., & Avtgis, T. A. (2010). *Rural trauma team development course* (3rd ed.). Chicago, IL: American College of Surgeons.

Kirkpatrick, D. L. (1994). *Evaluating training programs: The four levels.* San Francisco, CA: Barrett-Koehler Publishers.

Kirkpatrick, D. L., & Kirkpatrick, J. D. (2006). *Evaluating training programs: The four levels* (3rd ed.). San Francisco, CA: Barret-Koehler Publishers.

Medina, M. (2007). Providing feedback to enhance pharmacy students' performance. *American Journal of Health-System Pharmacy, 64,* 2542–2545.

Mehrabian, A. (1971). *Silent messages.* Belmont, CA: Wadsworth.

Polack, E. P., Richmond, V. P., & McCroskey, J. C. (2008). *Applied communication for health professionals.* Dubuque, IA: Kendall Hunt.

Salas, E., & Burke, C. S. (2009). Simulation for training is effective when . . . *Quality and Safety in Health Care, 11,* 119–120.

Ward, M., MacRae, H., Schlachta, C., Mamazza, J., Poulin, E., & Reznick, R. (2003). Resident self-assessment of operative performance. *American Journal of Surgery, 185,* 521–524.

Westberg, J., & Cason, H. (2001). *Fostering reflection and providing feedback.* New York: Springer Publishing.

Wood, B. (2000). Feedback: A key feature of medical training. *Radiology, 215,* 17–19.

part four

Medical Communication in Tributary Situations

chapter twelve

Informed Consent and Apology

chapter objectives

Upon completion of the chapter, the student should be able to:

1. Explain the informed consent process

2. Explain the NBAR acronym for informing a patient

3. Compare and contrast the different standards for determining an adequate amount of information given to a patient

4. Explain the five potential pitfalls of the informed consent process

5. Explain apology and the various philosophical, legal, and religious implications

For the past 30 to 40 years there has been a profound shift in the way that society perceives healthcare practitioners and the patient's relationship to the healthcare system as a whole. Within this time period, we moved from a system where the physician enjoyed total autonomy and power to one where the autonomy and power shifted to the patient and his or her individual right to be self-determined. With this societal shift in the perception of medicine and patient empowerment also came a simultaneous shift in legal and ethical perspectives. More specifically, healthcare providers operating in this "new" medical relationship paradigm had to account for legal issues that in earlier times were not considered as important, if they were considered at all. Issues such as how to control for risk, reduce existing risk, the role and responsibility of the patient in terms of being informed about choices and procedures available to them, and the responsibility of the healthcare practitioner when mistakes are made. This chapter is designed to expose the reader to how healthcare practitioners consider and effectively

© Syda Productions/Shutterstock.com

key terms

apology	event model	persuasion
coercion	informed consent	process model
crepe hanging	manipulation	

address risk; issues surrounding informed consent and how to go about the informed consent process; and the moral, professional, and legal aspects involved when medical mistakes are made. Finally, we present the concept of apology and the societal, legal, and religious factors that influence the process of apology. **Informed Consent**

To fully understand the concepts presented in this chapter, it is necessary to define some terms pertinent to understanding the content. Although many of these have been defined in earlier chapters, they are presented again in Table 12.1 as a refresher.

How much potential is there for medical mistakes to occur on any given day? One study focusing on an intensive care unit found that the average patient receives about 178 "activities" each day that all have the potential for harm as a result of system error. In the study of these 178 activities, on average 1.7 errors were made each day (Donchin et al., 1995). This number may seem small. However, when looking at "high reliability" organizations (such as NASA, the postal service, aviation, and banking), the following results would ensure that if there was a proficiency rate of 99.9% at O'Hare International Airport, the 0.1% error rate would equate to two unsafe landings each day, in the postal system 16,000 pieces of mail would be lost every hour, and in the banking system 32,000 bank checks would be deducted from the wrong bank account every hour. When put into this light, healthcare at its 99% proficiency rate does not seem all that safe.

Informed Consent

The Patient-Provider Power Shift: Informed Consent

| informed consent

A source (the provider) creating meaning in the mind of the receiver (the patient) as to what the source, either through a testing process (e.g., x-ray) or a procedure (e.g., operation), is planning to do.

Informed consent is defined as a source (the provider) creating meaning in the mind of a receiver (the patient) as to what the source, either through a testing process (e.g., labor, x-ray tests) or a procedure (e.g., operation), is planning to do. It is in the provider's ability to relay such meaning that constitutes the quality of the informed consent process. Therefore, we have the right of the patient to know relevant information concerning treatment being based on the communication competence of the provider to accurately relay such information. The legal precedence for the dramatic power shift from provider to patient in terms of informed consent was the 1914 case of *Schloendorff vs. The Society of New York Hospital.* **Two Cases** This case applies the **doctor knows best principle.** This principle holds that the doctor is the ultimate authority and is therefore beyond reproach by the patient regarding what is and what is not acceptable risk. The doctor in this case thought he was acting

| table 12.1 | Terms and Definitions Associated with Informed Consent and Apology |

Term	Definition
Adverse Event	Any injury caused by medical care. It does not imply error or negligence or poor quality of care, but rather is an undesirable outcome resulting from some aspect of diagnosis or therapy but not an underlying disease process.
Anchoring Error (Bias)	When a person latches onto the features of a patient's presentation that suggest a specific diagnosis. It is called "anchoring" because we are taught to always trust our first impressions. In some cases subsequent information through a process with the patient telling their story will prove inconsistent with the first impression, yet those who have anchoring bias tend to hold on to the initial diagnosis even in the face of disconfirmation.
Apology	An expression of remorse (deep sense of regret), shame (failing to live up to one's own standards), forbearance (commitment not to repeat the behavior), and humility (state of being humble, not arrogant).
Authority Gradient	The balance of power in decision-making. If there is a steep hierarchy (high authority gradient), expressing concerns, questioning, or simply clarifying instructions requires significant determination on the part of the team member who perceives his or her input as devalued and unwelcomed.
Close Call	An event or situation that did not produce patient injury but only because of chance (i.e., it had potential but was a missed incident).
Critical Incident	Events or occurrences that are significant or pivotal in either a desirable or undesirable way.
Error	Acts of commission, doing something wrong or by omission, failing to do the right thing that leads to an undesirable outcome or significant potential for an undesirable outcome.
Health Literacy	A constellation of skills that constitutes the ability to perform basic reading and numeric tasks for functioning in the healthcare environment and acting on healthcare information.
Latent Error	Less apparent failures of organization or design that contribute to the occurrence of an error or allow them to cause harm to patients (i.e., accidents waiting to happen).
Metacognition	Thinking about thinking.
Mistakes	Failures during intentional behaviors or incorrect choices. This can involve insufficient knowledge, failure to correctly interpret available information, or application of the wrong rule.
Near Miss	An event or situation that did not produce harm, but it is only by random chance that harm did not occur.
Negligence	An unanticipated event caused by error in the performance of duty.
Root-Cause Analysis	A structured process for identifying the causal or contributing factors underlying adverse events (i.e., any injury caused by medical care) or a critical incident (i.e., significant or pivotal incident in either a desirable or undesirable way).
Sentinel Event	An event causing or risking serious injury or death to the patient.
Standard of Care	What the average prudent clinician would be expected to do under certain circumstances.
Trigger	A signal for detecting a likely adverse event (e.g., if a patient receives Narcan to reverse the effects of narcotics, the patient probably received an excessive dose of narcotics and this would be a trigger for further investigation).

in the best interest of the patient, Mary Schloendorff, by removing a malignant tumor. However, this procedure was against the wishes of the patient, and, as a result, the court ruled that the doctor did in fact act against the wishes of the patient. Through this case it was determined that every adult human being who is of sound mind has the right to determine what should and should not be done to his or her body. With this precedent in place, a surgeon who performs an operation without his or her patient's consent is committing assault for which the surgeon is liable in damages. It took another 58 years for there to be a fully articulated definition of informed consent. In a 1972 case (*Canterbury vs. Spence*) a 17-year-old patient was experiencing shoulder pain. The surgeon suspected that the cause of the patient's pain was a ruptured disk in the neck and that surgery (i.e., cervical laminectomy) was necessary. Soon after the surgery the patient experienced paralysis from the waist down. The surgeon in this case argued that having to disclose the minute risks of a complication was not sound medical practice because it can potentially deter patients from having surgery. The judge in this case ruled that the doctor must disclose all risks that might materially affect the patient's decision. This changed the perspective from the doctor's right to disclose or not disclose information to the patient's right to know all reasonable information and outcome scenarios related to the procedure.

The concept of informed consent has three dimensions: *law, bioethics,* and *medicine's own understanding as to the nature of the doctor–patient relationship.* The legal dimension of informed consent holds that the practitioner has a duty to disclose information and obtain consent before administering treatment. One way (checklist) to do this is through what is known as the NBAR acronym: **Nature** of the procedure (whether it is a diagnostic or therapeutic treatment or what is going to be done to the patient), **Benefits** of the procedure (what this procedure will do to benefit you), **Alternatives**

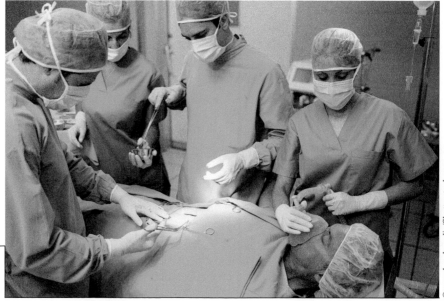

Doctors must disclose all risks that might affect a patient's decision to have surgery.

to the procedure (the alternatives to the proposed procedure and the associated risks and benefits with those alternatives), and **Risks** associated with the procedure (the more common risks in terms of those that are notable, those that are severe [major], and those that are likely [higher probability] to occur). The list of common risks should be as extensive and exhaustive as possible.

The bioethics dimension of informed consent is based on the philosophy of Immanuel Kant and holds that in order to act ethically, people must act with respect toward other people as if they were an intrinsically valued self-legislating being or beings that have autonomy (Kant, 2010). Although this autonomous approach may seem empowering by most counts, some people argue that not all people want to assume the burden of making such decisions (Schneider, 1998). In fact, Schneider argues that "bioethics has fallaciously reasoned that because the majority of people are thought to want to make health care decisions, not all people want that decision authority. On the other hand we neither want nor expect autonomy to lose its status as the centerpiece of bioethics, but that centerpiece should be a whole bouquet of concepts and not just a single flower of autonomy, however beguiling it may be" (p. 32).

Informed Consent in Action

Although the use of the NBAR acronym affords healthcare providers a standardized and efficient way to address informed consent, one comprehensive study showed that the informed consent procedure forms used in today's healthcare organizations are in many cases deficient. In a study of 157 hospitals throughout the United States, Bottrell, Alpert, Fischbach, and Emanuel (2000) reported that 26% of the informed consent forms contained all of the NBAR elements, 96% contained the *nature of the procedure,* 35% contained three of the NBAR elements, and two informed consent procedure forms contained none of the elements. These findings are especially important when combined with the fact that, even though some of the hospitals were included in this study were located in states that have legislative statutes requiring NBAR, these particular hospitals were no more likely to have the complete NBAR acronym on their forms.

When discussing informed consent, we invariably arrive at the question of "How much information is enough?" One could argue that given the complexities of the human body and possible complications that could result from any medical procedure, to be truly informed of all information would be a very arduous task. Generally speaking, there are three general ways to judge whether or not the amount of information is adequate. These include **reasonable physician standard,** which is based on what a typical physician would say about the intervention. Most research indicates that physicians tell patients very little regarding possible outcomes of the procedure. Another is **reasonable patient standard,** which is based on what the average patient would want or need to know to be an informed participant and understand the decision to be made. This patient standard can be more difficult to determine. Another variable is a patient's health literacy, which can range from

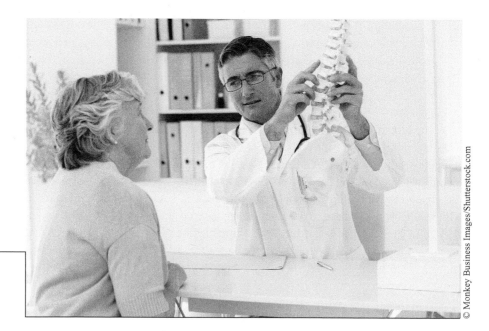

© Monkey Business Images/Shutterstock.com

How do you determine if the amount of information given to a patient is adequate for informed consent?

total literacy to total illiteracy (see Chapter 7). **Subjective standard** reflects how we standardize and tailor information to each individual patient. One way to overcome a patient's low literacy is to use face-to-face verbal dialogue along with visual aids such as video clips and print material (Sowden, Forbes, Entwistle, & Watt, 2001)

As with any concept presented in this book, medicine is not a monolithic concept; many contextual and situational factors alter or require a unique interpretation of any concept. For example, consider the unique surroundings of surgery versus obstetrics and gynecology, or any other specialty for that matter. All of these unique surroundings have unique factors that influence the informed consent process. This includes the *premedicated patient* who is in pain. Is it true that this patient cannot think clearly? Or perhaps pain relief might reduce emotional stress, thus allowing the patient to focus on the choices that he or she is making. However, if the premedication renders the patient unable to listen or understand the need for care, then it has negated the informed consent process. This presents a potential liability for the healthcare practitioner. However, if the physician and a witness can testify that the pain medication alone has not clouded the patient's thoughts, the pain medication should never be withheld from a suffering patient under the guise of first needing to get informed consent. There are unique situations in which patients experience pain. For example, consider a pregnant woman who has started labor. Would she be considered competent in terms of the informed consent process? In this unique situation, it is perfectly legitimate to obtain informed consent for an epidural placement (i.e., spinal anesthetic) in a patient who is in labor and therefore also in pain.

The conducting of research constitutes another unique situation, which is also known as an *investigational procedure*. In many hospitals throughout the United States and the world, an abundance of research is being conducted simultaneously with the treatment of patients. Such research requires extensive scrutiny by the *institutional review board,* which consists of people who try to ensure that any research being conducted is held to the highest standards regarding human dignity and respect. Finally, *cultural/linguistic factors* can also present unique situations. When faced with such a barrier, a culturally sensitive interpreter is required and should be present throughout the entire informed consent process to reduce the chances of a family member "sugar coating" the information, which is common in many cultures (e.g., Korean, Japanese, and Mexican American). In fact, Huyun (2002) believes that the physician should have a one-on-one conversation with the patient without the presence of family members using a culturally sensitive interpreter. An effort should be made to find out what the patient would like to know. Not all patients want to know all of the information. Posing a question such as "How much would you like to know?" allows the patient to demonstrate the level of autonomy with which he or she is comfortable. Such a question can afford the practitioner an opportunity to competently address the informed consent process in a way that is satisfying to the patient and reduces the chance that the information presented will neither overwhelm nor underwhelm the patient.

Problems in the Informed Consent Process

Five potential pitfalls can greatly confound the informed consent process. These pitfalls include *coercion, manipulation, persuasion, framing,* and *crepe hanging.* Coercion reflects the application of credible threat to obtain consent (e.g., if a doctor says to a patient, "If you refuse the Cesarean section that we have recommended and your baby dies, we will call the prosecuting attorney!"). Manipulation reflects the incomplete or less than truthful presentation of information such as lying or omitting vital information or deliberately deceiving the patient (e.g., "You can take your outdated antibiotics. They will be just fine."). Persuasion is a factor that when clearly distinguished from coercion and manipulation and not done to an excessive level is permissible and even desirable if the patient sees the practitioner as a trusted counselor. Persuasion is the process through which we create, shape, and reinforce the beliefs and attitudes of another person. For example, a patient may ask, "What would you do?" In this case, if the practitioner feels strongly that a particular course of action will be of most benefit to the patient, then subtle forms of persuasion may be used. Framing reflects the act of putting the information in ways that give it a particular perspective for the patient. How information is framed can have dramatic effects on the patient's decision-making. Compare the following two examples. A practitioner may say, "98% of the population with your condition lead productive lives" versus the practitioner saying, "There is a 2% chance that you may die from this disease." These two statements are both true, but they hold very different messages based simply on the framing choice of the practitioner. The final possible pitfall is crepe hanging, which reflects painting an overly bleak picture for the purpose of protecting the physician from possible litigation. For example, a practitioner who says "Absolutely nobody can repair this broken

coercion
The application of credible threat to obtain consent.

manipulation
The incomplete or less than truthful presentation of information such as lying or omitting vital information or deliberately deceiving the patient.

persuasion
The process through which we create, shape, and reinforce the beliefs and attitudes of another person.

crepe hanging
When the practitioner paints an overly bleak picture for the purpose of protecting the practitioner from possible litigation.

leg and expect a patient to be able to walk without a limp and pain after the operation" is maybe overstating the long-term prognosis of the injury in order to protect his or her professional and personal reputation. This type of behavior that serves to protect oneself from negative evaluation from others is known as **self-handicapping.** Self-handicapping is defined as the adoption of an impediment, either verbally or behaviorally, that serves to protect the person's self-esteem such that failure can be blamed on something other than the person's competence and success is seen as that much greater an accomplishment because of overcoming the handicap (Avtgis, Rancer, & Amato, 1998). In the case of the physician informing the patient about the broken leg, if the procedure does not turn out as the patient expected, the physician has already mentioned that "[a]bsolutely nobody can repair this broken leg and expect a patient to be able to walk without a limp and pain after the operation," thus protecting the physician's reputation in light of failure. However, if the patient should not limp and/or feel any pain, the surgeon is seen as that much more competent because he or she has overcome the probable outcome of lifelong disability that was explained to the patient prior to surgery.

What is a practitioner to do if the patient is incapacitated? In cases where there is a lack of mental capacities (e.g., mental illness, organic brain disease such as Alzheimer's or dementia, or an immature [generally younger than age 16] patient), a surrogate should act on behalf of the patient. This person should be familiar with the patient and aware of what the usual choices would be—that is, "How would the person act in his or her own self-interest?" The answer to this question should also be the same decision that the surrogate should make on behalf of the patient. If no such person is available to act on the patient's behalf, a guardian *ad litem* must be appointed through the social service/court process. This section presents but a few of the issues practitioners need to address when engaging in the informed consent process.

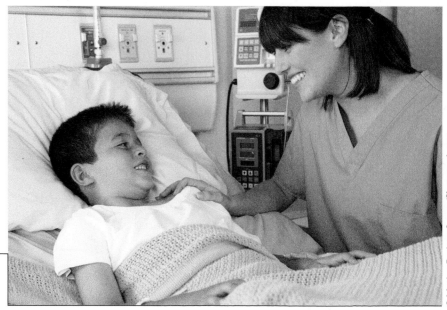

A surrogate must make medical decisions for some patients, including children.

Legal Implications of Informed Consent

Informed consent refers to a right afforded to the patient. Rights can generally be divided into **natural rights** and **civil rights** (Paine, 1791). Natural rights refer to rights that are organic in nature afforded to us because we are human. For example, the right to breathe (hopefully clean) air is considered a natural right. However, civil rights refer to rights afforded to us as members of a free society. For example, the right to a trial by jury is considered a civil right. Similarly, informed consent can be considered a civil right of the patient. In fact, the U.S. tort system is responsible for many breakthroughs in the disclosure of risks to patients and the overall empowerment of the patient. For example, as a result of litigation, the definition of informed consent was based on legal grounds by the state of Louisiana in 1975 in response to the *Canterbury vs. Spence* decision resulting in the Louisiana Informed Consent Law (*Canterbury & Spence,* 1972; Louisiana Uniform Consent Law, 1975; Madison, 1788). This law defines informed consent as "a consent to treatment (i.e., consent to an operation) obtained after adequate disclosure." This definition was challenged in 1989, resulting in the formation of the Louisiana Medical Disclosure Panel, which developed an extensive list of risks and liabilities for 127 different medical procedures.

Although we have discussed the "act" of informed consent and the types of information that are or are not appropriate to disclose during the consent-obtaining process, we did not yet discuss the manner in which the information is relayed. In an interesting book entitled *Risk Communication: Consent Delayed, Is Consent Denied?* Dr. Mark Hochhauser underwent a colonoscopy and reports being given a 10-page, 4,221-word document known as the Minnesota "Patient Bill of Rights Booklet" describing his rights as a patient. On closer examination of this information, he observed four significant things. First, although it is recommended that the readability be at an 8th grade level (see Chapter 7 on literacy), the patient rights document was written at a graduate school reading level. Second, although it is recommended that sentences used in these documents be "simple and normal," in the "Patient Bill of Rights Booklet" only 32% of the sentences were "simple and normal," whereas 68% of the sentences were complicated. Third, only 8% of the sentences were at an 8th to 10th grade reading level. Finally, 55% of the sentences were written at a graduate level, so much so that even with a Ph.D. degree Dr. Hochhauser could not understand these sentences. Also of interest in this account was the fact that before the document was presented, Dr. Hochhauser was lying down in a hospital gown with an IV in his arm. As can be concluded from this situation, not too many patients are going to stop a procedure that has progressed to the preparation phase even if they had a concern about the procedure.

Types of Informed Consent

The process of informed consent can be generally thought of in two different ways. The first way is through the event model, which views informed consent as a particular event that happens at one point in time. This approach assumes that patients are presented with the information at a single point in time and asked to endorse the fact that this process has occurred. This model is more concerned

| **event model** |
| A model of informed consent that views informed consent as a particular event that happens at one point in time. |

with determining whether or not the act of informed consent occurred; it is less concerned with whether or not the patient was actually informed about the procedure and the possible outcomes and risks associated with it. The second way to understand the informed consent process is through the **process model,** which assumes that being informed is a continuous active process that requires participation by the patient in medical decision-making. In this case, the patient is acted with, as opposed to acted on, as is the case in the event model. The patient is treated as a valuable member of the medical team. The process generally begins with an initial interview and explanation, with the patient being provided with written and explanatory materials. The patient is then asked to "teach back" the material to the practitioner. This process assures that the patient comprehends and understands the risks associated with the procedure. Through the patient being able to articulate in his or her own words the information presented by the provider, the patient, in effect, takes ownership of the process of informed consent. Although the process model is more time consuming than the event model, it gives the patients the opportunity to absorb the nature, benefits, alternatives, and risks of the procedures they have agreed to. This process also ensures a great level of personal autonomy and is the right thing to do regarding informing another human being of potential outcomes for his or her future.

Apology

The concept of apology is abstract and complex, with some people referring to it as an art and others referring to it as a science. Perhaps no other communication act is more complex than apology, which carries with it vulnerability,

How does the "teach back" process assure that the patient understands the risks associated with the procedure?

sensitivity, and honesty. Compound this complexity with a litigious society and a healthcare system that is already fraught with lawsuits. When considering these factors, the difficult act of apology becomes even more difficult. The concept of apology has been studied by researchers and philosophers for centuries with perhaps the most well-known quote coming from Alexander Pope (1711), who stated, "To err is human, to forgive is divine." This section will address apology from philosophical, ethical, legal, and religious perspectives.

Apology can be defined as an expression of **remorse** (deep sense of regret), **shame** (failing to live up to one's own standards), **forbearance** (commitment not to repeat the behavior), and **humility** (state of being humble, not arrogant). Within the healthcare literature, there is a misconception that apology is generally thought of as something that happens between a physician and a patient, not between other providers and a patient. This misconception is limiting in that in the contemporary technologically complex health care system, 80% of the care is provided by other (nonphysician) clinicians (Kizer, 2002). Given this, any provider may make or be responsible for error regardless as to whether there was injury to the patient. Because the nonphysician clinician is at a different, and most often lower, level of the healthcare hierarchy, they develop unique relationships with the patient and their families. Although an error may be a result of a glitch in "the system," these clinicians may be asked to apologize for such mistakes.

Apology, at least from a legal perspective, is no longer focused exclusively on the physician. Instead, members of the healthcare team responsible for any such error are now being held individually accountable. With this shifting responsibility to include all team members, people at all levels and positions in healthcare need to understand the philosophical and legal perspectives of apology.

| apology
Ar expression of remorse (deep sense of regret), shame (failing to live up to one's own standards), forbearance (commitment not to repeat), and humility (state of being humble, not arrogant).

Philosophical Perspective of Apology

The practice of medicine, by nature, is a constant moral exercise. However, this is never more apparent than when a mistake has been made. The healthcare practitioner has to achieve a dynamic balance between the tendency to be a perfectionist and the realization that it is human to make mistakes and that the practitioner is, indeed, human (Banja, 2005). When such mistakes are made, it is in our nature to first think of self-preservation. However, in the legal system, which is based on Judeo-Christian ethical principles, there is a different course of action. More specifically, we are instructed to disclose our mistakes, apologize, be repentant, and ask for forgiveness because everyone is capable of making mistakes. One thing that is not necessarily taught about mistakes is that it is less about the person who makes the mistake (i.e., the healthcare provider) and more about the person who was harmed by the mistake (i.e., patient). There is a natural tendency to be self-absorbed upon the realization that a person has made a mistake. It is important to understand that forgiveness can only be achieved by those who have been harmed, which in most cases is the patient or, in the case of death, the patient's family. Finally, forgiveness can be considered the final step on the part of the person who has been harmed to detach themselves from the trauma that has occurred. Therefore, there is no "timeline" for forgiveness because not all people are the same and neither are the mistakes that are made.

It is interesting to note that prior to the American Medical Association updating their Code of Medical Ethics, it was not part of professional ethics for the physician to accept honest responsibility (Bok, 1989). In fact, prior to the 1981 update, there was no code of medical ethics in any culture at any point in recorded history outlining such ethical behavior. When mistakes do happen, it should not be assumed that every patient and/or their family will litigate. However, this assumption is common among healthcare professionals. In fact, in a study examining the records of more than 30,000 patients, fewer than 2% of the patients who were injured by medical mistakes filed medical malpractice (liability) claims (Levine, 2002). In fact, Delbanco and Bell (2007) reported that when medical mistakes occur, the family of the patient often experiences three states. First, the family can experience a great deal of guilt. For example, a parent may be blaming themselves when the tonsillectomy performed on their child resulted in complications. Second, the family often experiences a fear of continued harm or retribution from the healthcare practitioner if the family is honest about their feelings. The degree to which the family experiences this is largely based on the relationship that has developed between the patient, the patient's family, and the practitioner. Finally, after a mistake has been detected, the family often experiences the physician or care providers engaging in avoidant behavior often resulting in a feeling of isolation. This is especially significant given that when this avoidant behavior occurs, it is usually during the time when the family needs the physician or care provider the most.

Truth-telling, and the research that it has inspired, has resulted in semantic differences that may seem subtle to an ordinary person but may mean a world of difference to the people involved in the truth-telling process. Truth-telling is the degree to which one discloses truthful events that are consistent with that person's perspective of the truth. Our society is filled with politicians and media celebrities who are constantly engaging in a "word game" when it comes to accepting responsibility. According to Bok (1982), how a person defines "truth-telling" affects how they go about engaging in truth-telling behavior. For example, if a physician is trained to see truth-telling in a narrow fashion, such as that truth-telling is not lying or the absence of lying, he or she may not disclose to the patient that an error has occurred. In this case, the physician rationalizes that he or she has not lied to the patient because there has been no breech of the truth-telling obligation. Therefore, the physician has fulfilled his or her ethical obligation. Consider a situation where a medical mistake has occurred that resulted in harm to the patient. The physician may inform the family that a "complication" has occurred. Through the narrow lens of our definition of truth-telling this is not lying, but it is drastically different when compared to the physician fully disclosing that there had been a medical mistake and, as a result of this mistake, the patient was harmed.

A second perspective of truth-telling was offered by Dietrich Bonhoeffer. This Christian theologian who was imprisoned during the Nazi rein for resistance against Hitler developed many interesting questions regarding truth-telling. More specifically, he reflects on those who suffer as a result of harm and to what degree the tangible or concrete responsibilities are toward those who suffer as a result of the actions of others. Bonhoeffer's approach is reflective of a "view from below" or a perspective from those who are injured as opposed to those who do the injuring. He believes that, in many cases, forgiveness may be an act of "cheap grace." In other words, there is a game disadvantage for the injured person or their family, especially in the case of death. The "view from below" is like a handicap in sports where one team begins the game at a disadvantage or in a less powerful position than the other team (e.g., the healthcare practitioner or the hospital). Bonhoeffer advocates that the remedy for any harm should be equivalent to the degree of human suffering that it caused (Enright & Kittle, 2000). Simply put, when a person commits small harm, there should be small remedy; when a person commits great harm, there should be great remedy.

Yet a third perspective was forwarded by philosopher Emmanuel Levinas, who argued that it is critical for a provider to understand that his or her actions caused harm to a patient and psychological pain on the patient's family. Thus, to truly understand the ramifications of medical harm, both the patient and the patient's family should not be viewed as an adversary to the well-being of the provider but as a source of information for the provider to understand "others" in the impact that the mistake has had on their lives. In a society that is quick to litigate, it becomes difficult for any provider, when faced with a medical error, to be "other" focused. Instead, there is a tendency to be focused only on his or her own personal and professional survival. Regardless of the philosophical perspective one takes to understanding forgiveness, apology, and the like, when there is a case of medical harm caused by a medical mistake, the system should avoid a default reaction to protect those healthcare professionals who have caused the harm over those who have been harmed. In the end, the ability to forgive is "a marker of psychological health and may be indispensible to healing relationships" (Enright & Kittle, 2000, p. 1621).

The Behavior of Apology

As has been stated throughout this book, communication involves three dimensions of what we think (*cognitive dimension*), what we feel (*affective dimension*), and what we do (*behavioral dimension*). This section is based on the behavior aspect of apology and how to engage with a patient and his or her family if a medical error does occur. Consistent with Judeo-Christian religious doctrine, a medical mistake should be managed through a three-step process. The first step is that of **confession,** which consists of complete truth-telling and a sincere **apology**. The second step is that of **repentance** and includes assurances that any medical, financial, or other needs of the injured patient or families will be addressed. The final step is that of **forgiveness,** which can only be granted by the injured party and often includes financial compensation in addition to a confession.

When apologizing, the acknowledgment openly identifies the mistake that occurred and identifies who made the mistake.

© bikeriderlondon/Shutterstock.com

In 2006, Dr. Aaron Lazare developed four steps to the apology process: *acknowledgement, explanation, apology,* and *reparation.* **Acknowledgement** refers to openly identifying the offense or mistake that occurred and identifying who made the mistake. **Explanation** refers to making a good-faith effort in trying to explain the offense while fully recognizing that phrases such as "There is no excuse" or "We are still trying to find out what happened" can be honest and dignified explanations in such circumstances. The third step is **apology** and, as defined before, reflects an expression of remorse (deep sense of regret about the behavior), shame (failing to live up to one's own standards), forbearance (commitment not to repeat), and humility (state of being humble, not arrogant). The final step is **reparation,** which reflects how one goes about rectifying the harm of the mistake and varies greatly from simply not charging for an appointment or scheduling an appointment to financial compensation. Lazare believes that apology has healing qualities and, as such, constitutes one of the more profound behaviors humans are capable of performing. Apology is a phenomenon that has been researched for centuries beginning in preliterate civilizations through to today's ethicists and philosophers. In fact, apology has been observed in the behavior of primates, which indicates that it truly is an important act in creating and maintaining relationships with others and may very well transcend human experience (DeWall, 1999).

It is now widely understood that when medical mistakes occur, more often than not they occur at a systemwide level. Systemwide errors reflect errors that are a function of not just the actions of one person, but also a lack of coordinated effort among and between the healthcare team. Figure 12.1 describes the process of how to determine origins of medical mistakes.

figure 12.1

Sources of Unanticipated Adverse Events

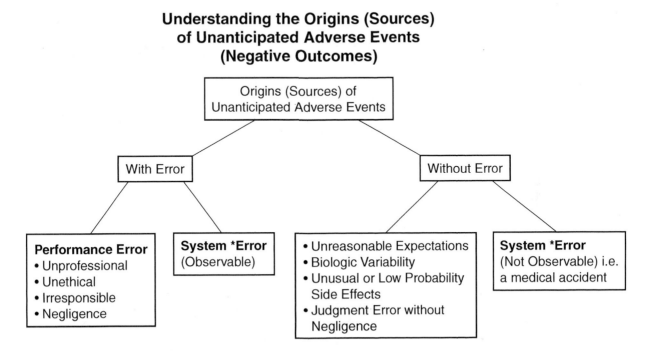

**Understanding the Origins (Sources)
of Unanticipated Adverse Events
(Negative Outcomes)**

Origins (Sources) of
Unanticipated Adverse Events

With Error

Without Error

Performance Error
• Unprofessional
• Unethical
• Irresponsible
• Negligence

System *Error
(Observable)

• Unreasonable Expectations
• Biologic Variability
• Unusual or Low Probability
  Side Effects
• Judgment Error without
  Negligence

System *Error
(Not Observable) i.e.
a medical accident

*To err is human (Institute of Medicine, 1999), the majority of errors are system (nonhuman errors)."

Source: Polack et al., (2008). Applied Communication for Health Professionals. Dubuque, IA: Kendall Hunt Publishing.

According to Gallagher, Denham, Leape, Amori, and Levinson (2007), when medical mistakes occur the apology process should be systemwide, which means that everyone from the CEO to nonphysician caregivers need to understand the importance of engaging in, and pitfalls associated with engaging in, apology. In fact, Gallagher et al. (2007) found in their study that 56% of physicians mentioned that there had been a "complication," whereas 42% stated that a "mistake" had been made (2% did not address the issue). This distinction between complication and mistake is more than just semantics. For example, if the physician was caught and the errors were obvious, 51% mentioned the mistake, but if the mistake was not so obvious, only 32% mentioned it. These data also appear to be influenced by the medical specialty that is practiced. Of specialists in internal medicine, 58% chose to report the medical error, whereas only 32% of surgeons would report it (Gallagher et al., 2007; Gallagher, Garbutt et al., 2006; Gallagher, Studdert, & Levinson, 2007). The conclusions to be drawn from these data are that when the medical error is obvious, the physician is more forthcoming with the information. It should be noted that a surgeon's willingness to disclose error is also based on the amount of prior training in disclosure and the degree of positivity associated with disclosure experiences in the past. If a surgeon has had experience with disclosure of error and that experience was a positive one for all parties involved, then the surgeon would tend to be more forthcoming than if the previous disclosure experience resulted in a traumatic experience for the parties involved.

A six-step guide for apology was developed by Shapiro (2006) and encompasses both compassion and care for the patient and the patient's family. Table 12.2 describes these steps.

Thus far, we have been referring to apology in theoretical and practical terms. We would like to present a personal story that serves to illustrate the plight that a family experiences when medical error occurs. Doug Wojciesak, a political consultant, was the brother of a 39-year-old man who died of a massive myocardial infarction (heart attack) as a result of gross medical error. He wrote that while his brother was dying on the operating table, the brother's doctor came out of the operating room, took one look at the patient's mother who was waiting in the hall, then ran the other way—literally. This experience prompted Wojciesak to develop the Sorry Works project, which is a national coalition advocating formal apology for medical errors as a possible solution to the medical liability debate. This coalition is made up of doctors, lawyers, insurers, patients, concerned citizens, policy experts, and media representatives. This coalition works together to advocate for full disclosure of medical errors. In its first year of website operation, *www.sorryworks.net* received more than 400,000 hits (Sorry Works, 2010).

Similarly, Wu (2010) advocates using a four-step approach known as the four As: *Acknowledge* the incident using plain language to explain what happened; *accept* responsibility on behalf of the institution or yourself, whichever is appropriate; *apologize* in a sincere and appropriate way; and *amend*

table 12.2	Six Steps of Apology
Step 1	Care for the patient. Assess the patient's condition and do what needs to be done immediately.
Step 2	Communicate about unanticipated adverse outcomes. Decide who is going to tell the patient and/or the patient's family. Prepare the communication in a way that is appropriate for the patient or his or her representative; this should be done as soon as possible but no more than 24 hours following the error event.
Step 3	Report the incident to the appropriate parties in the organization. Let all relevant parties within the organization know that an adverse outcome has occurred; then an institutional situation management plan should be employed.
Step 4	Check the medical record. Be sure objective details have been written in the record in a neutral, nonjudgmental language.
Step 5	Provide follow-up and closure. Relay any new information about the patient's condition to the patient or the patient's family and maintain an ongoing dialogue regarding patient care issues.
Step 6	Support the patient care team. There should be an institutional plan as to who is available and can provide needed support to staff members involved. This can include pastoral counseling, risk management counselors, administration, etc.

the situation by letting the patient and his or her family know what you are going to do in terms of root cause analysis and, if you are unsure as to what it is you are going to do, inform them that you will do an analysis and provide them with any information as soon as it becomes available. Do not negotiate monetary settlements at the time of initial contact. Any negotiation of monetary settlement is generally within the scope of risk management and not that of the apologizing physician. In addition to the different ways to approach the process of apology, Kidwell (2004) makes some additional suggestions to manage risk:

1. Try to contact the hospital risk manager prior to disclosing an apology.
2. Take a witness with you, such as a nurse or additional party.
3. Objectively document the results of the encounter.
4. If necessary, request counseling for your own emotional experience after offering the apology.

For further information on this topic refer to www.sorryworks.net and www.med.umich.edu/patientsafetytoolkit/disclosure.htm.

Legal Perspectives of Apology

In a society that is growing ever more litigious, we must include the legal ramifications of apology and what information, when included in the apology, can be a liability to the healthcare practitioner. When considering our mores and norms concerning medical error coupled with human nature, one can see how a healthcare provider would be reluctant to admit any wrongdoing to the patient or their family on the initial discovery of a medical error. However, recently there has been a cultural shift in the legal interpretation of apology. In 2003 a pivotal change in apology law was passed in Colorado. More specifically, the entire statement concerning the admission of fault or apology cannot be used against the apologizing physician in a court of law (Cohen, 2004). Cohen argues the law has both positive and negative aspects. Positive outcomes include the fact that apology will foster open and direct communication between the practitioner and the patient/patient's family, thereby speeding up settlement and preventing litigation. In opposition to the law, it may result in the promotion of insincere strategic apology. The Colorado law was implemented to promote an open, trusting, and caregiving relationship following any medical error. Further, failure to admit a mistake or failing to apologize can prompt a lawsuit for three important reasons. First, patients who experience an adverse outcome almost invariably desire to know what happened. If the medical provider does not provide such information, the patient may very well seek out advice from a malpractice attorney in an attempt to get such information. Many patients and their families are not only concerned with receiving an apology, but they also want to know what will be done to avoid the same situation occurring to another patient. Second, the doctor–patient relationship is based on trust and an assumption that the medical provider will "do no harm" (i.e., nonmalfeasance). Therefore, when a trusted medical caregiver becomes silent after the discovery of an error, this prompts feelings of suspicion and anger in the patient and his or her family. Finally, most patients demand dignity and respect from their healthcare provider. When a person injures another person, whether intentionally or unintentionally, the ethical behavior is for the person who does the harm to apologize and seek to remedy the situation in ways that exhibit dignity and respect toward the injured party.

In an interesting study assessing what patients would do if they were faced with different levels of medical error disclosure by their physician, Mazor, Simon, Yood, Martinson, Gunter, Reed, and Gurwitz (2004) revealed some intriguing findings. In the full disclosure scenario (i.e., the provider informing the patient of everything surrounding the error), patients reported a reduction in the likelihood of changing physicians, increased patient trust in the physician, increased satisfaction with the physician, and a positive emotional response toward the physician. This study also revealed that 83% of the patients, regardless of whether disclosure was full, partial, or none, favored financial compensation if harm had occurred.

Given that enforcement of code and standards of care are heavily regulated by state officials, each state varies in how apology is viewed from the legal standpoint. According to Lessard (2008), four different levels of legal exposure are associated with apology for medical error. Level I offers the least amount of protection, protecting only the words "I'm sorry" (regret and sympathy only); Level II offers some moderate protection against the expression of regret and liability (i.e., allows admission of fault). An example of a moderately protected expression may be "I'm sorry that my errors harmed you." Level III offers protection for only expressions of apology and expressions of fault are court interpreted. Level IV offers the most protection, with statements of apology, fault, and full disclosure being inadmissible. An example of such expressions could be "I am sorry (apology) that my error (liability) harmed you. I erred when I did XXX (disclosure) when I should have done YYY." Individual states (38 in 2011) and their protections are as follows:

Level I—Protection against regret-only states:

> California, Florida, Georgia, Indiana, Iowa, Massachusetts, Montana, Nebraska, Nevada, New Jersey, North Carolina, North Dakota, Ohio, Oklahoma, Oregon, Tennessee, Texas, Utah, Vermont, West Virginia

Level II—Some protection against the expression of regret states:

> Delaware, Idaho, Louisiana, Maine, Maryland, Missouri, New Hampshire, South Dakota, Virginia.

Level III—Protection against expressions of remorse and regret states:

> Hawaii, Kansas (pending)

Level IV—Protection against statements of fault and full disclosure states:

> Arizona, Colorado, Connecticut, Illinois, South Carolina, Washington, Wyoming.

The specific type of healthcare organization (e.g., public, private) also affects the type and amount of apology and disclosure that a practitioner can engage in. The Veterans Administration (VA) is one such healthcare organization. In 1987 there were two lawsuits against the VA, prompting them to pursue an "honest policy" toward error disclosure and apology. Before this, the common practice was to say nothing and fight with legal representation (Cantor, Barach, Derse, Maklan, Wlody, & Fox, 2005). Other hospitals followed suit, including the University of Michigan and the Dana Farber Cancer Center (Harvard Hospitals, 2006; Robbennolt, 2003) because this type of policy was seen as not only the right thing to do in terms of the patient, but also good for the overall reputation of the healthcare facilities and those that practice within them.

In sum, the legal ramifications of apology and disclosure are profound and will continue to exert great influence on healthcare providers' communication choices regarding medical errors. It appears from the data reviewed in this section that being forthcoming can have beneficial outcomes not only for the patient, but also for the healthcare practitioner.

Religious Perspectives of Apology

The religious perspective of apology is primarily concerned with what is right and wrong with regard to the humanity of medicine and the fact that people do indeed make mistakes. In doing so, however, people may take responsibility and make amends to the best of their abilities. To define something as a mistake, one has to see the action within the larger culture within which the mistakes are occurring. For example, the procedures used in the treatment of traumatic injuries on the battlefields of Iraq and Afghanistan may be different than those practiced within a hospital operating room. Without considering the specific context, words like "mistake" lose their meaning. Berlinger (2005) argues that the determination of medical error should be based on the following three-step process. First, seek to uncover the facts about the incident (i.e., the who, what, when, where, why, and how of the situation). Second, interpret the facts in reference to the standards and practices of the culture within which the incident took place. Third, describe the activities such that they might be understood by persons both inside and outside the cultures.

The basic assumption of such a mistake-determining process is that no one can know everything that must be known regarding medicine; to do so would make us God-like. Instead, healthcare professionals are human, and by nature, humans make mistakes. Berlinger believes that patients have a fundamental understanding of such a process. Further, it is suggested that when a mistake is made, the healthcare practitioner should avoid the propensity to take an adversarial position, which is often advocated by risk managers and lawyers. Instead, engage in whole truth-telling as opposed to spinning or limiting the truth. Finally, the practitioner should allow for both the expression of remorse and the feeling of remorse for harming a patient. According to the American Medical Association and the American College of Physicians, truth-telling after medical mistakes is a professional obligation required of all physicians (American College of Physicians, 2010). Some institutions seek to create a culture where this type of process can thrive. For example, the Catholic Health Care West healthcare system has a Philosophy of Mistake Management that does not provide for scapegoating behavior in that it is advocated that all healthcare professionals involved in the medical error, regardless of status, title, or power, be treated equitably in the aftermath of a mistake (Bayley, 2001).

Conclusion

This chapter reviewed the various issues associated with medical error, informed consent, and apology. The shift in societal perceptions of power regarding medicine, medical professionals, and the empowerment of the patient was presented. Informed consent was defined and its various dimensions of the legal, bioethical, and relational aspects were presented; all of these affect the informed consent process. The NBAR acronym was introduced as a means for streamlining the informed consent process, helping to ensure that the patient receives as much information as possible. The legal implications and the two models of informed consent (i.e., event model and the process model) were introduced and discussed in terms of their impact on how the informed consent process is conceptualized. The concept of apology and its various perspectives were presented. More specifically, the philosophical, legal, and religious perspectives were introduced to expose the sometimes vastly different views that the simple act of apology can take. This chapter is one that addresses some of the more difficult conversations healthcare practitioners can find themselves in, but it also provides step-by-step guidelines for engaging in difficult situations with utmost dignity and respect for the patient and the patient's family.

Questions for Discussion/Review

1. Define the informed consent process. Would you think it is considered a multidimensional concept?
2. Describe the events that occurred in the *Schloendorff vs. The Society of New York Hospital* and the impact that the outcome had on contemporary healthcare.
3. Explain the NBAR acronym and how it can affect the informed consent process.
4. Describe the three standards from which we measure whether or not the patient has received enough information.
5. Explain the five potential pitfalls that can greatly confound the informed consent process.

6. Compare and contrast the event model and the process model of informed consent.
7. Explain the concept of truth-telling and some of the various perspectives that can be taken regarding the disclosure of medical error.
8. List and define Lazare's four-step process for engaging in apology.
9. Explain the possible implications of state law regarding apology on the behavior of the healthcare practitioner.
10. Explain the religious perspective of apology.
11. List and describe Berlinger's three-step process for determining medical error.

References

American College of Physicians Ethics Manual. (2010). Retrieved January 2, 2011, from www.acponline.org/running_practice/ethics.

Avtgis, T. A., Rancer, A. S., & Amato, P. P. (1998). Self-handicapping orientation and tendencies toward verbal aggressiveness. *Communication Research Reports, 15,* 226–234.

Banja, J. (2005). *Medical errors and medical narcissism.* Boston, MA: Jones and Bartlett.

Bayley, C. (2001). Turning the Titanic: Changing the way we handle mistakes. *HEC Forum, 13,* 148–159.

Berlinger, N. (2005). *After harm: Medical error and ethics of forgiveness.* Baltimore, MD: The Johns Hopkins University Press.

Bok, S. (1982). *Secrets: On the ethics of concealment and revelation.* New York: Pantheon.

Bok, S. (1989). *Lying: Moral choice in public and private life.* New York: Random House/ Vantage Books.

Bottrell, M. M., Alpert, H., Fischbach, R. L., & Emanuel, L. L. (2000). Hospital informed consent for procedure forms facilitating quality patient-physician interaction. *Archives of Surgery, 135,* 26–33.

Canterbury vs. Spence, 464 F2nd 772; District of Columbia. (1972). Retrieved January 2, 2011, from http://paralegaltech.com/placement/employers/torts/courseware_samples/dutyOfCare1_ CanterburyVsSpence.asp

Cantor, M. D., Barach, P., Derse, A., Maklan, C. W., Wlody, G., & Fox, E. (2005). Disclosing adverse events to patients. *Journal of Quality and Patient Safety, 31,* 5–12.

Cohen, J. R. (2004). Toward candor after medical error: The first apology law. *Harvard Health Policy Review, 5,* 21–24.

Delbanco, T., & Bell, S. K. (2007). Guilty, afraid, and alone—Struggling with medical error. *New England Journal of Medicine, 357,* 1682–1683.

DeWall, F. (1999). *Ignorance about human reconciliation in peacemaking among primates.* Cambridge, MA: Harvard University Press.

Donchin, Y., Gopher, O., Badihi, Y., Sprung, C. L., Pizov, R., & Cotev, S. (1995). A look into the nature and causes of human error in the intensive care unit. *Critical Care Medicine, 23,* 294–300.

Enright, R. D., & Kittle, B. A. (2000). Forgiveness in psychology and the law: The meeting of moral development and restorative justice. *Fordham Urban Law Journal, 27,* 1621.

Gallagher, T. H., Denham, C. R., Leape, L. L., Amori, G., & Levinson, W. (2007). Disclosing unanticipated outcomes to patients: The art and practice. *Journal of Patient Safety, 3,* 158–165.

Gallagher, T. H., Garbutt, J. M., Waterman, A. D., Slum, D. R., Larson, E. D., & Waterman, B. M. (2006). Choosing your words carefully: How physicians would disclose harmful medical errors in patients. *Archives of Internal Medicine, 166,* 1585–1593.

Gallagher, Studdaert, D., & Levinson, W. (2007). Disclosing harmful medical errors to patients. *New England Journal of Medicine, 356,* 2713–2719.

Harvard Hospitals. (2006). *When things go wrong: Responding to adverse events.* A consensus statement of the Harvard Hospitals. Burlington, MA: Massachusetts Coalition for the Prevention of Medical Errors.

Hochhauser, M. (2002). Risk communication: Consent delayed, is consent denied? Retrieved October 20, 2003. http://bmj.bmjjournals.com/cgi/eletters/327/7417/731

Huyun, I. (2002). Waiver of informed consent, cultural sensitivity and the problem of unjust families and traditions. *Hastings Center Reports.* Retrieved January 2, 2011, from http://www.highbeam.com/doc/1G1-92201096.html.

Kant, I. (2010). *To err is human, to forgive is divine.* Retrieved January 2, 2011, from www.thinkexist.com/quotes/immanual_kant/

Kidwell, R.T. (2004) University of Pittsburgh Medical Center Mediation Program. Retrieved January 2, 2011, from www.post-gazette.com/pg/07066/767315-28.stm

Kizer, K. W. (2002). Patient centered care: Essential but probably not sufficient. *Quality and Safety in Healthcare, 11,* 117–118.

Lassard, D. (2008). Communication and the relationship to patient safety. In E. P. Polack, V. P. Richmond, & J. C. McCroskey (Eds.), *Applied communication for health professionals* (pp. 267–290). Dubuque, IA: Kendall-Hunt.

Lazare, A. (2006). Apology and medical practice: An emerging clinical skill. *Journal of the American Medical Association, 296,* 1401–1404.

Levine, C. (2002). Life but no limb: The aftermath of medical error. *Health Affairs, 21,* 237–241.

Louisiana Uniform Consent Law 1975, LA.R.S40: 13299-40. Retrieved January 2, 2011, from http://intrepidresources.com/html/informed_consent.html.

Madison, J. (1788). The Federalist Number 51. Retrieved January 2, 2011, from http://www.constitution.org/fed/federa51.htm.

Paine, T. (1791). The rights of man: A political pamphlet. Boston, MA: I. Thomas & E. T. Andrews.

Pope, A. (1711). An essay on criticism. Retrieved January 2, 2011, from http://poetry.eserver.org/essay-on-criticism.html.

Robbennolt, J. K. (2003). Apologies and legal settlement: Am empirical examination. *Michigan Law Review, 102,* 460–516.

Schloendorff vs. The Society of New York Hospital. (1914). Retrieved January 2, 2011, from http://wings.buffalo.edu/bioethics/schoen0.html.

Schneider, C. E. (1998). *The practice of autonomy: Patients, doctors, and medical decisions.* New York: Oxford Press.

Shapiro, E. (December, 2006). *Disclosing medical errors: Best practices from the "leading edge" in preparation for a workshop "Disclosure: What's morally right is organizationally right."* Presented at the 18th Annual IHA National Forum on Quality Improvement in Health Care, Orlando, FL.

Sowden, A. J., Forbes, C., Entwistle, V., & Watt, I. (2001). Informing, communicating and sharing decisions with people who have cancer. *Qualitative Health Care, 10,* 193–196.

Welcome to Sorry Works! Retrieved January 2, 2011, from http://sorryworks.net/default.

Wu, A. W. (2010). Removing insult from injury—Disclosing adverse events. Retrieved January 2, 2011, from http://webmm.ahrq.gov/perspective.aspx?perspectiveID=18.

Chapter thirteen

Professionalism, Ethics, Social Media, and Other Medical Communication Technologies

chapter objectives

Upon completion of the chapter, the student should be able to:

1. Explain the concept of ethos.

2. Explain the development of the healthcare profession.

3. Compare and contrast the various types of medical professions.

4. Compare and contrast the various documents associated with end-of-life care.

5. Compare and contrast the various religious perspectives regarding organ donation.

6. Explain new technology and its implication on health care.

7. Explain the use of electronic medical records and personal health records.

8. Explain the concept of SMART technology and the influence on health care.

Human beings have struggled with the questions of what is good in human nature and how to distinguish good from bad for centuries. History is replete with people who have struggled to do what they believe to be right even if it is in contrast to what others around them believe to be right. In contemporary health care, a myriad of legal and moral issues swirl around the healthcare practitioner daily. Concepts such as disclosure of human error, euthanasia, and abortion are a few of the many issues that are of great concern among healthcare practitioners. This chapter is designed to expose you to the concepts of professionalism and ethical standards as determined by not only our own moral compass but also the governing bodies that oversee health care in the United States. We will also explore the emerging technologies and how such technological breakthroughs influence the healthcare system as well as explore the informed consent process and apology.

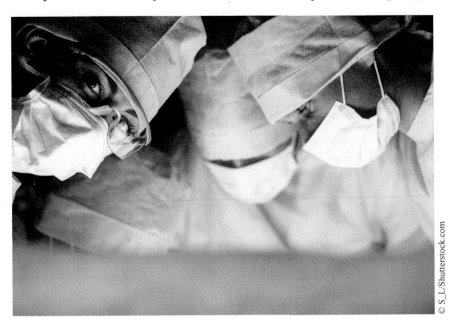

© S_L/Shutterstock.com

297

key terms

advance directives	ethos	living will
brain death	evidenced-based medicine	palliative care
clinical ethics committee	(EBM)	persistent vegetative state
coma	hospice	principle of totality
do not resuscitate order (DNR)	live donor	professionalism

Defining Professionalism

Professionalism

The degree to which a person exhibits and exceeds those standards and expectations set forth by the public they serve and the governing bodies that set such standards and expectations.

Professionalism is a fluid concept and can be defined as the degree to which a person exhibits and exceeds those standards and expectations set forth by the public they serve and the governing bodies that set such standards and expectations. When we use the term fluid, we are referring to a concept that is not static in nature. For example, a person is not always professional all of the time. Instead, we are referring to the ways in which people strive to do what is right and good on a daily basis. In an interesting study looking at the impact that the lack of professionalism in early career has on the later performance, Papadakis, Loeser, and Healy (2001) found that a lack of professionalism displayed by medical students predicted their degree of success in later practice. More specifically, medical students who had poor interpersonal skills (defined as the degree to which they got along with other members of the healthcare team) often were put on academic probation because of this very fact. Further, some evidence indicates that those who demonstrate a lack of professionalism early in their career at later times are often investigated by hospital oversight committees and state licensing boards. The result of such an investigation is often a recommendation for significant counseling/ intervention for the healthcare practitioner, which eventually can result in the loss of their license to practice.

According to Cohen, Cruess, and Davidson (2007), medical professionalism is a required alliance between the society and the profession of medicine. They ground their assertion on a document entitled *A Physician Charter: Medical Professionalism in the New Millennium,* which put forth a set of professional responsibilities that physicians, by way of respect and honor, are obligated to fulfill (ABIM Foundation, 2002). It is only through a strengthened relationship with society that professionalism can be sustained. By society we are referring to all parties involved in the medical system including advocacy groups, government officials, business leaders, insurance executives, and media outlets. Without fostering these relationships, it becomes difficult for society to understand the high level of autonomy required by physicians. In return for such a high degree of autonomy, the physicians vow to use scientific and medical expertise to only promote the interest and the welfare of their patients (Gough, 1957).

Cohen *et al.* (2007) caution healthcare practitioners about the economic seduction of commercial enterprises. For example, pharmaceutical companies and medical device manufacturers sometimes cloud scientific objectivity (in the name of economic gain). Such objectivity is required to ensure safe and effective medical care. These economic forces have the potential to obscure the design and purpose of continuing medical education programs, taint the science reported in medical journals, and obscure evidence and patient safety data. Presently, there are professional standards to combat such influences. More specifically, when giving a speech, presenting a conference paper, or any other similar activity, full disclosure to any economic link that they may have with a particular pharmaceutical or durable goods manufacturer must be made public.

To ensure public welfare, accountability, and social justice, a national discourse that fosters effective medical–societal alliances free of political, economic, and personal agendas must be enacted. Although this type of breakthrough may seem impossible to some, advances such as evidenced-based medicine (EBM) has emerged as the gold standard.

The identification of organizational strategies, structures, and change management practices that enable health practitioners to provide evidenced-based care to their patients and such efforts can result in fostering continuous quality improvement (CQI).

Evidenced-Based Medicine (EBM)

The identification of organizational strategies, structures, and change management practices that enable health practitioners to provide evidenced-based care to their patients.

Professional Ethos

One of the most important aspects of professionalism is the way in which people go about creating and maintaining their credibility and overall image. The concept of creating and maintaining an image has been of interest to scholars and researchers since antiquity. Aristotle used the term ethos to reflect the degree to which others perceive a person as being genuine and

Ethos

The degree to which others perceive a person as being genuine and having the best interest of their audience at heart.

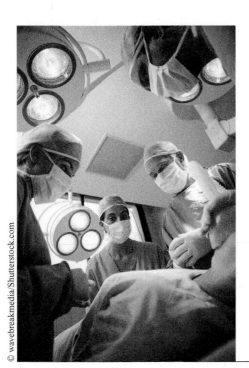
© wavebreakmedia/Shutterstock.com

Collaboration and coordination are of paramount importance when it comes to patient safety.

having the best interest of their audience at heart. More recent conceptualizations of ethos (source credibility) indicate that there are three dimensions to the concept: **competence,** or the degree to which a person is an expert in his or her respective field of study/practice; **trustworthiness,** or the degree to which a person is believable and worthy of trust; and **goodwill,** or the degree to which the person has the best interest of the audience at heart (McCroskey, 1966; McCroskey & Young, 1981; Teven & McCroskey, 1997).

The Professions of Medical Care

It is incredibly difficult to understand any complicated concept, let alone one as complex as the healthcare system, without first having an understanding of the roles that are played in such a system. Health care is an extremely complex interdependent combination of different professional backgrounds and roles. Each of these professions must have an understanding of the roles that other healthcare providers play in the delivery of healthcare for the system as a whole to function properly. It is critical for medical team members to understand the intercommunication and accountability necessary to have a system that is efficient and patient centered. For example, imagine being trained as a nurse with the best education regarding nursing but with little education as to the role of the other people you will be working with on a daily basis. Without such knowledge as to the roles that other people play in the healthcare process, regardless of how well trained a person is in nursing, this nurse will probably not be very successful. It is in this inter-silo knowledge or knowledge of the system as a whole where true teamwork can be realized. In this section, we will discuss some of the more common professions found in healthcare facilities. This is a fairly comprehensive, but not an exhaustive, list.

Each discipline within health care carries with it a world view or a way of interpreting the practice of medicine and those within it. However, when people from different disciplines come together as a team, a core set of responsibilities emerge that supersede any one discipline's view—the treatment and safety of the sick patient. For example, when treating a patient with a traumatic injury, a physician, nurse, physician assistant, and a surgical technologist are focused not on their own professional assumptions about the other medical team members, but on providing optimal care for the patient. As you review these different professions, consider how all of these healthcare professionals can come together in an effort to treat a sick patient. Needless to say, the concepts of collaboration and coordination are of paramount importance when it comes to patient safety. Table 13.1 defines each of these professions.

Ethical Practices for Medical Professionals

 According to Beauchamp and Childress (2001), there are four fundamental principles of ethical behavior in the practice of medicine. The Four Principles of Bioethics The first principle is that of **beneficence,** which reflects the primacy of the patient's welfare being paramount in the patient–provider

table 13.1	The Professions of Medical Care and Allied Medical Professions
Physician	A healer who views medicine as both an art and a science. They are trained as either an allopath (MD) or an osteopath (DO).
Physician Assistant	A practitioner licensed to practice medicine only under supervision of a licensed physician.
Dentistry	Trained in the evaluation, diagnosis and effective treatment of any disorder or condition associated with the mandible, oral cavity, or the sinuses.
Podiatry	Trained in the diagnosis, and treatment of disorders associated with the foot, ankle, and lower extremity.
Chiropractor (DC)	Trained in the diagnosis, treatment, and prevention of disorders of the neuromuscular system.
Optometry (OD)	Trained in the specialty of the eyes and related structures notably in the evaluation of vision, visual systems and vision information processing.
Nursing	Trained in the promotion of health, protection of health, prevention of illness and disease, and advocacy for patients, families, and communities. The training ranges from associate degree (e.g., GN) to doctorate degrees (e.g., Ph.D.).
Pharmacy	Trained in identification of potential and actual drug-related problems and preventing drug-related problems. They work with the patient to design, implement, and monitor medication.
Audiology	Trained in the science that evaluates hearing, balance, and other hearing-related disorders.
Speech and Language Pathologists	Trained in the evaluation and treatment of communication and swallowing disorders.
Healthcare Administration	Trained in the administration of public as well as private healthcare systems, hospitals, and hospital networks.
Healthcare Information Technology	Trained in the management of health information computerized systems and ensuring security of exchange information between providers, consumers, government, insurers, and oversight normative organizations.
Occupational Therapy	Trained in therapies that vary in scope and can include adapting utensils for making eating easier, creating splints for wrist pain, and providing other types of interventions that enable people to gain health and function.
Physical Therapy	Trained in facilitating each patient's achievement of goals for function, health, and wellness.
Dietician	Trained in human nutrition and regulation of diet that contributes to a healthy lifestyle.
Respiratory Therapy	Trained in the treatment of pulmonary medicine.
Radiologic Technology	Trained in creating medical images of human anatomy to aid radiologists in diagnosing and treating illness and injury.
Laboratory Professionals	Trained in various laboratory processes and include laboratory technicians and phlebotomists.
Medical Coder	Trained in analyzing and translating clinical statements into a classification system according to assigned standard codes.
Medical Assistant	Trained to perform the administrative and clinical tasks to keep the offices of health practitioners running smoothly.
EMT/Paramedic	Trained for pre-hospital treatment and range in training from Emergency Medical Technician to paramedics who are authorized to administer medication, start IV's, and provide advanced airway management.
Surgical Technologist	Trained to safely prepare and handle surgical instruments during surgical procedures.

(continued)

table 13.1   (continued)

Nursing Assistant	Trained to take care of personal patient needs and support the entire medical team in the proper care of the ill.
Social Work	Trained to assist individuals, their families, and significant others in regaining function when illness, disease, and disability result in changes in physical or mental state or the individual's role in society.
Counseling	Trained to rehabilitate patients with mental health issues and substance abuse.
Clinical Psychologist	Trained to provide behavioral and mental health evaluation and diagnosis of psychopathology.
Chaplaincy	Trained in listening grounded in religious philosophy with a strong belief in God and the power of prayer, is critical to the holistic healthcare team as this presence reminds the medical team and their families of the religious aspects of mortality.

How did the profession of the physician assistant evolve?

© Phovoir/Shutterstock.com

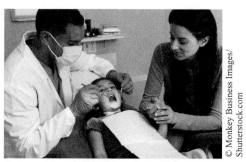

Dentistry is not only general practice; it includes subspecialties.

© Monkey Business Images/Shutterstock.com

Nursing is the largest of the healthcare professions.

© Jacob Lund/Shutterstock.com

Pharmacists may practice in a variety of different environments.

© wavebreakmedia/Shutterstock.com

A physical therapist performs a wide range of professional duties, from working with patients to performing workplace analyses.

© GagliardiImages/Shutterstock.com

Radiologists use radiologic technology to diagnose and treat illness and injury.

© anekoho/Shutterstock.com

relationship. Such a principle has been true since the days of Hippocrates. The second principle is **autonomy,** which reflects the right of the patient to make informed choices as to the nature of medical care, the alternatives available to the patient, the risks associated with the various alternatives, and the results of the suggested treatment. The third principle is that of **nonmalfeasance,** which means "do no harm." The final principle is that of **social justice,** or seeking to ensure that there is a fair distribution of healthcare resources among patients of all walks of life.

The Clinical Ethics Committee. The application and adherence to the four fundamental principles of ethical behavior in the practice of medicine within the hospital setting fall to the **clinical ethics committee**. Do Ethics Committees Always Help? Jonsen, Siegler, and Winslade (1998) outline an algorithmic decision-making process that can be applied to any clinical ethical dilemma. This decision-making process consists of four characteristics intrinsic to most ethical encounters: *medical indications* (i.e., the review of diagnosis and treatment options), *patient preferences* (i.e., the patient's values are integral to the encounter, which include both social and religious backgrounds), *quality of life* (i.e., the objective is to improve or address the quality of life for the patient), and *contextual features* (i.e., encounters occur in a wider context beyond provider and patient and include family, religious beliefs, legal constraints, hospital policy, insurance company regulations, etc.).

As a medical clinician working within the American healthcare system, ethical assistance usually is available in the form of an *ethics committee.* To a large degree, ethics committees became standard in hospitals following the New Jersey Supreme Court (1976) decision in the case of Karen Ann Quinlan. Ms. Quinlan was a young woman in a paralyzed persistent vegetative state for 10 years. In that court decision, the court suggested that hospital ethics committees may be the best place to discuss end-of-life decision-making as opposed to looking for the courts for such decisions (Kelly, 2004). Ethics committees provide written and personal support resources to decision-makers, provide opportunities for collaboration, and contribute significantly to the general ethical education of a hospital community.

Within the traditional hospital structure, ethics committees comprise physicians, nurses, social workers, pastoral care, administration, and members of the community at large. Such a group of people serve to determine *"what is the right thing to do?"* One frequent consideration for the ethics committee is to facilitate discussions; some issues may include the level of competency of the patient, to determine if the proper surrogate is making decisions for the patient, and whether or not there are cultural or religious issues to address. In any ethical dilemma, the hospital ethics committee questions the facts according to the patient's story, listens, reflects, and assists the patient or the patient's family to better understand the right thing to do according to what the patient would want. The ethics committee does not make final decisions or fix ethical problems. Instead, the committee serves in a recommendation (consultation) capacity to those people who have the final decision-making power (e.g., the patient or the patient's surrogate). The Ethical Clinical Consult

> **Clinical Ethics Committee**
>
> Is responsible for enforcing the adherence to the four fundamental principles of ethical behavior in the hospital setting.

We have mentioned but a few of the professions that constitute the healthcare system and those that work within it. As technology grows and society becomes more diverse in terms of patient needs, more professions will evolve as a result. Even in light of those existing diverse professions, the needs of the patient remain primary. The next section will discuss such patient needs.

Patient Needs

The constructs of ethics and professionalism are so closely related that it is almost impossible to distinguish between the two. Distributive Justice contends that the most important person in the medical encounter is the **patient.** The word patient is derived from Latin (*patiens)*, which means to endure, bear, or suffer and also includes vulnerability, anxiety, and dependency induced by changes in a person's health status. By this very definition, the patient relinquishes a high degree of control and autonomy. The patient is the one who is being acted upon by the healthcare professional. Therefore, it is imperative to understand the patient's perspective. Ethics and professionalism are contextually bound—that is, they are case specific and time bound. What was seen as ethical and professional in 1911 is different in 2016. There are also cultural influences as to appropriateness determination regarding standards of care. What is appropriate in the United States (a very individualistic culture) may differ from what is appropriate in more collectivist cultures (e.g., Latin American cultures). Figure 13.1 reports the results of a 2004 Harris Interactive poll revealing the following results about patient needs.

The financial costs associated with an inability to meet the needs of the patient are staggering. For example, in 2007 the average cost for caring for a patient in the United States was $6,096. This was approximately 16% of the gross domestic product of the country. When comparing this cost with other wealthy nations (i.e., Europe and Great Britain), the United States ranks highest in the world regarding cost per patient. In a study comparing the United States with the five other industrialized nations of Australia, Canada, Germany, New Zealand, and the United Kingdom, Frogner and Anderson (2006) used the following five categories: (1) *patient safety,* which reflects incidences of laboratory errors and delays in notifying patients of such mistakes (the United States was the most prone to error and least efficient in disclosing this to the patient); (2) *patient centeredness,* which reflects the patient leaving the physician's office with persistent questions (the United States was higher at 24% versus other countries that ranged from 15% to 20%); (3) *efficiency,* which reflects the number of times the patients were required to visit emergency rooms rather than having readily available primary care visits (the United States was highest at 24% with other countries being between 6% and 20%); (4) *equity,* which reflects the concept of social justice (e.g., if the patient cannot afford prescriptions, can he or she still have them filled?). In this category, the United States was higher at 26% with other countries ranging from 0% to 16%; and (5) *effectiveness* reflects the degree to which screenings, vaccines, mammograms, and so on are routinely given (the

figure 13.1

Needs of the Patient

1. My doctor treats me with respect: *Extremely important 85%* *Describes your doctor well 73%*
2. My doctor listens carefully to my health care concerns and questions: *Extremely important 84%* *Describes your doctor well 68%*
3. My doctor is easy to talk to: *Extremely important 84%* *Describes your doctor well 69%*
4. My doctor truly cares about me and my health: *Extremely important 81%* *Describes your doctor well 63%*
5. My doctor is up-to-date on the latest medical research and medical treatment: *Extremely important 78%* *Describes your doctor well 24%*

Source: Doctors' interpersonal skills valued more than their training or being up-to-date, Harris Interactive Poll. Wall Street Journal Online, 3, October 1, 2004.

United States excels in proactive/preventive health initiatives but falls below the other countries in the everyday delivery of health care) with particular reference to the distributive social justice required of medicine.

Professionalism and End-of-Life Issues

Perhaps in no circumstances are the communication skills of the healthcare practitioner more challenged than they are in end-of-life discussions with patients and families. As clinicians, such conversations more often than not take the form of standardized questions performed in a sequential manner. However, with end-of-life discussions, there are few rules because each patient, their story, and their situation are truly unique. Thus, the only real standard approach to such an event is the knowledge that there is no standard. Appropriateness is dictated by the patient, their situation, and their family. Several terms must be defined concerning end-of-life care to assist the healthcare practitioner when engaging in such conversations.

Advance Directives. **Advance directives** is a general term that refers to a patient's oral or written instructions about their future medical care in the event that they become unable to communicate those instructions by themselves. A written statement is prepared in accordance with state law, which addresses

Advance Directives

A general term that refers to a patient's oral or written instructions, about their future medical care in the event that they become unable to communicate those instructions by themselves.

the preferences for health care and treatment in the event that the person is incapacitated. The form of the advance directive will vary from state to state, but they typically consist of the living will, the durable power of attorney for health care, and the healthcare proxy.

Durable Medical Power of Attorney for Health Care.   The **power of attorney (POA-Health)** is a proxy directive (i.e., a legal document that designates a surrogate to make decisions on the patient's behalf if the patient becomes incapacitated for any reason). Such decisions may include life-support, organ donation, and the like.

| **Living Will**
| An instructional directive that varies according to context.

Living Will.   A living will is an instructional directive that will vary according to the specific context. This document serves as a person's desires to see a particular "conclusion" to their life story. However, given that situations, people, and relationships change suddenly and rapidly, experts advocate that advance care planning be viewed as a process in the patient–provider relationship (Lynn, Teno, & Phillips, 1997). This approach views the development of the living will not as a single encounter, but one that is based on a three-step process. The first step is that of *awareness,* which reflects the patient being aware of the need to share advanced care planning for decision-making processes with their designated surrogates (e.g., family or friends). The second step is that of *preparation,* which allows the patient to reflect on the situation and what issues may or may not be important to the patient and their family. For example, in a scenario where the illness is terminal, the patient may come to the conclusion that prolonging such an illness (e.g., experimental trials) may serve to deplete the finances of the family and thus refuse experimental treatment options. The final step is that of *taking action.* Lynn *et al*. (1997) recommend that the practitioner have an understanding of the patient's goals and aspirations. Such knowledge is believed to be vital for the physician and the interpretation of the durable medical power of attorney. One way to do this is through the Values Questionnaire, which assesses such patient characteristics (http://www.tcvermont.com/Questionaire. PDF, 2010). Whatever the case, most professionals advocate flexibility as circumstances—and possibly the priorities of the patient—change. **Advance Directive versus Living Will**

| **Do not Resuscitate Order (DNR)**
| A written order on the part of the healthcare provider that should be written with awareness as to the patient's quality of life, before they are in need of resuscitation and should include the patient's aspirations for quality of life after resuscitation.

Do Not Resuscitate Order.   The do not resuscitate order (DNR) is a written order on the part of the healthcare provider that should be developed with awareness as to the patient's quality of life before they are in need of resuscitation and the patient's aspirations for quality of life after resuscitation. This requires a candid conversation between the healthcare provider and the patient. According to Tomlinson and Brody (1998), there are three broad rationales for authorizing a DNR order. The first is *no medical benefit,* which reflects a determination made solely by the physician reflecting on the existing data as to what will and will not be of medical benefit to the patient. Families and patients sometimes have faulty assumptions about futile treatments and their "effectiveness." In such cases, the patient would be entitled to such "quack" therapies from their physician (Tomlinson & Brody, 1998). By the physician sharing such data with the family, requests for the "quack" therapies would decrease. The second rationale is *poor quality of life after CPR*. After the patient has arrested (i.e., sudden stoppage of the heart or breathing), even though they may survive being resuscitated, the patient may be in a persistent vegetative state. Many patients, when informed of such an outcome, may choose death over such a state of existence. The final rationale is *poor quality of life before CPR*. This reflects the health of the patient before they arrest and if that state is worth being restored to. For example, a patient with end-stage metastatic disease (cancer) may survive being resuscitated, but even a successful resuscitation would restore the patient to the end stages of cancer. Such an issue is for the patient, the patient's family, the healthcare provider, and perhaps the ethics committee to carefully consider.

Such conversations about DNR status are awkward and sometimes painful. Naughton, Davis, and von Gunten (2003) believe that any successful conversation about DNR needs to occur in an appropriate setting and must be discussed with empathy. As would be required for any ethical discussion, begin with an open-ended question (e.g., What are your desires concerning a do not resuscitate order?), use various methods of assessing the patient's comprehension and understanding of the information (e.g., Can you explain this information to me in your own words?), explore the patient's expectations regarding the future, discuss the actual DNR order (which may require recommendations on the part of the healthcare provider), respond to emotions in a caring and appropriate manner, and then establish a plan that requires the writing of specific and clear orders as to the wishes of the patient. You must inform/educate the patient. In a study of 12,000 patients on Medicare, Darnato et al. (2011) determined that of the elderly patients (i.e., those who are 65 years and older) placed on a ventilator, only 30% will survive. Further, the 30% who do survive do not have the same quality of life. The patient's ability to function in normal daily activities was reduced by 30% and mobility was reduced by 14%. Simply put, according to this data, if you are elderly and end up on a ventilator, you have a 30% chance of surviving, have one-third less ability to do desired activities and a 14% reduction in your mobility.

Although the DNR conversation is appropriate in a number of contexts, it is more appropriate in patients with acute reversible medical conditions as opposed to patients dying from progressive disease. Some people believe that the healthcare practitioner should consider other characteristics of the patients such as the patient's culture and religious beliefs and practices because these can have a major influence on end-of-life decisions. For example, according to Mebane, Oman, Kroonen, and Goldstein (1999), African-American physicians and patients are more likely than white physicians and patients to request artificial feeding, mechanical ventilation, or cardiopulmonary resuscitation if the patient is in a persistent vegetative state or terminally ill. An example of a religious influence can be seen in the Islamic tradition. More specifically, Muslims do not formally recognize brain death as death, and thus withdrawal of support in persistent vegetative state can be confounding (see Sarbill, LeGrand, Islambouli, Davis, & Walsh, 2001).

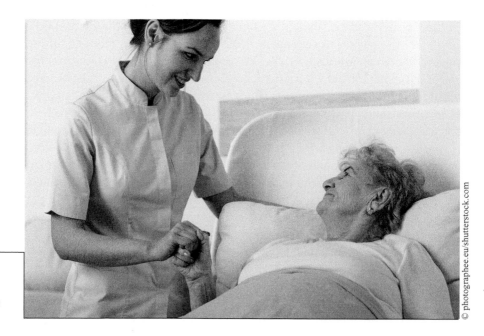

Hospice care places a special emphasis on adequate and appropriate pain control for the patient.

© photographee.eu/shutterstock.com

| Hospice

A type of care that focuses on relieving symptoms and supporting the patients and families when the patient has a life-limiting illness and generally has a life expectancy of six months or less.

| Palliative Care

Services that alleviate, lessen, or provide relief from symptoms that interfere with the quality of life in patients with serious illness whose life expectancy is undetermined.

| Brain Death

When the brain is no longer functioning in any capacity and will never again function.

Hospice and Palliative Care. The two services most commonly associated with end-of-life care are hospice and palliative care. Hospice refers to a type of care that focuses on relieving symptoms and supporting the patient and the patient's family when the patient has a life-limiting illness and generally has a life expectancy of six months or less. There is a special emphasis on adequate and appropriate pain control with hospice care. Palliative care refers to services that alleviate, lessen, or provide relief from symptoms that interfere with the quality of life when curative treatments are no longer effective or deemed too burdensome by the patient. The focus on palliative care is comfort, not aggressive pursuit of cure. Palliative care may be given at any time during the illness, and unlike hospice, which is generally at the very end stages (e.g., six months or less), palliative care can take place at any time from initial diagnosis on and can last for years.

Organ Donation

Perhaps no other aspect of medicine is more misunderstood than that of organ donation. Sometimes referred to as the "gift of life," many myths and half truths surround the situations in which a person is suitable to donate. By suitable we are referring to being physically, socially, and religiously compatible. As with other concepts discussed in this chapter, certain terms need to be defined to discuss this process. The definition of death is one that can take several different interpretations based on scientific, cultural, and religious assumptions. **Death** is defined as the end of the life of a biological organism. In this light, death can be referred to as an event or a condition. Brain death refers to when the brain is no longer functioning in any capacity and will never again function. This definition, under most state laws, can only be determined by two physicians independently examining the patient and generally following a diagnostic algorithm as outlined by medical/dental staff policy declaring that the patient is brain dead. Brain death can be caused by such things as blunt or penetrating trauma (e.g., auto accident or gunshot wound), cerebral aneurysm, drowning, or drug overdose. The result is a cessation of blood flow to the brain, the patient does not breathe spontaneously and requires a ventilator, and there is no pupillary response and no response to painful stimuli. A **coma** is a profound state of unconsciousness. It is derived from the Greek word *koma*. A **persistent vegetative state (PVS)** is a condition of patients with severe brain damage where coma has progressed to a state of wakefulness without detectable awareness.

For many families who experience a sudden traumatic accident, organ and/or tissue donation is the only positive experience in a tragic chain of events surrounding the loss of a loved one. There are different aspects to organ donation based on the state of the donor. A **live donor** generally refers to friends or family members who have compatible blood types and human leukocyte antigen (HLA) typing. Such compatible people are eligible for kidney donation. In the United States, three fourths of the patients in need of an organ transplant are waiting for a kidney. Most of these people will be on a waiting list for one to three years. More than half of these people will die before a matching organ becomes available (OPTN-SRTR Annual Report, 2006). Patients who are brain dead or those patients with no chance of recovery are donors of organs such as a heart, intestines, kidneys, lungs, liver, and pancreas. Patients who hearts are not beating (following cardiac death) can be donors of bone, tendon, corneas, heart valves, femoral veins, greater saphenous veins, pericardium (the covering of the heart), skin grafts, and sclera (the white of the eye).

Despite the autonomous directives set forth by the patient regarding organ donation, it is always in the best interest of all involved for the health-care practitioner to provide support and education to the family during this most painful time. It is not uncommon for family wishes to be in direct conflict with those predetermined directives of the patient. In fact, people frequently encounter many issues during the decision to donate organs. Table 13.2 illustrates some of these.

The experience of death is an event often bound in the philosophical and religious beliefs of the patient and his or her family. Such experiences can have a profound impact on organ donation decisions. Virtually every major organized religion, with the exception of *Shinto* (see www .donatelifecalifornia.org) permits organ donation whether it be on the premise that saving human life is a good thing or based on the individual patient's choice (www.organdonor.com, 2010).

In Catholic moral teaching, there was a holistic prohibition on the mutilation or injuring of the human body in any manner regardless of potential benefit. This policy was long-standing because the human body is believed to be created in the image of God. Thus, a diseased body part could not be removed to save the body. However, the **principle of totality** states that mutilation in one part of the body is legitimate in order to save the whole. For example, it would be deemed appropriate for a gangrenous left leg to be amputated to save

---

Coma

A profound state of unconsciousness.

Persistent Vegetative State (PVS)

A condition of patients with severe brain damage, where coma has progressed to a state of wakefulness without detectable awareness.

Live Donor

A person who has compatible blood type and human leukocyte antigen (HLA) typing.

Principle of Totality

A bioethical principle stating that mutilation in one body part is legitimate in order to save the whole.

a person's life. Thus, in accordance with the principle of totality, it was concluded that a person could mutilate his or her body in order to donate an organ (e.g., kidney) to save the life of another member of the human race as a whole (Kelly, 2004). In fact, the modern Catholic Church recognizes organ donation as a charitable act. However, it should be noted that organ donation is still prohibited if it threatens to disable or seriously injure the donor. According to the U.S. Conference of Catholic Bishops (2001), "The transplantation of organs from living donors is morally permissible when such a donation will not sacrifice or seriously impair any essential bodily function and the anticipated benefit to the recipient in proportion to the harm done to the donor. Furthermore, the freedom of the prospective donor must be respected, and economic advantages should not accrue to the donor" (Directive 30).

Similar to Catholicism, Judaism originally forbade postmortem organ donation. Jewish law prohibits the desecration of the dead body. It is assumed that the dead body must be treated with the utmost respect and that every body part, even if it is amputated, removed, or dismembered, must be appropriately buried. Similar to the body in death, Jewish law mandates a great respect for the living body, with no one being obligated to risk their own life to save another as would be the case in live organ donation. Live organ donation to save the life of another is believed to be a great act as long as the anticipated benefits to the recipient are not greater than the anticipated risks (Mackler, 2000).

Similar to both Catholicism and Judaism, the Muslim religion believes in the sanctity of the human life and permits organ donation as a means of preserving life (Bauer-Wu, Barret, & Yeager, 2007). The final major religion we will discuss is that of Jehovah's Witnesses, which do not prohibit church members from donating or receiving organs but do, however, mandate that the donated organs must be drained of the donor's blood prior to transplantation. By understanding these different religious perspectives, a communicatively competent healthcare practitioner can formulate appropriate messages that will accommodate such religious influences during very trying times for patients and their families.

Requesting an Organ Donation. One of the most challenging situations for a healthcare professional concerns the request for an organ donation in the absence of an advanced directive. There are, however, a few strategies and approaches that can make this request a mindful and compassionate act. First, *allow the family to grieve.* Although securing consent for organ donation is a noble goal, it is important not to further traumatize a grieving family by trying to obtain the consent. The family may have not fully accepted the fact that their loved one is deceased; give an appropriate time for grieving. Second, *time with the physical body is important.* For many families, spending time with the remains of their loved one is an important facet of the grieving process and should be fully respected by healthcare practitioners. Third, *educate the family about organ donation.* Focus on the positive aspects of the donation, such as it is a gift of life, while simultaneously framing such a message in a compassionate and understanding way. Fourth, *do not judge the family based*

table 13.2	Common Questions about Organ Donation

Question	Answer
Does the family have the right to override the predesignated donation?	Where online information is available and within the jurisdictions (states) where predetermination has been made, an organ retrieval agency does have the right to proceed with the organ donation in spite of the family's wishes. In those states where there is not a uniform registry available 24 hours a day, 7 days a week to healthcare providers and there is no driver's license designation or other form of organ donation consent, the family will be approached for consent.
Does age or preexisting medical condition relate to organ donation?	There are very few conditions that would exclude someone from donating organs. Any preexisting condition should be disclosed to the healthcare practitioner when discussing possible organ donation.
Is organ donation the same as whole-body donation?	Organ donation is not the same as whole-body donation. Whole-body donation refers to donating of the entire body to a medical school for the purpose of research or education, whereas organ or tissue donation is for use in living participants. Whole-body donation requires an instrument in the advanced directives, usually in the form of the Last Will and Testament.
Are there any restrictions about organ donations?	Depending on the jurisdiction, the donor may or may not predetermine where the organs will be used.
Will we as family members be told as to how the organs/tissues were used?	This is generally up to the in-state organ retrieval system. Frequently there is anonymous communication between the donor's family and the recipient. As a point of fact, a single organ donor can save up to 8 lives, with another 50 lives improving as a result of the donation.
How do you determine who received the organs?	Organs are distributed based on a complex medical formula by UNOS (the United Network for Organ Sharing). UNOS is a transplant patient waiting list. The basic components of compatibility include blood type, HLA (human leukocyte antigen) typing, and body weight and size (which are matched against a patient list).
Will the organs be sold?	The Uniform Anatomical Gift Act of 1984 makes buying and selling organs for the purpose of transplantation illegal in the United States. Strict regulations prevent any type of "black market," and illegal selling and trading result in large fines and imprisonment.
Will my family or estate be charged for the medical costs associated with donation?	There is no cost associated with the harvesting of organs or tissue that will be passed on to the donor's family.
Will the body be mutilated so that we cannot have an open casket viewing?	All current harvesting techniques are performed with great sensitivity as to the necessity of preserving the body such that open viewing remains an option.

on their decision. Whether or not the family consents to organ donation is solely up to them. Avoid attaching moral- or value-based characteristics on the family if they do or do not consent. Each case is different, as is each family's experience with the death of a loved one. Finally, *avoid coercion.* Informed consent is truly a shared decision-making process. The conversations with the family should be informative, educational, and supportive, not biased or judgmental in any way.

For the past 40 to 50 years there has been a profound shift in the way that society perceives healthcare practitioners and the patient's relationship to the healthcare system as a whole. Within this time period, we moved from a system where the physician enjoyed total autonomy and power to one where the autonomy and power shifted to the patient and his or her individual right to be self-determined. With this societal shift in the perception of medicine and patient empowerment also came a simultaneous shift in legal and ethical perspectives. More specifically, healthcare providers operating in this "new" medical relationship paradigm had to account for legal issues that in earlier times were not considered as important, if they were considered at all. Issues such as how to control for risk, reduce existing risk, the role and responsibility of the patient in terms of being informed about choices and procedures available to them, and the responsibility of the healthcare practitioner when mistakes are made. This chapter is designed to expose the reader to how healthcare practitioners consider and effectively address risk; issues surrounding informed consent and how to go about the informed consent process; and the moral, professional, and legal aspects involved when medical mistakes are made. Finally, we present the concept of apology and the societal, legal, and religious factors that influence the process of apology.

The concept of informed consent has three dimensions: *law, bioethics,* and *medicine's own understanding as to the nature of the physician–patient relationship.* The legal dimension of informed consent holds that the practitioner has a duty to disclose information and obtain consent before administering treatment. One way (checklist) to do this is through what is known as the NBAR acronym: **Nature** of the procedure (whether it is a diagnostic or therapeutic treatment or what is going to be done to the patient), **Benefits** of the procedure (what this procedure will do to benefit you), **Alternatives** to the procedure (the alternatives to the proposed procedure and the associated risks and benefits with those alternatives), and **Risks** associated with the procedure (the more common risks in terms of those that are notable, those that are severe [major], and those that are likely [higher probability] to occur). The list of common risks should be as extensive and exhaustive as possible.

The bioethics dimension of informed consent is based on the philosophy of Immanuel Kant and holds that in order to act ethically, people must act with respect toward other people as if they were an intrinsically valued self-legislating being or beings that have autonomy (Kant, 2010). Although this autonomous approach may seem empowering by most counts, some people argue that not all people want to assume the burden of making such decisions (Schneider, 1998). In fact, Schneider (1998) argues that "bioethics has fallaciously reasoned that because the majority of people are thought to want

© 2011, Condor 36, Shutterstock, Inc.

Physicians must disclose all risks that might affect a patient's decision to have surgery.

to make healthcare decisions, not all people want that decision authority. On the other hand, we neither want nor expect autonomy to lose its status as the centerpiece of bioethics, but that centerpiece should be a whole bouquet of concepts and not just a single flower of autonomy, however beguiling it may be" (p. 32).

Conclusion

This chapter presented some of the most important aspects of the medical profession; professionalism and the ethical standards that are all part of an internal striving for excellence. Societal changes have brought about different needs of the patient and the different needs of the healthcare professional. The various medical professions and the allied professions were presented and defined. Understand how and what the various people of the medical team do is vital to understanding the healthcare system in general.

The end of human life and processes that accompany such an event were presented and discussed. Special emphasis was given to the healthcare practitioner's ability to be professional, empathetic, and knowledgeable about the cultural and religious assumptions about death and the legal aspects associated with end-of-life care. The chapter concluded with a discussion of organ donation and the various issues that may arise. **Discussion Organ Donation**

Questions for Discussion/Review

1. Define professionalism and how the behavior of the healthcare provider can affect the patient, colleagues, and the healthcare system in general.
2. Briefly discuss the most important events in the historical development of medicine between the 19ᵗʰ and 21ˢᵗ centuries.
3. Explain how the Supreme Court decision in 1975 (i.e., *Goldfarb vs. United States)* profoundly changed the healthcare profession.
4. Explain the importance of any healthcare practitioner being knowledgeable about the expertise and training of all members of the healthcare team. What are some possible implications for the patient? The overall quality of care? The overall impact on healthcare team cohesion and competence?
5. Explain the four principles of ethical standards adopted by the American Society for Bioethics and Humanities (ASBH). Argue why each principle is important and how adhering to such principles can assist the practitioner, the patient, and the patient's family.
6. Describe the function of a clinical ethics committee.
7. List and define the four characteristics intrinsic to most ethical encounters.
8. In this chapter, many different end-of-life documents are discussed. Choose three of these documents, define each, and provide a scenario in which the absence of such documents can cause great difficulty for the people involved in making treatment decisions.
9. Explain the difference between hospice and palliative care. Provide an example for each.
10. Provide the definition of a "live donor" and how the organs that can be harvested differ from those harvested from a "dead donor."
11. Describe the "principle of totality" and its impact on organ donor decisions.

References

ABIM Foundation. (2002). Medical professionalism in the new millennium: A physician charter. *Annals of Internal Medicine, 136,* 243–246.

About Physician Assistants. (2010). *American Academy of Physician Assistants (AAPA).* Retrieved June 8, 2010, from http://www.aapa.org/about-aapa.

American Dental Association. (1997). *Dentistry definitions.* Retrieved June 5, 2010, from http://en.wikipedia.org/wiki/Dentistry.

American Nurses Association. (2010). *ANA's definition of nursing.* Retrieved June 4, 2010, from http://www.nursingworld.org/MainMenuCategories/certificationandaccreditation/aboutnursing.aspx.

American Physical Therapy Association (2001). Guide to physical therapist practice, (2nd ed.). *Physical Therapy, 81,* 13–27.

Bauer-Wu, S., Barrett, R., & Yeager, K. (2007). Spiritual perspectives and practices at the end-of-life. *Indian Journal of Palliative Care, 13,* 53–58.

Beauchamp, T. I., & Childress, J. F. (2001). *Principles of biomedical ethics.* New York: Oxford University Press.

Calman, K. (1994). The profession of medicine. *British Medical Journal, 309,* 1140–1143.

Cohen, J. J., Cruess, S., & Davidson, C. (2007). Alliance between society and medicine: The public's stake in the medical professionalism. *Journal of the American Medical Association, 298,* 670–673.

Edwards, D. F. (1997). The effect of occupational therapy on function and well-being. In C. H. Christiansen, & C. M. Baum (Eds.). *Occupational therapy: Enabling function and well-being* (2nd ed., pp. 556–574). Thorofare, NJ: Slack Inc.

Exploring Health Care Careers. (2010) Retrieved June 3, 2010, from http://www.fegpubco.com.

Freidson, E. (1993). *Professionalism: The third logic.* Chicago, IL: University of Chicago Press.

Frogner, B. K., & Anderson, G. F. (2006). *Multi-national comparisons of healthcare systems data, 2005.* New York: The Commonwealth Fund.

Goldfarb vs. Virginia State Bar (1975). 421 U.S. 773.

Gough, J. W. (1957). *The social contract: A Critical study of its development.* Oxford, England: Clarendon Press.

Harris Interactive poll. (2004). Doctors' interpersonal skills valued more than their training or being up-to-date. *Wall Street Journal On Line, 3,* 19.

Hepler, C. D., & Strand, L. M. (1989). Opportunities and responsibilities in pharmaceutical care. *The American Journal of Pharmacy Education, 53,* 7S–15S.

Jonsen, A. R., Siegler, M., & Winslade, W. J. (1998). *Clinical ethics: A practical approach to ethical decisions in clinical medicine* (4th ed.). New York: McGraw Hill, Inc.

Kelly, D. F. (2004). *Contemporary health care ethics.* Washington, DC: Georgetown University Press.

Kizer, K. W. (2002). Patient centered care: Essential but probably not sufficient. *Quality Safety Healthcare, 11,* 117–118.

Lynn, J., Teno, J. M., & Phillips, R. A. (1997). Perceptions by family members of the dying experience of older and seriously ill patients. *Annals of Internal Medicine, 126,* 97–106.

Mackler, A. L. (2000). *Life & death responsibilities in Jewish biomedical ethics.* New York: The Jewish theological seminary of America. New York organ donor network. Retrieved June 18, 2010, from www.donatelifeny.org.

McCroskey, J. C. (1966). Scales for the measurement of ethos. *Speech Monographs, 33,* 65–72.

McCroskey, J. C., & Young, T. J. (1981). Ethos and credibility: The construct and its measurement after three decades. *Central States Speech Journal, 32,* 24–34.

Mebane, E. W., Oman, R. F., Kroonen, L. T., & Goldstein, M. K. (1999). The influence of physician race, age, and gender on physician attitudes toward advanced care directives and preferences for end-of-life decision making. *Journal of the American Geriatric Society, 47,* 579–591.

National Association of Social Workers. (2010). *Standards for social work practice in health care settings.* Retrieved May 31, 2010, from http://www.socialworkers.org/practice/standards/NASWHealthCareStandards.pdf.

Naughton, M., Davis, M., & von Gunten, C. F. (2003). Discussing do-not-resuscitate status: Furthering the discourses. *Journal of Clinical Oncology, 19,* 3301–3302.

NCCB/USCC. (2001). *Ethical and religious directives for Catholic health care services* (4th ed.). Washington, DC: United States Conference of Catholic Health Care Services.

OPTN-SRTR. (2006). *Annual report.* Retrieved June 25, 2010, from http://www.donatelifeny.org.

Papadakis, M. A., Loeser, H., & Healy, K. (2001). Early detection in evaluation of professionalism, deficiencies in medical students: One school's approach. *Academic Medicine, 76,* 1100–1106.

Princeton WordNet. (2010). *Occupational therapy.* Retrieved June 25, 2010, from www.wordnet.princeton.edu/perl/webwn?5=occupation%20therapy.

Reich, W. (2010, June). *Rediscovering ancient consolation: Negative care, empathy, and the fundamental role of kindness in medicine.* Paper presented at the annual meeting of the Founders of Bioethics International Congress, Edinboro, PA.

Relman, A. S. (2007). *Rescuing America's health care.* New York: Public Affairs.

Sarbill, N., LeGrand, S., Islambouli, R., Davis, M. P., & Walsh, D. (2001). The terminally ill Muslim: Death and dying from the Muslim perspective. *American Journal of Hospice and Palliative Care, 18,* 251–255.

Starr, P. (1984). *The social transformation of American medicine.* New York: Harmony Books.

Stead, E. A. Jr. (2010). *The physician assistant's history center.* Retrieved June 8, 2010, from http://pahx.org/steadBio.html.

Teven, J. J., & McCroskey, J. C. (1997). The relationship of perceived teacher caring with student learning and teacher evaluation. *Communication Education, 46,* 1–9.

Tomlinson, T., & Brody, H. (1998). Ethics and communication in do-not-resuscitate order. *New England Journal of Medicine, 318,* 43–46.

Torstendahl, R. (1993). The transformation of professional education in the 19th century. In S. Rothblatt & B. Wittrock (Eds.), *The European and American university since 1800: Historical and sociological essays* (pp. 109–111). Cambridge, UK: Cambridge University Press.

United States Bureau of Labor Statistics. (2009). *Occupational outlook handbook 2010–2011 edition.* Retrieved June 3, 2010, from http://www.bls.gov/oco/ocos060.htm.

United States Department of Labor (2009). *Medical assistants.* Retrieved June 3, 2010, from http://www.bls.gov/oco/ocos096.htm.

www.donatelifecalifornia.org/about/facts. Retrieved June 25, 2010.

www.organdonor.com/hc3.asp. Retrieved June 25, 2010.

http://www.tcvermont.com/Questionaire.PDF. Retrieved June 25, 2010.

Zastrow, C. (2008). *Introduction to social work and social welfare: Empowering people* (9th ed.). Florence, KY: Brooks/Cole.

chapter fourteen

Medical Communication Technology: Currents and Futures

Chapter objectives

Upon completion of the chapter, the student should be able to:

1. Explain the impact that electronic health records and personal health records have on the healthcare system.

2. Understand the complexity of electronic medical records and electronic health records regarding privacy and security.

3. Understand how e-training is revolutionizing education in healthcare.

4. Explain the ways in which **SMART** technology is revolutionizing patient care.

5. Explain the three components that comprise the everyday practice of medicine (i.e., medical communication).

T he use of technology at all levels of society has paved the way for advancements and breakthroughs that were once unimaginable. The interface between man and computer has been nothing less than amazing in many disciplines such as science and medicine. For example, in the field of radiology, the two technologies of plane x-ray and computers were combined to form what is now known as computerized axial tomography (CAT). The CAT scan is revolutionary in that it allows physicians to evaluate both hard and soft tissues without having to perform invasive procedures. This is but one example of the application of technology and its impact on both the practice of medicine and the quality of healthcare delivery. This chapter will examine several technologies and technological applications being implemented to assist healthcare providers and patients alike.

© everything possible/Shutterstock.com

317

Key terms

anthropomorphic robot
asymmetrical cryptography
biometrics
CIA triad
e-learning
e-patients

electronic health record
 (EHR)
encryption
medical communication
mobile patient care assistant
 (MPCA)

personal health record (PHR)
smartphone
symmetrical cryptography
translational research
v-learning

Electronic Records

Computers have served not only to improve medical treatment, but also as a means to further empower the patient. Computer technology has enabled the patient to proactively research illness and disease and determine qualifications and reputations of healthcare practitioners. It also serves as a record keeper for a patient's health records. This section will introduce the concept of electronic records and how they are being utilized and experimented by healthcare practitioners and entire healthcare systems. In order for technology to be accepted as a benefit to both the provider and the patient, there must be some type of acceptance by the intended users. If patients and providers find the technology easy to use and useful, they will then continue to explore the **Future of Computers in Healthcare.**

| **Electronic health record (EHR)** |
| An electronic record that is considered the official document for patient management. |

According to Webb (2009), there is a clear distinction between the provider/supply side of record keeping, which is characterized by the **electronic health record (EHR),** and the patient side of record keeping, which is characterized by the **personal health record (PHR).** The EHR is the electronic record considered to be the official document for patient management, whereas the PHR is a document developed by the patient that contains the patient's personal healthcare information. **The Process of Going Electronic** Because one type of record is developed by the healthcare provider and one by the patient, these documents can be quite different from one another. The EHR is dynamic in nature in that it is interconnected to other medical treatment processes such as electronic prescribing and can serve as a resource for physician support for evaluation and treatment options based on the standard of care as defined by clinical protocols and guidelines. Further, the EHR can be accessed by the patient and certain aspects of the record can be modified by the patient. Such access and linking of different networks is believed to improve patient care because different members of the healthcare team, regardless of physical distance, all have access to the record (Electronic Health Records, 2010). By digitizing such a process, it is believed that caregivers will have more time to treat and listen to patients as opposed to being consumed by the standard paperwork. **How It Will Help the Patient** Theoretically, there would no longer be lost charts, duplicate records, and the unavailability of patient information that is common in the everyday practice of medicine. Some other benefits to this digitized record system would be the immediate availability of test results for both providers and

| **Personal health record (PHR)** |
| A document developed by the patient containing the patient's personal healthcare information. |

The EHR is the electronic record considered to be the official document for patient management, developed by the healthcare provider.

patients. Such an interconnected and efficient system should reduce the need and expense for transcription, the logistics of chart management, and the cost of record storage. Of course, all of these benefits are predicated on a system that does, in fact, function efficiently and offers a high degree of security not only across a hardwired network, but also throughout wireless networks around the world.

Although such a system may seem intuitively appealing, it does have associated costs. **The Financial Cost of Going Electronic** Webb (2009) estimates that implementing an electronic medical records/electronic health records (EMR/EHR) system in a primary care practice will take approximately 1 to 5 years to install, will cost about $44,000, and will take about 2.5 years for the system to pay for itself. However, once this process occurs, the system is believed to save the practice approximately $23,000 annually. More specifically, approximately 50% of savings would be realized in decreased personnel costs in the form of transcription (if voice recognition dictation is used) and chart management, with the other 50% of savings being attributed to increased revenue resulting from more accurate evaluation and management (EM) coding. In a Massachusetts study, analyzing 49 community practices, the researchers determined that the projected return over a five year period on the investment required for a single electronic health record system for a practitioner is approximately ($43,473) loss per physician (Adler, 2013).

Choosing the appropriate system can be a challenge. Most systems require a dramatic amount of new knowledge and effort from all members of the healthcare team. There are **web-based modules,** which are systems that are generally housed off site and can experience bandwidth limitations and inconsistent transfer speed based on the traffic of other healthcare practitioners who also use the vendor's server. Another option is a **practice-based**

system, which consists of a server that is housed within the specific healthcare facility and is owned and maintained by the healthcare facility. The practice-based system is more expensive both in up-front and maintenance costs. However, after the initial installation and testing, the maintenance costs tend to plane off, making annual maintenance costs less expensive than the fees commonly charged by web-based software vendors. Unlike the web-based systems, practice-based systems may be limited in situations where interconnectivity to other facilities is vital for patient care. For example, communicating information from varying office locations or from an office to a hospital can be adversely affected by system limitations. This is particularly prevalent when using voice dictation, submitting e-prescriptions, or ordering laboratory tests.

In a study investigating the efficacy of EMR/EHR systems, Greenhalgh, Potts, Wong, Bark, and Swinglehurst (2009) reached the following five conclusions. First, the EMR is excellent for patient billing, auditing, and general research. **Efficiency of EMR and Efficiency of EHR** Second, primary clinical work may be less efficient as a result of the expense and steep learning curve involved in adopting an electronic system. Both the expense and steep learning curve are attributed to 50% to 80% of failed attempts at implementing electronic health record systems. **Learning Curve** Third, paper is not an obsolete modality for record keeping and can offer more flexibility for many aspects of clinical work that are not available via traditional computerized record keeping systems. **Point Three** Fourth, the seamless integration between EMR/EHR systems is not likely to occur because human input of data will always be required and such human effort requires the contextualizing of information based on the specific situations in which medicine is practiced and, as such, is prone to human interpretation and error. **Integration** Fifth, computerized records can jeopardize the human side of nursing and medicine. As with any technology, computerized record systems can serve to obstruct the interpersonal dynamic that is believed to be critical for effective patient care. There can be considerable disequity in health information technology. Factors such as race, ethnicity, disabilities, low socioeconomic status, low literacy and advanced age can cause significant roadblocks. These populations are frequently at higher risk for chronic conditions and need for care. The Patient Protection and Affordable Care Act (PPACA) (Chapter 8, Focusing on Vulnerable Populations; http://govinfo.library.unt.edu/hcquality/meetings/mar12/papch08.htm) will expand this population to involve approximately 16 more million American adults thus having access to insured healthcare but based on the above listed factors meaningful access is challenging and will increase the digital divide (Kieschnik, 2011). **Potential for Obstruction**

The implementation of electronic records has indeed caught the attention of elected officials. On April 27, 2004, President George W. Bush issued an executive order that established the Office of the National Coordinator for Health Information Technology (ONCHIT) (Bush, 2004). This office is responsible for the full implementation of EMR/EHR systems by the year 2014. However, the reality of the situation is that full diffusion of this technology will more likely be achieved by the year 2024 (Ford, Menachemi, & Phillips, 2006). When it comes to the consumers of health care (i.e., patients), recent surveys indicate that 4 out of every 10 consumers are interested in creating an online personal health record (Konrad, 2009). Even in light of these data, in 2009 only 1.5% to 2% of the nonfederally funded hospitals had a comprehensive electronic medical record system, whereas 7.6% of these facilities owned a basic electronic document management system (i.e., a paper chart that is viewed on a computer monitor) (McDonald et al., 2003).

This lack of compliance with adoption of electronic health record systems is also influenced by the size of the healthcare facility. Research shows that only about 2% to 3% of small practices, defined as facilities having one to five members, have a fully functional EMR/EHR system. However, when there are 50 or more physician members within a facility, this number jumps to 17% (Goulde & Brown, 2006; Jha et al., 2009). One of the main reasons for this disparity based on healthcare facility size lies in the fact that most hospitals have to spend more than $100 million dollars for their EMR/EHR system. Further, this massive capital investment still does not enable the facility to fully integrate the system. Couple this with significant annual maintenance costs, and implementing such a system can be cost prohibitive (Feld, 2009). Of interest, a study of community healthcare centers (i.e., facilities that care for patients with low to no income) revealed that 28% of those surveyed reported having some sort of electronic record system, with 8% (versus 17% of the private sector) reporting having fully implemented electronic record systems (History of OSI, 2010).

Overall, the EMR and EHR are not only valuable tools for both the practitioner and patient, but they also are mechanisms that target efficiency necessary to combat the staggering costs of health care and the possible

© pisaphotography/Shutterstock.com

The larger the healthcare facility is, the more likely it has a fully functional EMR/EHR system.

reduction in medical error. Although initially cost prohibitive, the long-term prognosis of such systems seems to indicate a savings that may go far beyond the financials to include improved patient care and reductions in medical error. To put such savings potential into perspective, if the implementation of EMR/EHR systems were to improve the efficiency of health care just 1%, this would result in an annual savings of $22 billion for the healthcare system. Any cost-cutting measure is vital to a system where the total spending on health-care increased from 16% of the gross domestic product (GDP) in 2007, 25% of the GDP in 2025, and 49% of the GDP in 2082 (Congressional Budget Office, 2007; Orszag, 2008). Currently, Americans spend $2.2 trillion annu-ally on health care, and this figure is expected to rise considerably with each passing year.

So how can the healthcare practitioner manage a healthcare system that is constantly changing, resulting in changes in the everyday practice of medi-cine? How can the sacred medical encounter between the healthcare practi-tioner and the patient be integrated into the technological age of EMR/EHR systems and remain as human and relationally dependent as it has in the past? For such questions, we offer the following suggestions:

1. Consider using **open source software,** which allows you to copy, modify, use, and distribute patient information at approximately 50% of the imple-mentation costs and at a 65% reduction in maintenance costs (RPMS HER, 2010).

2. Utilize the **supplier–consumer economic metaphor** when discussing electronic health systems. This metaphor explains the financial and qual-ity-of-life benefits to all parties involved in the healing process. For exam-ple, start with the consumer in terms of saving costs through lifestyle change such as weight reduction, exercise, proper diet, stress manage-ment, and so on. Then address the supply side in terms of the trends in the demographics of healthcare providers. For example, the newer generations of healthcare providers are much more accepting and adaptable to new technology than older generations of healthcare practitioners. Thus, as one generation retires, there will also be an explosion in the adoption of elec-tronic record systems and other technologically dependent management systems.

3. Electronic health systems that are fully integrated enable the user to avoid the misuse of healthcare such as receiving duplicate services. For exam-ple, the National Center for Health Statistics report on the quality of care in patient safety indicated that in 2007, in 19 million healthcare visits, office-based physicians prescribed at least one potentially inappropriate drug and in 7.4% of all visits by adults age 65 and older (CDC, 2010). The report defines these potentially inappropriate medications as those that should generally be avoided in people 65 years or older because of the medication's ineffectiveness or because the medication poses an unnecessarily high risk for the patient when safer alternatives are avail-able. An electronic medical system that is fully integrated will help to sort out such potential problems, thus resulting in significant savings. In a

study by the Rand Corporation, it was found that once the electronic health records system is adopted and fully integrated, the potential savings could be upwards of $81 billion annually in healthcare costs, with the savings coming primarily from the reduction in the number of redundant tests, procedures, and treatment error (Gogolin, 2010). Federal government figures go even further, estimating that a fully computerized and integrated electronic record system can save the healthcare industry as much as $200 to $300 billion annually (Gogolin, 2010).

Complications of EMR/EHR

As the electronic medical record continues to grow in popularity throughout the healthcare system, the one big potential problem is the assurance of protecting the privacy of patient information. Given that electronic records contain the patient's name and other personal information, if these records fall into the wrong hands, it can have catastrophic consequences for the patient and the healthcare facility.

In addition to the obvious invasion of one's privacy, if electronic records were found to be vulnerable to either internal or external threats, such threats could jeopardize the entire future of electronic medical records. The American Health Information Management Association has defined specific legal issues of the electronic medical record, which include the validity of an electronic signature, defining who the actual custodian of the electronic record is, and what information can and cannot be released according to the Federal Health Insurance Portability and Accountability Act (HIPPA) (AHIMA, 2005). HIPPA specifically identifies **protected health information** as any information—be it oral or recorded in any form or medium. Such information can include data created by a healthcare provider, health plan, a public housing authority, an employer, a life insurer, a school or university, or a healthcare clearinghouse and is related to the past, present, or future physical or mental health condition of an individual. The protections for psychotherapy notes are afforded extra protection because they may have even greater stigmatizing effects for the individual.

For more than a century the healthcare system and its operation were monitored and maintained through a paper-based medical record system. Paper is considered a tangible document that can be identified as part of the patient's record of care. Such records can be and are reviewed for content, completeness, signatures, dates, and changes. Simply put, what you see in the record is the record. In contrast, the electronic medical record is markedly different because it is not based on physical documents. Instead, it is a transactional (back and forth communication) database that retains information over long periods of time (until deleted) and contains information for multiple care encounters with multiple data inputs from multiple locations. Further, these multiple inputs can occur simultaneously. Such challenges to system access and security have prompted the National Institute of Standards and Technology (NIST) to define **computer security** as "protection afforded to an automated information system in order to attain the applicable objectives of preserving the integrity, availability, and confidentiality of information system resources (this includes hardware, software, firmware, information/data and telecommunications)" (Kurtz & Vines, 2003, p. 345). NIST has outlined three security practices that they have defined as the CIA triad, which are the three dimensions of security domains (i.e., confidentiality, integrity, and availability) used to ensure computer network integrity for electronic medical record systems. **Confidentiality** is the security domain that requires private or confidential information not be disclosed to unauthorized individuals. The **integrity** security domain refers to the systematic and authorized maintenance of the system and reflects both **data integrity** and **system integrity.** Data integrity is the requirement that information and programs be changed only in a specified and authorized manner, whereas system integrity refers to the requirement that a system performs its intended function in an unimpaired manner that is free from deliberate or inadvertent unauthorized manipulation to the system. The final security domain is **availability** and refers to ensuring that systems work promptly and service is not denied to authorized users. Figure 14.1 illustrates this concept.

There are two major issues regarding this triad. First, the most vulnerable area for possible cyber hackers is within the software rather than the network system itself (SANS Institute, 2009). Second, there is a problem as to exactly who knows the encrypted codes of the system. Encryption is the transformation of plain text into an unreadable code or cipher text that serves as the basic technology used to protect the confidentiality and integrity of the data (Walsh, 2003). The two types of cryptography encryption consist of symmetrical cryptography and asymmetrical cryptography. Symmetrical cryptography uses the same secret key to encipher and decipher messages, whereas asymmetrical cryptography uses different keys, one to encipher and another key to

CIA triad

Three dimensions of security domains (i.e., confidentiality, integrity, and availability) used to ensure computer network integrity for electronic medical record systems.

Encryption

The transformation of plain text into an unreadable code or cipher text that serves as the basic technology used to protect the confidentiality and integrity of the data.

Symmetrical cryptography

Transformation of information using the same secret key to encipher and decipher messages.

Asymmetrical cryptography

Transformation of information using different keys, one to encipher and another to decipher the messages.

With a paper-based medical record system, what you see in the record is the record.

© bikeriderlondon/Shutterstock.com

decipher the message (Kurtz & Vines, 2003). Any implementation and use of an EMR/EHR system requires a **Certified Information System Security Professional (CISSP)**. The CISSP is a person who is credentialed through the International Information System Security Certification Consortium and is responsible for ensuring the confidentiality, integrity, and availability of the system (Schon, 2008).

Yet who gets access to information has always been a major issue of any medical record system regardless of whether it was paper or computer based. Harris (2002) believes that for any valid system to control access, the administrators of the system must follow the following four processes. The first is *identification,* or verifying the person who is wanting access. This can be done through things such as user ID. The second is *authentication,* or the use of a personal identification number (PIN), password, or pass code or may include a smart card or biometric measures such as fingerprinting or an iris scan. Third is *authorization,* or the determination as to what information the user can access. For example, a physician may have access to other portions of the system that the volunteer working at the front desk would not be able to

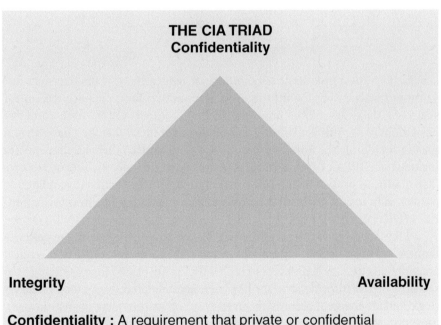

THE CIA TRIAD
Confidentiality

Integrity   **Availability**

Confidentiality : A requirement that private or confidential information not be disclosed to unauthorized individuals.

Integrity: Data integrity is a requirement that information and programs are changed only in a specified and authorized manner. System integrity is a requirement that a system performs its intended function in an unimpaired manner, free from deliberate or inadvertent unauthorized manipulation of the system.

Availability: A requirement intended to ensure that systems work promptly and service is not denied to authorized users.

figure 14.1

The CIA Triad

Source: Dougherty, M. (2010). The 10 security domains (updated). Journal of the American Health Information Management Association, 81, 57–61.

© william casey/Shutterstock.com

Physicians may be authorized to see portions of the medical records that are not accessible to other staff.

access. The final process is *accounting,* or determining if the user has just cause to be accessing the information. Accounting for a person's reason for accessing data may be the most challenging because just because someone has a right to see privileged information does not mean that they have a valid reason for doing so. Some of the most significant challenges that remain include the HIPPA (1996) security rule that mandates specific sets of *security* (safeguards to protect health information) and *privacy* (national standards to protect individuals' medical records and other personal health information) rules (DHHR, 2010).

A few specific directives of the HIPPA law directly pertain to the patient's request for information. Patients have the right to access, copy, and request amendments to their health records (DHHR, 2000). Such requests include the redisclosure of information that has been accumulated from other facilities (e.g., outside medical records received from other providers or institutions). Such provisions regarding patient information requests were further expanded with the passage of the 2009 American Recovery and Reinvestment Act (ARRA), which allowed for patients to be provided with a transfer of their health information in electronic format on request. Further, patients have the right to restrict the access to or disclosure of their health information. According to a meta-analytic study by Ross and Lin (2003), by providing the patient with the right to review his or her medical record, the result should be an enhanced flow of information between patients and their providers and a reduction in errors as well as an increase in the quality of health care. A meta-analysis is a method of analysis where instead of using data from a specific study, you use the data from many previous studies that have already been conducted. For example, if we wanted to investigate the impact of fluoride on oral health, instead of assessing 100 people for our study, we may simply gather all of the previous studies on the subject and use the findings of each study as a specific data point. By performing meta-analyses, researchers can get a more accurate sample as to what the true findings are in the population (not just in their sample). More specifically, Ross and Lin (2003) uncovered five points of interest, consisting of the following:

1. In the United States only 0.4% of medical inpatients and outpatients requested to see their records (Altman, Reich, Kelly, & Rogeres, 1980).
2. Patient access to his or her clinical record does not appreciably increase workload for the healthcare provider (Elbourne, Richardson, Chalmer, Waterhouse, & Holt, 1987).
3. The most consistent finding across all studies is that patient-accessible medical records enhance patient–provider communication.
4. The overall impression from the meta-analysis was that patient-accessible medical records are unlikely to cause harm to patients and have the potential for modest benefits.
5. Patient-accessible medical records, in addition to offering the opportunity to correct errors in the medical records, may also allow the patient to *introduce* errors through unauthorized changes to the electronic medical record (Anwar & Mahoney, 2000). A real-life example of this occurred when a patient altered her record, resulting in an unnecessary Cesarean section procedure.

The complexity of protecting the EMR/EHR has prompted the American Information Management Association (AHIMA) to develop a model for protecting health information, known as the AHIMA Bill of Rights.

Legal Implications

To date, there remains great concern as to the legal standards regarding the exchange of health information (i.e., jurisdictional issues). For example, if a record is sent from a healthcare facility in West Virginia to a healthcare facility in Montana, who has jurisdiction over the record? Given that the standards of medical practice are constantly changing as a result of the implementation of electronic medical record systems, there will undoubtedly be mistakes made and, as a result, litigation will increase. Further, the health information officers will be held liable for such damages as the case law involving electronic health records continues to evolve. According to Terry and Francis (2007), one way to navigate such legal issues, such as challenges to autonomy and the personal and professional responsibility on the part of the provider, is to address such issues *prior* to the implementation of any electronic health record system. More specifically, three assumptions must be understood before any system is implemented. First, the data belong to the patient, not the provider (Brailer, 2005). Second, the ethical perspective of autonomy must be protected under law. Third, to ensure such autonomy may require limitations on other aspects of electronic health records such as limited interoperability and limited comprehensiveness. Simply put, far too often the interests of hospitals, insurance companies, and government have trumped the interests and participation of the patient; therefore, when considering electronic medical record systems, err on the side of the patient. Terry and Francis (2007) argue that an independent oversight agency (similar to the Australian Privacy Commissioner used in the Australian medical system) should be legislatively charged with ensuring compliance and establishing data protection guidelines. Such an agency should be a body that is free of political influence and serves to educate patients and providers about codes of conduct and dispute resolution in constructive ways that avoid litigation such as providing an ombudsman to ensure fair and impartial processes (an official in charge of investigating a patient's complaints). Such processes are currently being utilized in Australia, Canada, New Zealand, and the United Kingdom.

Other Technological Factors in Healthcare Communication

The concept of technology includes aspects such as education, training, and treatment. The following sections introduce how various aspects of health care are benefitting from such technological advancements.

E-Patients

In the world of contemporary medicine, patients have more information-seeking options than ever before. Such options, of course, vary in credibility and perspective, but nonetheless, more patients are utilizing technology to seek out information about health and illness and for social support (Wright, 2002). It is estimated that 61% of adults seek out online information pertaining to healing, with approximately 20% of them going to social network sites such as Facebook and Twitter to facilitate health- and illness-related conversations that serve to bring together people of like mind and experience (Fox et al., 2009). Such patients are known as **e-patients**, which reflects when patients utilize technology for social support and social networking resources that are specific to their disease or medical situation. The information garnered through such social networking is not necessarily medically specific, but issues such as whether or not your concerns are justified, whether these concerns resonate or make sense to others in the same situation, and whether the support seeker is doing the right thing. Such information-seeking behavior on the part of the patient has resulted in the creation of hundreds of disease specific sites. For example, the website Patients-likeme.com has specific support and information resources for people with disorders or diseases ranging from ALS (Lou Gehrig's disease) to bipolar disorder and depression. These venues serve many medical and psychosocial functions for the patient and their family.

| **E-patients**

Patients who utilize technology for social support and social networking resources that are specific to their disease or medical situation.

© Jenny Sturm/Shutterstock.com

e-patients seek online information and sometimes social network sites to access resources that are specific to their disease or medical situation.

E-Training

Training and development for new employees is perhaps one of the most recurring, unpredictable, and expensive pursuits that hospitals must undertake. The amount of time and money involved in teaching healthcare professionals at all levels is vast and requires a degree of consistency to ensure that the same information gets relayed to the different personnel in the same way. One of the most effective ways to do this is through technology. E-learning is a type of learning that is technology dependent and does not require face-to-face interaction, as is necessary in traditional learning environments. According to Carbonaro, King, Taylor, Satzinger, Snart, and Drummond (2008), computer-based technology is a vital element for effective teaching of the necessary skills and knowledge required to educate clinically competent healthcare students. Such manifestations of technology can take the form of computer courses available that may include *continuing medical education* (CME) requirements for computer-based simulations of particular situations and procedures. In fact, computer-based simulation can assist in the development of both technical and nontechnical skills that are readily transferred to real-world practice. Most academic medical centers provide the nursing and medical student, the allied health professional, and the resident experience in simulated environments prior to experience with live patients (Mili, Barr, Harris, & Pittiglio, 2008).

Most recently there has been a movement to a more advanced type of e-learning called v-learning, which entails the user to act within a three-dimensional landscape as an avatar that serves as a virtual simulation of

| **E-learning**

A type of learning that is technology dependent and not requiring face-to-face interaction as is necessary in traditional learning environments.

| **V-learning**

Learning that entails the user to act within a three-dimensional landscape as an avatar that serves as a virtual simulation of "real-world" situations.

Computer-based simulation can assist in the development of skills that are readily transferred to real-world practice.

"real-world" situations. This type of three-dimensional experience is also known as *second life* and allows users to create entire "lives" without the consequences associated with performing such behaviors with real patients. In other words, the virtual experience is perhaps the closest thing to real-life interaction that can enable a healthcare professional or student in the health sciences to explore different approaches to situations without having the "real-life" accountability or liability. Although this technology seems as if it would be intuitively effective for teaching in the healthcare professions, no reliable data are available to confirm or deny such a finding (Linden Labs, 2008; Second Life Blogs, 2009). V-learning is indeed being utilized in many scientific communities including aerospace and engineering. Within the medical community, such technology is being utilized to instruct patients on how to perform a self-administered breast exam (Ruic, 2009) and is expected to be utilized for a variety of other health-related applications in the future.

E-Therapy

Technology of all kinds has been utilized to assist patients with disabilities and in the rehabilitation/therapeutic realm. There are literally thousands of examples of applied technology that improves the lives of people afflicted with physical and mental disorders. We will highlight one such application being used in the treatment of depression. A team of researchers from Harvard Medical School, Beth Israel-Deaconess Medical Center, and Dartmouth Medical School have developed the Virtual Space Station (Thomas, 2008). This technology can detect a person's stress, negative mood states, and fatigue, which are all indications of clinical depression. The treatment is known as **Problem Solving Treatment (PST)** and includes a multimedia approach that incorporates graphics and video featuring a psychologist who leads the patient through a problem-solving treatment algorithm and provides feedback regarding the patient's adherence to the treatment. The treatment algorithm is as follows:

1. Make a problem list.
2. Select which problem you want to work on.
3. Set goals and brainstorm how to reach the goals.
4. Look at social exchange (costs and rewards) to determine the benefits and costs of any possible solution.
5. Create an action plan.
6. Implement the action plan.

Using such technology to address a growing social problem such as depression can have a significant impact on the availability of treatment and on how that treatment is administered. To put this in perspective, approximately 31% of patients who visit a primary care provider display symptoms of depression. This technologically administered treatment can take place in a physician's office or in the privacy of the patient's home. Furthermore, this technology can enable people who are depressed and in remote locations or in locations where there is a shortage of mental health professionals to have access to treatment (Sackett, 1997). The applicability of this system goes beyond the treatment of depression and can potentially be adapted to treat many psychosocial problems. The patient can be provided with a flash drive that will run the appropriate treatment program on any standard computer, thus providing the patient with control over the information and the subsequent treatment process.

Handheld Technology

Just as the mobile phone has revolutionized the way people communicate and relate to one another, smart phone technology may very well do the same for the practice of health care. The **smart phone** is a communication device that is able to transmit data and images through time and space. The word "Smart" is an acronym for **S**elf-**M**onitoring, **A**nalysis, and **R**eporting **T**echnology. Physicians and clinics in remote areas are now able to transmit data to distant sites and, through telemedicine, be guided through difficult clinical situations and scenarios in real time. Something as basic as an x-ray is now on digital scanning systems known as a Picture Archiving and Communication System (PACS) and can be transmitted via Smart phone technology. Before such technology was available, films were created for the x-ray image without a digital record. Such films would have to be signed out, transported to each healthcare practitioner, and then returned to the place of origin. This process could take hours, if not days. Today, this process can take seconds. The two platforms of computers and cell phones are rapidly converging, and the Smart phone is an early manifestation of this technological convergence.

In an everyday application of Smart phone technology, a healthcare provider, a patient's family, and a nurse manager for an insurance company can all use Smart phone technology to keep track of appointments and the outcomes of those appointments. In the case of chronic diseases such as

| Smartphone
A communication device that is able to transmit data and images through time and space. SMART is an acronym for Self-Monitoring, Analysis, and Reporting Technology.

hypertension and diabetes, this technology can monitor medication schedules and other vital patient information (DeAvila, 2010). Such monitoring can afford greater independence for senior citizens and those suffering from chronic disease. Researchers believe that Smart phone technology can serve as a cognitive assistant to the elderly, who have diminishing cognitive skills and frequently suffer from forgetfulness (Burdette, Herchline, & Olher, 2008). More specifically, there are three Smart phone applications that can serve an assisting function for the patient. First is **mobile patient care assistant (MPCA),** which provides the user with reminders to perform necessary tasks. Second, a **general reminder system (GRS)** reminds people when to take medications, attend physician's appointments, and so on. The GRS can also be equipped with a mobile bar code scanner that is attached to the Smart phone to verify whether the patient is taking the correct medication. The third application is the **augmented awareness system (AAS),** which serves an environmental function controlling household appliances, lighting, doors, and monitoring abilities such as signaling when a visitor is at the door.

Perhaps one of the most versatile applications for Smart technology is the **smart card.** This credit card-shaped device contains a small microprocessing chip embedded within it that can serve innumerable functions for the user (Smart Card Alliance, 2010). Such a technology should reduce medical errors in that the card will contain all of your relevant medical history and medications and establish your identity, yet it is protected by security features such as a personal identification number, fingerprint, or iris scan so that use and the information contained therein is restricted to the user. For example, when a patient arrives at a physician's office or hospital, a simple swipe of the smart card (after proper identification authorization) will bring up all of the patient's information, insurance information, name and location of your physician, and

mobile patient care assistant (MPCA)

A smart phone application that provide users with reminders to perform a necessary task or tasks.

How will technology change the way you check in for an appointment at your doctor's office?

© Tyler Olson/Shutterstock.com

the like. Such a technology will also offer the patient immediate access to his or her medical records. Similar to the check-in process options people have at an airport, the use of smart card check-in will circumvent long waiting times and ensure proper medical record information. It is amazing that 10 out of every 17 deaths from medical error are a result of identity errors (wrong patients) (Hess, 2005). In summary, Smart phones, smart cards, and smart hospitals are the future of healthcare delivery, with technological advances occurring daily.

Social Media

In 2015, PEW 87% of the population uses the Internet. Of these users, younger users tend to attain medical information through social media significantly more than older populations. Approximately 97% of the 18–29 year olds using social media. By far the greatest use of medical social media is to gather health information (PEW 2007/2012) and approximately 35% of U.S. adults try to ascertain what their diagnosis may be through online methods (PEW 2013). It is not just patients that use social media but 94% of physicians communicate with their patients through cell calls, e-mails and remote medical monitoring devices (Terry, 2001). The use of social media can be quite tricky in terms of protected health information thus requiring secure portal access and encryption systems such that the provider is complicit with HIPAA laws [HIPAA, 1996] where there are consistent standards of documentation, handling and privacy. In order to avoid HIPAA offenses, there are four critical areas of compliance that involve secure data centers, encryptions, recipient authentication and audit controls (Wieczorek, 2015).

Text messaging can be a very efficient asynchronous means of communication but it must be safe and compliant thus it requires a very sophisticated security system (Brooks, 2015). The British Medical Association in 2011, advised all physicians to avoid Facebook, Linkedin, Twitter, et al. As a case in point, the *Boston Globe* (2011) reported a Rhode Island physician violated HIPAA regulations for posting patient information on her Facebook page and she was fired as well as reprimanded by the State Medical Board after she posted (Facebook) about a trauma patient.

In summary, professionalism requires that the healthcare provider never use unencrypted information for communication or any type of discussion about protected health information (Wieczorek, 2015).

Biometrics

In a 2010/2011 survey from the Computer Security Institute, it is noted that only about 20% of those surveyed are in any way dependent upon biometric technology (Richardson, 2010). Current evidence reveals that individuals are mostly dependent upon passwords and PINs.

Biometrics is the study of biological features unique to individuals. The most prominent technologies are fingerprint, facial identification, and iris (the colored part of one's eye) identification. A fourth technology, palm vein

Biometrics
The study of biological features unique to individuals.

matching, is currently under evaluation. These methods have been evaluated and deemed valid by the U.S. National Institute of Standards and Technology (Biometrics, 2010). Biometric technology is affordable, portable, and safe. Fingerprint, voice and facial recognition were considered gold standards but they are not foolproof. For example, with the development of the iPhone 5S and its associated finger scanning technology, was compromised by a German hacker who was able to create 3-dimension replicas of fingerprints using high definition photo scanning (Rockwell, 2013). The person being evaluated via biometric assessment is not encumbered with having to carry identification documents or devices with identification chips (e.g., smart cards). Biometrics is already used in certain governmental agencies and is being implemented in several healthcare systems throughout the United States. Biometrics will serve to further improve patient safety by ensuring accuracy regarding the identity of a particular person regardless of cultural, language, or other differences that can impair accurate identification.

Telehealth

Telehealth refers to the practice of healthcare via a satellite link between fixed stations to deliver healthcare that would otherwise need to be performed in a face-to-face environment. Telemedicine literally means "healing at a distance" through the Latin "medicus" and Greek tele (Strehlee & Shabde, 2006). This is particularly relevant in that chronic illnesses are expected to spiral between now and 2023 with a 40% increase in heart disease and a 50% increase in both cancer and diabetes (partnership to fight chronic disease, 2009).

When looking at a cohort of 3000 patients with congestive heart failure, using telehealth as well as decision support software, readmissions were reduced by 44% and the program generated a cost savings of more than $10 million over a six year period (Kulshreshtha et al., 2010).

Consider this example, communication between a remote health clinic and major university teaching hospital is easily established, making diagnosis and consultation more cost and time efficient. This type of medicine is especially effective in the treatment of chronic diseases such as diabetes (i.e., high blood glucose) and hypertension (i.e., high blood pressure). Telehealth is especially effective because it can also allow for the practitioner to monitor, diagnose, and consult with the patient remaining in their home or within their living facility without the burden of having to drive great distances for such services. This is especially important regarding chronic diseases in light of the fact that 80% of all healthcare costs and 7 out of every 10 deaths in this country are attributable to either diabetes or hypertension (Lohr, 2009).

Perhaps one of the major drawbacks of telemedicine, beyond technological considerations, would be the fee structure for healthcare practitioners who practice such medicine. Currently, healthcare practitioners work in a fee-for-service healthcare system, and telemedicine is currently not reimbursable. However,

Medicare is instituting a pilot program investigating ways for reimbursement that are based on health outcomes regardless of the mode in which care is delivered (e.g., telemedicine versus face to face) with a special emphasis on treatment of chronic disease. This new type of reimbursement is known as **pay-for-performance** and is predicated on improved health outcomes as opposed to simply rendering a service regardless of outcome.

Robotics in Healthcare Delivery

Although robots and robotic technology have been used for decades in the production and manufacturing of durable medical goods and pharmaceuticals, this technology has experienced little experimentation in the everyday delivery of health care. Is it possible for robots to deliver health care to patients in a way that adequately substitutes for human interaction and care? One such effort is that of *Pearl the Nurse*. Pearl is an anthropomorphic robot, or a robot that looks human (Figure 14.2).

anthropomorphic robot

A robot that looks human.

Pearl was developed through a collaboration of researchers at the University of Michigan, University of Pittsburgh, Stanford University, and Carnegie Mellon University with the realization that by the year 2020, 50 million people will be older than age 65 and in need of care from an industry that will sorely lack qualified healthcare professionals. Pearl is the second prototype to Flo—the first anthropomorphic robot, named after Florence Nightingale, that looked much like an alien (similar to the creature from the movie E.T.) whose ears spun every time she was thinking.

Pearl, however, has a more human look with a pearly sheen to her skull and an electronic mouth that is able to display four settings ranging from a big smile to sticking out her tongue. She has eyebrows to enhance her expression, and she blinks every 5 seconds with her eyes twitching slightly to give her a more natural look. Pearl is equipped with sonar detectors, laser range finder, mapping software, and two separate computers to calculate where she is to go next. Some of her other navigational skills include the ability to assist people who are lost or confused and need help finding their way to destinations such as the cafeteria, their room, and so on. She has also been used in chronic care settings. This amazing machine can identify any conflicts regarding what the patient is supposed to do in terms of daily activities and what the patient actually does. When such discrepancies appear, Pearl makes decisions about when to remind the patient about the situation. With a cost of about $100,000, such robot caregivers are far from cost effective in terms of being implemented system-wide. However, according to Dr. Martha Pollack, future generations of such robots will be able to do the following: (a) Remind elderly patients to visit the bathroom, take medication, drink, eat, or see the physician; (b) connect patients with caregivers through the Internet; (c) collect video and audio data and monitor the well-being of the patient such as in the case of chronic disease, including heart failure and sugar diabetes; (d) and manipulate objects with an articulated arm. Such objects may include kitchen appliances such as a refrigerator, washing machine, and microwave ovens. Such a feature is especially important in light of the fact that *arthritis* is the main reason that elderly

Courtesy of Personal Robotic Assistants for the Elderly Project

figure 14.2

Is it possible for robots to deliver adequate healthcare to patients?

individuals give up independent living (Pollack et al., 2002). However promising, robots can never replace the empathetic touch or clinical intuition of a human nurse. Right now robots have difficulty operating in complex and unpredictable work environments such as that experienced in a fast-paced acute care hospital. Further, they are incapable of synthesizing information in novel situations the way that a human nurse is able to.

Another arena in health care for robotic use is within the operating room. More specifically, the well-known *da Vinci surgical robotic system* is of great assistance in minimally invasive (laparoscopic) surgery. Knight and Escobar (2014) analyzed the cost of robotic surgery particularly in doing hysterectomies [removing of a woman's uterus]. Whereas the morbidity was similar, the robotic technology costs an additional $2189.00 compared to the traditional laparoscope used in minimally invasive surgery. **Minimally invasive surgery** utilizes small incisions that often result in decreased pain, decreased recovery time, and shorter hospital stays. Another similar system is known as *Penelope,* which was once used for surgical procedures; however, system complications rendered it less useful for this purpose so the system was reconfigured to wash, sterilize, and count surgical instruments.

Taken as a whole (although robots such as *Pearl* cannot substitute for the human aspect of health care and the special healing relationship that commonly develops between the patient and their provider) there is added value to the use of such technology. An example of this would be Palomar Pomerado Health, a hospital system in San Diego, CA, that was scheduled to open a brand-new, $917 million facility in 2012. In this facility, there will be video camera-equipped robots that will allow physicians and nurses to

© Photographee.eu/Shutterstock.com

No matter how "lifelike" they can be made, robots will never replace the empathetic touch of a human nurse.

make virtual rounds with patients from afar. The efficiency of these robots is yet to be determined, but the annual maintenance costs to the hospital will be approximately $96,000 for each robot.

The Future of Healthcare Communication: Concluding Thoughts

The study of communication in the everyday practice of medicine concerns the complexities of individuals, relationships, organizations, and political and social structures. To say the least, this is a difficult task that must be focused and based in scientific inquiry. It is on these assumptions that we believe the future of the study of communication in the everyday practice of medicine is best referred to as medical communication. Medical communication is communication which involves **contextual communication**, **medical informatics**, and **health communication.** Contextual communication is the pragmatic approach to the daily navigation through the interpersonal encounters according to the context between all healthcare providers, their patients, and their colleagues. Medical informatics is the computer-based transference, retrieval, and storage of information. Health communication is the multi-channel dissemination (e.g., face to face, print, radio, video, and Internet) that is rhetorical in nature because its main functions are to inform and persuade.

We firmly believe that the future of medical communication will be a dynamic combination of these three subdivisions with the focus of all three being receiver dependent. However, to achieve clarity and fulfillment of the

medical communication

The pragmatic approach to the everyday navigation through and the interpersonal encounters between all healthcare providers, their patients, and their colleagues.

translational research

Research that includes collaboration from two or more disciplines focusing on a specific idea, concept, or problem.

different objectives set forth by this tripartite of medical communication, there needs to be translational research (i.e., research that includes collaborators from two or more disciplines focusing on a specific idea, concept, or problem) between healthcare practitioners and researchers in the social sciences to create the concepts and processes that increase satisfaction, reduce liability, and reduce overall cost to our healthcare system. Dr. Eric Topol, a cardiologist who is Professor of Innovative Medicine at the Scripts Institute in California in his new book, The Patient Will See You Now, (Topol, 2015) feels that the future will be controlled by the patient. The concept of "physician knows best" in his opinion is gone forever, that a SMART phone with proper apps will substitute and transmit any relevant physiologic data to the physician without the patient being present in person. Sick people will be cared for with their own portable sensors. There will be web pages with sequenced genes that can determine the genetic pattern which will distinguish who might or might not benefit from a particular drug. There will be small computers that can be swallowed and travel through your body to track any health data in real time such that major catastrophes like a heart attack, diabetes or even cancer can be detected before they happen according to genomic data. Clearly, patients who advocate for their own health rather than being passive fair better, but physicians are trusted counselors and people who are ill have a primal need to be cared for.

In a *New York Times* editorial by Abigail Zugger, MD, January 5, 2015, the author counters that in spite of translational research and computerization of the patient, "sick people have a primal need to be cared for, almost always, the sickest patients find that relinquishing the tough decisions to someone else brings huge relief... there are many wonderful things to do in this world other than keeping track of your organs. Sometimes it makes sense to have someone do it for you" [page D5, *The New York Edition*].

As you have read through this book—*Medical Communication: Defining the Discipline*—you have probably come across concepts that were familiar, common sense, strange, novel, unthinkable, and unimaginable. The vast majority of the concepts and research discussed within this book were the fruit of the translational research and collaboration between a surgeon and communication researcher. We believe that this approach to the study of communication in the everyday practice of medicine is the best way to improve the humanity involved in the process of healing others and to reducing errors.

Questions for Discussion/Review

1. Compare and contrast the electronic health record (EHR) with the personal health record (PHR). Do you have experience with either of these record types? Explain.

2. Explain some of the complications with implementing electronic medical records (EMR) and EHRs.

3. Explain the three security dimensions of the CIA triad and how each is distinct from one another. Have you ever witnessed a breeching of a patient's or your own privacy regarding medical records in any of these dimensions? Explain.

4. Compare and contrast the two types of cryptography used in the electronic transfer of medical information.
5. Discuss some of the legal implications involved in using electronic medical records. In your opinion, can these issues ever be resolved?
6. Explain how patients (e-patients) utilize technology when seeking out health information. Describe the types of technology that you use when seeking out health information.
7. Explain Smart phone technology and how some of the applications of the technology are being used to assist patients and improve patient care.
8. Explain how telehealth can be especially beneficial for healthcare professionals in rural areas.
9. Discuss how robotics is changing the way health care is delivered. Do you think that there will be a loss of the "human aspects" of medicine as a result of implementing such technology?
10. Define medical communication, and explain the three dimensions that make up such a discipline.

References

AHIMA eHIM Work Group. (2005). Defining the legal health record. "The legal process in electronic health records." *Journal of the American Health Information Management Association, 76,* 96A-D.

Adler, Milstein, J., Green, C.E., Bates, D.W. (2013). A Survey Analysis Suggest that Electronic Health Records Will Yield Revenue Gains for Some Practices and Losses for Many. *Health Affairs*, 32(3); 562–570.

Altman, J. H., Reich, P., Kelly, M. J., & Rogeres, M. P. (1980). Sounding board. Patients who read their hospital charts. *New England Journal of Medicine, 302,* 169–171.

Anwar, K., & O'Mahony, F. (2000). Patient access to their records: Rights or risks? *British Journal of Obstetrics and Gynecology, 107,* 141–142.

Benabio, J. (2013). Commentary: Friending patients on Facebook. ACS Surgery News. Retrieved on June 26, 2015 from http://www.acssurgerynews.com/opinions/editorials/single-article/commentary-friending-patients-on-facebook/812e395453dbecdcc2a72c9b371a8afa.html

Biometrics. (2010). *Eye controls.* Retrieved January 3, 2011, from http://www.eye-controls.com/technology.

Brooks, (2015). "Healthcare Texting in a HIPPA Compliant Environment: Texting Speeds Communication but Could Put You at Risk," Andrew A. Brooks, MD, American Academy of Orthopedic Surgeons. Retrieved on June 24, 2015 from http://www.aaos.org/news/aaosnow/aug12/managing5.asp

Burdette, S.D., Herchline, T.E., & Olher, R. (2008). Practicing Medicine in a Technologic Age: Using SMART Phones in Clinical Practice, *Clinical Infectious Disease, 47,* pp. 117–122.

Bush, G. W. (2004). *Executive order: 13335. Incentives for the use of health information technology and establishing the position of the national health information technology coordinator*. Retrieved January 3, 2011, from http://findarticles.com/p/articles/mi_m2889/is_18_40/ai_117325469/.

Carbonaro, M., King, S., Taylor, E., Satzinger, F., Snart, F., & Drummond, J. (2008). Integration of e-learning technologies in an interprofessional health science course. *Medical Teacher, 30,* 25.

Carnegie Mellon University. (2010). *Cover story: Pearl the NurseBot helps the elderly at home.* Retrieved January 3, 2011, from http://www.carnegiemellontoday.com/article.asp?aid=155.

Chapter 8, *Focusing on Vulnerable Populations*; Retrieved on May 26, 2015 from http://govinfo .library.unt.edu/hcquality/meetings/mar12/papch08.htm.

Conaboy, C. (2011). For doctors, social media a tricky case. *Boston Globe*. Retrieved on June 26, 2015 from http://www.boston.com/lifestyle/health/articles/2011/04/20/for_doctors_ social_media_a_tricy_case/

Congressional Budget Office. (2007). *The long-term outlook for health care spending*. Retrieved January 3, 2011, from http://www.cbo.gov/ftpdocs/87xx/doc8758/11-13-LT-Health.pdf.

Davis, F., Bagozzi, R. & Warshaw, P. (1989). "User acceptance of computer technology: A comparison of two theoretical models", *Management Science 358*; 982–1003.

DeAvila, J. (2010). How's your health? Wall Street Journal. Retrieved on June 26, 2015 from http://www.wsj.com/articles/SB10001424052748704259304575043583691241828

Dougherty, M. The 10 Security Domains (AHIMA Practice Brief). JAHIMA. Retrieved on June 26, 2015 from http://www.advancedmedrec.com/images/The10SecurityDomains.pdf.

Elbourne, D., Richardson, M., Chalmer, S. I., Waterhouse, I., & Holt, E. (1987). The Newbury Maternity Care study: A randomized controlled trial to assess a policy of women holding their own obstetric records. *British Journal of Obstetrics and Gynecology, 94,* 612–619.

Electronic Health Records. (2010).

Feld, S. (2009). *Repairing the health care system: The electronic medical record (EMR) stimulus fiasco: Part III.* Retrieved January 3, 2011, from http://stanleyfeldmdmace.typepad .com/repairing_the_healthcare_/2009/05/the-electronic-medical-record-emr-stimulus-fiasco-part-3.html.

Ford, E. W., Menachemi, N., & Phillips, M. T. (2006). Predicting the adoption of electronic health records by physicians: When will health care be paperless? *Journal of the American Medical Information Association, 13,* 106–112.

Fox, S, Zickuhr, K, & Smith, A. (2009). Twitter and Status Updating, Fall 2009. Retrieved on June 26, 2015 from http://www.pewinternet.org/2009/10/21/twitter-and-status-updating-fall-2009/

Furnell, S. & Clarke, N. (2014). Biometrics: Making the Mainstream, *Technology Today*, 2014(1); 5–9.

Gogolin, J. (2010). *Electronic health records: Has their time come?* Retrieved January 3, 2011, from http://poland.emc.com/leadership/business-view/electronic-health-records.htm.

Gould, M. & Brown, E. (2006). *Open source software: A primer for health care leaders.* RetrievedJanuary3,2011,fromhttp://www.chcf.org/publications/2006/03/open-source-software-a-primer-for-health-care-leaders.

Greenhalgh, T., Potts, H. W. W., Wong, G., Bark, P., & Swinglehurst, D. (2009). Tensions and paradoxes in electronic patient record research: A systematic literature review using the meta-narrative method. *Milbank Quarterly, 87,* 729–788.

Harris, S. (2002). *CISSP certification (CISSP Certification All-in-one, Exam Guide, Boot camp edition.)* Berkley, CA, McGraw Hill/Osborne.

Hess, R. (2005). Identity crisis. *For the Record, 17,* 34.

HIPAA Act of 1996. Retrieved on June 26, 2015 from: http://www.hhs.gov/ocr/privacy/hipaa/ administrative/statute/hipaastatuteped.pdfHistory of OSI. (2010). *Open source initiative.* Retrieved January 3, 2011, from http://www.opensource.org/history.

http://www.hipaa-101.com/

Jha, A. K., DesRoches, C. M., Campbell, E. G., Donelan, K., Rao, S. R. & Ferris, T. G., *et al.* (2009). Use of electronic health records in U.S. hospitals. *New England Journal of Medicine, 360,* 1628–1638.

Kieschnik, T., &Raymond, B. (2011). *How Can Health IT Promote Health Equity in Patient-Centered Care, A Round Table Discussion*. March 7-8, 2011, Washington, D.C., Kaiser Permanente Institute for Health Policy.

Knight, J. & Escobar, P. F., (2014). *Cost and Robotic Surgery in Gynecology in the Journal of Obstetrics and Gynecologic Research*, Volume 40, 12–17, January 2014.

Konrad, W. (2009). Some caveats about keeping your own electronic health records. *New York Times*, April 17, 2009. Retrieved January 3, 2011, from http://www.nytimes.com/2009/04/ 18/health/18patient.html.

Kulshreshtha, A., Kevdar, J., Goyal, A., Halperne, F., & Watson, A.G. (2010). Use of Remote Monitoring to Improve Outcomes in Patients with Heart Failure: A Pilot Trial. *International Journal of Telemedicine Applications.*

Kurtz, R. L., & Vines, R. D. (2003). *CISSP prep guide (Gold edition).* Indianapolis, IN: Wiley.

Linden Labs. (2008). *Second life usage demographics.* Retrieved January 3, 2011, from http://www.bananaverse.com/2008/05/07/second-life-usage-demographics/.

Lohr, S. (2009). *GE and Intel working on remote monitors to provide home health care.* Retrieved January 3, 2011, from http://www.nytimes.com/2009/04/03/health/03health.html?scp=1&sq=GE%20and%20Intel%20working%20on%20remote%20monitors%20to%20provide%20home%20health%20care&st=cse.

McDonald, C. J., Schadow, G., Barnes, M., Dexter, P., Overhange, J. M., & Mamlin, B., et al. (2003). Open-source software in medical informatics, why, how, and what. *International Journal of Medical Information, 69,* 175–184.

Mili, F., Barr, J., Harris, M., & Pittiglio, L. (2008). Nursing training: 3D game with learning objectives. *First International Conference on Advances in Computer-Human Interaction* (pp. 236–242). Sainte Luce: IEEE Computer Society.

National Center for Health Statistics. (2010). *Centers for Disease Control.* Retrieved January 3, 2011, from http://www.cdc.gov/nchs.

Orszag, P. R. (2008). *The overuse, underuse, and misuse of health care.* Before the Committee on Finance, United States Senate, July 17, 2008, Congressional Budget Office, Washington, DC. Retrieved January 3, 2011, from http://www.cbo.gov/ftpdocs/95xx/doc9567/07-17-Healthcare_Testimony.pdf.

Partnership to Fight Chronic Disease. *The Impact of Chronic Disease on U.S. Health and Prosperity: A Collection of Statistics and Commentary* [Internet, Washington, D.C., pfcd; 2009 @ http://www.fightchronicdisease.org/sites/fightchronicdisease.org/files/docs/2009AlmanacofChronicDisease_updated81009.pdf.

Pollack, M, Brown, L., Colbry, D., Orosz, C., Peintner, B., Ramakrishnan, S., Engberg, S., Matthews, J., Dunbar-Jacob, J., McCarthy, C., Thrun, S., Montemerlo, M., Pineau, J., & Roy, N. (2002). Pearl: A mobile Robotic Assistant for the Elderly. Retrieved on June 26, 2015 from http://www.ai.sri.com/~peintner/papers/aaai02wkshp.pdf

Recovery Act. American Recovery and Reinvestment Act. (2009). Retrieved on June 26, 2015 from http://www.recovery.gov/arra/About/Pages/The_Act.aspx

Pew Research Center. U.S. Smartphone Use in 2015. Retrieved on June 24, 2015 from http://www.pewinternet.org/2015/04/01/us-smartphone-use-in-2015

Richardson, R. 2009 (2010). 15th Annual 2010/2011 Computer Crime and Security Survey. Computer Security Institute, Retrieved June 24, 2015, from http://gatton.uky.edu/FACULTY/PAYNE/ACC324/CSISurvey2010.pdf.

Rockwell, M., (2013). *The Fight Against Biometric Spoofing, FCW,* retrieved at http://fcw.com/articles-2013/10/28-biometric-spoofing.aspx?p=1, retrieved 4-17-15

Ross, S. E., & Lin, C. (2003). The effects of promoting patient access to medical records: A review. *Journal of the American Medical Informatics Association, 10,* 129–138.

RPMS HER for Community Health. (2010). *Community Health Network of West Virginia.* Retrieved January 3, 2011, from http://www.chnwv.org/Home/tabid/36/Default.aspx.

Ruic, R. (2009). *How the Internet is changing health care: From Twitter to Second Life to Facebook, patients now have access to more health information that ever before. Forbes.* Retrieved January 3, 2011, from http://forbes.com/2009/07/30/health-wellness-internet-lifestyle-health-online-facebook.html.

Sackett, B. L. (1997). Evidence-based medicine. *Seminars in Perinatology, 21,* 3–5.

SANS Institute. (2009). *The top cyber security risks.* Retrieved January 3, 2011, from http://www.sans.org/top-cyber-security-risks/.

Second Life Blogs. (2009). *M. Linden's interview with the BBC.* Retrieved January 3, 2011, from http://blogs.secondlife.com/community/press/blog/2009/11/20.

Smart Card Alliance. (2010). *Healthcare applications.* Retrieved January 3, 2011, from http://www.smartcardalliance.org/pages/smart-cards-applications-healthcare.

Strehlee, M., & Shabde, N. (2006). One Hundred Years of Telemedicine: Does This New Technology Have a Place in Pediatrics? *Archives of Diseases in Children,* 91 (12); 956-959.

Terry N., 2001. E-mail patients? Don't be nervous. Do be careful. Med Econ 78:83, 86-88, Terry, N. & Francis, L. (2007). *Ensuring the privacy and confidentiality of electronic health records.* Retrieved on June 26, 2015 from http://illinoislawreview.org/wp-content/ ilr-content/articles/2007/2/Terry.pdf

Thomas, B. (2008). September 24th National Space Biomedical Research Institute. Retrieved January 3, 2011, from http://democrats.science.house.gov/Media/File/Commdocs/hearings/2008/Space/24apr/Pickens_Testimony.pdf

Topol, Eric (2015). *The Patient Will See You Now*, Basic Books. New York, NY.

U.S. Department of Health & Human Services. (2000). *Standards for privacy of individually identifiable health information*, billing code 4150-04M, Federal Register, 82461-82829 (IV/V CFR parts, 160-164).

U.S. Department of Health & Human Services. (2010). *Health information privacy. HIPAA* administrative simplification statute and rules. Retrieved January 3, 2011, from http:// www.hhs.gov/ocr/privacy/hipaa/administrative/index.html.

Walsh, T. (2003). *Selecting and implementing security.* Retrieved January 3, 2011, from http:// campus.ahima.org/audio/2008/RB011708.pdf.

Webb, M. (2009). Considering an EMR? Electronic medical record implementation. *The Bulletin of the American Association of Neurologic Surgeons.* Retrieved June 26, 2015 from http://www.aans.org/en/AANS%20and%20JNSPG%20Publications/AANS%20 Neurosurgeon/AANS%20Neurosurgeon%20Issues/2009/2009%20-%20Issue%201/ Considering%20an%20EMR%20Electronic%20Medical%20Record%20Implementation .aspx

Wieczorek, S. M. (2015). Risk Factors in Social Media, 35th Annual Respiratory Conference at the Slopes, March 4 2015.

Wright, K. B. (2002). Social support within an on-line cancer community: An assessment of emotional support, perceptions of advantages and disadvantages and motives for using the community from a communication perspective. *Journal of Applied Communication Research, 30,* 195–209.

Zugger, A., Patient Health Thyself: The Patient Will See You Now, Envisions a New Era of Digitally Perfected Care, January 5 2015, *New York Times* at http://www.newyorktimes. com/2015/01/06/science/the-patient-will-see-you-now-envisions-a-new-era-of-digitally-perfected-care retrieved 1-13-15.

Glossary

Abstractness. Refers to the level of concreteness of the information and the capacity of the person to think in abstract terms.

Abuse. Behavior that results in humiliation or degradation or shows a lack of dignity or respect for another person.

Accentuating. A function of nonverbal communication that reflects the use of nonverbal behavior to emphasize particular points of a message.

Accident or Overt Human Aggression. A type of naturally caused illness and includes auto accidents, gunshot wounds, and stab wounds.

Acculturation Phase. A phase of the medical internship process that reflects the newcomer becoming a member of the new culture and starts to reflect the verbal and nonverbal behaviors of the new culture.

Acknowledgment. Openly identifying the offense or mistake that occurred and who made the mistake.

Active Listening Skills. Necessary training skills reflecting the ability to interact and listen to many different types of people at different levels of expertise and organizational status. Such skills include listening for comprehension and paraphrasing the input of others into the overall theme of the training module.

Adaptation. Whether or not the information or stimuli is useful or adaptable to the receivers' needs.

Adaptors. A type of kinesic behavior that refers to behavior that people use to "cope" with different situations.

Adjustment Phase. The phase of the medical internship process reflecting the newcomer becoming more comfortable with his or her surroundings and ability to successfully navigate through the new environment and culture.

Adult Basic Education (ABE). Adult education that primarily targets reading, writing, and math skills that are at high school level or below.

Adult Education. Any education that is targeted toward adult populations; also known as andragogy.

Advance Directives. A general term that refers to a patient's oral or written instructions about their future medical care in the event that they become unable to communicate those instructions by themselves.

Adventurousness. A personality trait that is the degree to which a person likes to experience new and novel situations.

Adverse Event. Any injury caused by medical care. It does not imply negligence or poor quality of care; rather, it is an undesirable outcome resulting from some aspect of diagnosis or therapy; not an underlying disease process.

Air Producing Mechanism. A function of the respiration process of language production needed to produce language by providing currents of air to the vocal cords.

Affect Displays. A type of kinesic behavior that refers to voluntary and involuntary movements that reveal a person's emotional display.

Affection. A motivation for communicating where people communicate to express caring or concern or to let others know you appreciate them.

Affirming Communication. Communicating in a way that verbally and nonverbally validates the self-concept of another person.

Agreeableness. A dimension of the big five that refers to the degree to which people are compassionate, pleasant, good-natured, warm, and sympathetic.

Aggressive Communication. Any interpersonal behavior that applies force physically or symbolically in order, minimally, to dominate and perhaps damage or, maximally, to defeat and perhaps destroy the locus of attack.

Alternative Medicine. Non-mainstream treatments that are not proven by scientific inquiry nor evidence-based inquiry and are sometimes chosen by patients over the more orthodox treatments.

Alternatives. Part of the NBAR acronym for effectively obtaining informed consent, referring to the risks and benefits associated with the alternatives to the proposed procedure.

Alzheimer's Disease. A degenerative neurological disease that generally affects people age 65 and older. One contributing factor to the disease is believed to be a beta-amyloid protein.

Ambiguous Messages. Messages that are imprecise and ripe for misunderstanding.

Amiable Style. A communication style that reflects being high in responsiveness and low in assertiveness.

Amoral. Something that is without moral characteristic.

Amygdala. A part of the brain associated with friendship, love, affection, fear, rage, and aggression and identifying possible danger in an effort for self-preservation *(fight or flight)*.

Analytic Style. A communicator style that reflects being low in responsiveness and low in assertiveness.

Anchoring Bias. When a person latches onto the features of a patient's presentation that suggests a specific diagnosis.

Andragogy. The art and science of adult learning.

Androgyny. A person's tendency to appropriately use both masculine and feminine communication styles.

Angular Gyrus. A part of the human brain that stores memory for words and written language.

Animist Culture. A cultural belief in the existence of spirits that are separate from the body.

Anterior Cingulate Cortex. A part of the limbic system that, when stimulated, elicits vocal activity.

Anterior Temporal Cortex. A higher level cortex, which, along with the prefrontal cortex, is responsible for the expression of emotion during social interaction and assists in the ability to remain rational as opposed to being entirely emotionally driven in our behavior.

Anterior Thalamic Nucleus. A part of the human brain associated with emotion. It is responsible for emotional reactivity.

Anthropomorphic Robot. A robot that looks human.

Apathetic Moderate Argumentative. A person who has a low motivation to approach arguments and a low motivation to avoid arguments.

Apology. An expression of remorse (deep sense of regret), shame (failing to live up to one's own standards), forbearance (commitment not to repeat), and humility (state of being humble, not arrogant).

Application Stage. Feedback stage reflecting the actual implementation of the improvement plan into the everyday practice of healthcare.

Appreciative Inquiry (AI). A newer approach to organizational development that focuses on doing things right and using those things to build the future of the organization.

Appreciative Listening. When we listen in order to form a connection to the other person or object (e.g., music or poetry).

Appropriateness. A dimension of communication competency that reflects the ability to engage in polite and socially acceptable behaviors when communicating.

Arcuate Fasciculus. A dense fiber tract that connects Broca's area and Wernicke's area.

Argument Approach. A motivation that reflects the degree to which we approach argumentative situations.

Argument Avoidance. A motivation that reflects the degree to which we avoid argumentative situations.

Argument Skills Deficiency Model. People resort to verbal aggression because of a lack of motivation to engage in argument and a lack of skill in creating a cogent argument.

Argumentativeness. A generally stable trait that predisposes an individual in communication situations to advocate positions on controversial issues and to attack verbally the positions other people take on these issues.

Articulation. A component of the voicing mechanism that depends on the throat, palate, tongue, lips, and teeth.

Artifacts. A nonverbal communication factor referring to things that people wear in addition to clothes that can communicate information to another person.

Asperger's Syndrome. Part of the autism spectrum where the person has social and communication problems but is considered to be high functioning because they often show a normal or superior intelligence.

Assertiveness. A global trait where a person tends to be interpersonally dominant and forceful in order to achieve personal goals in socially appropriate ways. The degree to which people are able to stand up for their position or rights.

Assertiveness Continuum. A gender orientation range that reflects the degree of a person's masculinity.

Assigned Power (Legitimate Power). Power that is officially granted to you by some overarching organization or authority.

Asymmetrical Cryptography. Transformation of information using different keys, one to encipher and another to decipher the messages.

Attention. A focused type of consciousness resulting in a heightened sensitivity to stimuli.

Attention Deficit Hyperactivity Disorder (ADHD). A disorder of focus and behavior associated with a decrease in frontal lobe activity.

Attention Span. Part of selective attention referring to the amount and intensity a person can exert on incoming stimuli.

Attractiveness. The degree of appeal a person has regarding physical, task, and social qualities.

Attribute As Sufficient Cause Model. A model of stigma that reflects the qualities or traits seen as deficient or discrediting the moral being or moral character of the affected person.

Auditory Cortex. A part of the human brain responsible for interpreting auditory information from the ears and transmitting that information to the parietal lobe. Also involved in long-term memory storage.

Augmented Awareness System (AAS). A smart phone application that serves as an environmental function controlling household appliances, lighting, and doors and monitoring abilities such as when a visitor is at the door.

Authoritarianism. A personality trait where people tend to rely on structure and rules for determining what is right and wrong.

Authority Gradient. The degree to which there is a balance of power in decision-making.

Autism. A neurological developmental disorder resulting in impairment of communication and repetitive or stereotyped patterns of behavior, interests, and actions.

Autism Spectrum. The degree of severity in the symptoms of autism characterized by different combinations of developmental factors.

Autonomics. A dimension of nonverbal behavior referring to how involuntary signs communicate a person's internal state.

Autonomy. Principle that reflects the right of the patient to make informed choices as to the nature of medical care, the alternatives available to the patient, the risks associated with the various alternatives, and the results of the suggested treatment.

Availability. A security domain ensuring that systems work promptly and service is not denied to authorized users.

Avoidance. Part of the ethnocentrism spectrum reflecting a person who wants little or nothing to do with people of other cultures.

Awareness. The radar for consciousness and is defined as the continuous monitoring of inner and outer environment such that stimuli may be registered in consciousness without being the center of focus.

Back-Stabbing. A covert and indirect conflict behavior where the destructive properties are difficult to measure or control.

Behavior. The actual laughter, smiling, guffawing, tittering, giggling, or any other reaction that is stimulated by the humorous message generated by the source (relating to humor); level 3 of training assessment concerning the degree to which the behavior of the trainee has actually changed as a result of having attended the training.

Behavior Activation System. An appetitive motivational system that activates or influences us to behave when we encounter a reward or punishment from the environment.

Behavior Inhibition System. An aversive motivational state that inhibits our behavioral response to punishment or nonrewarding or novel situations.

Behavioral Objectives. The things that the learners or trainees are expected to do or perform at the conclusion of the training.

Behaviorally Involved. An assumption of adult education where the learner engages in activities to concretize the lessons.

Beneficence. The act of doing good for your patients. A principle that reflects the primacy of the patient's welfare is paramount in the patientÐprovider relationship.

Benefits. Part of the NBAR acronym for effectively obtaining informed consent referring to the good points of having the procedure.

Biases. Part of selective perception reflecting the cognitive controls that people place on incoming stimuli that influence the interpretation of the stimuli into a desired path.

Biological Time Orientation. A time orientation based on biological preferences for time; also known as circadian rhythms.

Biometrics. The study of features unique to individuals.

Blood Oxygen Level-Dependent Contrast (BOLD). A technique used in neuroscience imaging (e.g., functional magnetic resonance imaging) that assumes changes in the oxyhemoglobin concentration of the blood reflect whether the tissue of interest either is or is not functioning.

Bodily-Kinesthetic Intelligence. A form of IQ referring to the ability to learn and execute physical movement.

Brain Death. When the brain is no longer functioning in any capacity and will never again function.

Brain Plasticity. The capacity for change or malleability of the brain.

Broaden-and-Build Theory of Positive Emotions. A theory that assumes experiences of positive emotions broaden people's momentary thought-action repertoires, which in turn serves to build their enduring personal resources ranging from physical and intellectual resources to social and psychological resources.

Broca's Aphasia. A syndrome where a person is able to comprehend language yet unable to produce the desired speech.

Broca's Area. Part of the left inferior frontal cortex responsible for speech production.

Brodmann's Classification System. A system of mapping the cerebral cortex into 50 distinct areas. Each area is classified with the letters BA followed by the specific area of the brain. For example, Broca's area is identified as BA 44-45.

Build Relationships. A goal of communication where people seek connectedness to others, build social and professional networks, and utilize them for functional purposes.

Bullying. Activity that is repeating and defined as offensive by the receiver. These behaviors are intentional, vindictive, or malicious or undermine a person or a group of people.

Burnout Syndrome. A general malaise with increased feelings of being emotionally exhausted, of detachment from both colleagues and patients, and of professional failure.

CA-Group. A dimension of communication apprehension defined as the fear or anxiety associated with communication in group settings.

CA-Interpersonal. A dimension of CA defined as the fear or anxiety associated with communication in dyadic situations.

CA-Meeting. A dimension of communication apprehension defined as the fear or anxiety associated with communication in formal meeting settings.

CA-Public. A dimension of CA defined as the fear or anxiety associated with giving a public speech.

Case Study. A training vehicle allowing the application of knowledge that was presented earlier in the training.

Cerebral Cortex. The surface of the brain that shares electrical communication with both the midbrain and the brain stem. Responsible for speech, vision, movement, and memory.

Certified Information System Security Professional (CISSP). A person credentialed through the International Information Systems Security Certification Consortium and responsible for ensuring the confidentiality, integrity, and availability of the system.

Channel. The mode with which the message is sent. The means by which a message is conveyed from the source to the receiver and concerns the five senses (hear, see, taste, touch, smell).

Chaplain. An educated listener grounded in religious philosophy with a strong belief in God and the power of prayer.

Choleric Humor. An angry type of humor associated with bile.

Chronemics. A nonverbal factor focusing on the study of time and how people use time to communicate.

Chronodynamics. A study of nonverbal behavior focusing on how people use color to communicate.

CIA Triad. Three dimensions of security domains (i.e., confidentiality, integrity, and availability) used to ensure computer network integrity for electronic medical record systems.

Cingulate Cortex (Gyrus or Limbic Lobe). A part of the human brain made up of both the primitive brain and modern brain. Responsible for behaviors such as finding food, self-preservation, motivation, and emotional behavior.

Cingulate Gyrus. A part of the human brain associated with emotion. It is responsible for coordinating smell and sights associated with pleasant memories and reactions to pain and the regulation of aggressive behavior.

Cingulate Sulcus. Separates the frontal (front) and parietal (side/lateral) parts of the brain.

Circadian Rhythms. The biological determination of when a person functions best, consisting of three different time frames of being an owl (night), sparrow (morning), or sprowl (anytime).

Civil Rights. Rights that are afforded to people because they are a member of a free society.

Clinical Ethics Committee. Responsible for enforcing the adherence to the four fundamental principles of ethical behavior in the hospital setting.

Close Call. An event or situation that did not produce patient injury but only because of chance (i.e., it had potential but was a missed incident).

Close-Ended Question. A question that forces the patient into a fixed response with little or no opportunity for elaboration.

Cochlea. Part of the hearing process; a snail-like structure containing three connected fluid-filled areas in the ear.

Cochlear Nerve. Part of the hearing process; part of the auditory nerve that transmits impulses from the ear to the portion of the brain responsible for sound processing.

Coercion. The application of credible threat to obtain consent.

Coercive Power. Control over the distribution of punishment depending on whether the person complies with the wishes of the person in power.

Cognitive and Meta-Cognitive Ability. A dimension of self-assessment concerning the ability of the trainee to learn new information and the ability to retrieve that information accurately and quickly from their memory.

Cognitive Chunking. The grouping of related information in a way that is easy for a person to commit to both short-term and long-term memory.

Cognitive Neuroscience. A scientific discipline concerned with the mind as it is manifested in the human brain.

Cognitive Response. (In the process of humor) Our interpretation and thought process about the incoming stimuli.

Cognitive Restructuring. A treatment of communication apprehension that focuses on the reinterpretation of thoughts or cognitions associated with communication situations. Through restructuring the apprehensive or threatening thoughts turn into nonapprehensive and nonthreatening thoughts, the overall anxiety associated with the communicative event will decrease.

Cognitively Involved. An assumption of adult education where we strive to get the learner to think about the information.

Coma. A profound state of unconsciousness.

Commitment. Having all healthcare members committed to a mission of creating and maintaining a safe and violence-free workplace and a culture that reflects willingness to actively aid and assist others in pursuing such a mission.

Communication. The process of a source stimulating meaning in the mind of a receiver by means of verbal and nonverbal messages.

Communication Apprehension (CA). A communication trait that refers to the degree of fear or anxiety associated with either real or anticipated communication with others.

Communication Can Break Down. A misconception of communication that assumes communication is something that can break or be in need of repair when in fact communication is a fluid process that is ever present.

Communication Competency. The ability to relay information in an effective and socially appropriate way or understanding how communication works.

Communication Is a Good Thing. A misconception of communication that assumes communication is always something that is good in nature when in fact it should be considered amoral.

Communication Is a Natural Ability. A misconception of communication that assumes people have an innate capacity to be effective communicators when in fact a large part of competent communication is a learned skill.

Communication Is a Verbal Process. A misconception of communication that assumes that communication is all verbal when in fact communication involves both verbal and nonverbal behavior.

Communicator Style. The way people use verbal and nonverbal behavior to signal how literal meaning should be taken, interpreted, filtered, or understood.

Communication Trait. An abstraction constructed to account for enduring consistencies and differences in message-sending and message-receiving behaviors among individuals.

Communication Will Solve All of Our Problems. A misconception of communication that assumes that all problems are a result of misunderstanding when in fact problems can be belief and value based, and as such, no amount of communication can rectify the problem.

Competence. The degree to which a person is believable and worthy of trust.

Competent Communication Is Effective Communication. A misconception of communication that assumes effectiveness is the only factor in determining competent communication when in fact competent communication is a function of both effectiveness and appropriateness.

Complementary Medicine. Supportive methods used to complement the evidenced-based treatment as established by scientific inquiry.

Complementing. A function of nonverbal communication that reflects the use of nonverbal behavior to complement verbal messages.

Complexity. The amount and details of the information and the capacity of the person to process complex information.

Componential Intelligence. A factor of the triarchic theory of intelligence and refers to the mental abilities more closely related to traditional concepts of intelligence, such as a score on an IQ test.

Comprehensive Listening. Listening for the totality of the message.

Computer Security. Protection afforded to an automated information system to attain the applicable objectives of preserving the integrity, availability, and confidentiality of information system resources.

Computerized Axial Tomography (CAT). An imaging technique of human tissues using thin slices of x-ray images to provide three-dimensional images of the body's internal organs.

Concierge Medicine. The practice of medicine whereby a physician takes care (for a retainer fee) of a small panel of patients, makes house calls, and is available 24/7.

Concordant Decision. A decision that is mutually agreed to by both the healthcare practitioner and the patient.

Concreteness. Part of selective attention referring to the concept that people pay attention to communication that affects them or that which they can relate to.

Confession. Part of the Judeo-Christian doctrine that advocates when medical mistakes are made the truth should be told, told completely, and accompanied by a sincere apology.

Confidentiality. Security domain reflecting that private or confidential information not to be disclosed to unauthorized individuals.

Conflict. An intrapersonal and interpersonal state where people perceive that they are in an opposing position or are actually in an opposing position from another person in a particular situation or on a particular issue.

Conflict Behavior. The ways that people proact and react to a state of conflict.

Conflicted Dyad. Two people who are in a conflict with one another.

Conflicted-Feelings Moderate Argumentative. A person who has a high motivation to approach arguments and a high motivation to avoid arguments.

Connectional Power. Power that is based on the degree to which a person has influential networks deemed valuable by others.

Conscientiousness. A dimension of the big five that refers to the degree to which people are dependent, organized, reliable, and responsible.

Consciousness. The state of existence that requires both attention and awareness to outside sources of energy.

Constraining Environment. A dimension of environment that reflects surroundings that are restrictive physically or psychologically.

Consumerism. A verbal trigger agent that is a shift in healthcare-seeking behavior in that patients will seek out the best fit for their healthcare needs.

Contagion. The rapid transmission or spread of disease from one person to another.

Context. An environment that serves as a triggering event, allowing people to enact the stored information from memory.

Contextual Communication. The pragmatic approach to the daily navigation through interpersonal encounters according to the context between all healthcare providers and their patients.

Contextual Intelligence. A factor of the triarchic theory of intelligence and refers to the ability to be practical or display "street smarts."

Contingency Theory. A leader's success is contingent on situational demands, such as whether the leader should have a task or employee focus, and the degree to which the leader has influence and control in a given situation.

Continuous Quality Improvement (CQI). A process based on evidenced based standards that are derived by the scientific method and result in improvement of patient care.

Contradicting. A function of nonverbal communication whereby the nonverbal behavior sends the opposite message to what is being communicated verbally.

Control. A motivation for communicating where people communicate to get others to do something or to gain compliance.

Coprolalia. Inappropriate expression of obscene words and derogatory remarks associated with Tourette's disorder.

Coronary Artery Disease. The clogging of the arteries of circulation to the heart; also known as CAD.

Corpus Callosum. The connector portion separating the right and left sides of the brain that allows the two hemispheres (sides) to communicate and coordinate activities.

Cortical Resource. Any attribute of the brain that assists in information processing.

Course Delivery. A major area of training involving the actual presentation of the instructional content.

Courtship Readiness Cues. A type of kinesic behavior exhibited in courtship situations and may include readiness cues.

Crepe Hanging. When the practitioner paints an overly bleak picture for the purpose of protecting the practitioner from possible litigation.

Crew Resource Management (CRM). A management system based on the concept of error that results from a breakdown in interpersonal communication, leadership, and decision-making.

Critical Incident. Events or occurrences that are significant or pivotal in either a desirable or undesirable way.

Critical Listening. Listening that is associated with the evaluation of the message or information.

Cross-Cultural Communication. Communication behaviors across cultures from different nations.

Cultural Empathy. The ability to show other people that you have an understanding of how someone else is feeling in a way that reflects the specific cultural influences that comprise that person's experience.

Cultural Level of Uncertainty Reduction. A level of uncertainty reduction that consists of making assumptions about other people based on easily recognizable yet sometimes insignificant characteristics.

Cultural Sensitivity. The ability to demonstrate an awareness of the cultural influences of another person.

Cultural Time Orientation. A time orientation based on culture and contains technical, formal, and informal factors.

Culture. The traditions, customs, norms, beliefs, values, and thought patterning passed down from generation to generation.

Culture Shock. The degree to which a person feels trauma related to the experience of a new culture.

Culture Shock Phase. A phase of the medical internship process marked by feelings of despair and depression that occurs between the third and sixth months in the environment.

Cytoplasm. The substance that fills the cell.

Data-Analysis Skills. A necessary training skill reflecting the ability to evaluate and properly interpret the data obtained from the trainees.

Data-Gathering Skills. A necessary training skill that reflects the ability to assess the needs of the trainees and the trainer's progress, and both the quality and effectiveness of the overall training.

Data Integrity. The requirement that information and programs be changed only in a specified and authorized manner.

Death. The end of the life of a biological organism.

Deception. The interpersonal act of distorting, altering, or omitting information from another person or person(s).

Decoding. The process of interpreting and evaluating the source's messages. The process of taking the stimuli that have been received and giving those stimuli meaning through individual interpretation and perception.

Delegating Style. A style of training where trainees have high levels of both job and psychological maturity.

Dentistry. The evaluation, diagnosis, prevention, and treatment of diseases, disorders, and conditions of the soft tissues of the jaw, the oral cavity, maxillofacial area, and the adjacent structures as to their necessary impact on complete overall health.

Deoxyribonucleic acid (DNA). Bytes of biologic instruction containing information such as specific physical traits, psychological traits, communication traits, and temperaments.

Diagnosis and Feedback Stage. Feedback stage reflects the identification of deficiencies where the person is in need of improvement.

Discrimination. Undesired or unreciprocated behavior degrading a person's dignity and based on demographic categories such as race, gender, and social status.

Discriminative Listening. When we listen in order to distinguish between different elements of a message or when we are in a "learning state."

Disdain Explanation of Verbal Aggressiveness. When people resort to verbal aggression as a result of an intense dislike or hatred toward a person or object.

Disease Framework. A primary focus on the patient's history, physical examination, and laboratory factors that contribute to a medical diagnosis in an effort to develop adequate treatment.

Disparagement. Part of the ethnocentrism spectrum reflecting a person who displays a great deal of prejudice and intolerance for people of other cultures.

Distant Environment. A dimension of environment that reflects surroundings that create distance and are impersonal.

Do Not Resuscitate Order (DNR). A written order on the part of the healthcare provider that should be written with awareness as to the patient's quality of life before they are in need of resuscitation and should include the patient's aspirations for quality of life after resuscitation.

Doctor Knows Best Principle. A principle that holds that the doctor is the ultimate authority and is therefore beyond reproach by the patient regarding what is and what is not acceptable risk.

Document. A dimension of literacy that reflects the ability to integrate or make sense of information requiring a person to be able to read and synthesize information so as to be able to follow instructions.

Dogmatism. A personality trait where people are rigid in their belief systems as to what is right and wrong.

Driver Style. A communication style that reflects being low in responsiveness and high in assertiveness.

Duchenne Display. The smiling that occurs as a result of humor.

Duration. Part of selective attention referring to extremely short or extremely long communication encounters that tend to decay people's attention.

Dyslexia. A reading disability that affects a person's ability to accurately process graphic symbols.

E-Health. The use of Internet, email, and other mediated technologies in the healthcare realm.

E-Learning. A type of learning that is technology dependent and not requiring face-to-face interaction as is necessary in traditional learning environments.

E-Patients. Patients who utilize technology for social support and social networking resources that are specific to their disease or medical situation.

Ear Canal. Also known as the external auditory canal, which funnels the sound into the eardrum that then vibrates the three bones of the middle ear.

Early Start Denver Model (ESDM). A behavioral therapy focusing on improving social interaction and communication skills in children with autism through constant interaction with significant people within the child's social world.

Ectomorph. A somatype that reflects a body that is tall and slender with poor muscle tone.

Education. The process of imparting knowledge to others.

Educational Approaches. The knowledge of the various pedagogical tools and theories available to the trainer for designing the most appropriate and effective training.

Effective Assessment. The ability to develop, implement, analyze, and interpret the outcomes from measures given to the trainees.

Effectiveness. A dimension of communication competence that reflects the ability to achieve one's goals.

Eight-Factor Model of Intelligence. A multidimensional concept of intelligence including linguistic, logical-mathematical, spatial, bodily-kinesthetic, musical, interpersonal, intrapersonal, and naturalistic intelligences.

Electroencephalograph (EEG). A technique of measuring electrical impulses from the scalp. These impulses are measured in millivolts.

Electronic Health Records (EHR). An electronic record that is considered the official document for patient management.

Elicitation Stage. Feedback stage that asks the person being evaluated how they view not only their performance or behavior, but also their thoughts and feelings experienced during this performance.

Emblems. A type of kinesic behavior that refers to gestures that can be used instead of verbal messagesÑstandalone gestures.

Emotional Contagion. The process of a person's emotive state influencing the emotive state of another person or persons in a similar way.

Emotional Maturity/Emotional Intelligence. A personality trait that reflects the degree to which people are able to understand, recognize, regulate, and productively utilize their emotions.

Emotional Reactivity. A process that refers to how people respond to pleasant and unpleasant events.

Emotional Response. (In the process of humor) The affective reaction to amusement and pleasure. The pleasant psychological shift also known as mirth.

Empathy. An ability to show another person that you have an understanding of how they are feeling; identifying with someone else's emotional experience.

Employee Burnout. Feelings of overwhelming exhaustion, frustration, anger, and cynicism associated with work.

Encoding. Process of conceiving an idea, determining your intent, and selecting the meaning you wish to attach to the message.

Encryption. The transformation of plain text into an unreadable code or cipher text that serves as the basic technology used to protect the confidentiality and integrity of the data.

Endomorph. A somatype consisting of a round body with a large abdomen.

English As a Second Language (ESL). Teaching efforts targeted at people whose first language is something other than English.

Environment. A nonverbal factor that reflects how both man-made and natural surroundings influence human behavior and communication.

Equality. The lowest level of disparity on the ethnocentrism spectrum, making the probability of effective communication quite high.

Error. Acts of commission; doing something wrong or by omission; failing to do the right thing that leads to an undesirable outcome or significant potential for an undesirable outcome.

Escape. A motivation for communicating where people communicate to avoid or delay engaging in other activities.

Ethnocentrism. Belief that the customs and practices of one's own culture are superior to those of other cultures.

Ethos. The degree to which others perceive a person as being genuine and having the best interest of their audience at heart.

Eustachian Tube. A part of the ear that connects the throat and mouth area and equalizes pressure on both sides of the eardrum.

Event Model. A model of informed consent that views informed consent as a particular event that happens at one point in time.

Evidence-Based Data. Research that is data driven and derived through the scientific method.

Evidenced-Based Medicine (EBM). The identification of organizational strategies, structures, and change management practices that enable health practitioners to provide evidence-based care to their patients.

Exhaustion and Stress. Physical and psychological response to overwhelming stimuli that has been associated with elevated heart rates and blood pressure.

Experimental Intelligence. A factor of the triarchic theory of intelligence and refers to the ability for creative thinking and problem-solving.

Expert Power. Power earned by a person who is perceived as knowledgeable and trustworthy with regard to a specific topic.

Explanation. Making a good-faith effort in trying to explain the offense while fully recognizing that phrases such as "There is no excuse" or "We are still trying to find out what happened" can be honest and dignified explanations.

Expressive Style. A communication style that reflects being high in responsiveness and high in assertiveness.

External Locus of Control. The tendency to see events in life as resulting from chance, luck, or fate.

Extraversion. A dimension of the PEN model of the big three model of personality and reflects the degree to which people range on a continuum from being outgoing (high in extraversion) to being socially avoidant (low in extraversion).

Facilitation Skills. Necessary training skill reflecting the ability to guide discussion and topic direction of the group while also making sure that those who wish to contribute are recognized and their contribution is valued and synthesized into the overall theme of the training module.

Familiar Environment. A dimension of environment that reflects surroundings where people regularly inhabit.

Fate. The belief in ominous sensations or feelings that something is going to happen and there is nothing that can be done to stop it from occurring.

Feedback. Any information via verbal or nonverbal communication that is sent in reaction to a message.

Feedback-Induced Adaptation. A source can adapt to a receiver's feedback by altering his or her subsequent messages and responses.

Feminine. A classification representing tendencies that are traditionally associated with women such as cooperation, nurturing, responsiveness, and relationally focused.

Fight or Flight System. A primal response that prompts the body to stand up to danger (fight) or to flee from the danger (flight).

Flexibility. The demands of the external environment, which include the level of openness, adaptability, and change and a person's ability to select, receive, and process such information.

Flip chart. A fundamental instructional aid that allows for the recording of ideas and responses from training participants and for relaying important instructional content.

Forbearance. Commitment not to repeat the behavior that brought about the mistake.

Forgiveness. Part of the Judeo-Christian doctrine that advocates when medical mistakes are made it is up to the patient and the patient's family and may include financial compensation rather than a mere confession.

Formal Environment. A dimension of the environment that reflects surroundings that are sterile and formal.

Formal Overt Decision-Making. Highest level of symmetrical power and reflects the nurse making decisions in a spirit of shared power.

Formal Time. Reflects the keeping of time in a socially standardized way such as through days, months, years, etc.

Formative Feedback. Feedback targeted at performance improvement and occurs before or during job performance.

Framing. Chunking data and information into small bites with frequent breaks to verify patient comprehension. The act of putting information in ways that give it a particular perspective for the patient.

Framingham Heart Study. A ground-breaking study of cardiology and stroke revealing that females have a greater probability of stroke and diminished poststroke recovery than men.

Friendship Touch. A dimension of haptics referring to touch that indicates that another person is a close friend or more than an acquaintance.

Front-Stabbing. A conflict behavior that is overt, is direct, and leaves no ambiguity as to the person's intent (i.e., to cause you personal and/or professional harm).

Frontal Lobe. A part of the human brain responsible for handling motor skills (including speech behavior) and cognitive functions of higher thinking and reasoning.

Functional Magnetic Resonance Imaging (fMRI). An imaging technique using large amounts of magnetism to generate images of activated tissue through measurement of the oxyhemoglobin concentration of the blood.

Functions of Nonverbal Communication. A study of nonverbal communication that focuses on how nonverbal behavior assists us when communicating.

Future-Time Ordering. A type of psychological time orientation based on what is coming in the future.

Galvanic Skin Response. A measure of physiological arousal measuring electrical conductance found in the skin, which is controlled by the sympathetic and parasympathetic nervous systems.

Gastroenterology. A medical specialty focusing on the treatment of disorders found in the gut.

Gelastic (Laughter) Epilepsy. A rare seizure disorder of the hypothalamus and the frontal and temporal lobes that can manifest as general arousal and movement disorders in addition to inappropriate laughter.

Gelotology. The study of laughter as a science.

Gender. A person's self-representation as a man or woman or how that person is responded to by social institutions based on the individual's gender representation.

General Intelligence (G-Factor). A conceptualization of intelligence that assumes intelligence is unidimensional and universal across people.

General Reminder System (GRS). A smart phone application that provides users with reminders when to take medications, attend doctor appointments, etc. The GRS can also be fitted with a mobile bar code scanner to verify the user's accuracy in taking scheduled medication in the proper doses.

Generalized Human Trait. Traits that are generalizable to any person in any place.

Generative Learning. Type of learning that entails not only learning the process, but also how the process contributes to the function of the entire organization.

Genetic Explanation of Verbal Aggressiveness. Verbal aggression is an expression of a person's temperaments.

Gesundheit Institute. A healthcare facility founded in 1971 by Hunter Campbell on the principles of the complementary and alternative (holistic) effects of humor.

Goodwill. The degree to which the person has the best interest of the audience at heart.

Grade Level. Average literacy skill associated with each grade in the KÐ12 American public school system.

Great Man Theory of Leadership. Assumes that there are common leadership attributes that all effective leaders possess.

Groups. Several individuals with individual interests and individual concerns working together with one another.

Gyri. The folds of the brain.

Hand-Off Communication. Information exchanged between the outgoing party and the incoming party regarding health and general information pertaining to patients and patient care.

Haptics. The study of nonverbal behavior that focuses on touch and how touch functions in communication.

Health Communication. The multichannel dissemination (e.g., face-to-face, print, radio, and Internet) that is rhetorical in nature because its main functions are to inform and persuade.

Health Literacy. A constellation of skills that constitutes the ability to perform basic reading and numerical tasks for functioning in the healthcare environment and acting on healthcare information.

Healthcare Communication. The study of communication in the everyday practice of medicine that involves medical communication, medical informatics, and health communication.

Healthcare Facility. Any place where there is a regular practice of medicine and healing regarding physical and psychological illness.

Healthcare Knowledge Acquisition. The adoption and integration of new knowledge in order to perform healthcare functions.

Healthcare Skill Acquisition. The adoption or refinement of behavioral skills and processes associated with the delivery of quality healthcare.

Healthcare Training. The process of acquiring the necessary knowledge and skill required to function in healthcare roles effectively.

Hearing. A physiological process that occurs when sound waves enter the ear canal and vibrations are converted to electrical signals sent to the brain.

High Argumentative. A person who has a high motivation to approach arguments and a low motivation to avoid arguments.

Highlighting of Information. A factor in long-term memory that assumes information that is highlighted tends to be more memorable than that which is not.

Hippocampus. A part of the human brain associated with memory, especially long-term memory.

Homophily. The degree of closeness that a person feels with another person and can be based on things such as ethnicity, sex, place of origin, socioeconomic status, etc.

Honeymoon Phase. A phase of the medical internship process that reflects the first 3 months of the internship where the person feels like a special guest who is there for a pleasant visit.

Hospice. A type of care that focuses on relieving symptoms and supporting the patients and families when the patient has a life-limiting illness and generally has a life expectancy of 6 months or less.

Hostility. A globally destructive trait expressed in interpersonal communication as irritability, negativity, resentment, and suspicion.

Humility. A state of being humble, not arrogant.

Humor. Any communication perceived by any of the interacting parties as humorous and leads to laughing, smiling, and a feeling of amusement.

Hypothalamus. A part of the human brain associated with emotion. It is responsible for thermal regulation, sexuality, combativeness, hunger, and thirst. This brain structure is further divided into lateral regions (responsible for emotions such as pleasure and rage) and medial regions (responsible for emotions such as aggression and displeasure).

Illness Framework. A primary focus on the affective state of the patient's fears, anxieties, expectations, feelings, and perceptions about illness in an effort to develop adequate treatment.

Illustrators. A type of kinesic behavior that refers to body movements that are generally in the hands and serve to add meaning to a message.

Immediacy. The degree of perceived physical and psychological closeness or distance between people in a relationship.

Improvement Plan Stage. Feedback stage requiring the creation of a document containing specific strategies as to how to improve performance.

Inclusion. A motivation for communication where people communicate to combat loneliness or to feel connected to others.

Incus. Also known as the anvil, which is the middle bone in the ear and involved in the hearing process.

Indifference. Part of the ethnocentrism spectrum reflecting the tendency for a person to not pay attention to the culture or subcultures of other people because of a desire to communicate with people of their own culture.

Individual Human Trait. Traits that specific people possess as a result of genetics or heredity.

Infections. A type of naturally caused illness and includes HIV/AIDS, leprosy, tuberculosis, and polio.

Influence Others. A goal of communication where people seek to exert influence over others in an effort to get them to do what we want them to do.

Informal Covert Decision-Making. When a nurse carries out the orders from the physician but with open disagreement.

Informal Overt Decision-Making. When a nurse is invited to offer opinions but on an informal basis.

Informal Time. A type of culture time orientation that reflects the nuance concepts as it is calibrated by the individual, not the society as a whole.

Information Scanning. The way in which people identify and attribute significance to bits of information in the environment.

Informational Power. Power that is based on a person who possesses or has access to information that others deem valuable.

Informational Reception Apprehension (IRA). A tendency to process information reflecting a pattern of anxiety and antipathy that filters informational reception, perception, and processing, and/or adjustment (psychologically, verbally, physically) associated with complexity, abstractness, and flexibility.

Informed Consent. A source (the provider) creating meaning in the mind of the receiver (the patient) as to what the source, either through a testing process (e.g., x-ray) or a procedure (e.g., operation), is planning to do.

Instructional Design. A major area of training involving the development of content lessons and modules that will be presented.

Instructional Objectives. The things that the learners or trainees are expected to know at the conclusion of the training.

Instruments. An effective means for gaining insight into the trainer and the trainee concerning their attitudes, beliefs, behaviors, and retention of knowledge.

Integrative Medicine. The concept of intertwining disciplines such as psychology, communication, and the humanities with traditional medicine to better deliver healthcare.

Integrity. Security domain reflecting the systematic and authorized maintenance of the system containing data inquiry and system integrity.

Intellectual Inflexibility. The degree to which people are unwilling to consider different points of view.

Intelligence. The ability to understand complex ideas, to adapt effectively to the environment, to learn from experience, to engage in various forms of reasoning, and to overcome obstacles by taking thought.

Intercultural Communication. Communication that occurs between people who are members of different cultural groups.

Interethnic Communication. Communication between members of different ethnic groups; not necessarily people from different countries, political systems, etc.

Internal Locus of Control. The tendency to see events in life as being a result of personal ability and purposeful effort.

International Communication. Communication between governmental bodies of different cultures.

Interpersonal Communication. Any communication that occurs between two parties.

Interpersonal Communication Is Intimate Communication. A misconception of communication that assumes that all talk between two people is intimate when in fact it is only the disclosure of highly personal information that constitutes intimate communication.

Interpersonal Communication Skills. Necessary training skill reflecting the ability to demonstrate appropriate and effective interpersonal behavior that facilitates open and honest communication between you and the trainees. This requires an appreciation of diversity in thought and perspective and the ability to show empathy.

Interpersonal Behaviors (Rules). The understanding of how people successfully utilize particular behaviors.

Interpersonal Intelligence. A form of IQ referring to the ability to communicate and engage in effective social relationships with others.

Interpretation. The making sense of and relaying of culturally sensitive oral communication.

Interracial Communication. Communication between people of different racial groups.

Intimate Communication. Communication that involves disclosure of significant information from one or both interaction partners.

Intimate Distance. A category of personal space reflecting a closeness of 0 to 18 inches.

Intimate Level of Uncertainty Reduction. The lowest level of uncertainty reduction experienced by a person because it requires knowledge of the higher levels of uncertainty reduction plus the ability to tailor messages in a way that fully accounts for the potential reaction of the other person.

Intracultural Communication. Communication between members of the same culture or subculture.

Intrapersonal Intelligence. A form of IQ referring to the ability to understand one's self, including emotions and cognitions.

Intrapersonal Noise. Psychological states of the sender and/or receiver that can impede the successful transmission of a message.

Involvement. Part of selective exposure referring to the more involved a person is with a topic, the more likely the stimuli related to that topic will be attended to.

James-Lang Theory of Emotion. A theory that assumes emotion is not a cause of physiological occurrences but a reaction to them.

Job Maturity. A person's level of both knowledge and skill needed to perform a task.

Kayser Fleischer Ring. A symptom of Wilson's disease in which a brown ring forms around the iris (colored portion) of the eye indicating an accumulation of copper.

Kinesics. The study of nonverbal behavior that focuses on how people use body movements to communicate.

Knowledge Acquisition. Training that focuses on what people need to know about a particular policy or procedure.

Laboratory Professionals. An allied medical profession that involves working within a laboratory. Personnel can be medical technologists, medical laboratory technicians, and phlebotomists.

Lack of Prior Experience. When people do not have previous similar experience with which to compare present stimuli, they are less likely to be preprogrammed to tune into certain types of messages over others.

Lack of Redundancy. Part of selective perception where messages are bound or constricted as a result of lack of repetition or use of another communication channel.

Lack of Schema. Part of selective perception reflecting a lack of organizing ability.

Language. A human communication system usually consisting of words (symbols), syntax (word sequence), and grammar (rules for use).

Language Barrier. The inability to relay effective and appropriate communication through verbal behavior.

Latent Error (Latent Condition). Less apparent failures of organization or design that contribute to the occurrence of an error or allow them to cause harm to patients.

Laughter. A physiological experience that is considered a behavior.

Leader-Member Exchange Theory. Relationship quality between superiors and subordinates is determined by the quality of their communication exchanges.

Learned Helplessness. An acquired disorder where a person experiences a disconnect between their own effort and the connection of that effort to successfully achieving goals.

Learning. The acquisition of information that was not previously known; level 2 of training assessment concerning the degree to which trainees learned from the training.

Lecture. The most common form of training vehicle in that it is one such delivery device that is most identifiable with people.

Left Inferior Frontal Cortex. The area of the human brain responsible for language production. Also known as Broca's area.

Left Posterior Superior Temporal Cortex. The area of the human brain responsible for the processing of auditory signals and language comprehension. Also known as Wernicke's area.

Linguistic Intelligence. A form of IQ referring to the ability to use language as an aid to thinking and when communicating with others.

Lipophilic. Characteristics of a drug reflecting the degree to which it dissolves or is stored in fat deposition.

Listening. The process of receiving, constructing, deriving meaning from, and responding to spoken and/or nonverbal messages.

Listening Apprehension. Fear associated with either anticipated or real listening situations.

Literacy. An individual's ability to read, write, and speak English and compute and solve problems at levels of proficiency necessary to function on the job and in society; to achieve one's goals and develop one's knowledge and potential.

Live Donor. A person who has compatible blood type and human leukocyte antigen (HLA) typing.

Living Will. An instructional directive that varies according to context.

Lizard Brain (Brainstem). The most primitive portion of the brain; also known as the brain stem. Responsible for breathing, heart rate, and sleeping patterns.

Locus of Control. A personality trait that reflects the degree to which people interpret events in their life as being a result of personal ability and purposeful effort.

Logical-Mathematical Intelligence. A form of IQ referring to the ability to think logically and to solve mathematical problems.

Love or Intimate Touch. A dimension of haptics referring to touch that indicates a powerful bond with another person.

Low Argumentative. A person who has a low motivation to approach arguments and a high motivation to avoid arguments.

Low Literacy (Limited Literacy). Having a reading level at or below 7th grade or having deficiencies in both reading and writing such that necessary personal and work-related tasks suffer.

Ludic. A type of mood primarily controlled by the limbic system and is characteristic of playful and relaxed behavior and feeling.

M-Time (Monochronic Time). A time orientation indicating the valuation of time and view time as a commodity to be maximized.

Machiavellianism. A personality trait that reflects the degree to which people will say and do whatever needs to be said and done in order to achieve a desired goal or outcome.

Magnetic Resonance Imaging (MRI). An imaging technique that uses large amounts of magnetism to generate images of soft tissues within the body.

Magnetoencephalography (MEG). An imaging technology that uses magnetic detection coils with the assistance of an extremely sensitive instrument called the superconducting quantum interference device (SQUID). MEG is able to directly analyze the nervous system at the cellular level.

Malleus. Also known as the hammer; a lever that vibrates the incus.

Mammalian Brain (Midbrain). A part of the brain that sits atop the brain stem and is responsible for behaviors that are more representative of animal behavior than that of exclusive human behavior. Also known as the midbrain. Responsible for fighting behavior, fleeing behavior, feeding behavior, and reproductive behavior.

Managed Care Industry. A verbal trigger event that is a moderator between healthcare provider and patient and has been shown to undermine that trust between the patient and physician.

Management. The active containment of situations where aggression is about to take place or has just started to occur.

Manipulation. The incomplete or less than truthful presentation of information such as lying or omitting vital information or deliberately deceiving the patient.

Marasmus. A disease prevalent in the 19th and early 20th century that resulted from a lack of human touch and contact.

Masculine. A classification representing tendencies that are traditionally associated with men such as competition, aggression, assertiveness, and focusing on a task.

Matter. Entity that can be either solid (e.g., Earth), liquid (e.g., water), or gas (e.g., air) in nature.

McCroskey Model of Communication. A model of communication that expanded the concept of noise to include the two processes of encoding and decoding in the source, the receiver, the primary channel, and the feedback channel.

Meaning. The idiosyncratic way in which people make sense of stimuli.

Medical Assistant. An allied medical profession that involves performing the administrative and clinical tasks that keep the offices of licensed health practitioners running smoothly.

Medical Communication. The pragmatic approach to the everyday navigation through and the interpersonal encounters between all healthcare providers and their patients.

Medical Informatics. The computer-based transference, retrieval, and storage of information.

Medical Method of Intelligence. A determination of IQ based on anatomical, physiological, and pathological signs of inferior intelligence.

Melancholy Humor. A depressing humor associated with black bile.

Mesomorph. A somatype that reflects a triangular athletic body that is muscular and firm with good posture.

Message. The information being sent.

Meta-Analysis. A type of study that investigates the results of previous studies on a certain topic to determine a common statistic or tendency across studies.

Metacognition. Thinking about thinking.

Microexpressions. Brief, involuntary facial expressions shown on the face of humans when they are trying to conceal or deceive.

Mimetics. A study of nonverbal behavior that focuses on how facial expressions are used, interpreted, or filtered during human interaction.

Mindfulness. The process of being aware of your behavior and basing your behavior on a specific situation as opposed to simply enacting a generic script used for a variety of situations.

Mindfulness Meditation. A meditation that emphasizes the quality of being fully present and attentive to the moment during everyday activities.

Minimally Invasive Surgery. A procedure that utilizes small incisions that often result in decreased pain, decreased recovery time, and shorter hospital stays.

Mirth. The pleasant psychological shift when one experiences humorous communication.

Mistakes. Failures during intentional behaviors or incorrect choices and can involve insufficient knowledge, failure to correctly interpret available information, or application of the wrong rule.

Mobile Patient Care Assistant (MPCA). A smart phone application that provide users with reminders to perform a necessary task or tasks.

Models of the Stigmatization Process. A way to typify stigma that was proposed by Irving Goffman.

Monochronic Time (M-Time). Societal time orientation where time is viewed as a commodity to be maximized and time delay is seen as wasted.

Musical Intelligence. Form of IQ referring to the ability to discern among pitch, rhythm, and other aspects of music.

Mutuality Model. A society that values equality among all members of a group or society. In medicine, the concept that traditional power structures need to be flattened and power de-emphasized with equality among all members.

Mystical Retribution. A type of supernatural-caused illness that reflects the belief that a disease is caused or spread as a result of some deviant behavior or social practice.

Narrative Medicine. The utilization of the patient's story regarding illness in the development and application of medical treatment.

Natural Causation. Cause of illness that is naturally occurring such as infection, stress, organic deterioration, accident, or human aggression.

Natural Killer (NK) Cells. Cells that are capable of killing cancer cells while leaving normal cells intact.

Natural Rights. Rights that are organic in nature that are afforded to us because we are members of the human race.

Naturalistic Intelligence. A form of IQ referring to the ability to identify patterns in nature and to determine how individual objects fit into the larger whole or pattern.

Nature. Part of the NBAR acronym for effectively obtaining informed consent referring to the nature of the procedure.

Near Miss. An event or situation that did not produce harm, but it is only because of random chance that harm did not occur.

Negative Reinforcement. Performing or witnessing a behavior or event that brings about an undesired or detrimental outcome.

Negligence. An unanticipated event caused by error in the performance of duty.

Neurogenesis. The brain's ability to newly generate neurological connections.

Neuron. A nerve cell that sends electrical signals throughout the body.

Neuroscience. A scientific discipline concerned with the nervous system including structure, function, evolution, development, genetics, biochemistry, physiology, pharmacology, informatics, computational neuroscience, and pathology.

Neuroticism. A dimension of the big three model of personality and is the degree to which people range on a continuum from being potentially unstable (high neuroticism) to being emotionally stable (low neuroticism).

Neutral Moderate Argumentative. A person who is moderate in both argument approach and argument avoidance.

Newest Vital Sign (NVS). A bilingual measure of health literacy (in both Spanish and English) that involves having a patient read a nutrition label on a container of ice cream and then they are asked six questions about what they have read.

Noise. Anything that can get in the way of or serve to encumber the communication process.

Nonmalfeasance. The act of doing no harm to your patients.

Nonserious Social Incongruity. A concept of spontaneous laughter based on safe surprise or being surprised in a good or non-threatening kind of way that may elicit laughter or a smile.

Nonverbal. All other aspects of communication that do not involve words.

Nonverbal Barrier. The inability to relay effective and appropriate communication through nonverbal behavior.

Nonverbal Immediacy. The degree to which people use nonverbal communication to increase the physical and psychological closeness or distance between people in a relationship.

Novelty. Part of selective attention referring to the fact that things that are unusual or out of the ordinary will tend to get our attention.

Nucleus. A group of nerve cells.

Nursing. A profession involving the protection, promotion, and optimization of health and abilities; prevention of illness and injury; alleviation of suffering through the diagnosis and treatment of human response; and advocacy in the care of individuals, families, communities, and populations.

Occupational Therapy. A profession that enables people to do the day-to-day activities that are important to them despite impairments, activity limitations or participation restrictions, or risks for these problems.

Occipital Lobe. A part of the human brain responsible for processing information from the eyes and immediately transferring this to the parietal lobe for comprehension and to the frontal lobe for speech production.

Occulesics. A study of nonverbal behavior that focuses on how the eyes are used to communicate.

OCEAN Model of Personality. The big five model of personality contains dimensions of conscientiousness, agreeableness, open to experience, extraversion, and neuroticism.

Olfactics. A study of nonverbal behavior that refers to how people use scent and smell as a means of communicating and interacting with others.

Open-Ended Question. A question that gives the opportunity for the patient to answer in ways, allowing for more elaborate and extensive explanations.

Open Source Software. Software that allows you to copy, modify, use, and distribute patient information at approximately 50% of the implementation costs and at a 65% reduction in maintenance costs.

Openness to Experience. Part of the OCEAN model of personality that reflects the degree to which people seek out varied experiences, are imaginative, and are creative.

Orientation and Climate Stage. Feedback stage requiring advanced notice to all parties who are to receive feedback, providing an affirming atmosphere that is conducive to learning and providing a full explanation as to what exactly will be covered.

Orthographic Memory. Memory centers associated with the retention of letters and symbols.

Overqualifying Questions. Questions that are asked in a way that makes the person who asks the question appear unsure and powerless.

P-Time (Polychronic Time). A time orientation where time is relative and is not a commodity to be consumed but something to mark the passing of days, years, etc.

Pain. An unpleasant sensory and/or emotional experience associated with actual or potential damage to bodily tissue.

Palliative Care. Services that alleviate, lessen, or provide relief from symptoms that interfere with the quality of life when curative treatments are no longer effective or deemed too burdensome by the patient.

Paralanguage. All the verbal communication behavior we use besides the actual words to send messages.

Paralinguistics. A category of vocalics that are comprised of vocalizations that are difficult to measure.

Parietal Lobe. A part of the human brain responsible for receiving and processing all touch and pain sensation from the body.

Participative Style. A style of training where trainees have high levels of job maturity and low levels of psychological maturity.

Participatory Education. Education that fosters a team concept between the teacher and the learner such that the student becomes an active agent in acquiring necessary skills.

Past-Time Ordering. A type of psychological time orientation based on reliving past events.

Paternalistic Decision. A decision that is made by the healthcare practitioner and forced on the patient.

Paternalistic Model. A society that values traditional hierarchy and structure. If a doctor was held in high esteem and his or her actions were not questioned or scrutinized, this would be representative of a paternalistic society.

Pathological Laughter. A range of behavior from laughing at politically incorrect jokes to laughter as a manifestation of chromosomal aberration or diseases such as mania, schizophrenia, mood-related disorders, Alzheimer's disease, Pick's disease, and Wilson's disease.

Patient. A derivative of the Latin word meaning to endure, bear, or suffer and also includes vulnerability, anxiety, and dependency that is induced by changes in a person's health status.

Patient Distrust. A verbal trigger event that results in patients doubting the effectiveness of medical treatment and, as such, underutilizing available healthcare services.

Pay-for-Performance. A reimbursement system based on health outcomes regardless of the mode in which care is delivered.

Pedagogy. The art and science of child learning.

Pedagogy Method of Intelligence. A determination of IQ based on education or acquired knowledge.

Peer Review Method. A process in which institutions and programs are reviewed by other experts in other institutions and programs of equal professional status.

PEN Model of Temperament. Known as the big three model of personality consisting of psychoticism, extraversion, and neuroticism.

Persistent Vegetative State (PVS). A condition of patients with severe brain damage where coma has progressed to a state of wakefulness without detectable awareness.

Personal Distance. A category of personal space reflecting a closeness of 18 inches to 4 feet.

Personal Health Record (PHR). A document developed by the patient containing the patient's personal healthcare information.

Personal Report of Communication Apprehension (PRCA). A 24-item measure developed to assess a person's overall communication apprehension, communication within groups, communication within meetings, communication at the interpersonal level, and communication in a public setting.

Persuasion. The process through which we create, shape, and reinforce the beliefs and attitudes of another person.

Pharmacodynamics. The study of how drugs interact.

Pharmacokinetics. The study of how drugs work.

Pharmacy. A profession concerned with the identification of potential and actual drug-related problems, resolving actual drug-related problems, and preventing drug-related problems.

Phlegmatic Humor. An apathetic humor associated with mucus.

Phonemes. Any sounds that are distinct to a language.

Phonological Memory. Memory centers associated with the recall of language sounds and style.

Phonology. The study of the articulation process.

Physical Attractiveness. A dimension of attractiveness and refers to the degree to which a person's physical characteristics are desirable to others.

Physical Noise. Aspects of the physical environment (e.g., busy city street) that can adversely affect the successful transmission of a message.

Physical Response. (In the process of humor) The behaviors we engage in to physiologically express our amusement.

Physical Stigma. Any physical attribute that serves as a marker resulting in the marginalization of the person solely based on that physical attribute.

Physical Therapy. A profession that focuses on restoring, maintaining, and promoting optimal physical function and quality of life related to movement and health.

Physician. A healer who views medicine as both an art and a science involving biomedical research and technology to diagnose and treat disease and illness.

Physician Assistant (PA-C). A health practitioner licensed to practice medicine only under the supervision of a licensed physician.

Pick's Disease. A degenerative brain illness that causes dementia, usually begins after age 40, generally involves the frontal and temporal behavioral centers of the brain, and accounts for approximately 5% of all cases of progressive dementia.

Pinna. External ear; a series of folds that serve to harness the external sound waves and assist in harnessing the sound into the ear canal.

Plain Language (Simple Language and Easy-to-Read Language). Writing that is comprehensible at the 8th grade level or below; often contains large font.

Pleasantry. A form of spontaneous humor that is a milder form of humor that may or may not elicit laughter but likely will result in a smile.

Pleasure. A motivation for communicating where people communicate for entertainment or social functions.

Plot. Part of narrative medicine reflecting the organizing line or the thread that makes the narrative possible.

Political Skills. A necessary training skill reflecting the ability to determine potential personality and relational difficulties among trainees given that most groups that require training have a history of working together.

Polychronic Time (P-Time). A time orientation where time is relative and is not a commodity to be consumed but something to mark the passing of days, years, etc.

Position Emission Tomography (PET). An imaging technology that uses radioactive isotopes (added to a tracer such as glucose) to determine cellular activity. The more glucose consumed, the greater the cellular activity. The less glucose consumed, the less cellular activity.

Positional Cues. A type of kinesic behavior concerning how a person positions his or her body in relation to others.

Positive Reinforcement. Performing or witnessing a behavior or event that brings about a desired or beneficial outcome.

Positron Emitting. A characteristic of a tracer that is introduced into the body by some active molecule such as glucose. This is used in PET imaging technology.

Power of Attorney (POA-Health). A legal document that designates a surrogate to make decisions on the patient's behalf if the patient becomes incapacitated for any reason.

Powerless Language. Language that communicates to the other person insecurity, low power, low status, and low expertise.

Practice-Based Systems. A server housed within the specific healthcare facility and owned and maintained by the healthcare facility.

Preassaultive Tension State. A point in a situation where verbal and physical aggression is about to be triggered; marked by anxiety, a rigid or stiff body posture, clenching of the teeth and/or fists, and other signs of physiological arousal.

Prefrontal Cortex. A higher-level cortex responsible for the control of emotion during social interaction and assists in the ability to remain rational as opposed to being entirely emotionally driven in our behavior.

Prejudice. A prejudgment of people based on stereotyping.

Present-Time Ordering. A type of psychological time orientation based on the here and now.

Presentation Software (PowerPoint). Presentation vehicle that allows for the use of text, pictures, sounds, video, and animation in content delivery.

Presentational Skills. A necessary training skill reflecting the ability to be dynamic, be energetic, and channel the proper communication behaviors in an effort to create an atmosphere conducive to learning and enhancing trainer credibility.

Primacy Principle. In persuasive communication the concept that messages presented first will be most memorable and most persuasive.

Primary Auditory Cortex. The area through which we organize and convey a message.

Primary Language. The first acquired language and the language that is most used within one's home.

Primary Mental Abilities Test. A determination of IQ assessing verbal comprehension, numerical ability, spatial relations, perceptual speed, word fluency, memory, and reasoning.

Principle of Totality. A bioethical principle stating that mutilation in one body part is legitimate in order to save the whole.

Private Environment. A dimension of environment that reflects surroundings that are more intimate in nature.

Proactive Scanning. A person's tendency to identify and assign significance to data that may/will be used in future decision-making.

Problem Solving Treatment (PST). A treatment of clinical depression that involves a multimedia approach that incorporates graphics and video featuring a psychologist who leads the patient through problem-solving algorithms and provides feedback regarding the patient's adherence to the treatment.

Process. Something that is ongoing with no real beginning and end.

Process Model. A model of informed consent that views informed consent as a continuous active process requiring participation by the patient in medical decision-making.

Professional Touch. A dimension of haptics referring to the type of touch experienced when you visit a doctor, dentist, or any person who uses touch in a professional capacity.

Professionalism. The degree to which a person exhibits and exceeds those standards and expectations set forth by the publics they serve and the governing bodies that set such standards and expectations.

Prose. A dimension of literacy that reflects the ability to find information and follow instructions.

Prosody. Vocal qualities that are easily measureable.

Protected Health Information. Any information, be it oral or recorded in any form or medium.

Proxemics. An area of nonverbal behavior focusing on how people use space to communicate.

Proximity. Part of selective exposure reflecting the easier the access a person has to a stimulus, the more likely it is to be noticed.

Psychological Level of Uncertainty Reduction. A level of uncertainty reduction that focuses on the other person's attitudes, beliefs, and values.

Psychological Maturity. A person's degree of self-efficacy and willingness to accept the responsibility of acquiring and implementing the new information and skills being taught in the training.

Psychological Method of Intelligence. A determination of IQ based on direct observation and assessing behavior that is considered intelligent in nature.

Psychological Time Orientation. A time orientation based on ordering events of the past, present, and future.

Psychological Violence. The intentional use of power that may include the threat of physical force against another person or group of people.

Psychoneuroimmunology (PNI). The study of basic interactions between the nervous system and the immune system and the subsequent effects or lack of effects of these interactions on disease development or progression.

Psychopathological Explanation of Verbal Aggressiveness. Aggression is a product of repressed hostility toward another person.

Psychoticism. A dimension of the PEN model or big three model of personality and reflects the degree to which people range on a continuum from being socially likable (low in psychoticism) to socially irritating and aggressive (high in psychoticism).

Public Distance. A category of personal space reflecting a closeness of 8 feet to the point where a person is beyond our vision and hearing.

Quantitative Ability. A dimension of literacy that reflects the ability to find numbers and be able to perform basic calculations, which requires understanding numeracy and the skills to perform as directed by the calculation.

Radioisotopes. An isotope that is radioactive because of an unstable nucleus that emits radiation during its delay to a more stable form.

Radiologic Technology. A profession that creates medical images of human anatomy to aid radiologists (physicians) in diagnosing and treating illness and injury.

Rapid Estimate of Adult Literacy in Medicine (REALM). A measure designed to accurately assess a patient's level of health literacy.

Reaction. Level 1 of training assessment consisting of the more primitive aspects of evaluation, which concern perceptions and feelings about the training.

Reactive Scanning. The tendency to identify and assign significance to data only after a problem or situation requiring a decision presents itself.

Reading Anxiety. The degree of anxiety a person experiences when reading information.

Reasonable Patient Standard. A standard based on what the average patient would need to know in order to be an informed participant and understand the decision to be made.

Reasonable Physician Standard. A standard based on what a typical physician would say about this intervention.

Receiver. The person(s) who attends to and decodes the message in an effort to make sense of it and is bound by the same factors that influence the sender.

Recency Principle. In persuasive communication the concept that messages presented last will be most memorable and persuasive.

Reduce Uncertainty. A goal of communication where people seek to reduce feelings of vulnerability or reduce the unknown.

Redundancy. When a message is sent in the same way with the same channel, in different ways using the same channel, and in different ways via another channel. Also in selective retention, referring to the more someone uses or accesses something, the more likely they are to remember it.

Referent Power. People complying with the wishes of another person for no other reason than to gain their approval or to please them.

Regulating. A function of nonverbal communication that assists in turn-taking behavior, starting and stopping conversations, and changing topics.

Regulators. A type of kinesic behavior that serves to coordinate turn-taking behavior during conversation.

Reinforcement. Part of selective exposure referring to the more desired outcomes are experienced with certain stimuli, the greater the probability that the stimuli will be attended to in the future.

Relaxation. A motivation for communicating where people communicate to help induce a state of relaxation.

Remorse. A deep sense of regret.

Reparation. Reflects how one goes about rectifying the harm of the mistake and varies greatly from simply not charging for an appointment or scheduling an appointment earlier than originally scheduled due to financial compensation.

Repeating. A function of nonverbal communication occurring when the nonverbal behavior is an actual replication of the verbal messages.

Repentance. Part of the Judeo-Christian doctrine that advocates when medical mistakes are made, full assurance that any medical, financial, or other needs of the injured patient or families will be addressed.

Respiration. The first process in the production and projection of symbolic language and involves air-producing, voicing, and articulation mechanisms.

Respiratory Therapy. A profession that involves the assessment and treatment of breathing disorders such as emphysema, asthma, and bronchitis.

Responsiveness. The degree to which people show compassion, empathy, and "other" orientation for another person.

Responsiveness Continuum. A gender orientation range that reflects the degree of a person's femininity.

Results. Level 4 of training assessment concerning the degree to which the training assisted the organization in achieving the larger goals.

Review Stage. Feedback stage consisting of making sure that the person understands and agrees with all that has been presented and developed during the previous five feedback stages.

Reward Power. Control of reward and the discretion to dispense rewards based on the ability of a person to comply with the wishes of the powerful.

Rhett's Disorder. A disorder that is part of the autism spectrum of disorders that appears at around 6 to 18 months of age, resulting in the loss of communication skills, purposeful hand motion, and development of a stereotyped hand posturing.

Risk Communication. A specialized type of interpersonal communication that involves the exchange of critical information of possible health outcomes and occurs between the healthcare practitioner and the patient.

Risks. Part of the NBAR acronym for effectively obtaining informed consent referring to notable risks, severe risks, and risks most likely to occur as a result of the procedure.

Role Play. A training vehicle that affords the trainees the opportunity to apply the knowledge and skills they have just acquired.

Root-Cause Analysis. A structured process for identifying the causal or contributing factors underlying adverse events (i.e., any injury caused by medical care) or a critical incident (i.e., significant or pivotal incident in either a desirable or undesirable way).

Rule of 16. A principle for PowerPoint slides that holds that there should be no more than 16 words on any given slide because any more can result in sensory overload for the trainees.

SBAR. A pneumonic device developed to increase the efficiency of information exchange, thus reducing the chance of human error. SBAR stands for Situation, Background, Assessment, and Recommendations.

Sabotage. When someone consciously or unconsciously undermines or destroys another person's physical property, personal integrity, professional integrity, credibility, and/or self-esteem.

Safety and Health Training. The adoption of aggression diffusion techniques and the knowledge of the detrimental effects of aggressive communication.

Sanguine Humor. A cheerful type of humor associated with the blood.

Sarcasm. A paralinguistic device that communicates to the receiver that the meaning of the message being sent should be the opposite of the meaning inferred by the spoken word.

Scapegoat Model. A model of stigma that reflects the labeling of people who deviate from accepted social standards.

Schema. Factor of selective retention reflecting the need for an idea or experience to have an assigned place to be stored in the brain.

Second-Life Experience. A type of role play where people are trained in the use of computer-simulated or virtual health environments in which they are embedded within a complete milieu of a healthcare environment where the choices they make bring about differing consequences.

Selective Attention. A hurdle in information processing reflecting which stimuli actually gets our attention.

Selective Exposure. A hurdle in information processing referring to a person's conscious or unconscious decision to place himself or herself in a position to receive messages from a source.

Selective Perception. A hurdle in information processing of attributing meaning to some messages while ignoring others.

Selective Recall. A hurdle in information processing and communication referring to how people store information.

Selective Retention. A hurdle in information processing and communication reflecting the ability, or inability, to store information in long-term memory.

Self-Concept. A dimension of self-assessment that reflects the level of general self-worth that the trainee holds.

Self-Efficacy. A dimension of self-assessment that reflects the degree to which the trainee believes that he or she has the capacity to accomplish a particular act or achieve a particular goal.

Self-Handicapping. The adoption of an impediment, either verbally or behaviorally, that serves to protect the person's self-esteem such that failure can be blamed on something other than the person's competence and success is seen as that much greater an accomplishment as a result of overcoming the handicap.

Sell Style. A style of training where the trainees have some level of psychological and job maturity and are reluctant to be told what to do, yet they are not motivated to take initiative on their own.

Semantics. The analog language or meaning of the words that are used. The process of attributing meaning to language, messages, or symbols.

Sensitivity. Part of the ethnocentrism spectrum reflecting the concept that one person is aware of the ethnocentrism of another person and tailors the communication accordingly.

Sentinel Event. An event causing or risking serious injury or death to the patient.

Serial Position Effect. In persuasive communication the concept that messages, according to when they are presented, can be more memorable and persuasive (i.e., information presented near the beginning and at the end of the message).

Sex. The classification of living things as man or woman according to their reproductive organs and functions aligned by chromosomal complement.

Sexual Arousal Touch. A dimension of haptics that reflects touching others in a sexual way or for sexual gratification.

Sexual Harassment. Unreciprocated or unwanted behavior of a sexual nature that offends the victim or makes the victim feel threatened, embarrassed, or humiliated.

Shame. Failing to live up to one's own standards.

Shyness. A predisposition to be timid and reserved when engaged in social situations.

Simulated Patient Technique. A type of role play where the patient is acting in ways that are consistent with a given directive.

Single Photon Emission Computerized Tomography (SPECT). An imaging technology for assessing functional information about the brain using radioisotopes. SPECT is especially effective in researching or assessing dementia, cognitive decline, psychiatric disorders, mood disorders, anxiety, autism, and attention deficit disorders.

Situational CA. Anxiety experienced when communicating in a specific situation or with a specific person or persons.

Situational Leadership Perspective. Leadership style should be based on both the employee's psychological maturity and job maturity.

Size. Part of selective attention referring to the fact that things that are out of normal proportion will draw our attention.

Skill Acquisition. The adoption or refinement of behavioral skills and processes associated with the delivery of quality healthcare.

Skill of Understanding the Adult Learner. A necessary training skill that reflects the ability to apply the basic concepts of andragogy and the learning tripartite of cognitive, affective, and behavioral components.

Smart Card. A credit cardÐshaped device that contains a small microprocessing chip embedded within it that can serve innumerable functions for the user.

Smart Phone. A communication device that is able to transmit data and images through time and space. SMART is an acronym for Self-Monitoring, Analysis, and Reporting Technology.

Social Attractiveness. A dimension of attractiveness based on a person's communication abilities and social networks.

Social Cognition. A dimension of self-assessment that reflects the ability to accurately compare your own thoughts and behaviors to those of others.

Social Distance. A category of personal space reflecting a closeness of 4 to 8 feet.

Social Justice. The principle that advocates the fair distribution of healthcare resources.

Social Learning Explanation of Verbal Aggressiveness. Verbal aggressiveness is developed as a result of modeling our behavior after significant others in the immediate environment and the media.

Social Level of Uncertainty Reduction. A level of uncertainty reduction that consists of information based on things such as a person's sex and age.

Social Stigma. Any social attribute that serves as a marker resulting in the marginalization of the person solely based on that social attribute.

Social Touch. A dimension of haptics referring to touch during routine social exchanges.

Social Work. An allied medical profession that involves assisting individuals, their families, and significant others to regain function when illness, disease, or disability results in changes in their physical state, mental state, or their role in society.

Sociocommunicative Orientation (SCO). A person's self-perception of his or her communicative behavior.

Sociocommunicative Style (SCS). How other people view your communicative behavior.

Somatype. A classification of a person's body type and consists of endomorph, mesomorph, and ectomorph.

Sound. Created when an object vibrates in nature.

Source. The person who encoded the message and sends it to the receiver.

Source Message Channel Receiver (SMCR). Communication model proposed by David Berlo that highlights the concepts of source, message, channel, and receiver.

Spatial Intelligence. A form of IQ referring to the ability to use images that represent special relations between and among objects.

Spontaneous Humor. Humor that arises out of ordinary situations and is usually a witty remark or ludicrous action inspired by the circumstances at hand.

Standard of Care. What the average prudent clinician would be expected to do under certain circumstances.

Stanford-Binet IQ Assessment. The standardized measure for assessing general intelligence.

Stapes. The stirrup bone, which is involved in the physiology of hearing. This bone vibrates against a window-like structure that vibrates the fluid in the cochlea and in turn sound is amplified.

Stereotyping. A sense-making behavior that requires people to make generalizations in order to make sense of the people and cultures that exist around them.

Stigma. A mark of disgrace that people can attach to something they regard as unacceptable.

Stimulus. (Relating to humor) The thing that stimulates a humorous response in another person or persons.

Stress. A type of naturally caused illness and includes depression, burnout, and organic deterioration (e.g., Alzheimer's disease).

Subjective Standard. The standard of how we standardize and tailor information to each individual patient.

Substituting. A function of nonverbal communication where nonverbal messages are used in place of the verbal messages.

Sulci. The grooves of the brain.

Summative Feedback. Feedback that reflects a postbehavioral assessment where feedback takes the form of an evaluation or judgment of an already-existing performance behavior.

Superconducting Quantum Interference Device (SQUID). An instrument used in MEG imaging to measure extremely weak signals (e.g., subtle changes in electromagnetic energy such as that found in the human brain).

Supernatural Causation. Causes of illness that are supernatural in nature such as fate, contagion, and mystical retribution.

SupplierÐConsumer Economic Metaphor. A metaphor that explains the financial and quality-of-life benefits to all parties involved in the healing process.

Surgical Technologist. An allied medical profession that involves safely preparing and handling surgical instruments during surgical procedures.

Symmetrical Cryptography. Transformation of information using the same secret key to encipher and decipher messages.

Synaptic Connection. The structure and connection that permits chemical and electrical signals to travel to another cell.

Synchrony. High level of commonality that communicators share as a result of being from the same culture; includes common verbal and nonverbal behaviors.

Syntax. The orderly sequence of the digital (actual) words that are used.

System Integrity. The requirement that a system performs its intended function in an unimpaired manner free from deliberate or inadvertent unauthorized manipulation of the system.

Systematic Desensitization. A treatment for communication apprehension that utilizes relaxation techniques in order to build a greater threshold for the experience of apprehension associated with the specific communication.

Tag Questions. Questions attached to the end of a statement, such as "you know?" or "right?"

Talkaholism. A predisposition to engage in compulsive communication behavior.

Task Attractiveness. A dimension of attractiveness that reflects being drawn to someone because of what they do.

Taste. A study of nonverbal behavior focusing on the role of taste in communication.

Teams. Individuals who come together to produce a joint product.

Technical Time. A type of cultural time orientation that is scientific in nature.

Telehealth. The practice of healthcare via a satellite link between fixed stations to deliver healthcare that would otherwise need to be performed in a face-to-face environment.

Tell Style. A style of training where the trainees are low in both psychological and job maturity.

Telling Is Communicating. A misconception of communication that assumes that telling someone something is reflective of competent communication when in fact it is a sender-centric communication practice.

Temperament. A person's default or overall reaction to stimuli in their environment.

Temporal Lobe. A part of the human brain responsible for processing auditory information from the ears.

Territoriality. An area of nonverbal behavior referring to how people use and organize their personal space.

Test of Functional Health Literacy in Adults (TOFHLA). A measure of health literacy that requires the patient to read passages in which every fifth to seventh word is deleted and the patient must insert the correct word from a choice of four words.

Thalamus. A part of the human brain that modulates the sensory processing of emotional reactivity.

The More You Communicate, The Better. A misconception of communication that assumes the greater the quantity of communication, the better the outcomes when in fact it is the quality of communication that matters.

Theory of Arousal and Cognitive Factors. A theory of humor that assumes humor is not just a present stimulus, but also a recollection of past experiences, the reality of the present, and the anticipation of the future that is collated into generating and arousing pleasure.

Theory of Interpersonal Communication Motives. A theory that assumes people develop expectations about communication and as such engage in interpersonal communication for any one of six reasons.

Therapeutic Humor. A type of humor based on mindfulness, empathy, and compassion and consists of any intervention that promotes health and wellness by stimulating a discovery, expression, or appreciation for the absurdity or incongruity of life and life's situations.

Therapeutic Listening. The ability to listen to both the message and all of the emotional and psychological information that accompanies it.

Therapeutic Writing. An exercise designed to allow the practitioner to fully express his or her experience with a patient.

Threat. The overt or implied promise of physical or psychological force resulting in the person fearing psychological or physical harm or other perceived retribution.

Time Out. A planned period of quiet and/or interdisciplinary discussion focused on key procedural details such as in the operating room.

Tourette's Disorder. A genetic disorder resulting in a tick disorder such as eye blinking, coughing, throat clearing, sniffing, and facial movement affecting approximately 1% of children.

Training. The acquisition of knowledge and skills necessary for individuals to perform effectively on the job.

Training Goals. General statements as to what the trainee is expected to learn or do.

Training Objectives. Easily measurable and often specific skills that are demonstrable.

Trait Theory of Leadership. Leadership qualities believed to be within the personality of the person.

Traits. Enduring characteristics that uniquely distinguish one person from another person.

Translation. The making sense of and relaying of culturally sensitive written communication.

Translational Research. Research that includes collaboration from two or more disciplines focusing on a specific idea, concept, or problem.

Triarchic Theory of Intelligence. A theory of IQ that assumes intelligence is composed of three factors consisting of componential intelligence, experimental intelligence, and contextual intelligence.

Trigger. A signal for detecting a likely adverse event.

Trustworthiness. The degree to which a person is believable and worthy of trust.

Truth-Dumping. Providing too much information, resulting in the patient feeling overwhelmed.

Truth-Telling. Providing the patient enough information so that the information is complete and the patient is satisfied.

Uncertainty Management Theory (UMT). A theory that explains how people react to health-related uncertainty.

Understand. A goal of communication where people seek to understand and interpret the world around them.

Unintentional Humor. A form of spontaneous humor that results when the person has no intention of making another person laugh, but it just occurs.

Unproblematic Subordination. When a nurse carries out the doctor's orders without question and does so in a subordinate fashion.

Utility. Part of selective exposure referring to the more useful a stimuli is to a person, the more likely it is to be noticed.

V-Learning. Learning that entails the user to act within a three-dimensional landscape as an avatar that serves as a virtual simulation of "real-world" situations.

Ventral Medial Prefrontal Cortex (VMPFC). An area of the brain located over the eye sockets associated with moral judgments in everyday situations.

Verbal. Aspects of communication that include syntax (i.e., the digital or the actual words that are used) and semantics (i.e., the analog or meaning of the words that are used).

Verbal Aggressiveness. A predisposition to attack the self-concept of individuals instead of, or in addition to, their positions on topics of communication.

Verbal Qualifiers. Language that is used at the beginning of a message that detracts from the credibility of the sender.

Verbal Trigger Agents. Factors that, when present, result in an onset of verbal and potentially physical aggression.

Versatility. The degree to which people can adapt their assertiveness and responsiveness to specific people and specific situations.

Visual Cortex. A part of the brain responsible for receiving visual stimuli from the environment. For example, the written word will stimulate the visual cortex but then is transferred to other parts of the brain for interpretation and translation.

Voicing Mechanism. A function of the respiration process of language production whereby vocal cords tighten to produce vibration.

Warm Environment. A dimension of environment that reflects surroundings that are comfortable and casual.

Web-Based Module. Systems generally housed off site that can experience bandwidth limitations and varying transfer speed based on the traffic of others users who also use the vendor's server.

Wernicke's Aphasia. A syndrome where a person is able to comprehend language yet is unable to produce the desired speech.

Wernicke's Area. A part of the left posterior superior temporal region responsible for language comprehension.

Wide Range Achievement Test (WRAT). A general literacy measure that assesses a person's ability to read words, comprehend sentences, spell, and compute solutions to math problems.

William's Disorder. A chromosomal disorder whereby those affected possess somewhat "elfin-like" faces and are excessively social appearing, extremely communicatively competent, and dynamic.

Willingness to Communicate (WTC). A person's willingness to initiate communication with others.

Wilson's Disease. A disorder of copper metabolism whereby copper accumulates in the brain causing tremors, abnormal muscular activity and movements, emotional liability, and involuntary laughing and crying eventually resulting in progressive dementia.

Witnessing. Being in the presence of an event that is significant to one or all of the parties involved.

Witticism. A form of spontaneous humor deliberately designed to entertain by clever and original spontaneity.

Words Have Meaning. A misconception of communication that assumes that meanings are in words when in fact meanings are in people.

Worksite Analysis. Conducting a comprehensive review of all aspects and procedures of healthcare, including the physical, psychological, and social factors present in the delivery of healthcare.

Written Communication Skills. A necessary training skill reflecting the ability to create relevant objectives, persuasively arrange content, and provide concise and interesting documents.

Xenophobia. The fear of strangers.

Index

A

AAS. *See* Augmented awareness system (AAS)
Abstractness, 213
Abuse, 189
Accentuating, 100
Accept, 290
Accounting, 326
Accreditation Council for Graduate Medical Education (ACGME), 10, 145, 235
Acculturation phase, 138
Acknowledgement, 288, 290
ACS. *See* American College of Surgeons (ACS)
Active listening skills, 259
Adaptation, 72
Adaptors, 103
ADHD. *See* Attention deficit hyperactivity disorder (ADHD)
Adjustment phase, 138
Adult basic education (ABE), 162
Adult learning, 258–259
Advance directives, 305–306
Advanced Trauma Life Support (ATLS), 257
Adventurousness, 60
Adverse event, 209, 210, 277
Affect displays, 103
Affirming communication, 198
Affordable Care Act, 231
African Americans, 133
  DNR request by, 307
  intracultural communication and, 131
  trust by, 146
Ageism, 123
Agency for Health Care Quality Research, 4
Aggression
  concept of, 187
  nursing and, 195
  reporting of, 195
Aggressive communication
  behavior encompassed by, 189
  causes of, 189–191

defined, 188–189
  diffusion of, 196–199
  events triggering, 193–195
  origins of, 191–192
  susceptibility to, 188–189
Agreeableness, 49
AI. *See* Appreciative inquiry (AI)
Air producing mechanism, 46
Alzheimer's disease, stress and, 144
AMA. *See* American Medical Association (AMA)
Ambiguous messages, 71
American College of Surgeons (ACS), 5, 223, 257
American Information Management Association (AHIMA), 323, 327
  Bill of Rights, 327
American Medical Association (AMA), 257
American Recovery and Reinvestment Act (ARRA), 326
American Society for Surgery of the Hand (ASSH), 257
Amiable style, 86
Amygdala
  autism and, 64
  emotions and, 34
Analytic style, 86
Anchoring error (bias), 277
Andragogy, 258
Androgyny, 60
Angry gestures, 103
Angular gyrus, 30
Animist culture, 135
Ankylosing spondylitis, 183
Anterior cingulate cortex, 32
Anterior temporal cortex, 32
Anterior thalamic nucleus, 33
Anthropomorphic robot, 335
Aphasia, 36
Apology
  behavior of, 287–291
  definition, 277, 285, 288, 290
  legal perspectives, 291–293
  philosophical perspective, 285–287
  religious perspectives, 293–294
  six-step guide, 290
Appreciative inquiry (AI), 217–218, 227
Appreciative listening, 224
Arcuate fasciculus, 36

Argumentativeness
  assertiveness and, 192
  defined, 192
  development of, 196
  motivations for, 196
Argument skills deficiency model, 198
Arousal and cognitive factors, theory of, 183–184
ARRA. *See* American Recovery and Reinvestment Act (ARRA)
Arrogant conflict, 199
Articulation, 46
Artifacts, 107
Asians, 131
  health awareness of, 132
  humor and, 186
  patriarchy bias of, 142
  trust by, 146
Asperger's syndrome, 63
Assertiveness
  argumentativeness and, 192
  continuum, 86
  defined, 59
Assessment
  effective, 257
  health literacy, 169–171
  IQ, 65
  training, 267–270
Asymmetrical cryptography, 324
Attention, 216
  brain and, 67–68
  selective, 68
  spans, 67–68
Attention deficit hyperactivity disorder (ADHD), 62
Attractiveness, 105–106
Attributes, 71, 145
Audience. *See* Learners
Auditory cortex, 30
Augmented awareness system (AAS), 332
Authentication, 325
Authoritarianism, 60
Authority gradient, 186, 277
Authorization, 325–326
Autism spectrum
  brain structures and, 64–65
  characterization of, 62–63
  features of, 62–63
Autonomics, 116–117